About This Book

This book starts where you are likely to start—at the beginning. The design ensures that you learn the user and programming concepts when you need them, as you need them, as you start your exploration of the UNIX® C Shell.

By following the book's examples, you will learn various techniques to accomplish tasks that build on each other until you have mastered the basics of the C Shell. If you faithfully follow the book, you will learn how to use the C Shell's command line and how to write shell scripts to perform your common everyday tasks.

All you need is a UNIX login, and you are ready to go.

Who Should Read This Book?

Anyone interested in learning to use the C Shell will find something of value in this book. This book is aimed at helping the UNIX novice; in addition, it can be used by the experienced UNIX users to write script.

For both, this book covers the C Shell from the basics—such as command line editing, creating and using aliases, and the history command—to more advanced subjects, such as programming scripts.

This book is for you, if one or more of the following is true:

☐ You are interested in learning more about your UNIX account.

☐ You've just heard that your company is switching to UNIX.

☐ You need to create batch programs to perform a task various times of the day or on demand.

☐ You need to automate some of your everyday, mundane tasks.

Conventions

To help guide you through the daily topics and draw your attention to important information, several special easy-to-see icons are used in this book.

 Note: Here you will find interesting information that can make your use of the C Shell more effective.

 Tip: Read these boxes for useful shortcuts and techniques for being more efficient with the C Shell.

 Caution: These boxes focus your attention on problems or side effects that can occur in specific situations.

In addition, you will find useful advice in the Do/Don't boxes and clear explanations of command syntax in the book's Syntax boxes. With this book and 14 days, you can put yourself well on the way to mastery of the C Shell.

Teach Yourself the UNIX® C Shell
in 14 Days

Teach Yourself the
UNIX® C Shell
in 14 Days

David Ennis
James C. Armstrong, Jr.

SAMS
PUBLISHING

201 West 103rd Street
Indianapolis, Indiana 46290

To my wonderful wife, Perriann, and my terrific children, Courtney and Craig.—David Ennis

To, Dr. and Mrs. Nag. Sime eorum laboribus, non essem qui sum.—James Armstrong

Copyright © 1994 by Sams Publishing

FIRST EDITION

International Standard Book Number: 0-672-30540-2

Library of Congress Catalog Card Number: 94-66641

97 96   4 3 2

Interpretation of the printing code: the rightmost double-digit number is the year of the book's printing; the rightmost single-digit, the number of the book's printing. For example, a printing code of 94-1 shows that the first printing of the book occurred in 1994.

Composed in AGaramond and MCPdigital by Macmillan Computer Publishing

Printed in the United States of America

Trademarks

Publisher
Richard K. Swadley

Associate Publisher
Jordan Gold

Acquisitions Manager
Stacy Hiquet

Managing Editor
Cindy Morrow

Acquisitions Editor
Rosemarie Graham

Development Editor
Scott Parker

Production Editor
Deborah Frisby

Editor
Tonya Simpson

Editorial Coordinator
Bill Whitmer

Editorial Assistants
Carol Ackerman
Sharon Cox
Lynette Quinn

Technical Reviewer
Larry Schumer
Mark Sims

Marketing Manager
Gregg Bushyeager

Cover Designer
Dan Armstrong

Book Designer
Alyssa Yesh

Director of Production and Manufacturing
Jeff Valler

Imprint Manager
Juli Cook

Manufacturing Coordinator
Paul Gilchrist

Production Analysts
Dennis Hager
Mary Beth Wakefield

Graphics Image Specialists
Tim Montgomery
Dennis Sheehan

Production
Carol L. Bowers
Georgiana Briggs
Mona Brown
Cheryl Cameron
Mary Ann Cosby
Elaine Crabtree
Mike Dietsch
Rob Falco
Stephanie J. McComb
Chad Poore
Casey Price
Brian-Kent Proffitt
Linda Quigley
Kim Scott
O. Dennis Wesner

Indexer
Charlotte Clapp

Overview

Contents

6   Customizing the User Environment   133

7   File Redirection, Pipes, and Filters   159

9   C Shell Built-In Commands, Part II   231

Acknowledgements

The idea that I could be an author never occurred to me until I was approached to write this book. Now, incredibly, it is finished and many people are deserving of thanks for helping to make this book a reality:

Duke Luper, for putting my name in the right place at the right time to get me noticed.

Rosemarie Graham, for seeing the potential in me that I did not realize existed and for her advice, support, and encouraging words through thick and thin.

Frank Catone, for introducing me to Duke Luper and cheering me on when opportunity knocked.

Scott Parker, for his development comments.

Mark Sims, for his technical editing, keeping me accurate.

Deborah Frisby and Tonya Simpson, for their editorial support from start to finish to make the book happen.

All of the many people at Sams who contributed their skill and expertise to make my words look great.

My daughter Courtney and son Craig, for putting up with a dad more absent than present. I love you both very much.

Most of all, thanks to my wife Perri, who suffered through the long hours over the months I was working on this book—working herself, running the household, raising our son, and surviving a move, with surprisingly good spirits. Thank you for your patience, caring, support, encouragement, and love. I couldn't have survived it without you.

—David Ennis

First, thanks to Toni Morgan, Wes Morgan, Phil Harbison, and Chris Stassen for assistance in debugging some of the sample programs.

A special thanks to the team at SAMS, for making the book all that it can be.

At times, the schedule did feel like a boot camp! Deserving special mention is Rosemarie Graham, who worked with me to keep me on my deadlines.

Jordan Gold deserves many thanks from me for letting me get my nose in the door with *UNIX Unleashed*. You aren't getting rid of this camel easily!

I'd like to thank Dave Taylor for believing in my writing skills even before I did, and for the opportunity to start writing, both at SunWorld and with SAMS.

My friends all deserve a mention, but there just isn't room for all of you. Special kudos go to Nancy Colucci, Curtis Hill, Curtis Jackson, Dorothy Nelson, Belinda Frazier, and James Ross.

I'd like to thank both Nyssa and Leela for their patience with me these last few weeks.

Finally, I'd like to thank my parents for providing me with the upbringing necessary to be a creative and productive person, and my sister Lillian for listening when I complained.

—James Armstrong

About the Authors

David Ennis

David Ennis began programming 22 years ago. For the last 17 years, he has been an independent consultant working in the Los Angeles area. He first learned of UNIX and C in the late 1970s, and, intrigued, he read books and articles to stay informed. Ten years ago while working for Hughes Aircraft Company, he got his first exposure to UNIX and has been involved with all aspects of it since that time. He has worked as an administrator, developer, consultant, and trainer for a number of companies, including several in the Fortune 500. During the late 1980s, he also taught UNIX and C, hoping to help others learn more about this unique operating system. His experience with UNIX has been on a wide variety of platforms, ranging from PCs to mainframes, and an equal variety of UNIX versions, including BSD 4.1 to 4.3, SunOS, HP-UX, and AIX on RS6000s, PCs, and 370s. He authored Days 1 through 7 and the Appendixes.

James C. Armstrong, Jr.

James C. Armstrong, Jr. is a UNIX software consultant with extensive experience with both the Internet and GUI development. A graduate of Duke University, he attended graduate school at the University of St. Andrews in Scotland, and he has worked for several industry leaders, including Bell Labs and Tandem. He is based in Silicon Valley, where he lives with his two cats. On the weekends, he enjoys nature, photography, and backcountry exploration. He authored Days 8 through 14.

Introduction

You're at the beginning of this book, a two-week course to teach yourself the UNIX C Shell. The fact that you are reading this introduction indicates your interest in UNIX and specifically in the C Shell. This book is not just for those who are new to the UNIX system. It is also for those who may have used one of the other available shells and who want to know more about the C Shell. Whatever the level of your experience, this book will help you gain the knowledge of this popular UNIX command shell.

This book, unlike many others about UNIX and shell programming, focuses on learning just the C Shell—not just programming the C Shell, but all aspects of using it as an interactive user, as well as for writing scripts. It is not a reference, dry and lifeless, nor is it an overview of the subject, breezing past point after point with hardly more than a glance. In *Teach Yourself the UNIX C Shell in 14 Days*, each day has its own chapter, dedicated to a topic or a small group of related concepts.

If you browse through this book, you will find that it is filled with many examples illustrating the topic of the day. There are Notes, Tips, Cautions, and Do/Don't boxes placed throughout the book, but what you will find most of all is information and guidance to help you become an accomplished user of the C Shell.

You have an advantage if have access to a system that is running UNIX, but that is not a requirement for you to benefit from this book. If you have access to a UNIX system, it has, hopefully, the C Shell available on it, so you can try out each of the new ideas presented as you progress through the book. The first few days are oriented to the user working at the terminal or workstation. They guide you through the C Shell features that are intended to make using the shell and UNIX easier and therefore more enjoyable. By the end of the first week, you will know a great deal about the C Shell and be ready to put it to work.

The second week rounds out your training and then begins the applied portion of the book, where your newly found knowledge can be put to use. You will see many examples of practical ways to use the C Shell, both interactively at the terminal and by writing tools in the form of shell scripts.

At the end of each day's lesson, there is a summary to help you review and reinforce the day's material. The summary is followed by a list of related UNIX topics, where concepts and commands that will help you more fully understand the C Shell are highlighted, with suggestions for further reading or investigation. I recommend that you take the opportunity to study these sections and learn more about these related areas of UNIX.

There is also a Q&A section, where questions are asked and answers given on the day's lesson. It is a chance for more detailed review of the material presented for the day. The Workshop, which rounds out the end of each day, is divided into two sections, Quiz and Exercises. Unlike the Q&A section, there are no answers given here in the chapter. The questions and exercises are intended to make you think and be creative. At the end of the book, in Appendix F, you will find the answers to the Quiz questions and examples of the Exercise results.

Before You Start

First of all, take a deep breath. You are about to begin your expedition in search of expertise. Remember, though, that this is not school and you will not be graded. Reading this book to learn about the C Shell is for yourself and nobody else. You will get out of this book what you put into it.

I hope that you will find this book easy to read. Every effort was made to make the material easy to understand and the explanations clear and concise. Enjoy the adventure of learning something new and make it a positive experience.

Even though this book is not a reference, it is packed with information. As you progress through each day, make notes in the margins. Write down the experiments you did, the side trips you took, and the results you found. Make the book a source of learning now and a source of personalized reference in the future.

One of the reasons that there is the "Related UNIX Topics" section at the end of each day is that you cannot learn about the C Shell in a vacuum. Yes, there are commands that are built into the shell, but you will use many more commands that are a part of UNIX outside the shell. One aim of this book is to help you learn about the C Shell; but it is also intended to teach you a bit more about UNIX and to stimulate your interest to learn even more about UNIX, as you also learn about the C Shell.

I have worked with UNIX for more than 10 years now, as a user, a system administrator, and a developer. I have had the opportunity to work for not only companies that develop applications to run under UNIX, but also companies that develop the UNIX operating system itself. UNIX is a never-ending experience, and even for the experienced user there is always something new to be learned. I hope that I can pass on to you some of my knowledge and experience through this book.

1

This first week covers the fundamentals. It gets you started by covering topics that you can put to work immediately. You will be able to apply what you learn right at the terminal keyboard and see results, which I hope will keep you enthusiastic about learning more about the C Shell.

This week starts, appropriately, an introduction to give you an overview and an idea of what to expect from the C Shell. The first day tells you about the C Shell and why it is the shell you should choose to use with your UNIX system. The following is a list of the topics for the first week and a brief overview of the lesson for each day.

Day	Overview
1	In "Introducing the C Shell," you will get a bit of history and an overview of the C Shell's features and facilities. You will find out how to determine your default shell and how to make the C Shell your default, if it's not already. Also, you will be introduced to the history mechanism of the shell and learn how to modify a previous command and run it.
2	This chapter, "Metacharacters," presents these special characters that you will use to punctuate many of the commands you run while using UNIX. There are five different groups of metacharacters used in the C Shell. All five groups are discussed in detail, explaining each metacharacter with examples, tips, and cautions.
3	This chapter, "Command Substitution, Aliases, and Filename Generation," jumps right in with applications for some of what you learned on Day 2. Day 3 shows you what you can do with metacharacters for command substitution and filename generation. Aliasing, a key facility of the C Shell, is also presented on this day, again with examples, tips, and cautions.
4	In "Shell Variables, Part I," you return to foundation material for later in the book. Shell variables are explained, and you will learn the difference between local and global variables. Here and in Day 5 the special built-in variables of the C Shell are presented. Day 4 starts with the variables that can be assigned values. Shell variables, used to control the operation and tailor the environment of the C Shell, are important to understand, both for interactive use of the shell as well as for programming to write shell scripts.
5	"Shell Variables, Part II" continues with the lesson started on Day 4. This day's lesson covers the remaining built-in variables of the C Shell, those that act like switches, having only an ON or OFF state. Each of these is explained, with examples to illustrate their use. Day 5 then presents numeric variables and arithmetic operators, which in combination can be used to perform arithmetic in shell scripts. Finally, pattern matching operators and file inquiry operators are explained, as always, with examples, tips, and cautions.
6	"Customizing the User Environment" applies what you have learned in the first five days. Here you will learn about the C Shell startup files—.cshrc, .login, and .logout. You will find out what

these files do and how you can change them to change the options and operation of your C Shell sessions. Tips and techniques, examples and suggestions, are used liberally to give you ideas about changes you can make to these files to tailor your own user environment.

7   "File Redirection, Pipes, and Filters" ends the first week of your exploration of the C Shell. File redirection extends the capability of UNIX commands, enabling you to change the source and destination of data from most commands. Pipes give you the power to build more complex commands of your own by connecting multiple commands together to make a new tool. Filters are an important component of a pipeline and are presented to round out this day's lesson. A behind-the-scenes look at how UNIX implements these features helps you in understanding them as well as applying them.

At the end of each day's lesson there is a Q&A section, in which questions and their answers are given to help you review the material you just learned. After that, you will find Quiz questions and Exercises, which you can work on your own to test your knowledge of the topics just presented. Appendix F, "Answers to Quizzes and Exercises" presents the answers to the quiz questions and to some of the exercises. In many cases, the exercises are more like "thought-provoking" questions to give you some direction for inquiry on the current topic. I encourage you to review the Q&A section and work all of the Quiz questions. Make an effort to allocate some time to tackle the Exercises and explore where they take you in the C Shell and UNIX.

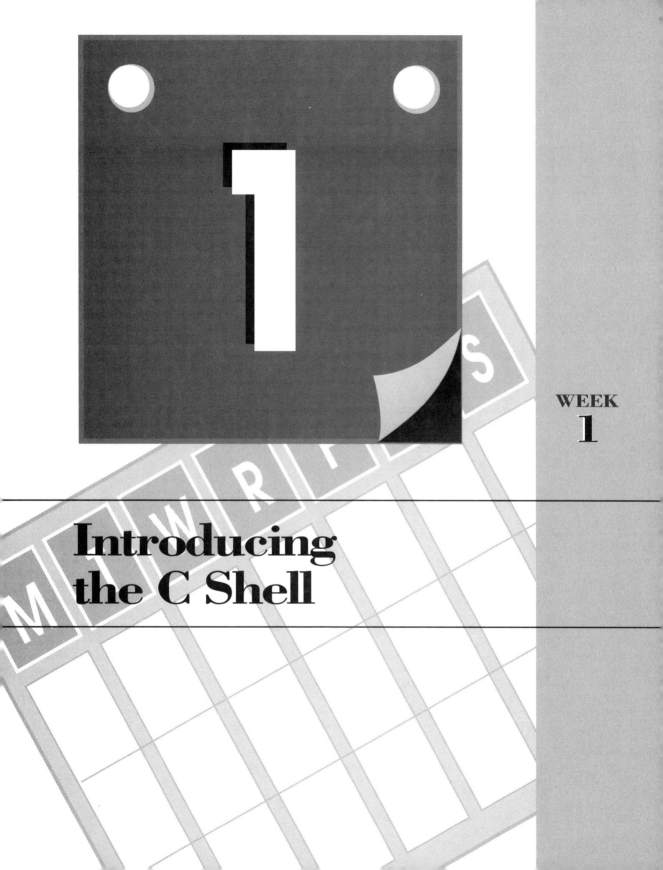

Introducing
the C Shell

Introduction to Day 1

This chapter will introduce you to the C Shell. In the following pages, you will learn what the C Shell is and why you would choose it over the other command shells available with your UNIX system. The different C Shell options, how to use the shell interactively at your terminal, and how to use the C Shell noninteractively for shell scripts are covered in this chapter. You will find out how to determine the setting of your login shell and how to change your current login shell to be the C Shell.

The remainder of this chapter is devoted to a feature that first set the C Shell apart from other UNIX shells—command history. At the time the C Shell was introduced, no other shell provided this type of facility. You will learn about history events, how to recall them, modify them, and reuse them. This feature is one that you will likely find useful as you progress through this book. If you choose to continue using the C Shell, the history event feature will be a valuable tool as you use UNIX for work or pleasure.

Setting Today's Goals

Today you will learn how to

☐ Determine whether the C Shell should be your choice for a login shell

☐ Start the C Shell for use at your terminal and for scripts

☐ Use the different command-line options of the C Shell

☐ End the C Shell

☐ Determine your login shell and temporarily or permanently change it

☐ Use the command history facility of the C Shell to reuse previous command events

☐ Modify history events

What Is the C Shell?

When you enter commands at the command prompt on your terminal screen using the UNIX operating system, you are interacting with a special-purpose program. In UNIX, the programs that process the system's commands are called *shells*. This book teaches you how to use a specific shell program called the C Shell.

When UNIX was first written and put to use at AT&T Bell Labs in the early '70s, it too had a command shell. This early UNIX went on to become the System V that is the dominant standard in the industry today. The same command shell—named the Bourne Shell, after its author Stephen Bourne—is still used and distributed today with every version of UNIX.

In 1978, a copy of UNIX was given to the Computer Science Department at the University of California at Berkeley. Under a contract from an agency of the United States government, the students and faculty developed the first 32-bit virtual memory version of UNIX. As part of that effort a new command shell, dubbed the *C Shell*, was written. This new shell provided a number of features that were not available with the Bourne Shell.

The new functionality added to the C Shell was designed to benefit the interactive user. Two important additions were the history mechanism, allowing the user to reuse and modify previously executed commands; and job control, which provided for more control over tasks initiated by the user. A third very visible change made with the C Shell was the new programming language for writing shell programs, or *scripts*.

The architects of Berkeley UNIX and the C Shell patterned the shell programming language for their new shell after the C programming language. Their aim was to make writing shell programs easy for users, many of whom already were proficient in the C programming language. If you are familiar with the now popular C programming language, you will find writing shell scripts for the C Shell easy, because doing so is much like writing a C program.

Why Use the C Shell?

The original UNIX system and the first Bourne Shell were designed and written by programmers mainly for users who were programmers. In today's terms, the original versions of UNIX were *no frills*. The users of these early systems were more concerned with developing the operating system, with its commands and tools, to accomplish the tasks that were a part of their everyday jobs than in making it user friendly. User facilities were developed and enhanced only after the UNIX system left the confines of the Bell Labs and entered the world of academia and, later, the public marketplace.

Depending on the type of user that you are and the nature of the job for which you are using UNIX, you will have a varying amount of contact with the shell. You may be a user who sees only a menu of selections and the programs behind the selections. If this is the case, then it matters very little which shell you choose, because your interaction with it will be minimal if not nonexistent. If, on the other hand, you are logging on and dealing directly with the shell on a day-to-day basis, then your choice of shells becomes very important.

As you complete each chapter of this book, you will become more comfortable and proficient with the commands and features of the C Shell. The hallmark features of the C Shell—command history and job control, as well as the C-like programming language—will be important labor savers, and perhaps even sanity savers. When you find that you don't have to retype entire command lines if you've used them just moments before, you will appreciate the history mechanism.

You will learn about C Shell job control at the end of this book. Using job control, you will start a procedure, answer its questions, interrupt it, and put it in the background, freeing up your terminal to do other work while the procedure processes behind the scenes. If the job needs input, it will inform you. You can then bring it back, supply the data or answers, and then return it to the background. On a simple terminal without windowing, this helps you be more productive. Even with windowing, you can do more work with your existing open windows.

Now, back to the question, Why use the C Shell? Well, if anything I have said in the last few paragraphs appeals to you, then you should use the C Shell. None of the features just discussed are a part of the Bourne Shell. There are other shells, available on some UNIX versions, that incorporate some or all of these features in one form or another. The difference between those other shells and the C Shell is that, if you move from one version of UNIX to another, you can't depend on finding those other shells. The two command shells you will find in all versions of UNIX are the Bourne Shell and the C Shell.

Changing Your Login Shell

I hope that you are reading this book because you have an interest in the C Shell. If you are going to work with the C Shell, you can make it your default shell or start it each time you want to change temporarily from your default to the C Shell. The next section shows you how to determine whether you have the C Shell as your default, and how to change to or from it, if you choose.

Determining Your Login Shell

When you log in to your system, UNIX starts a shell, which is the program that displays your initial command prompt for the session. That shell is referred to as your *login shell*. Your system administrator set up your account on the system and chose your login shell. The name and location of that shell—its pathname—is maintained by UNIX in the system password file. Exiting the shell logs you out of the system.

The password file contains information describing your account on the system: your login name or account, password, user ID number, group number, and home directory. Another field contains descriptive information, which could be your full name, a work phone number, your office location, or other pertinent information, in a free format. The last item in your account record is your default, or login, shell, which is kept as a full pathname like /usr/bin/csh.

There are two easy ways for you to find out which shell has been set up as your default shell. One way is to look in the password file in your account record to see what is in the last field in the record. This always contains the path of the default shell. The password file is /etc/passwd. If you use the UNIX grep command—a text searching program—you won't have to look through the entire password file to locate and display your record. To use grep, you enter the following command (here shown in bold) on your system:

```
1 % grep David /etc/passwd
davide:AQ1#BpsGN&mY:100:20:David Ennis, x5021:/usr/davide:/usr/bin/csh
2 % _
```

> **Note:** The grep command searches for patterns in text. The pattern can be simply literal text, such as in the preceding example where I searched for my account name, davide. The text usually is found in one or more files that you specify to grep on the command line. The file was /etc/passwd in my example. With no options selected, the default behavior of grep is to display any lines of text that contain the match pattern. The line of text that follows the grep command, beginning with davide, is the text that was located in the password file.
>
> The password file contains records, which are lines of text, one for each login account on the system. Each account record contains seven fields delimited with colons (:). The seven fields contain the following information :
>
> 1. Account name (davide).
>
> 2. Encrypted password (AQ1#BpsGN&mY).
>
> 3. User ID number (100).
>
> 4. Primary group number (20).
>
> 5. Descriptive information (David Ennis, x5021).
>
> 6. Home directory path (/usr/davide).
>
> 7. Default shell path (/usr/bin/csh).

9

If you examine the line displayed by the grep command, you will see your default shell at the end of the line, just after the last colon (:) character. My default shell is, of course, /usr/bin/csh, otherwise known as the C Shell. In the next sections, you will learn how to change your default shell. If you choose to make a change in your default shell selection, this field in the password file is where the change is made. The next time you log in to the system, your choice takes effect.

There is a second method used to determine your default shell setting. When you log in to the system and your login shell is started, it sets a special shell variable to the value of your current shell. Variables are the topic of Day 4, "Shell Variables, Part I" and Day 5, "Shell Variables, Part II." The specific variable that you are interested in, called $shell, always contains the value of your current shell.

The system looks at the last field in your password record to find your default shell. When you examine $shell from a login shell, the value of your current shell is the same as your default shell setting. The easiest way to look at a shell variable is to use the shell's built-in command echo to display its contents. The echo command and the rest of the C Shell's built-in commands are the topic of Days 8, 9, and 10 of this book. Enter echo $shell on your system to find out the setting of your default shell:

```
2 % echo $SHELL
/usr/bin/csh
3 % _
```

The shell echo command displays the contents of the shell variable $shell. In the preceding example, you see that mine is set to /usr/bin/csh, which is the same as what is in my password file record displayed earlier. After you have chosen and changed your default shell setting, it will not change unless you or your administrator alters it.

A qualification to this statement has to be made if you are working in a networked environment where you have access to more than one system. It is possible for you to have a different default shell setting on another host that you have access to over the network. This is especially true if the machine is from a different vendor, or if it is administered by a different person, group, or organization. You will want to check those hosts in the same manner and perhaps change your default shell on those hosts, so that you are using the same shell on all systems that you access. This will make using UNIX much easier for you.

Setting Your Regular Default Shell

Now that you know what your default shell setting is, how can you change it if you want to do so? There is a UNIX command which does just that for you. The chsh command,

which stands for *change shell*, enables you to change the setting for your default shell. When you use chsh to make a change to your default, the change does not take effect until you log out and then log in once again. At that time, you will have the shell that you selected as your login shell. Although chsh is not a part of the C Shell, its syntax is shown here so you will know how to change your default shell setting before you go further in the book.

The syntax for the chsh command is

```
chsh default-shell-path
```

where the *default-shell-path* is the full file pathname of the command shell program that you want to use as your default shell. Check with your system administrator if you cannot locate the shell of your choice.

Example: chsh /usr/bin/csh

When you use the chsh command to change your default shell, it changes the contents of the last field of your password file record to reflect the new shell pathname you entered on the command line. This change stays in effect until the next time you use chsh to change your default to another value. This change is what I like to call *temporarily permanent*, because it can be modified but is otherwise permanent. Next I will show you how to quickly change your current shell without using chsh. This change is *temporary* in the true sense of the word.

Caution: When you use chsh to change your default shell setting, be sure that you properly spell the pathname for your new shell. If you misspell any part of the pathname and don't catch your error before logging out of the system, your logon will fail when you attempt to log in the next time. Most likely, the system will be unable to locate the file that you give to chsh and will not be able to start a login shell for you. The only way to fix this is to contact your administrator and ask to have the pathname corrected in your password entry. So be careful!

Temporarily Changing Your Shell

Occasionally, you will need to change your shell to one that is different from your default shell. If the change is short-term, you do not want to use chsh, having to log out and log in again simply to change your shell for a short period of time. There is a simpler solution that I'll present to you now.

Whenever you run any command in UNIX from the command prompt, your current shell process is paused, while your entered command is run. When your command finishes, your current shell process is started again, and it displays a new prompt for your next command. You can take advantage of this behavior of UNIX to temporarily change your shell to a different command program.

To make this temporary change, at your command prompt you simply enter the command name of the new shell you wish to run. If, for example, you find that your default shell is the Bourne Shell, and you want to run the C Shell at this time, enter csh at the command prompt. The next prompt you see will be coming from the C Shell and not from your default Bourne Shell.

```
$ csh
% _
```

> **Note:** In the preceding example, it may not be readily apparent to you that I have switched shells. I have given you a subtle hint in the command prompts that are shown. The first prompt, a dollar sign ($), is the typical Bourne Shell prompt. The second prompt, a percent sign (%), is typical of the C Shell. Later in today's lesson, you'll learn about history events and event numbering. On Day 6, "Customizing the User Environment," you'll learn how to include this event number in your command prompt to help you recall history events. When your command prompt includes this event number, you'll have a better visual clue that you have changed to a new shell. Your event number will then change from its current value back to one (1) with the start of a new shell process.

When you have finished using the C Shell and want to return to your original shell process, you only need to end the C Shell. Ending the C Shell is covered in detail later in today's material.

Starting the Shell

Now it's time to look at the different ways that you can start the C Shell, the options that are available to you, and how you can take advantage of them. The next few sections

introduce you to the two modes in which the shell operates—interactive and noninteractive. The interactive mode is used when you are using the shell at your terminal. The noninteractive mode of the C Shell is used when you run a shell script, where the shell takes its commands from the script file. The syntax for the C Shell is shown in the following syntax box, with all of the options available for starting the program. These options are reviewed later in today's lesson.

The syntax for the csh command is

```
csh [-bcefinstvVxX] [argument...]
```

The csh command has twelve option flags, shown in the square brackets, that affect the operation of the shell. Some of these options are more appropriate to either the interactive or noninteractive mode of operation of the shell, but none are limited to one or the other. Each of the options is explained briefly here and in more detail where appropriate later in the book.

OPTIONS

-b   Marks the end of options that are applied to the C Shell. Options after this one are passed to the script or command started by the shell. This permits passing options to a script without confusion.

-c   Reads commands from the first filename *argument* (which is required). Any arguments following the filename are placed in $argv, the argument-list shell variable.

-e   Exits from the shell if a command ends abnormally or returns a nonzero exit status.

-f   Starts the C Shell fast by inhibiting the reading of the .cshrc file and, if the shell is a login shell, the .login file upon startup. This accelerates the startup of the shell.

-i   Forces interactive mode. The shell prompts for command-line input, even if standard input is not apparently a terminal device.

-n   Interprets but does not execute commands. Used to check the syntax of C Shell scripts for errors.

-s   Uses standard input to read commands.

-t   Takes a single command line as input. The backslash character (\\) may be used at the end of each line to allow continuation of the command on following lines.

Syntax

-v	Sets the $verbose shell variable, enabling echoing of command input after history substitutions (and before other substitutions) have been made, but before the command is executed.
-V	The same as -v except that $verbose is set before the shell reads .cshrc.
-x	Sets the $echo shell variable, enabling echoing of command input after all substitutions have been made.
-X	The same as -x except that $echo is set before the shell reads .cshrc.

Except for -c, -i, -s, and -t, the first argument that is *not* an option is assumed to be the name of a command or script. This argument is passed as argument zero, the name of the command program. Subsequent arguments are added to the argument list for the command or script.

Interactive Use of the C Shell

You will likely use the C Shell most often in its interactive mode, while you are sitting at the keyboard entering commands to get your computer to do your bidding. Each time a C Shell is started, it looks in your home directory for its configuration files. These files, .cshrc and .login, contain commands that are executed by the shell.

When the system starts your first shell, the *login* shell, it does so by prefixing a dash (-) to the name of the shell to change the name. This acts as a special flag to the login shell so that it can read the .login file if it exists in your home directory.

If you look at the syntax for the csh command, you'll notice that it has many options. You may think that, because the system starts your login shell, you don't have the ability to set any of these options. This is not the case, however. There is a method available by which you can set these options for your login shell if you choose to. Using the special variables, you can set these options either temporarily, for a single session, or permanently, where they will be set every time you log in to the system.

To set an option on temporarily, you can simply set its corresponding shell variable at a command prompt in your login shell, or any other shell. The option remains in effect until it is unset or the current shell session is ended. It is not reinstated for later shell sessions unless you specifically set it again at the command prompt.

For any option that you want to be in effect for all of your interactive shell sessions, the method is basically the same. You set the options by setting the shell variables. The difference is that each time the shell starts, it—rather than you—sets the variables at the command prompt. To do this, you put the commands to set the variables in one of your

startup files, .cshrc or .login. You'll learn more about these two files and how they affect the operation of the shell on Day 6.

Noninteractive Use of the C Shell

Whenever you write and use a C Shell script or use a C Shell script written by someone else, you are using the shell noninteractively. The main difference between the two modes—interactive and noninteractive—is that the noninteractive shell does not issue prompts for input from the terminal. You can execute a single command, supplied as an argument on the command line, or a shell script containing multiple commands, in this mode.

Using the shell noninteractively, you have several choices for setting any necessary options, whether you are running a single command or a shell script. You can choose to

1. Add the option to the command line when you invoke a single command or script using csh directly.

2. Use the set command within a shell script to set the shell variable corresponding to the desired option.

3. Set the option on the first line of a shell script where you want to be able to invoke a script by name without using the csh command (this is covered in more detail on Day 12, "Applied C Shell Programming, Part I").

Command-Line Options

The options of the C Shell give you control over how the shell operates. As you learned earlier, you can set options individually, through the use of command-line options or option-related shell variables. In this section, I'll give you a brief overview of each option of the C Shell. In the remainder of the book, the options are revisited and explained in more detail when they relate to the current topic.

Break Option, -b

When you choose to invoke a command or script from the command line using the csh command directly, there are situations when you want to pass options or arguments both to the C Shell and to the command being executed by the shell. To do this properly, you often must separate the options to csh from those intended for the command being executed by the shell. The -b option is used to signal the end of the options intended for the C Shell and the beginning of those directed at the command being invoked.

In the following example, the options -f and -v are passed to and processed by the csh command, whereas the options -q and -x are passed to the script myscript for whatever processing it may do:

```
3 % csh myscript -f -v -b -q -x
4 % _
```

This separation happens by a special arrangement in which the csh command takes the options up to, but not including, the -b option for itself and passes the options after the -b option to the command that it is executing.

Script File Option, -c

If you want to start the shell in a noninteractive mode and direct it to take its command input from a file, you would use the -c option. This informs the shell that the first filename argument (that is, not an option flag) should be read for commands to be executed. Any arguments that appear on the csh command line after this first argument are placed in the special shell variable $argv, which is the argument list variable.

In the following example, the -c tells the shell that scriptfile contains the commands that it should read and execute:

```
4 % csh -c scriptfile -v -a infile1 infile2
5 % _
```

The options and file arguments that follow scriptfile on the command line are put into the $argv argument-list variable for use by the commands within scriptfile. The difference between this example and the one for the -b option is that here only the -c is processed as an argument to the csh command. In the case of scriptfile, it may not otherwise be clear to the C Shell that this file contains commands, so you use the -c option to indicate that fact to the shell. Later, you'll learn methods by which you can specify unambiguously that a file is a shell script, and thus not need this option.

Exit-Upon-Error Option, -e

The -e option modifies a default behavior of the C Shell when executing shell scripts. Normally, if a command being executed from within a shell script returns a nonzero exit status, or abnormally terminates, the script continues to execute, unless directed otherwise by the logic of the script. If the -e option is included when you start the csh command or the script file itself, execution of the script ceases immediately when a command within the script terminates abnormally or returns a nonzero status.

For some simpler scripts, this eliminates the need to test the outcome of each command executed as part of the script. If you want your script to exit immediately when an error occurs, use this option. If it is necessary to take additional steps when a command fails within a script, these steps should be explicitly written in the script, and the -e option should not be used.

Fast Start Option, *-f*

When the csh command startup processing occurs, one step the C Shell takes within that startup is to read and process commands found in the .cshrc file from the user's home directory. Normally, the contents of the .cshrc file are used to tailor the interactive environment of the user. These commands often are not appropriate for the noninteractive environment, and on occasion they may even cause errors to occur. The -f option tells the csh command to skip the reading of this file, typically resulting in a faster startup of the shell process. The -f option is used most often on the special first line of C Shell scripts.

Forced Interactive Option, *-i*

The -i option causes the shell to prompt for input even if it appears that its input (standard input) is not a terminal (character-special device). If you are trying to use the C Shell from a terminal-like device but you can't get a prompt, you can try this option to get the shell to issue you a prompt.

Nonexecution Option, *-n*

If you are writing a shell script and want to check it for syntax errors, you can use the -n option. With this option, the shell will parse and interpret all of the commands in your script but will not execute them. If there are errors in the script, the parsing and interpreting will report them, as it would during a regular execution. Unlike the regular execution of a shell, script processing proceeds to the end of the script regardless of whether errors are encountered and reported.

Standard Input Option, *-s*

With the -s option, the shell takes its input from standard input. If this option is used with the csh command invoked from within a script file, the shell process that is started takes its commands from the lines immediately following the csh command line until an *end-of-file* is encountered. If this option is used starting csh at the command prompt,

17

the shell takes its input from the terminal, but not prompt for input as it normally does. This option is rarely used.

Single Command-Line Option, *-t*

The usual behavior of the shell is to read multiple command lines from its input source. The -t option causes the C Shell to read a single input line from standard input. The backslash (\) can be used at the end of each line to escape each newline character for continuation of the command line on subsequent lines.

Verbose Option, *-v*

The -v option causes the C Shell to set the verbose shell variable. When the verbose shell variable is set, the shell echoes each command just after all history substitutions have been made and before any other substitution processing is done on each command line. This option is used when there is a need to debug shell scripts and view what the C Shell is doing as it processes each command line within the script. The -v option is not usually left on a script that is used regularly, for it produces a considerable amount of output on most scripts.

Verbose *.cshrc* Option, *-V*

If you have not set the -f option, the C Shell first reads the startup file .cshrc before reading the first line of your script. At times, while debugging a script, you want to view what the C Shell is doing during this processing prior to reading your script. Like the -v option, the -V option causes the shell to set the verbose shell variable and to echo commands just after history substitutions have been made. The important difference between the two verbose options is that this one, -V, sets the verbose shell variable before the shell starts to read the .cshrc startup file. This allows you to view the processing that the shell performs on your startup file and that could be affecting how your script executes.

Echo Option, *-x*

The -x option causes the C Shell to set the echo shell variable. When the echo shell variable is set, the shell echoes each command after *all* substitutions—history *and* metacharacter—have been made and just before the command is executed. The -x option, like the -v option, is also used when there is a need to debug shell scripts and view

what the C Shell is doing as it processes each command line within the script. The -x option also is not usually left on a script that is used regularly, for it produces considerable amounts of output on most scripts.

Echo *.cshrc* Option, -X

In a manner like that of the -V option, the -X option causes the C Shell to set the echo shell variable prior to the start of reading the .cshrc startup file. As with the -x option, the -X option echoes each command line after *all* substitutions have been completed. The -X option is also not left on scripts that have been debugged; it too produces volumes of output.

Ending the Shell

When you are ready to end the C Shell, you can simply enter exit at the command prompt. This terminates your current shell. If that happens to be your login shell, you are logged off of the system, and a login prompt appears, as in this example:

```
% exit

Welcome to UNIX

Login: _
```

Another way to end the C Shell is to enter ^D, that is, to hold down the Control key while you type the letter D. ^D, also represented as Control-D, is the UNIX end-of-file (EOF) character, and when the C Shell sees the EOF on input, it takes that to be the end of the *command file* and terminates. This can be a dangerous way to end the shell.

Some UNIX commands can accept input from the terminal rather than from a file specified on the command line. To indicate to these commands that you are finished with input, you use the same ^D EOF character. If you were to accidentally enter an extra ^D, your shell would end when you least expect it to end. To avoid this, the C Shell has a special shell variable that acts as a switch to disable ^D for exiting the shell. That special variable is $ignoreeof, which, as it name implies, tells the shell to ignore the EOF character.

To find out whether you have this switch set, you can use the set command to display all of your shell variables and their current settings. See the example in the next section to see what the output looks like. In that example, you'll see that there is a line with the word ignoreeof on it. This indicates that the $ignoreeof shell variable is in fact set to ON. If it were not set to ON, you would not see ignoreeof in the list displayed by the set command.

On Day 6, you'll learn more about a special file, .logout, that you can use to configure special processing that occurs when you exit from your login shell and log out of your system.

Command History

You will recall that, at the start of this day, I mentioned command history as a useful and distinguishing feature of the C Shell. In this section, I'll show you how you can set up the C Shell to keep a history. Also, I'll show you how to recall commands, modify them, and reuse them to make working interactively with the C Shell more productive and easier.

Setting the History Variable

The first step in using command history is to set the C Shell $history variable. This shell variable sets the number of commands that the shell keeps in its history, before discarding the oldest saved command. You can set the variable to any number, but typically you set it initially to a reasonable value like 50. Later, as you become more experienced using the C Shell, you will likely increase this number so that you can keep a bigger backlog of command history.

First you can check to see if, in fact, you have the $history variable set. Your system administrator may have given you a startup file, as part of the initial configuration of your account, that included a command line to set this variable for you. To find out whether you already have $history set, you can use the C Shell set command to show all of the currently defined variables. Here is an example:

```
5 % set
argv        ()
cwd         /usr/dave
history     20
home        /usr/dave
ignoreeof
noclobber
path        (/bin /usr/bin /usr/dave/bin /usr/lib .)
prompt      ! %
shell       /bin/csh
status      0
term        vt100
6 % _
```

> **Note:** What you will see when you enter the `set` command at your command prompt will probably be different from what is shown in the example, but in general this is similar to what you will see. The first column is the name of the variables that you have set in your current shell session. The second column is the value that the variable contains. Notice that two of the variables, `ignoreeof` and `noclobber`, do not have values. These are special variables that behave like switches. When they appear in the list they are ON, and when they are absent from the list they are OFF. These and the other reserved shell variables are explained in detail during Days 4 and 5.

In the output displayed in the preceding `set` command example, notice that there is a line that begins with `history` and has the number 20 after it. If you see a similar line in the output from your `set` command, then you know that you have the command-history feature enabled for your shell sessions. Don't worry now about the value set for your `$history` variable. If it is set, the value is likely to be something reasonable and will be adequate for working the examples that follow. If you choose, you can edit your `.cshrc` file and change the value setting for the `$history` variable.

Viewing History

The C Shell has a command that you can use to look at your history list at any time from the command prompt. That command is `history`, and when entered, it displays all of the commands in your history list, up to the number set in the `$history` variable. Consider this example:

```
6 % history
1  grep David /etc/passwd
2  echo $shell
3  csh myscript -f -v -b -q -x
4  csh -c scriptfile -v -a infile1 infile2
5  set
6  history
7 % _
```

When you enter the `history` command at your shell prompt, your output will be different from what I have shown here but should look similar in format. What you see is a list of the command history, those commands that you have entered at the shell prompt since you logged onto the system. Your output may not have all of the commands that you have entered if the number exceeded the value of your `$history` variable. In that case, you will see only the most recent commands listed. For example, if your `$history` is set to 20, but you have entered 30 commands since you started on the system, your history list would start with command number 11 and end with command number 30.

The commands contained in your history list are referred to as *events*. You should have noticed in the last example that each of these events has a number shown next to it in the output from the `history` command. These numbers are called *event numbers* and are important because this is how you identify the command in history that you want to reuse and possibly modify. Throughout the remainder of this book, I will use the terms *event* and *event number* to refer to command lines in the history list and the number associated with them.

Recycling Events

The simplest thing you can do with history events is to repeat them unchanged. Say, for example, you want to use the UNIX command `ls` to look for all the files that end with `.txt`. You might want to find files like this in several subdirectories. To do so, you would enter at your command prompt the command in the following example:

```
7 % ls *.txt
memo.txt
test.txt
welcome.txt
8 % cd stuff
9 % !7
ls *.txt
letter.txt
tutorial.txt
10 % _
```

In this example, you see that there were three files in the current directory that end in `.txt`. In event 8, I used the `cd` command—which you will learn more about on Day 8, "C Shell Built-In Commands"—to change the current directory to one called `stuff`. Event 9 then does something interesting. It recalls event 7, the `ls` command, which then displays the two files in directory `stuff` that end in `.txt`.

The syntax for the history recall commands is shown here. All of the commands begin with the exclamation character (!), sometimes called a *bang*. This character informs the C shell that what follows refers to a history event.

To recall an event by its event number, use this syntax:

```
% !event_number
```

To recall the *last* event, use the following syntax:

```
% !!
```

To recall an event by a relative event number, use

```
% !-relative_event_offset
```

where the `relative_event_offset` is subtracted from the current event number to get the number of the event to be recalled.

To recall an event by text content, use this:

```
% !text_string_beginning_of_event
```

or this:

```
% !?text_string_contained_in_event[?]
```

The following sections explain in greater detail how to use these variations on recalling history events.

Recalling by Event Number

One of the easiest ways to recall events is by event number. You saw an example of this in event 9 where I typed !7 to recall event number 7. When you recall history events, the C Shell always first displays the event being recalled. If you look again at event 9, you see that the ls command from event 7 is displayed before it is executed, producing the output shown in the example. This permits you to verify the command that was executed as a result of the recall.

Depending on the setting of your $history variable, you might on occasion try to recall an event that the shell has discarded. When the number of events exceeds the value in $history, the shell discards the oldest command before adding the newest one to the list. If you reference an event that is no longer in the history list, the shell returns the command prompt with no action taken.

Recalling the Last Command

In the preceding syntax box, you saw that there is a special case for recalling the *last* command executed. Because frequently you will want to repeat the same command immediately, this special method is provided to make doing this recall easier. To recall the last event. use !! at the command prompt.

Recalling by Relative Event Number

Frequently, you will want to repeat an event that you performed a few commands earlier. It might even still be displayed on your terminal screen, or you remember that it was three

commands ago. The C Shell allows you to recall events relative to the current event number by typing the bang (!) followed immediately (no spaces, please) by a minus (-) and the number of events back that you want to recall. If you want to recall the command three events ago, you would enter !-3:

```
10 % !-3
ls *.txt
memo.txt
test.txt
welcome.txt
11 % _
```

Do the simple arithmetic to find that the current event (10) minus 3 is equal to 7, which is the original `ls` command that looked for files ending in `.txt`. The event recalled is echoed as always and then executed, producing the output listing all of the files that match.

Recalling by Event Text

Once you get more comfortable with recalling events and you increase the setting of your `$history` variable to, say, 100, it will become more challenging for you to remember the event number of some command that you did an hour ago and now want to repeat. For just this situation, the C Shell has yet another way to recall events.

Instead of following the bang with an event *number*, you can follow the bang with the name of the command that you want to recall. The shell searches backwards from the most recent event until it finds a match. That event is then displayed and executed. The one restriction is that the text must match exactly to the beginning of the command line originally entered. For example, to recall by text the `echo` command from event 2 (see earlier in this chapter), you would use `!echo`:

```
11 % !echo
echo $shell
/bin/csh
12 % _
```

The shell searches backwards through the history list until it finds an event that starts with `echo`. If it does find a match, it displays the event and then executes the command. In event 11, I recalled the most recent event that began with the string `echo`. The shell displayed the command, `echo $shell`, and then performed the command, producing the output `/usr/bin/csh`.

Because this method only matches to the initial characters of an event, it is not always easy for you to use to recall the specific event you have in mind. So the C Shell provides an alternate way to match an event using text rather than an event number. In this

method, as in the last, you use the bang and the text you want to match, but between the bang and the text, you put a question mark (?). This tells the shell that you want to match the most recent event that *contains* the text *anywhere* in the event string. Perhaps you have done more `ls` commands since the one you are interested in recalling, but they had different match strings than the one you want. You can recall an older event by matching to a string *within* the event, instead of strictly at the beginning. You would do so by using a command like that shown in the following example:

```
12 % !?myscript
csh myscript -f -v -b -q -x
13 % _
```

In this example, I recalled event 3 from earlier in the chapter by matching to the string `myscript`. If I had tried to match to the beginning of the line with `!csh`, I would have recalled event 4 instead, because it was the more recent event that matched to `csh` at the start of the command. With this method, I was recall the event I wanted by matching to text *contained* within the event.

Optionally, you can follow the match text by another question mark (?). This is required only when you want to follow the match text with new text to be appended to the recalled event. The additional question mark is then needed to tell the C Shell where the match text ends and the appended text starts:

```
13 % !?myscript? appended_filename
csh myscript -f -v -b -q -x appended_filename
14 % _
```

Here I recalled the same event as before, but I also added a filename, `appended_filename`, to the end of the command as part of the action of recalling the event.

Modifying Previous Events

Thus far, you have learned how to recall events to repeat them without change. Now you'll see how you can make changes to an event as part of the recall commands you have learned.

Words Within Events

Before you can modify previous events, you must know how to specify which word or words in the event you want to change. This section shows you how to make changes to one or more words in an event when you recall it from the history list.

Table 1.1 lists the C Shell *word designators* and a brief description of what each one indicates when used in recalling an event for modification.

Table 1.1. Event word designators.

Designator	Description
#	The entire command line entered up to this point.
0	The first input word (the command).
n	The *n*th argument on the command line.
^	The first argument on the command line (that is, 1).
$	The last argument on the command line.
x–y	The range of words from word *x* to word *y*.
-*y*	The range from 0-*y*.
*	All of the arguments, or a null value if just one word is in the event (that is, just a command).
*x**	Abbreviates *x* - $.
x -	Like *x** but omits word $.

Modifying Previous Events

When you enter new commands or recall previous ones from the history list, you can include selected words from previous commands. The most common history substitution that you will use is to include the last argument from the previous command in a new command. Typically, the last argument of a command is a filename that you want to reuse on the next command. To see how this can be done, look at the following example:

```
14 % ls testfile.txt
testfile.txt
15 % cat !$
This is the text that was in a file 'testfile.txt'
in my home directory /usr/dave. I will use this file
in examples where I want to look at text in a file.
16 % _
```

In this example, I first did an `ls` command to see that the file `testfile.txt` exists. The `ls` command displayed the filename, showing that the file is present. Then I included the same filename, `testfile.txt`, in the next command, which I entered by using the history word designator `!$` in place of a filename with the command `cat`. The shell made the substitution of the last word from the previous command onto this command line, and the result was to display the contents of the file on my terminal.

You could also just as easily use the word modifier !^ to indicate that the first argument in the previous command should be substituted. In the last example, because there is only one argument, the first and last argument are the same, so the result would be identical. In all cases, history word modifiers must be prefixed with the bang character to indicate that a history reference follows.

In the last example, using just the bang (!), I referenced the most recent event. If you need to reference an earlier event, you have to further qualify the modifier in the command. If you want to use the ls command on the files that were referenced in event 13, you could use the following command:

```
16 % ls !13:$ !13:^
ls appended_filename myscript
appended_filename
myscript
17 % _
```

In this example, I substituted the last argument word and the first argument word on the ls command. The shell echoed back the resulting command after the substitution and then it executed the command. The filenames that appear, appended_filename and myscript, are the results displayed by the ls command.

Once again, there is a another way I could have done the last example and still have received the same results. Rather than using the event number in the substitution, I could have used one of the forms of text recall, as I did in the simpler examples earlier in this section. Then, in place of the event number !13, I could have used either !csh to match on the command name or either !?myscript or !?appended_filename to match to text within event 13.

Lastly, you can use one of the word range designators to include some portion of the arguments from a previous event in your current command. I will leave that to you as an exercise to experiment with independently as you explore the possibilities of history substitutions and event modification.

Summary

In Day 1, you were introduced to the C Shell and presented with many reasons why it should be your default shell, the one that you use in your day-to-day work on the UNIX system. I showed you how to find out what your default shell is set to and how to make the C Shell your default shell.

You learned about the two modes of operation of the shell: the interactive mode, in which you receive command prompts from the shell at your terminal; and the noninteractive mode, in which the shell is processing a script file that contains C Shell and UNIX commands. Ways to end the C Shell were also demonstrated, and the options for starting up the C Shell were presented with brief explanations.

The last part of Day 1 introduced the C Shell's command history facility. You were shown a number of methods for recalling events from history and how to modify those recalled events. I also presented the event word designators that enable you to use selected words from previous events in a new command.

In Day 2, "Metacharacters," you will learn about shell metacharacters, which are used in filename generation, pattern matching, input and output modification, and much more. This material will be the foundation upon which your effective use of the C Shell will be based.

Related UNIX Topics

This chapter presented some new concepts and commands. Here is a list of some of these concepts and topics, with suggestions for sources of further information.

Dot Files: Consult Appendix E at the end of this book for examples of the "dot" files—.cshrc, .login, and .logout. You can modify these files to customize your shell environment. Doing so is covered in Day 6.

Other Shells: Look in Section 1 of your UNIX manuals for the man pages for the more and pg commands. Determine which of these commands is available on your system, and learn more about the different capabilities of these versatile commands.

Q&A

Q What are some of the features that distinguish the C Shell from the Bourne Shell?

A The C Shell has a history facility, by which you can recall command lines that were previously executed. You can then repeat those command lines or modify them and execute the modified version. Additionally, the C Shell provides a job control capability that gives you the ability to exert more control over your background processes. This feature is covered in the last chapter of the book.

Q What is the command that I would use to change my default shell? Where is the C Shell usually found on UNIX systems?

A The command used to change your default shell is chsh. To use this command, you give it a single argument, which is the pathname of the shell that you want to have as your new default. On some systems, the C shell is in /bin/csh, whereas on others you will find it in /usr/bin/csh. Typically, if your system is Berkeley-kernel based, the first path applies. On the other hand, if yours is a System V-based kernel system, look for the C Shell in /usr/bin/csh.

Q How can I quickly repeat the last command that I entered?

A The quick way to do that is with the history recall of !!. All history substitutions begin with the exclamation, or *bang*, character (!), and the second exclamation mark is a short hand for the previous command.

Q How can I make a quick change of one word of the last command and rerun it?

A The Quick Substitution character is the carat (^). Enclose first the string you want to change in carats, followed by the string to replace it with, and a closing carat (for example, ^change_this^to_that^). The first occurrence of the search string will then be replaced by the second, and the resulting command line will then be executed.

Workshop

The Workshop provides several sections to aid you in reviewing the topics covered in today's lesson. There is a quiz section to help you reinforce your understanding of the material presented in Day 1 and exercises to give you practice applying what you have learned. Take the time to review these questions and exercises, so that you understand the concepts before you begin the next day's lesson. The answers are provided in Appendix F, "Answers to Quizzes and Exercises."

Quiz

1. How can you find out what the settings are for your shell variables?

2. What is the difference between the two modes of C Shell operation?

3. How would you recall an event in each of the following ways?

    a. By event number

    b. By searching for a command word

    c. By searching for a word within the command line

4. How would you include the first argument from your last command line on your next command line?

5. How would you include the last argument from your previous command on your next command line?

Exercises

1. Experiment with event modification.

2. Work with substituting words from previous events into new commands.

3. Find out more about the capabilities of using word ranges to include more than one or less than all of the words from a previous event.

Metacharacters

Introduction to Day 2

Throughout this book, and in all aspects of the C Shell, you will encounter various special characters. These special characters are referred to as *metacharacters*. They have special meaning to the shell in a number of different contexts. Metacharacters are the subject of today's lesson. Learning about the different types of metacharacters is key to becoming a proficient C Shell user.

Setting Today's Goals

Today, you will learn about

- [ ] Syntactic metacharacters

- [ ] Filename metacharacters

- [ ] Quotation metacharacters

- [ ] Input/Output metacharacters

- [ ] Expansion substitution metacharacters

- [ ] Other metacharacters

- [ ] Using metacharacters as normal characters

Metacharacters in the C Shell

As you learn more about using the C Shell, you will frequently use metacharacters. The shell has groups of characters which, in different contexts, have special meaning or significance. These special characters are called metacharacters.

The operation of the C Shell is affected by metacharacters. Metacharacters play an important part during the period when the shell is processing a command line, before it executes the command line. The different groups of metacharacters affect separate aspects of command-line processing.

The following sections introduce you to each of the different kinds of metacharacters employed by the C Shell. You will have the opportunity to explore the effects each group has on the command line. Today's lesson shows you how you can use them to enhance your use of the shell, both in writing scripts and in entering commands interactively at your terminal.

## 2

Syntactic Metacharacters

The first group of metacharacters, *syntactic metacharacters*, are used as special punctuation characters between and around commands. They are used to combine multiple UNIX commands to make a single logical command. Syntactic metacharacters provide a way to effect conditional execution of a command or commands, based on the outcome of a previous command.

In later parts of this book, you'll learn more about processing commands in background and the concept of "jobs" in the C Shell. A syntactic metacharacter is important to these distinctive aspects of the C Shell. Table 2.1 lists each of the syntactic metacharacters, with a brief description of its function. Each syntactic metacharacter is explained in detail following the table, with examples illustrating where and how the metacharacter is used.

Table 2.1. Syntactic metacharacters.

Metacharacter	Description of Function
;	Separator between sequentially executed commands.
¦	Separator between commands that are part of a pipeline. In a pipeline, commands execute sequentially. The output of the command to the left of the separator becomes the input to the command that follows the separator.
( )	Used to isolate commands separated by semicolons ; or pipelines ¦. The commands within the parentheses, executed within their own subshell, are treated as a unit and appear to be a single command. Enclosing a pipeline in parentheses allows it to be included within other pipelines.
&	Background command indicator. Tells the shell to execute the commands as a background process.
¦¦	Separator between commands, in which the command following the ¦¦ is executed only if the preceding command fails.
&&	Separator between commands, in which the command following the && is executed only if the preceding command succeeds.

Joining Commands with ;

Using the semicolon (;) as a separator between commands enables you to put two or more commands together on the same line. The commands are executed sequentially, as though each were on a separate script line or as though each were individually entered at multiple command prompts.

By itself, this separator is used for cosmetic reasons in a script to put more than one command on a line. At a command prompt, it permits you to enter several commands to be executed sequentially, without the need to wait for each to complete before entering the next.

In the following example, the pwd command prints the current working directory, showing that it is my home directory /usr/dave.

```
1 % pwd
/usr/dave
2 % cd tools/myscripts ; ls
backuphomedir
findbyname
whois
3 % pwd
/usr/dave/tools/myscripts
4 % _
```

Next, using the semicolon separator, I joined a cd command to an ls command on the same line. The two commands are executed sequentially. First, the cd command changes directories to my tools/myscripts subdirectory, and then the ls command displays the names of the files in that directory. Another pwd command is done, showing that the current working directory is still /usr/dave/tools/myscripts.

Tip: Using the semicolon (;) metacharacter to join related command lines in scripts is useful for visually associating them together on a single line.

This separator is also useful for including more than one command in the definition of an alias. Aliases are explained in detail in tomorrow's lesson, "Command Substitution, Aliases, and Filename Generation."

Here, in the following example, I have defined an alias myscripts that duplicates the cd and ls commands used in the previous example.

```
4 % alias myscripts "cd tools/myscripts ; ls"
5 % pwd
```

```
/usr/dave
6 % myscripts
backuphomedir
findbyname
whois
7 % pwd
/usr/dave/tools/myscripts
8 % _
```

The two commands are joined using the semicolon separator to let the shell know that there are two distinct commands. Without the semicolon separator, the ls command would look as if it were a second argument to the cd command. This would cause the shell to issue an error message, because the cd command accepts only a single argument.

Without the semicolon, the shell cannot easily tell where one command ends and the next one begins. This separator character clearly indicates the boundary between commands. Another use of the semicolon is to separate commands that are to be grouped using the parentheses. The parentheses syntactic metacharacters are explained later in this lesson.

Caution: The UNIX find command has an option, -exec, that takes a command string as its argument. The find command wants the command string terminated with a semicolon so that find can tell where the command string argument ends and the next option or command begins. When you use the find -exec option from the C Shell, you need to remember that the semicolon character needs to be escaped with a backslash (\) character. The backslash escape character tells the C Shell not to interpret the character that follows as a metacharacter. Unless you "escape" the semicolon, the shell will process the semicolon as a metacharacter, and the find command will not get the semicolon on its command line. This results in an error message issued by the find command.

Creating Pipelines with |

Pipes and pipelines are one of the unique features of UNIX. Before pipes and pipelines were available, the output of one command would have to be captured to a file before it could then be used as the input to the next command. This was cumbersome and created additional overhead with opening and closing files and the attendant disk I/O to first write and then read the file. Additionally, you needed to provide for cleaning up these temporary work files after you were finished. Using pipes eliminates the additional disk I/O, as well as the need to clean up work files.

```
 8 % who > /tmp/who.$$
 9 % sort < /tmp/who.$$
craig          tty08     May 10 10:20
dave           tty07     May 10  8:00
fred           tty03     May 10  9:58
george         tty05     May 10 11:47
kathy          tty09     May 10  8:17
mary           tty02     May 10 13:35
10 % rm /tmp/who.$$
11 % _
```

Pipes and pipelines are explained in detail on Day 7, "File Redirection, Pipes, and Filters." Here I'll give you a brief introduction to the use of the pipe (¦) syntactic metacharacter. To easily understand what this separator character does, imagine connecting the output from one command to the input of a second command using a section of pipe. The data flows from the first to the second command without being written to the disk.

In the following example, the who command is executed, producing a report of the users that are currently logged in to the system. Each line shows the account name of a user, the terminal port he or she is working on, and the date and time that he or she logged in to the system. On the next line, event 12, the who command is again executed, but this time the output is piped to the UNIX sort command. The same report is produced, but now it is sorted by user account name rather than by the terminal port column, which is the default for the who command.

```
11 % who
mary           tty02     May 10 13:35
fred           tty03     May 10  9:58
george         tty05     May 10 11:47
dave           tty07     May 10  8:00
craig          tty08     May 10 10:20
kathy          tty09     May 10  8:17
12 % who ¦ sort
craig          tty08     May 10 10:20
dave           tty07     May 10  8:00
fred           tty03     May 10  9:58
george         tty05     May 10 11:47
kathy          tty09     May 10  8:17
mary           tty02     May 10 13:35
13 % _
```

Many UNIX commands, known generally as *filters*, take their input from stdin and write their output to stdout. The special filenames stdin and stdout refer to the default input and output sources for all UNIX commands. The default for stdin is the keyboard, and the default for stdout is the terminal display. With pipes you can connect multiple filters, creating a pipeline. New commands can be created by using pipelines in alias definitions.

In the following example, I first create an alias, whoison, that takes the output of who and pipes it to sort. The UNIX sort command, in the absence of a sort key, sorts the entire record. In this case the output of sort is essentially sorted by the user name in the first column. On the second line of the example, I now use my new alias whoison. As you can see, the output of who is sorted by the user name.

```
14 % alias whoison "who | sort"
15 % whoison
craig           tty08      May 10 10:20
dave            tty07      May 10  8:00
fred            tty03      May 10  9:58
george          tty05      May 10 11:47
kathy           tty09      May 10  8:17
mary            tty02      May 10 13:35
16 % _
```

Combining Commands with ()

On some occasions, you need to isolate a pipeline or sequence of semicolon-separated commands from the rest of the command line. The following example illustrates a case where parentheses are needed to achieve the desired results.

```
cd ~dave/tools/myscripts; tar cf - | (cd ~dave/tools/newscripts; tar xvpf -)
```

In this example, the current working directory is changed to ~dave/tools/myscripts. The tilde (~) metacharacter, explained in detail later in this chapter, is expanded to the home directory of the user name it precedes. Next, the tar command is used to create an archive of this directory and any subdirectories. The archive is output to stdout, which is specified with the f - portion of the options to tar. Following the pipe is a pair of commands enclosed in parentheses.

The parentheses start a subshell to process the commands. The output from the previous command is supplied through the pipe as the input to the subshell. The first command that the subshell processes is the cd command, which changes the working directory to /usr/dave/tools/newscripts. Because the cd command doesn't take its input from stdin, the output from the pipe is passed to the next command, tar. This tar command expects to extract an archive from stdin, again specified by the f - option.

The result is to make a copy of the subdirectory tree from /usr/dave/tools/myscripts on down, and place that copy at /usr/dave/tools/newscripts. The advantage of this method is that the tar command maintains all of the attributes of the original files, time, permissions, owner, group, and date. Using the UNIX cp command would have copied the files but with the current date, time, permissions, owner, and group, based on the current user's environment.

Executing Commands in Background with &

UNIX supports running programs at the command prompt in foreground and detached from the prompt in background. In foreground, the prompt does not reappear until the current command line completes execution. When you put a command or commands in background, the shell prompt reappears at once. The background job runs separately to completion, while you execute additional commands in foreground.

Background commands are entered in the same way as foreground commands, with the addition of a special metacharacter, the ampersand (&). The ampersand character is the last character of a command line. It indicates to the C Shell that you want the command to be run in background.

The following example shows a long format directory-listing command that recurses through all subdirectories, `ls -lR`.

```
17 % ls -lR > /tmp/longlist &
[1] 1021
18 % _
```

The output from this command is redirected to a file /tmp/longlist. If the output were not redirected to a file, it would be displayed at your terminal while you were attempting to enter additional commands in foreground. By redirecting the output to a file, you can examine it later, after the command has completed executing in background. File redirection is the topic of Day 7.

The line following event 17 has the number 1 in square brackets, followed by the number 1021. When you put a command in background using the ampersand, the C Shell always responds with two pieces of information. The number in brackets is the job number, in this case 1. The number following it is the process ID of the command, which is 1021 for the `ls` command that was entered. The job number can be used to control the background process. For more information on jobs and controlling background processes, see Day 14, "Jobs."

The ampersand syntactic metacharacter can also be used to place pipelined commands in background, as in the following example:

```
19 % who ¦ sort -o /tmp/whoison &
[2] 1033 1034
20 % _
```

In event 19, the two commands, `who` and `sort`, are both placed in background, with the output of who still linked to the input of sort as described earlier. If you already have one or more background jobs running, the shell returns the next higher job number, [2] in this example. Notice also that because there are actually two commands on the command line, the shell returned two process IDs, 1033 and 1034, belonging to who and sort respectively.

Caution: Earlier, you learned how to enter multiple commands on a single input line using the semicolon (;) metacharacter. If you want to put any of those commands in background, you would replace the semicolon with an ampersand. Keep in mind, however, that you will then lose the sequential processing of the commands; they will all be running in background at the same time. If you need to maintain sequential processing with the semicolon, and you also want to run the commands in background, enclose the entire set of commands in parentheses and follow the closing parenthesis with the ampersand metacharacter. Thus

```
20 % cd tools/myscripts ; ls > /tmp/myscripts.$$
21 % _
```

becomes

```
21 % ( cd tools/myscripts ; ls > /tmp/myscripts.$$ ) &
[3] 1057
22 % _
```

Notice that there is only a single process ID for the two commands, cd and ls. Because the commands are enclosed in parentheses, the shell starts a subshell to process the commands. The process ID is for this subshell and not for the commands within the parentheses. They are run attached to the subshell in its 'foreground,' despite the fact that the subshell itself is running in background.

Conditionally Executing Commands with | | and &&

The C Shell supports two special metacharacter pairs that enable conditional execution of commands based on completion status. Very often in shell programming you need to determine whether to run a command, based on the results of a previous command's execution. The syntactic metacharacter pairs double pipes (¦¦) and double ampersands (&&) give you that ability.

Separating two commands with ¦¦ causes the C Shell to test the status of the first command and execute the second only if the first command fails. With && the reverse is true. The second command is performed if, and only if, the first command succeeds.

In the following example, the output of who is piped to grep, which searches for the word frodo. If grep fails to find frodo in the output of who, a message is echoed to that effect.

```
22 % who ¦ grep frodo ¦¦ echo "User frodo is not logged on."
User frodo is not logged on.
23 % _
```

Notice that there is no restriction against having more than one command before the ¦¦, but only the status of the last command in any multicommand sequence is evaluated.

> **Tip:** You can use these operators in many creative ways within your shell scripts. To give you an idea, here is an excellent example in which the remainder of the iteration is skipped, using the continue command, based on the outcome of a command within a `foreach` loop:
>
> ```
> foreach filename ( * )
>     grep -v '1994$' $filename && continue
>     sort $filename >> /tmp/prior_years
> end
> ```
>
> The contents of each file `$filename` are searched to see whether it contains lines that end with 1994. If no lines ending in 1994 are found, that file is skipped, using the `continue` command. The continue command skips to the `end` statement, which starts the next iteration of the `foreach` loop. Each file containing lines ending in 1994 is sorted and the output appended to a file named `/tmp/prior_years`.
>
> This use of the && and ¦¦ metacharacters makes your C Shell scripts more concise and easier to code and read. An alternative—using an `if` statement to test `$status`—is readable and understandable but not as compact.
>
> Similarly, these metacharacters can be used with `break` within loops and `breaksw` with switches, to control when the regular behavior of these commands is to be modified.

Filename Metacharacters

The next group of metacharacters—filename metacharacters—are used on command lines to form match patterns for filename substitution. They are used to identify or form abbreviations. On Day 3, "Command Substitution, Aliases, and Filename Generation,"

you will learn more about the use of these metacharacters. Table 2.2 lists each of them with a brief description of its function. This section introduces you to filename metacharacters, briefly explaining the use and function of each in matching UNIX filenames and identifying abbreviations, with examples.

Table 2.2. Filename metacharacters.

Metacharacter	Description of Function
?	Filename-expansion character that matches any single character.
*	Filename-expansion character that matches any sequence of zero or more characters.
[ ]	Filename expansion designating a character or range of characters that, as a class, are matched against a single character. A range is shown by the first and last characters in the range separated by a dash (-).
{ }	Used for abbreviating sets of words that share common parts.
~	Used to abbreviate the path to a user's home directory.

Matching a Single Character with ?

Frequently, files are created with some form of serialization as part of the filename. For example, the initial data file for an application might be named something like gl_data.01. This could be the general ledger data for the first month of the year. The next file would then be named gl_data.02, and so on as the year progresses. If I want to use the ls command to get information on all of these data files, I could type the following command:

```
23 % cd acctdata
24 % ls -l gl_data.01 gl_data.02 gl_data.03 gl_data.04 gl_data.05
-rw-r--r--  1 dave     users     2420 Jan 31 17:05 gl_data.01
-rw-r--r--  1 dave     users     2204 Feb 28 16:58 gl_data.02
-rw-r--r--  1 dave     users     2532 Mar 31 17:12 gl_data.03
-rw-r--r--  1 dave     users     2380 Apr 30 16:45 gl_data.04
-rw-r--r--  1 dave     users     2466 May 31 17:25 gl_data.05
25 % _
```

After changing my working directory to acctdata, I used the ls command to show the sizes and dates of each gl_data file for the first five months of the year. If these were the only files that existed to date, I could have entered the following shorter version of the command, and I would have received the same output.

```
25 % ls -l gl_data.??
-rw-r--r--  1 dave     users      2420 Jan 31 17:05 gl_data.01
-rw-r--r--  1 dave     users      2204 Feb 28 16:58 gl_data.02
-rw-r--r--  1 dave     users      2532 Mar 31 17:12 gl_data.03
-rw-r--r--  1 dave     users      2380 Apr 30 16:45 gl_data.04
-rw-r--r--  1 dave     users      2466 May 31 17:25 gl_data.05
26 % _
```

Each of the question-mark metacharacters matches to a single character, no more, no less. So, the pattern gl_data.?? would match to the string gl_data., followed by any combination of two characters. The characters can be any character from the printable portion of the ASCII character set.

One of my favorite and frequent uses for the question-mark metacharacter is to find all of the *dot*, also called *silent*, files in a directory. These files are called silent because the ls command normally does not display them. They begin with a dot or period (.) as the first character of the filename. These files typically are used by various UNIX commands for configuration data and startup scripts.

Often, when you use these filenames as arguments to UNIX commands, you want to explicitly avoid the special files called *dot* (.) and *dot dot* (..). These are special directory files that point to the current directory (.) and its parent directory (..). Many commands produce unpredictable, unexpected, and frequently undesirable results when given one or both of these files as arguments.

To get all of the dot files and avoid these special directories, use the match pattern .??*. If you analyze this pattern, you will see first the dot, which directly matches the initial character of all of the silent files you want to select. The dot is followed by two question-mark metacharacters. This is key, because the two of these characters together force the selected filenames to have at least two characters following the initial dot, thus eliminating *dot* (.) and *dot dot* (..). Finally, there is a trailing asterisk, which matches zero or more additional characters for the remainder of any of the filenames.

In the following example, I illustrate the use of the match pattern .??*, which was described previously. First, in event 26, I use the cd command without an argument to ensure that my current working directory is my home directory. Next, I use the ls command with the filename match pattern .??* so you can see the effect of this particular combination of metacharacters. The output of the ls command shows a list of only my *dot* files. This list does not include the files *dot* (.) and *dot dot* (..), because they are less than three characters in length, and the match pattern .??* requires matching filenames to be at least three characters long.

```
26 % cd
27 % ls .??*
.cshrc
.exrc
.login
.mailrc
.newsrc
.profile
28 % _
```

Matching Zero or Many Characters with *

In the last example, I used the metacharacter pattern .??* to find all of the silent files in my home directory. Notice that the last character in this expression is the asterisk (*) metacharacter. This special character matches zero or more characters that can occur in a filename, with the exception of the period or dot (.). To match a period or dot, you must explicitly place it in the pattern, such as in the previous example.

The asterisk metacharacter can be used anywhere in the match pattern: at the beginning, in the middle, or at the end. It is probably the most frequently used filename metacharacter. The following list illustrates the use of this metacharacter.

Match Pattern	Description
*.c	This pattern, with the asterisk at the beginning, matches all C language source code files that end with .c, such as main.c, getline.c, my_sub.c, Read.c, and put1char.c.
ar_*.dat	With the asterisk in the middle of the pattern, with literal characters at the beginning and end, all files that begin with ar_ and end with .dat with any kind and number of characters in between will match. All of the following would match this pattern: ar_january.dat, ar_config.dat, ar_backup.dat, and ar_proof.dat.
gl_data.*	The asterisk metacharacter placed at the end of the pattern matches all files that begin with gl_data. The type and number of characters following the asterisk does not matter, because the asterisk matches zero or more of any character (except .). This pattern would match the files that were found in event 24 earlier in today's material: gl_data.01, gl_data.02, gl_data.03, gl_data.04, and gl_data.05.

Matching a Class of Characters with *[]*

The square-bracket ([]) filename metacharacters define a list, or class of characters, that are the allowable matches for a single character position. This list, or class, can contain a character range—two characters separated by a dash (-). A range includes the starting and ending characters used in its definition.

When a match pattern includes a character class definition, the shell substitutes each member in the class, one at a time, for the brackets and their contents. Any filename that matches the resulting pattern is included as an argument on the command line.

Character classes enable you to create match patterns that are more exact than those using just the question mark (?) and asterisk (*) metacharacters presented previously. The following list illustrates some of the different ways you can use character classes to match groups of files.

Match Pattern	Description
`[A-Z]*`	Matches all files that start with a capital letter. The range A-Z matches any of the letters from A to Z inclusively.
`*[aeiou]`	Matches any file that ends in a lowercase vowel.
`chapter*[24680].txt`	Matches all even-numbered chapters.
`page.[2-48]`	Matches page.2, page.3, page.4, and page.8.
`[A-Za-z][0-9]*`	Matches all files that begin with a letter (lowercase or uppercase), followed by a digit and zero or more other characters.

As these examples illustrate, the square-bracket character-range metacharacters ([]) provide a great deal of flexibility and the power to create match patterns tailored to exact requirements. Rather than having to enter a long list of filenames on a command line or resorting to other means to create the list, you can use character classes for concise match pattern definition.

Abbreviating Filenames with *{}*

You have learned about the filename metacharacters ?, *, and [], which you can use as shortcuts to form filenames. Using combinations of these metacharacters, you can form more specific match patterns that expand to the filenames you want on the command line. In some cases you cannot get the exact set of filenames you need using just these metacharacters. Often in these cases you can target the precise set of filenames required using the curly bracket ({}) metacharacters. Using the curly brackets alone or combined with the other filename metacharacters you learned today, you can form more complex filename expressions.

The curly brackets ({}) contain a comma-separated list of items consisting of one or more characters. Each item in the list is used in turn to expand to a filename that matches the full expression in which the brackets are included. Unlike the square-bracket metacharacters, the items in this list are not sorted. For example, a{f,e,d}b expands to afb, aeb, and adb, in this exact order. The following examples illustrate how these special metacharacters are used to abbreviate filenames.

In earlier examples, you saw filenames such as gl_data.05, in which the 05 indicated that the file contains data for the month of May. These files are a small part of an accounting system that has applications for payables, receivables, payroll, inventory, and sales, in addition to the general ledger system. Each of these applications has data files that begin with a two-character code for the application: gl for general ledger, ap for accounts payable, ar for accounts receivable, pr for payroll, sa for sales, and in for inventory.

Changing to the directory that contains these data files and entering the ls command shows all of these data files for each of the applications that are part of the accounting system:

```
29 % cd acctdata
30 % ls -l *data.*
-rw-r--r--  1 dave    users       3640 Jan 31 17:05 ap_data.01
-rw-r--r--  1 dave    users       3424 Feb 28 16:58 ap_data.02
-rw-r--r--  1 dave    users       3752 Mar 31 17:12 ap_data.03
-rw-r--r--  1 dave    users       3500 Apr 30 16:45 ap_data.04
-rw-r--r--  1 dave    users       3686 May 31 17:25 ap_data.05
-rw-r--r--  1 dave    users       4210 Jan 31 17:05 ar_data.01
-rw-r--r--  1 dave    users       4004 Feb 28 16:58 ar_data.02
-rw-r--r--  1 dave    users       4322 Mar 31 17:12 ar_data.03
-rw-r--r--  1 dave    users       4170 Apr 30 16:45 ar_data.04
-rw-r--r--  1 dave    users       4256 May 31 17:25 ar_data.05
-rw-r--r--  1 dave    users       2420 Jan 31 17:05 gl_data.01
-rw-r--r--  1 dave    users       2204 Feb 28 16:58 gl_data.02
-rw-r--r--  1 dave    users       2532 Mar 31 17:12 gl_data.03
-rw-r--r--  1 dave    users       2380 Apr 30 16:45 gl_data.04
-rw-r--r--  1 dave    users       2466 May 31 17:25 gl_data.05
-rw-r--r--  1 dave    users       6530 Jan 31 17:05 in_data.01
-rw-r--r--  1 dave    users       6314 Feb 28 16:58 in_data.02
-rw-r--r--  1 dave    users       6642 Mar 31 17:12 in_data.03
-rw-r--r--  1 dave    users       6490 Apr 30 16:45 in_data.04
-rw-r--r--  1 dave    users       6576 May 31 17:25 in_data.05
-rw-r--r--  1 dave    users        420 Jan 31 17:05 pr_data.01
-rw-r--r--  1 dave    users        404 Feb 28 16:58 pr_data.02
-rw-r--r--  1 dave    users        532 Mar 31 17:12 pr_data.03
-rw-r--r--  1 dave    users        480 Apr 30 16:45 pr_data.04
-rw-r--r--  1 dave    users        466 May 31 17:25 pr_data.05
-rw-r--r--  1 dave    users       5150 Jan 31 17:05 sa_data.01
-rw-r--r--  1 dave    users       5234 Feb 28 16:58 sa_data.02
-rw-r--r--  1 dave    users       5262 Mar 31 17:12 sa_data.03
-rw-r--r--  1 dave    users       5110 Apr 30 16:45 sa_data.04
-rw-r--r--  1 dave    users       5196 May 31 17:25 sa_data.05
31 % _
```

You saw that using the question mark and asterisk metacharacters, you can select all of the files for an application, for example, pr_data.* to get all of the payroll data files. You also learned that with the square bracket metacharacters, you can get a more specific subset of all of the data files. You might use a[pr]data.* to list all of the files for accounts payable and accounts receivable. If you needed to list the files for sales as well as receivables and payables, you would need to combine a[pr]data.* with sa_data.* on the command line, as in the following example.

```
31 % ls a[pr]data.* sa_data.*
-rw-r--r--  1 dave    users     3640 Jan 31 17:05 ap_data.01
-rw-r--r--  1 dave    users     3424 Feb 28 16:58 ap_data.02
-rw-r--r--  1 dave    users     3752 Mar 31 17:12 ap_data.03
-rw-r--r--  1 dave    users     3500 Apr 30 16:45 ap_data.04
-rw-r--r--  1 dave    users     3686 May 31 17:25 ap_data.05
-rw-r--r--  1 dave    users     4210 Jan 31 17:05 ar_data.01
-rw-r--r--  1 dave    users     4004 Feb 28 16:58 ar_data.02
-rw-r--r--  1 dave    users     4322 Mar 31 17:12 ar_data.03
-rw-r--r--  1 dave    users     4170 Apr 30 16:45 ar_data.04
-rw-r--r--  1 dave    users     4256 May 31 17:25 ar_data.05
-rw-r--r--  1 dave    users     5150 Jan 31 17:05 sa_data.01
-rw-r--r--  1 dave    users     5234 Feb 28 16:58 sa_data.02
-rw-r--r--  1 dave    users     5262 Mar 31 17:12 sa_data.03
-rw-r--r--  1 dave    users     5110 Apr 30 16:45 sa_data.04
-rw-r--r--  1 dave    users     5196 May 31 17:25 sa_data.05
32 % _
```

Using the curly bracket metacharacters, you can shorten the expression and not have to use two separate patterns to match these three sets of files. Because they all contain data in the middle and because all end with the month digits, their only difference is in the first two characters. If you use {ar,ap,sa}data.*, the command will expand to the exact set of files that you need:

```
32 % ls {ar,ap,sa}data.*
-rw-r--r--  1 dave    users     3640 Jan 31 17:05 ap_data.01
-rw-r--r--  1 dave    users     3424 Feb 28 16:58 ap_data.02
-rw-r--r--  1 dave    users     3752 Mar 31 17:12 ap_data.03
-rw-r--r--  1 dave    users     3500 Apr 30 16:45 ap_data.04
-rw-r--r--  1 dave    users     3686 May 31 17:25 ap_data.05
-rw-r--r--  1 dave    users     4210 Jan 31 17:05 ar_data.01
-rw-r--r--  1 dave    users     4004 Feb 28 16:58 ar_data.02
-rw-r--r--  1 dave    users     4322 Mar 31 17:12 ar_data.03
-rw-r--r--  1 dave    users     4170 Apr 30 16:45 ar_data.04
-rw-r--r--  1 dave    users     4256 May 31 17:25 ar_data.05
-rw-r--r--  1 dave    users     5150 Jan 31 17:05 sa_data.01
-rw-r--r--  1 dave    users     5234 Feb 28 16:58 sa_data.02
-rw-r--r--  1 dave    users     5262 Mar 31 17:12 sa_data.03
-rw-r--r--  1 dave    users     5110 Apr 30 16:45 sa_data.04
-rw-r--r--  1 dave    users     5196 May 31 17:25 sa_data.05
33 % _
```

Using the curly brackets more than once in an expression is permitted and can be used to good advantage to abbreviate filenames. The expression s{a,e,i,o,u}{n,t} expands

to san, sen, sin, son, sun, sat, set, sit, sot, and sut. Combined with the other filename metacharacters—?, *, and [ ]—you can use the curly bracket metacharacters to create expansion patterns to suit your needs.

Home Directory Abbreviations with ~

The tilde (~) metacharacter is a special character that expands to a user's home directory path. When the tilde is used by itself, the C Shell replaces it with your home directory path. The tilde can also be followed immediately by the name of a user on your system. In this case, the shell replaces the tilde with the path of that user's home directory.

In the following example, I first confirm my current working directory using the pwd command. The output from pwd shows that I am in the directory /tmp. In event 34 I change directories to the acctdata subdirectory within my home directory. To do this, I use cd with the path ~/acctdata. The tilde is expanded by the C Shell to my home directory. Once again I confirm my current directory using pwd, and you can see that it has changed to /usr/dave/acctdata. The C Shell replaced the tilde with /usr/dave, which is my home directory path. In event 36 I again change directories, but this time I use tilde with the account name of a different user. Using pwd once more shows me that I am in the home directory of the user dennis, which is /usr/dennis. The C Shell replaced the entire expression ~dennis with the home directory path for the user name that followed the tilde.

```
33 % pwd
/tmp
34 % cd ~/acctdata
35 % pwd
/usr/dave/acctdata
36 % cd ~dennis
37 % pwd
/usr/dennis
38 % _
```

Using the tilde in shell scripts permits you to make them adaptable. It eliminates the need to hardcode paths to user directories or to perform an elaborate lookup to find a user's home directory.

Note: When you use the tilde by itself to get your own home directory, the C Shell returns the value contained in the built-in shell variable $home. When you use the tilde followed by a username, the C Shell looks up the user in the /etc/passwd file and returns the home directory path found in the user's password record.

Quotation Metacharacters

There are three quotation metacharacters, used to selectively control when metacharacters from other groups are protected from expansion or interpretation by the C Shell. Judicious use of these characters allows construction of more sophisticated scripts. Table 2.3 introduces these three characters and describes the function of each.

Table 2.3. Quotation metacharacters.

Metacharacter	Description of Function
\	Prevents the following character from being interpreted as a metacharacter by the shell.
"	Prevents the string of characters enclosed within a pair of double-quote characters (") from being interpreted as metacharacters. Command and variable expansion are not affected by the double quotes.
'	Prevents the string of characters enclosed within a pair of single-quote characters (') from being interpreted as com mands or metacharacters.

Escaping Metacharacters with \

When the shell interprets or expands metacharacters, they no longer appear on the command line when execution begins. "Escaping" individual metacharacters prevents them from being interpreted by the shell, and they remain for the command to process when execution begins. The following examples and their explanations will illustrate some of the uses for the backslash (\) metacharacter.

```
38 % set quoted=\"quotes\"
39 % echo $quoted
"quotes"
40 % set unquoted="noquotes"
41 % echo $unquoted
noquotes
42 % _
```

This example shows how escaped quotes can be used to produce strings that contain quotes themselves. The variable $quoted is assigned the value of \"quotes\". Because the quotes are preceded by backslashes, they are "escaped" and are not interpreted by the shell; they remain to be part of the value assigned to the variable. Using echo to display the contents of the variable $quoted, you can see that the value retains the quotes.

Next, the variable $noquotes is set to the string "noquotes". Notice that the quotes are not escaped with backslashes. Again using echo to display the variable contents, you can see that this time the quotes were removed by the shell before the assignment was made. Using the backslash to escape quote metacharacters is helpful when the contents of a variable are to be passed to another script or command, where the contents can then be interpreted and expanded.

Protecting Metacharacters with "

The backslash, used to protect individual metacharacters, must be placed before each and every character that is to be escaped. For a limited number of characters, using the backslash is not unreasonable. For a longer string of characters, you can use the double quotes (") to enclose the entire string. All of the metacharacters in the string will be protected from interpretation and expansion by the C Shell.

Quoted strings can contain normal characters, metacharacters, and shell variables. Although the quotes protect the metacharacters from expansion, commands and shell variables will still be expanded even when enclosed within quotes. The following example shows how quotes protect metacharacters from expansion.

```
42 % set inside="test text"
43 % set outside="* $inside !"
44 % echo $outside
* test text !
45 % _
```

Putting variables with in shell variables

Notice that the asterisk and exclamation metacharacters were not expanded, but the variable $inside was expanded by the shell. When the resulting string, assigned to $outside, is displayed, it shows these metacharacters surrounding the contents of the variable $inside.

Protecting Commands, Variables and Metacharacters with '

The single quote (') metacharacter is much like the double quote ("). It too protects metacharacters from being expanded. Additionally, it protects variables from expansion, and it prevents normal characters from being interpreted as commands.

In the following example, in events 45 and 46, variables $text1 and $inside are set to values:

```
45 % set text1="contents of text1"
46 % set inside="double quotes show $text1"
47 % echo $inside
double quotes show contents of text1
```

49

```
48 % set inside='single quotes hide $text1'
49 % echo $inside
double quotes hide $text1
50 % _
```

Notice that $inside includes $text1 in its string. When $inside is displayed using echo, you can see that $text1 was expanded in event 46 because the double quotes don't protect variables. In event 48 the same assignment is made, but this time the string is enclosed in single quotes. When $inside is displayed again, you see that this time the variable $text1 was protected and shows as a literal within the string.

Input/Output Metacharacters

When any UNIX program is executed, whether it is a shell or another command, it starts with three open files: standard input, referred to as stdin; standard output, referred to as stdout; and standard error, referred to as stderr. Many UNIX commands known as filters expect their input from stdin and write their output to stdout.

The input/output metacharacters, used for file redirection and pipes, are one of the distinctive features of UNIX. With these metacharacters, you can direct the output of a command to a file or you pipe it through other UNIX commands. You can also cause a command to take its input from a disk file or a pipe rather than from your keyboard. Additionally, with these metacharacters, you can merge stderr with stdout. Table 2.4 lists these metacharacters and describes the function each performs. Following the table is an introduction to these metacharacters. On Day 7, they are presented again in detail.

Table 2.4. Input/Output metacharacters.

Metacharacter	Description of Function
< name	Redirected input to command is read from name.
> name	Output from command is redirected to name. If name exists, it is overwritten.
>& name	Output from stderr is combined with stdout and written to name.
>! name	Output from command is redirected to name. If name exists, it is overwritten. This form is used when you want to override the effect of the $noclobber variable.
>&! name	Output from stderr is combined with stdout and redirected to name. If name exists, it is overwritten. This form is used when you want to override the effect of the $noclobber variable.

Metacharacter	Description of Function
>> *name*	Output from command is appended to the end of *name*. If $noclobber is set and *name* does not exist, an error message is issued.
>>& *name*	Appends output from stderr, combined with stdout and appended to the end of name.
>>! *name*	The same as >>, used when $noclobber is set. When name does not exist, it is created without an error being issued.
>>&! *name*	Appends output from stderr, combined with stdout and appended to the end of *name*. The same as >>& used when $noclobber is set. When *name* does not exist, it is created without an error being issued.
<< *word*	Input is read from stdin to the shell, up to the first input line that contains only *word*. No command, filename, or variable substitution is performed on *word*. Before any expansion or substitution is done on each input line, the line is examined for *word*.
¦	Creates a pipeline between two commands. The output of the command to the left of the pipe (¦) is connected to the input of the command to the right of the pipe.
¦&	Creates a pipeline between two commands, with the output from both stderr and stdout of the command to the left of the pipe (¦) combined and connected to the input of the command to the right of the pipe.

Handwritten annotations: "error Log" (left margin near >>& name); "read in only up to — word —" (near << word); "error processing" (near ¦&)

The input/output metacharacters are referred to as redirection characters. They are used to redirect input and output from their standard sources to or from files or other commands. These metacharacters can also be used to combine or merge the output of standard error, where diagnostic and error messages are sent, with the regular output that goes to standard output.

Input Redirection with <

Input to commands typically comes from one of two sources—the keyboard or a filename supplied as an argument on the command line. Some UNIX commands take input from a file if given, but read from stdin if no file is present. Other commands *only* take their input from stdin. You can supply input to such commands from a file that you have prepared by using the less than (<) metacharacter.

Consider the following example:

```
50 % mail mary < memo.24may
51 % _
```

The UNIX mail command reads input from stdin and doesn't accept a filename argument. Normal use of mail permits you to start typing your message immediately after entering the command. The example illustrates an alternative in which a message to be sent to user mary is redirected from a file named memo.24may. You have the option to use the UNIX editor vi to prepare your message in advance rather than typing it on the fly with no editing capability other than the backspace key.

The UNIX cat command is one that reads from either a file or from stdin. Event 51, in the following example, uses input redirection to provide input to cat, whereas event 52 uses a file argument to cat:

```
51 % cat < testtext
This is the contents of the file testtext
which I use in examples to display what's
inside a file with a UNIX command.
52 % cat testtext
This is the contents of the file testtext
which I use in examples to display what's
inside a file with a UNIX command.
53 % _
```

You can see that both methods provide the same results.

Output Redirection with >, >&, >!, or >&!

Output from UNIX commands typically goes to stdout. Many commands write their error messages and informational messages to stderr. This allows you to use redirection to capture output to a file and still receive errors or information messages at the terminal.

The following examples illustrate the different output redirection metacharacters.

```
53 % grep -i david /etc/passwd > /tmp/david.pass
54 % cat /tmp/david.pass
davide:A01#BpsGN&mY:100:20:David Ennis, x5021:/usr/davide:/usr/bin/csh
55 % set noclobber
56 % grep -i david /etc/passwd > /tmp/david.pass
file exists
57 % grep -i david /etc/passwd >! /tmp/david.pass
58 % grep -i david /etc/passwd >& /tmp/pass.error
59 % cat /tmp/pass.error
file exists
60 % _
```

In event 53, the grep command is used to search the /etc/passwd file for lines containing the word david. The -i option has grep do the search in a case insensitive mode, so David matches as well as david. The output from grep is redirected to the file /tmp/david.pass. Using cat to display the contents of /tmp/david.pass, I see the account record that matches the search string.

Next, the built-in shell variable $noclobber is set. You should recall that when this switch variable is set, it prevents an existing file from being overwritten by file redirection output. When the same grep command is repeated with the output file existing, an error message is displayed and nothing is written to the output file. Changing the redirection to >! and repeating the command permits the file to be overwritten without an error message.

In event 58, with the file still existing and $noclobber still set, the grep command is repeated. This time the redirection is done with >&, which merges stderr with stdout. The grep command, as in event 56, issues an error message, but this message is not displayed at the terminal. The >& redirection caused the message to be written to the file /tmp/pass.error. Using cat to display this file shows that the error message from stderr did in fact go to the file. Though not shown in the example, redirection with >&! will overwrite a file if it exists with $noclobber set.

Input Redirection Within Scripts Using <<

The input metacharacters (<<) enable you to redirect lines from a script to the input of a UNIX command within the script. Input redirection done in this manner is known as a *here document*. This manner of input redirection has several common uses within scripts. It can be used to output multiline messages from a script without the need to use multiple echo commands. The input metacharacters can also be used to supply repeatable command input to UNIX text-processing utilities such as sed, ed, or ex.

The input (<<) metacharacters are followed by *word*, which is a unique set of characters that marks the end of input lines to the here document. Each of the input lines, read by <<, is examined for a match to *word* before any other substitutions or metacharacter expansions are performed. Because variable substitution and metacharacter expansion is done on the here document text, you can include shell variables in the text and dynamically customize the message text or commands.

As the following example illustrates, the here document can be used to create output that reflects the values of current shell variables.

```
60 % echo <<END_WELCOME
Hello $user
Your current directory is $PWD
```

Where is the script Specified?

53

```
Have a good day.
END_WELCOME
Hello davide
Your current directory is /usr/davide
Have a good day.
61 % _
```

Examples later in this book will show more ways to take advantage of here documents in scripts.

Expansion/Substitution Metacharacters

The expansion/substitution metacharacters act as special indicators to the C Shell. There are four of these metacharacters. Table 2.5 lists each of these with a brief description.

Table 2.5. Expansion/Substitution metacharacters.

Metacharacter	Description
$	Variable substitution indicator. A word preceded by the $ is interpreted by the C Shell as a variable, and the contents of that variable are substituted for the string $word.
!	History substitution indicator. The exclamation character precedes all history event references.
?	History substitution modifier. The question mark character, preceded by the exclamation character (!) and followed by a word, indicates that the most recent event which contains the word is to be substituted.
:	Precedes substitution modifiers.

You have already learned about the exclamation (!) and question mark (?) metacharacters on Day 1 in the discussion of history events. The dollar sign and colon metacharacters are used with shell variables and are the topics of Day 4, "Shell Variables, Part I" and Day 5, "Shell Variables, Part II."

Other Metacharacters

The two metacharacters in this group don't fit any of the classes that you were introduced to today. One is used to indicate to the C Shell that the balance of the input line on which

it occurs is a comment. The other is a special prefix for identifying jobs on commands related to job control. On Day 14, these related commands, where you will use this prefix, will be presented in detail.

Using Metacharacters as Normal Characters

As you have learned in today's lesson, metacharacters used as part of command arguments are expanded by the C Shell and replaced by the results of that expansion. Therefore, they cannot be used directly on a command line and retain their original form. The command

```
echo *
```

results in the display of a sorted list of filenames in the current directory or the error message No match if there are no files. You will not see the asterisk displayed by echo because it was expanded by the C Shell. To allow the asterisk to be displayed, you must place it between single quotes or use a backslash before the character to protect it from the shell:

```
echo '*'
```

or

```
echo \*
```

There are three metacharacters that cannot be *quoted*, or *escaped*, using single quotes:

☐ The exclamation mark (!)

☐ The backslash (\)

☐ The single quote (')

To protect these metacharacters, you must use the backslash character for each instance.

```
61 % echo \'This is a quote\'
'This is a quote'
62 % echo 'Surprise\!'
Surprise!
63 % echo '\\backslash\\\*asterisk'
\backslash\*asterisk
64 % _
```

Notice in event 63 that the backslash is doubled for protection to produce a \ on output.

Summary

Today's lesson presented the C Shell's metacharacters—special characters used on command lines and in shell expressions. You were introduced to syntactic metacharacters, filename metacharacters, quotation metacharacters, input/output metacharacters, and expansion/substitution metacharacters. Metacharacters are used frequently in UNIX and with the C Shell. Successful use of metacharacters brings you to a new level of sophistication as a C Shell and UNIX user.

Tomorrow's lesson will introduce you to the C Shell alias facility. With aliases, you can define new commands, redefine old ones, and create abbreviations and synonyms for UNIX commands. Day 3 will also show you more on how to use the filename metacharacters you learned today for filename generation on C Shell command lines. Command substitution will also be presented, showing you how you can embed another UNIX command in your command line using its output as an argument.

Related UNIX Topics

This chapter presented some new concepts and commands. The following is a list of some of these concepts and topics, with suggestions for sources of further information.

Filename Generation:	Day 3 provides you with more detail on the use of filename metacharacters for filename generation.
File Redirection:	Day 7 explores the use of input/output metacharacters in file redirection and also the construction of command pipelines.
Background Jobs:	Day 14 explains the C Shell job control facilities and how you can use them to monitor and manage background jobs.

Q&A

Q What is the difference between the use of the semicolon (;) and the pipe (¦) as separators between commands?

A The semicolon metacharacter connects sequentially executed commands, permitting you to enter more than one command on a line. It is also used within the parentheses metacharacters as a separator. There is no direct

interaction between one command and the next when the semicolon is used as a separator.

The pipe metacharacter establishes a connection between two commands, where the output of the first command becomes the input to the second command. The two commands run concurrently, as opposed to sequentially as with the semicolon metacharacter.

Q How do you place a command in background?

A Any command can be executed in background simply by ending the command line with the ampersand (&) metacharacter. This indicates to the C Shell that the command should be processed in background. Not all commands are good candidates for background processing. Any command that requires input from stdin or output to stdout will stop when input is required and will output information back to the terminal as it is running. To avoid these problems, you can use file redirection, with < for input and > for output, to give the command alternates for stdin and stdout.

Q Why are files that begin with a dot (.) not found with the asterisk (*) metacharacter?

A The answer is somewhat historic. UNIX filenames that begin with a dot, referred to as *silent files*, include the special directory files *dot* (.) and *dot dot* (..), as well as the various startup files and configuration files. Startup files, such as .login and .cshrc, used by the C Shell for configuration when logging on or starting a new subshell, are not often changed or accessed. When you use the UNIX ls command, they are omitted from the list unless the special -a option is included.

Because silent files are rarely of interest and frequently cause problems when included on a command line and processed by a command, the asterisk metacharacter excludes matching the dot so that they are not part of the expansion. If you need or want to have these files on a command line or in a directory list, use the expression .??* to get all but the files *dot* (.) and *dot dot* (..).

Workshop

The Workshop provides several sections to aid you in reviewing the topics covered in today's lesson. There is a quiz section to help you reinforce your understanding of the

material presented for Day 2 and exercises to give you practice applying what you learned. Take the time to review these questions and exercises, so that you understand the chapter's concepts before you begin the next day's lesson. The answers are provided in Appendix F, "Answers to Quizzes and Exercises."

Quiz

1. How would you conditionally execute one command if another fails? How would you execute the second command only if the first command succeeded?

2. How would you list all of the files in /bin that start with a vowel? How would you list the ones that start with a consonant?

3. What is a shortcut to get to a subdirectory of your home directory? How would you get to the home directory for another user using the same method?

4. What is the difference between the double quote (") and single quote (') metacharacters when the string they enclose contains metacharacters?

5. How do you override the effects of $noclobber being set when you do file redirection?

6. How do you combine the outputs of stdout and stderr using file redirection?

Exercises

1. Think of some different ways to use here documents in a shell script.

2. Change directories to /bin and experiment with filename metacharacters to get directory listings for selected subsets of the command files.

Command Substitution, Aliases, and Filename Generation

Introduction to Day 3

In the first day's lesson, as a part of your introduction to the C Shell, you saw how the shell history mechanism enables you to recall and edit recently executed commands. Today you will see a different labor-saving feature of the C Shell: command aliasing.

Setting Today's Goals

Today, you will learn how to

- [ ] List current aliases

- [ ] Create command synonyms

- [ ] Redefine existing commands

- [ ] Create new commands with the `alias` command

- [ ] Include arguments in your aliases

- [ ] Remove existing aliases

- [ ] Generate filenames with special shell characters

- [ ] Use command substitution

Aliasing Defined

The C Shell alias facility provides the capability for you to customize how UNIX commands behave when you invoke them. Aliases are similar to macro definition capabilities in other languages. You created aliases in the C Shell by using the `alias` command. The `alias` command is typically used in the `.cshrc` startup file. The reason for this is that aliases don't exist from one shell instance to another; that is, they are not inherited. Because of this behavior, aliases must be redefined for each shell instance , and this is done in the `.cshrc` startup file. Startup files, including `.cshrc`, are discussed in Day 6, "Customizing the User Environment."

DO	DON'T

DO place alias definitions in your `.cshrc` startup file.

DON'T place alias definitions in your `.login` startup file.

Caution: The C Shell reads the entire .cshrc file each time it starts. Placing a large number of commands in the .cshrc file, including aliases, tends to slow the startup of your shells. As you will see, aliases can be an important tool in making your use of UNIX more enjoyable. Don't be afraid to experiment with aliases as you learn more about them. Keep in mind the slow-down at shell startup I just described and do not go overboard defining new aliases for everything that you might possibly want to do with UNIX. Try to limit your aliases to those that you will use frequently.

The syntax for the `alias` command is

```
alias [alias name [command definition]]
```

where *alias name* is what you type to use your new alias, and *command definition* is the command that you want performed when you invoke your alias. The `alias` command associates your alias name with the command definition.

Example: `alias rm rm -i`

Note: In the preceding syntax description, the example, which aliases the `rm` command, is actually an excellent alias for the novice UNIX user. By forcing the `rm` command to include the `-i` option, you ensure that you will be asked to verify that you want to remove a file before it is actually deleted. Likewise, the `cp` (copy) and `mv` (move/rename) commands also accept a `-i` option with the same behavior.

With this simple `alias` command, you will be able to do the following:

- [ ] List the definition for one or all of your current aliases
- [ ] Rename an existing command (create a synonym)
- [ ] Redefine an existing command
- [ ] Create a new command

Listing Aliases

To display a list of all of your current aliases, type the `alias` command by itself at the command prompt.

```
1 % alias
del     rm
ll      ls -l
print   lpr
2 % _
```

> **Note:** Pipe the output of the alias command through a pager such as more when you list all of your aliases; this helps you view them a screen page at a time.

To display the alias for a single command, type the `alias` command, followed by the name of the alias you wish to see. You might have defined a synonym alias for the UNIX `rm` command called `del`. To see just this single alias definition, type `alias del` at the command prompt.

```
2 % alias del
del     rm
3 % _
```

Aliasing Existing Commands

UNIX has an extensive command set, numbering hundreds of commands. The easiest alias you can create is a synonym for one of these commands. Perhaps you cannot remember that the UNIX command to rename a file is `mv`, which stands for "move." You might choose to create an alias for this command, which you will call "rename." This will be a synonym for an existing UNIX command. Then when you type `rename` at the command prompt, `rename` will behave like the UNIX `mv` command. To create such an alias, type `alias rename mv` at the command prompt.

```
3 % alias rename mv
4 % _
```

Users often create synonym aliases to save keystrokes on frequently used commands. A common example is to alias the `history` command to the single-letter alias name `h`. This same alias-synonym method can save your sanity when you frequently misspell or mistype a command. I would often find myself mistyping the UNIX paging command

more as "mroe." After getting frustrated once too often, I created the following alias to eliminate seeing the error message `Command not found: mroe`.

```
4 % alias mroe more
5 % _
```

As illustrated in the `rename` alias that I created in history event 3, you can make UNIX look more like another operating system with which you are more familiar. This too can be a sanity saver for the new UNIX user. You can do things such as alias the UNIX `ls` command, which displays a listing of the files in a directory, with an alias called `dir`, which is used in the DOS system on PCs to likewise display a listing of the files in a directory.

Note: Because aliases are defined in a user's `.cshrc` startup file, each user can have his or her own set of aliases without conflicting with those of other users.

Redefining Existing Commands

As you become more comfortable and familiar with UNIX and its many commands, you will begin to have preferences for the options you use to invoke them. Another use of the `alias` command is to redefine an existing command specifying options as well as the command as part of the alias.

In the following example, I have redefined the `ls` command to always include the option `-F` whenever the `ls` command is invoked.

```
5 % alias ls 'ls -F'
6 % _
```

You can use techniques similar to this to tailor your own UNIX environment. In the preceding example—creating an alias that redefined `ls` so that it always included the `-F` option—I changed my environment so that `ls` always behaves the way that I want it to behave. The `-F` option causes `ls` to flag directories with a slash (/) suffix, executable files with an asterisk (*) suffix, and symbolic links with an at-sign (@) suffix. This helps to make these types of files stand out in the output from `ls`.

Caution: Using aliases can be very helpful in an interactive shell environment, but there are cases where aliases can create problem situations. Aliases that redefine common UNIX commands, such as ls, may cause some shell scripts to fail. If a script is expecting the default behavior from a command that has been aliased, it may not run correctly because of the alias. A work-around to this problem is presented on Day 6, "Customizing the User Environment," and in the sample .cshrc file shown in Appendix E. The work-around involves testing to determine whether or not the current shell is interactive, and only defining aliases when the shell is interactive. Then any script will work properly because it will not have your alias definitions to contend with when it is running.

Note: The ls command has many useful options. You can start with the aliases given in Table 3.1 and build on them with changes to suit your own needs. In most cases, the options can be combined with each other without restriction.

Table 3.1. Useful aliases for the ls command.

Alias Name	Definition	Description
lf	ls -FC	List files with file type flags, in multiple columns.
la	ls -a	List all files, including dot files.
lA	ls -A	List all files, except the dot files.
ll	ls -l	List files in long format, showing permissions, owner, size, date, and full filename.
lt	ls -lt	Same as above but sorted in date order.

> **Note:** There are some restrictions on creating aliases.
>
> You can not create an alias for a command and call it `alias`. Attempting to do this will earn you an error message.
>
> You cannot create an alias that references itself more than once. When you do this, you create an alias loop, and the C Shell tells you so with an error message.
>
> To end on a positive note, you *can* have an alias that references another alias.

Creating New Commands with the *alias* Command

In the previous sections, you saw how synonym aliases can simplify the use of existing commands. As you progress through this book, you will learn about the more advanced capabilities of the C shell. On Day 7, "File Redirection, Pipes, and Filters," you will explore *pipes*, which let you combine two or more commands to create a new tool to accomplish a task. On one hand pipes are a powerful tool, but on the other hand they make commands longer and more prone to typing errors. Here's a tailor-made use for aliases!

You might find that there are some more involved command sequences that you are using frequently. To make typing easier, the obvious thing to do would be to create an alias with a new name that defines your special set of commands. Let's try a simple example. You learned on the first day that you can set a shell variable to indicate how many history events the shell should maintain. To make the most advantage of command editing, you want to keep sufficient history. The disadvantage of keeping a lot of history is that it all gushes out on the display when you use the history command. A solution to this problem is to pipe the output of the history command through one of the UNIX pager commands such as more. To do this, you would enter command shown in event 6:

```
6 % history ¦ more
  1  set history=100
  2  ls
  3  date
  4  who
     .
     .
     .
 19 cd testdata
```

```
 20  wc -l monday.data
 --More--(47%)
7 % _
```

> **Note:** The command more was added to the UNIX command set as part of
> the enhancements made at the University of California at Berkeley. There is
> another command with a similar function called pg and referred to as
> "page." It is distributed with systems that are based on the System V UNIX
> from AT&T. Check on your system to see which of these handy commands
> you have available. Don't be surprised to find that you have both of them.
> Take time to study the man pages for these commands because there is more
> to them than just simply "paging." For the remainder of this book, I will use
> the more command as a pager in all examples. Because the topic of this book
> is the C Shell, which was developed at UC Berkeley, it is only reasonable to
> use the pager that was developed there too.

The first screenful of commands are displayed, and then more (or whatever pager you
selected) displays a prompt and waits for you to respond before continuing. Using this
method gives you the opportunity to review what has been displayed and then proceed
when you are ready. If you define an alias for this command sequence, the sequence can
then be repeated with the simple alias name you assign to it.

With the following alias, you can get your paged history output by typing hp instead of
the longer two-word piped command sequence:

```
7 % alias hp 'history ¦ more'
8 % _
```

Another useful history alias that you can define replaces more with a different UNIX
command called tail. The tail command shows you the last lines of a file or of the
contents that the tail command receives through stdin. The default number of lines
that tail will output is 10, but that can be changed with a command line option -#,
where # is the number of lines to be displayed. The following alias causes the last 10 lines
of history to be displayed:

```
8 % alias h 'history ¦ tail'
9 % _
```

Caution: Don't forget to enclose your multiword aliases in single quotes. Failing to do this will get you unexpected results. For example, in event 7 shown earlier, without the quotes the shell takes your input to mean that you want an alias of hp, with a command definition of history, and that you want to pipe the output of the alias command (of which there is none) through the pager more. This is not exactly what you intended. In this case, the example without the quotes would not be syntactically wrong, so the shell would not give you an error. Other instances would likely result in an error message.

One of my favorite uses for an alias is to create a mnemonic command that I can use to change directories to a location that I go to often. This might be a data directory or the source directory where all the programs and scripts for a project are maintained. In some instances, the path to get to this location is many levels deep in the UNIX file hierarchy. This is another opportunity to save myself from my bad typing and make my life easier. Here's my alias:

```
9 % alias cdsrc 'cd /usr/dave/project/source'
10 % pwd
/usr/dave
11 % cdsrc
12 % pwd
/usr/dave/project/source
13 % _
```

In events 7 and 8 earlier, I created aliases that combined two UNIX commands together with the shell's pipe character (¦). This takes the output of the first command and uses it as the input of the second command. In event 7, I used a command, more, to pause the output of the history command after each screen so that I could examine the output at my own pace. There is another way in the C Shell to combine commands: use a semicolon (;) to separate each command from the next. When the shell sees the semicolon, it knows that one command has ended and another is about to begin. Here are some examples of useful aliases that combine commands by use of semicolons:

```
13 % alias pl 'pwd;ls'
14 % pl
<Your current working directory is displayed here on this line>
<Followed by a listing of the files that are in that directory>
<The ls output could go on for many lines.>
@@@
15 % _
```

The new alias pl, named for the first letters of the two combined commands, displays where you are with the pwd command and then lists the contents of the directory with the ls command. The command pwd stands for *print working directory*. It always shows you the directory that you are in when it is run. If you reference a filename on any command without qualifying the directory that the file is in, the first place that is examined is this directory. Note the difference between this alias and the others created earlier using the pipe character (¦). These two commands, combined with the semicolon, do not share their input and output with each other. Instead, simply one command is performed and then the other. The output from each is displayed at your terminal and any input that is required must be supplied either from the keyboard or from a file (see Day 7).

Note: More on the pwd command and current and working directories can be found in later chapters. In Day 4, "Shell Variables," there is a discussion of the shell variable $cwd, which contains the value of the current working directory. This shell variable is one that is often put to good use in defining effective shell aliases. Look at the sample dot files (.cshrc in particular) that are provided in Appendix E, "Examples of *Dot* Files," for many examples of aliases using these commands and shell variables.

Caution: Throughout the remaining lessons, additional aliases will be shown that make use of the new material presented in that lesson. Rather than attempt to present all of these aliases now, before their contents have been explained, I will instead show them in the lesson context that defines their function. Be sure to study these aliases so that you fully understand how they are defined and how they can be put to use to make your use of UNIX easier and more enjoyable. The dot files presented in Appendix E contain all of the aliases that are defined in the book. You can use the sample .cshrc file as an easy reference, as well as a good example.

Including Arguments in Your Aliases

Earlier in today's material you learned how to create a variety of simple aliases. Those simple aliases do not allow any variability. When you use them, they always do exactly

the thing each and every time. Now you will learn how to include arguments in your aliases. This will allow you to pass parameters from a command line that invokes an alias to the commands within the alias.

You will often substitute arguments into an alias using special characters to tell the shell to insert all of the command line parameters at a single point in the alias. In the previous day's lesson, you learned how metacharacters are used. The exclamation point (!) is the metacharacter that signals a reference to history events. Table 3.2 shows some of the metacharacter combinations that are useful in defining aliases.

Table 3.2. Event-designator metacharacters used in aliases.

Metacharacters	Effect Within an Alias
!^	Inserts the first argument from the command line.
!*	Inserts all of the arguments from the command line.
!x-y	Inserts a range of words; from word x to word y.
!x*	Like x-$ ($ is the last argument) above.
!x-	Like x* except that word $ is omitted.

Note: Alias substitution metacharacters include the C Shell history word modifiers that you learned on Day 1. You can insert a specific word from the command line at a desired location within your alias, if required. In some instances, you might create an alias that you will use with several parameters and want to use those parameters in more than one spot in your alias. This case would call for using the word modifiers. There are examples of this in the .cshrc shown in Appendix E. Examine the examples closely to get ideas for creating your own advanced aliases when the need arises.

Caution: Recall from Day 2, "Metacharacters," that the exclamation (!) character indicates the start of a history substitution. It tells the shell that the following metacharacters define which elements of a selected history event are to be substituted at this point in a command or alias definition. In the case of

> alias definitions, you typically don't want the substitution to happen until the
> alias is used, so don't forget two important steps in defining a successful alias:
>
> 1. Always enclose your command-definition string in single quotes. It
>   never hurts to do this when in doubt, and usually it is the difference
>   between an alias that works properly and one that doesn't.
>
> 2. Don't forget to properly protect metacharacters that you don't want
>   interpreted now. You do this with the backslash escape character (\).
>
> Remembering these two points will help you avoid frustrations when you
> create aliases and use UNIX commands interactively and in scripts.

Now let's look at some ways that you can use alias substitution in your own aliases. In
event 9 earlier, I created an alias called cdsrc, which simply invoked a UNIX cd
command to change directories to my own project source directory. For confirmation
of the change, I did a pwd command to display the location to which I had changed. If
you like the idea of getting that confirmation display every time you do a cd command,
you can create a new alias to redefine the cd command to do just that. You would enter
the alias shown next in event 15:

```
15 % alias cd 'cd \!^;pwd'
16 % _
```

Let's look closer at this alias and see what it does and why. The part of this alias that you
have not seen before is the metacharacter sequence \!^ after the cd in the command
definition string. In Table 3.2, you see that !^ is replaced with the first argument from
the command line. You should also remember from Day 1, when you learned about
history event modification, that the first word of the command line, word 0, is the
command name itself and that the command arguments, options, and parameters start
with word 1. So in your new alias for cd, the first word—the directory to which you want
to change—is substituted into the alias at the point indicated by the !^ metacharacters.

Just ahead of the !^ metacharacters is another important metacharacter, the backslash
(\). You should remember this metacharacter from Day 2. It is often referred to as the
escape character because it allows the character which follows it to "escape" special
interpretation by the C Shell. In this case, you are protecting the bang, or exclamation
point (!), metacharacter. Because this metacharacter has special significance to the shell,
you need to escape it to ensure that your alias performs as expected. If you do not escape
the bang in this manner, the shell replaces it with the current event number when the alias
command is processed. This is not what you want to happen. You want the bang

character to be interpreted when the alias is invoked, not when it is defined. When the bang is substituted with the event number, the caret (^) is orphaned. The bang and carat metacharacters need to travel as a pair in order to have proper significance to the shell.

> **Caution:** I specifically picked the metacharacters !^ in the cd alias defined above (where others might choose to use !*) for a good reason. If you use more than one argument in a cd command, the shell gives you an error. By using the !^ metacharacters instead of !*, I have protected myself from getting an error with my alias, because only the first argument word will be substituted, even if I mistakenly enter more than one word on the command line. But you may choose to use the !* instead. This way the shell will give you an error rather than assume you are correct and attempt the change to the directory specified by the first word you entered. Note the distinction here and the choice you have in specifying how your aliases behave.

Now you'll examine some different ways that you can use this new capability. You'll look at several different UNIX commands that are excellent candidates for aliasing with argument substitution. I'll show you some different ways to define aliases, which will make using these sophisticated UNIX commands easier for even the advanced user. These aliases will be better labor savers and will simplify repetitive use of the same command.

The find command is a very powerful tool available to the UNIX user. It is used to search all or a portion of the UNIX directory hierarchy for files that meet specified criteria. The find command has many options, used to specify the search criteria, and a syntax that differs from that used by a majority of UNIX commands. Often users discover that they are utilizing the same find command frequently—which makes it an excellent candidate for an alias! Let's look at a simple, but helpful, alias for the find command.

The find command's first argument specifies the starting point in the directory tree, for the search. This is then followed by options and their parameters, which specify the criteria that a file must meet to be considered found, and an action to be taken for each file that meets that criteria. First, look at a simple case of the find command that I will then alias:

```
16 % find ~ -name '*.memo' -print
/usr/dave/documents/first.memo
/usr/dave/documents/second.memo
/usr/dave/documents/test.memo
17 % _
```

This `find` command starts at my home directory and searches it and all of its subdirectories for matches to the specified criteria. The starting point is indicated by the special tilde (~) metacharacter. The shell expands the tilde to my home directory pathname, so the displayed filenames actually show that path rather than the tilde itself. The first option, `-name`, specifies the criteria for matching a filename. The `-name` option requires that an argument follow the option to supply the match criteria. In my command, that criteria is `'*.memo'`, which says that I want to match any filename that starts with any characters (*) and ends with the string `.memo`. At the end of the `find` command is the action option `-print`, which instructs the command to display each filename found that matches the name criteria. It's simple once it's explained! Now you can explore how to add some flexibility to the `find` command by creating an alias that you can use to find any filename in your own home directory. Consider these examples:

```
17 % alias findhome "find ~ -name '\!^' -print"
18 % findhome '*.memo'
/usr/dave/documents/first.memo
/usr/dave/documents/second.memo
/usr/dave/documents/test.memo
19 % findhome '*.ltr'
/usr/dave/letters/landlord.ltr
/usr/dave/letters/mother.ltr
/usr/dave/letters/test.ltr
20 % _
```

Notice that when I used my new `findhome` alias in event 18 with the argument `*.memo`, it found the same filenames as when I typed the `find` command directly in event 16 above. When I used `findhome` again in event 19, now with a different argument of `*.ltr`, it still works as expected and locates files that match my criteria.

Note: The `find` command is one of the more powerful in the UNIX command set. It will be well worth your time to investigate this command further either in the UNIX manuals or in a book on UNIX, such as *Teach Yourself UNIX in a Week*, where the `find` command is discussed in some detail. Although the `find` command is a little more difficult to understand and master than the typical UNIX command, the benefits derived from gaining working knowledge of the `find` command are worth the effort.

I would like to add a note of caution regarding the `find` command. If you use this command to do indiscriminate searches of the entire file system (or even a large subset of it), you are likely to find out about the surly side of your system administrator and possibly your fellow users. The `find` command has its good purposes, but it can also use up a considerable amount of system resources to simply browse the file system.

Next, to illustrate a point, let's make a change to the `findname` alias to give it just a bit more flexibility. My original alias definition specified that the command should start its search with my home directory. Now I'll modify the alias so that I can choose where the search should start, as well as the filenames to be located. To do this, I need to use a different set of metacharacters from the list shown in Table 3.2. I now need to have a *pair* of metacharacter specifications, one for the starting point and one for the filename. My new `findname` alias is shown here:

```
20 % alias findname "find \!^ -name '\!2*' -print"
21 % findname ~ '*.memo'
/usr/dave/documents/first.memo
/usr/dave/documents/second.memo
/usr/dave/documents/test.memo
22 % findname ~ '*.ltr'
/usr/dave/letters/landlord.ltr
/usr/dave/letters/mother.ltr
/usr/dave/letters/test.ltr
23 % findname /bin '*.txt'
24 % _
```

Take a look at this alias and see what makes it tick. If you look again at Table 3.2, you'll see that the metacharacter pair `!^` gets substituted by the first argument word of the current command line (not the command name itself, because the command name itself is word 0). This will substitute the starting path (~ in events 21 and 22 and `/bin` in event 23) into my new `findname` alias, after the `find` command name and before the `-name` option. My file-match criteria (`*.memo` in event 21, `*.ltr` in event 22, and `*.txt` in event 23) will be substituted for the `!2*` metacharacter pair, immediately after the `-name` option. Notice that there is no output from event 23. This is not because my alias failed or is somehow broken, but rather because there are no files in `/bin` that end in `.txt` to match my criteria, so the `find` command had nothing to report!

Caution: Notice in this last alias, as well as the previous alias for `findhome`, that the entire alias was enclosed in double quotes (") and the metacharacters in single quotes ('). You need to enclose the entire alias in quotes so that the shell knows to take all of the words as part of the alias command definition. At the same time, you need to specially quote the metacharacters for the parameter to the `-name` option. This special handling is to ensure that the metacharacters will not be interpreted by the shell now or when the `find` command is executed when the `findname` alias is used. The `-name` option requires that metacharacters in its parameter be quoted in single quotes so that the shell will not attempt to expand them. If this were not done, the shell would attempt to expand the metacharacters and would potentially replace them with multiple filenames that matched the criteria. The other possibility is that the shell would attempt the expansion, find *no* files that matched in the current directory, and substitute *no* names. Either of these cases—multiple names or no names—would result in an alias that gives syntax errors. So you need to quote the metacharacters in single quotes, which tells the shell not to expand the metacharacters. This lets the `find` command use them internally to match each file it locates, while searching the directory tree.

How the Shell Processes Aliases

For a moment, let's take a break and look at how the shell processes your command lines when you have aliases defined. I hope that when you understand a bit of what the shell is doing when it gets a command line with an alias, you will find writing successful alias definitions to be easier. Don't worry, though; this will not be detailed and complex, but rather a quick overview of the steps and processes that the C Shell takes when it processes a command line. Keep in mind also that these same steps and processes occur regardless of whether the command gets to the shell from the keyboard via an interactive shell session or from a line within a shell script.

Caution: There is one exception to the similarity of processing an interactive command and of processing a command line from a script. Often, a C Shell script will be invoked with the option `-f`, for "Fast Start," which has the effect of telling the C Shell to skip reading `.cshrc` and, if applicable, `.login` upon startup to process the shell script. This is done to significantly speed up the processing of the script by reducing the time needed to get the shell going. This has the negative side-effect of not reading in your alias definitions. So, although I stated that the processing steps for interactive commands is the same as for scripts, you usually will not use aliases in your scripts if you want to invoke them with this Fast Start option. Also, it is not as beneficial to use aliases in scripts, because scripts are typed in only once and then reused themselves, so the savings in using aliases is not the same as it would be with interactive commands.

When you enter a command at the shell prompt and press the Enter key, what does the shell do that makes aliases work? Each time the shell processes a command line, one of the first steps is alias substitution. To do this step, the shell takes the first word of the entered line and searches the table of aliases to see if that word matches one of the alias names. If a match is found, then the shell takes the next step—substituting the alias. This is done as a simple text substitution not unlike what you might do in your editor or word processor. The shell replaces the first word of your command line, the alias name, with the command definition of the alias. Once the command definition is in place in the input buffer, command processing starts over again. It is in this manner that the shell allows for nested aliases, in which one alias uses another alias in its command definition.

Once all possible alias substitutions have been made to your entered command, the shell starts the next step in the process. Part of the previous step also inserted your metacharacters, if there were any in the substituted aliases, into the command buffer. Now the shell will search the buffer looking for metacharacters. Metacharacters may not have been placed there by aliasing, but you may have typed them in at the command line. Either way, the shell now examines these metacharacters and makes any substitutions that are required. It is at this point that your command-line parameters are used to replace the `!*` and `!^` metacharacter pairs that you used in your alias definitions. The shell takes the appropriate parameter words from the originally typed command and replaces the metacharacter pairs with these words. When all the metacharacter substitution has been completed, special handling for any file-redirection metacharacters is performed. Then the shell is finally ready to submit the command buffer to the kernel for execution.

Note: You can take advantage of the way the shell handles aliases to turn them off on a case-by-case basis. Earlier, I defined the alias for `ls` in event 5, which forces `ls` to always include the `-F` option. If you want a directory list without this option but don't want to undo your alias, enter your command as `/bin/ls`. This word pattern will fail to match your alias, and `ls` will behave in its default manner. This will work to temporarily disable any alias.

Note: On Day 5 you will learn about the `echo` and `verbose` switches and shell variables. When you are creating more complex aliases with substitution, it is often interesting and informative to be able to see what the shell is doing with the alias that you defined. A trick to aid in debugging your aliases is to set the echo or verbose switches ON by setting either one or both of these variables. Then the shell will display more information to your screen. Setting echo will display the command line before it is expanded, and setting verbose will display the line after the history substitutions are done but before any further substitutions are made. You will likely get the most benefit from setting verbose ON to debug your aliases.

Unaliasing an Alias

In the first part of today's material, you learned how to create command aliases. Now you will find out how to *unalias*, or delete an alias. You might be asking yourself why you would want to delete an alias after going to the trouble of creating it. If you have typed at the command prompt the examples I have given so far, they are still temporary and will go away when you log off your computer session. In order to make them permanent, you would need to enter them into your .cshrc file so that the shell will read them in each time it is started. Perhaps after experimenting with an alias you decide that you don't want to keep it, but you don't want to log off just yet. Using the unalias command, you can remove the alias without logging off.

There can be another source for the aliases you see when you type in the alias command by itself to list your current aliases. Your system administrator may have created some system-wide aliases by putting them in a special system file /etc/cshrc. You might find that one or more of these aliases is not to your liking. Perhaps even worse, you find that a system-wide alias causes one of your own newly created aliases to behave poorly, and you'd rather have your own alias work properly than have the other alias. You can remove the other alias before or after you define your own new alias. To do this, you would include an unalias command in your .cshrc to remove the system-wide alias that is causing the problem.

Syntax

The syntax for the unalias command is

```
unalias alias name
```

where alias name is the name of the alias that is to be deleted. Take note of the fact that, whereas the alias command does not require an argument and will then list all currently defined aliases, the unalias command *must* have an argument. If you do not supply an argument to unalias, you will receive the following error message:

```
unalias: Too few arguments
```

Filename Generation

When you use UNIX commands, you probably are going to be performing some operation or process against one or more files on your system. Often it is possible and desirable to abbreviate the filenames that you want to process. The shell then takes your abbreviation and expands it to generate a complete list of the files that will be processed by your command. To create these abbreviations, you use another set of metacharacters specifically set aside for this purpose. You learned about these filename metacharacters in the previous day's lesson. Here I'll discuss again, in more detail, how to apply these characters when using commands. Table 3.3 lists each of these special characters used for abbreviating filenames.

Table 3.3. Filename metacharacters.

Metacharacter	What It Matches in a File Abbreviation
*	Matches any (zero or more) characters.
?	Matches any single character.
[...]	Matches any single character in the enclosed lists or ranges—where a list is a string of characters and a range is any two characters separated by a minus sign (-) and includes all the characters in between based on the ASCII collating sequence.
{str,str,...}	Expands to each string, str, in the comma-separated list, where str can be literal characters or any valid filename matching pattern.
~[username]	Expands to the home directory that is contained in the variable home if no username is supplied. Otherwise, it expands to the home directory for the username following the tilde. This home directory is found in that user's password entry.

Caution: The patterns *, ?, and [...] are the only ones that imply pattern matching. An error results if there is no filename that matches any pattern. If the first character of a filename is not a metacharacter, it must be explicitly matched. The same applies to the slash (/), in that it too must be explicitly matched.

When any one or more of these special filename metacharacters appear on a command line, the shell expands the arguments that contain them into a list of filenames that match the given expression. This list is then substituted for the metacharacters in the command line before the command is executed. The expansion of these filename metacharacters happens after the expansion of aliases, as described earlier.

Now that all of the details are out of the way, take a look at these metacharacters and see how they can be put to good use. Actually, I have already snuck by you a few instances of using metacharacters without really talking much about them. Filename metacharacters are easy to use once you understand them and see a few examples.

The first metacharacter, and probably the easiest and most intuitive one to use, is the asterisk or star character (*). This character matches zero or more characters in the position that it occupies. Say, for example, I want to get a listing of all the C source code files in my current directory. The convention for files containing C source code is that they end with what is called a *file extension* of .c. To get a directory listing of all of these files, I would use the following metacharacter expression on my ls command:

```
24 % ls *.c
main.c
addone.c
chgone.c
delone.c
listone.c
25 % _
```

You can see that there are five files ending in .c in the directory. The star metacharacter at the beginning of the expression matched one or more characters of each of these files, and the .c matched the end of each of the filenames, as I wanted. If I wanted to find all of the files that contained the letter *d* in the filename, I would use the command ls *d*:

```
25 % ls *d*
addone.c
addone.o
delone.c
delone.o
header.h
26 % _
```

Here you see that I got some of the same files as before and a few new ones that I did not get the last time. I have some *object files* in the directory because I have been working on my program. These are the files that have the extension .o. There is another file, called a *header file*, that has an extension of .h. What these files are and what they contain is not important to this discussion or to the subject of this book. What is important is that they contain the letter *d* in their names, and the ls command matched them as I requested.

Notice that the number of letters before the d in these filenames is different. The *
metacharacter matches zero or more characters, so I got delone.c, matching zero
characters before the d, and I got addone.c matching one character before the d, and I got
header.h matching three characters before the d, and so on. The * character is good for
cases where there is a lot of variability in the names of the file that you want to match.

For the situations in which you want to be more specific in matching a name or group
of names, you can use the ? character, which matches one, and only one, character in its
position, not zero and not two or more. If you were to use the ? metacharacter in the
expression ls ???one.c, you would see how the ? character differs from the * character
in matching:

```
26 % ls ???one.c
addone.c
chgone.c
delone.c
27 % _
```

Notice that the filenames displayed all have three characters to begin with, followed by
the characters one.c. The filename listone.c was not displayed because it has four
characters before the characters one.c. So the question mark metacharacter enables you
to narrow down the expression of which filenames you want to include in your list.

On occasion, there might be cases in which even with the question metacharacter you
cannot get the exact match to the list that you want on your command line. Now you
can bring into play the next weapon in your new metacharacter arsenal. The brackets
[...], also called *square brackets* to distinguish them from another bracket metacharacter,
allow you to specify a list or range of characters that can appear in a character position.
So, like the ? metacharacter, the brackets match only a single character in their position.
Unlike either the ? and the * metacharacters, the brackets further specify exactly which
characters can appear in that position to be a match.

In event 25, you saw that there were source files, ending in .c, and object files, ending
in .o, in my directory. You also saw that there was a header file, which ends in .h. Suppose
that you want to get a list of only the source and object files, and not the header files or
any other files that may be in this directory. How would you do that with the
metacharacters you have learned so far? The following example shows how you can
achieve the desired results using the star and bracket metacharacters:

```
27 % ls *.[co]
main.c
main.o
addone.c
addone.o
chgone.c
chgone.o
```

```
delone.c
delone.o
listone.c
listone.o
28 % _
```

This expression matched all of the files that started with any number of any characters but ended with a period (.), followed by either one of the characters *c* or *o*. I did not get header.*h* because it has the wrong ending character. You can do an experiment and look only for those files that have a six-character base name, followed by the extension, and again include both source and object files:

```
28 % ls ??????.[co]
addone.c
addone.o
chgone.c
chgone.o
delone.c
delone.o
29 % _
```

Notice this time that, by using the question mark metacharacter along with the brackets, I got all of the six-character filenames, excluding main and listone because they are either more or less than six characters in length.

Another frequent use of the brackets is to select filenames, based on whether some of the letters in the filename are uppercase or lowercase or specific combinations of both. You might choose to create filenames based on the type of file or some other criteria, where you would use uppercase letters in the filename. This gives you the advantage of separating these files from the rest in a general ls command and also lets you use metacharacters, as you are about to see, to specifically select these files from the rest:

```
29 % ls [A-Z]*
Makefile
30 % _
```

Notice in this example that I matched just one file. This file begins with an uppercase letter. I did not get any of my source or object files or the header file because all of those files begin with lowercase letters. I can use a variation on this technique to select file-names that include a digit in a specific position; that variation is to use the range [0-9]. I can get the pattern of all letters—without digits or special punctuation characters—by using the bracket pattern [A-Za-z]. Be careful to not fall into the trap of using [A-z] as a pattern, because there are other nonletter characters in the collating sequence between *Z* and *a* that might get you some unexpected results.

Even with these three metacharacters—the asterisk, the question mark, and the brack-ets—there can be times when you cannot easily create an expression to match exactly those files that you want and no others. The {} metacharacters, referred to as curly

brackets or braces, provide another powerful matching tool to generate the exact list of filenames that you want on a command line. Unlike the square brackets, curly brackets can match more than one character position. Another difference is that the curly brackets contain a comma-separated list of strings of varying lengths. These strings can be either literals (that is, non-metacharacters) or matching patterns composed of the metacharacters discussed previously. It is even possible to have a null string, as I will discuss later.

With the curly bracket metacharacters, if you used the command `ls l{i,o,a}st`, you might encounter the following list of filenames:

```
30 % ls l{i,o,a}st
list
lost
last
31 %
```

Here the letters *i*, *o*, and *a* were each in turn substituted in place of the second character to form each of the three filenames. Notice that no sorting of the list is performed, unlike the usual `ls` command output with the previous metacharacters. In the following example, you see that it is not required that each element of the curly bracket list be the same length as the other elements. The example also demonstrates the power and flexibility that the curly brackets give to filename generation using metacharacters:

```
31 % ls a{,r,bou,f}t
at
art
about
aft
32 %
```

In the output of event 31, the letters a and t were "sandwiched" around each of the list items within the curly braces to make a filename. Notice that the first element is null (that is, it contains no characters), and therefore results in forming the word at, which in this example matched to a file of the same name. This is perfectly valid and legal and often necessary to get the exact list of filenames desired.

In an example earlier in this lesson, you saw how to use the tilde (~) metacharacter. This character is a special shorthand metacharacter unique to the C Shell. Used by itself, it results in the user's home directory name, contained in the shell variable `$home`, replacing the tilde character in the command. If the tilde is followed immediately by a valid username, with no spaces between the tilde and the name, it is replaced by the home directory of that user, found by doing a lookup in the password file. This shortcut is especially handy because, on many systems today with multiple disks, a user's home directory is often not a subdirectory of /usr or even in the same part of the filetree as your own home directory. If you use the tilde, then there is no guessing as to the exact location of your home directory or that of another user. You can try several interesting examples to prove to yourself that this is true. Do the following examples on your system and note the results:

```
32 % echo ~
<the path of your home directory is displayed here>
33 % cd /
34 % ls
<a listing of the files that are in the root directory>
35 % _
```

You should get a listing of the files in the root directory of your system.

```
35 % ls ~
<a listing of the files that are in your home directory>
36 % _
```

You should get a listing of the files in your home directory.

```
36 % cd; pwd
<the path of your home directory is displayed here>
37 % ls
<a listing of the files that are in your home directory>
38 % _
```

You should get the same listing of the files in your home directory as before.

```
38 % ls ~root
<a listing of the files in your system's root directory (/)>
39 % _
```

You should get the same listing of the files in the root directory as before.

```
39 % echo ~root
/
40 % _
```

In event 32, you used the shell's echo command to see what the tilde expanded to and got a response that matched our home directory path. You should not see /usr/dave unless by coincidence your name is dave or david and your system administrator created your directory with the same name. Where I indicated, you should see the directory listings of the files in your home directory and of those found in the root directory (/) on your system. The contents of these two directories varies, so rather than give you some example of what is on my system, I will leave it to you to do the comparison.

The *glob* Command and the *noglob* Variable Switch

A unique term is used to describe the process of expanding metacharacter expressions to form filenames. That term, *globbing*, is the source of the name of a command called glob

and a shell variable switch called `noglob`. They are both related to each other and to the topic you have just completed—filename generation.

The `glob` command is used within scripts to perform metacharacter expression evaluation on a supplied string. The string is expanded based on the all of the rules presented earlier in today's lesson. The result of this expansion is a list of the filenames that match the expression. Each of the filenames in this list is separated by a null character, and no carriage return is placed at the end of the list. The `glob` command is typically used to build a shell variable array list of filenames, which the script can then use for a variety of purposes. Using `glob` is a shorthand method to build lists, saving the shell programmer from having to use the `ls` command to generate the list.

Syntax

The syntax of the `glob` command is

```
glob wordlist
```

where *wordlist* is a whitespace-separated list of expression strings.

Command Substitution

Command substitution is indicated by the substitution metacharacter (`), also called a *grave accent*, *back quote*, or *backtick*. To use command substitution, you enclose a valid UNIX command within the back quotes on a command or script line. The shell first executes the command within the back quotes before filenames on the command line are expanded. The output resulting from executing the enclosed command is substituted for the entire back-quoted expression in the command line. Evaluation of filenames then occurs, followed by the remainder of steps the shell performs in processing a command line. This provides a unique tool for generating a list of filenames that filename metacharacters alone cannot match.

The UNIX `grep` command is used to do string searches of the contents of one or more files based on a match pattern supplied on the command line, along with the filenames to be searched. One option of `grep` is particularly useful, in combination with the command substitution capability of the shell. The `grep` command displays the lines found in the files that contain the match string for which you are searching. Each line is prefixed with the name of the file in which the string was found.

Rather than receive this potentially verbose output, the `-l` option to `grep` causes it to list only the names of the files that were found to contain the match string. Using this option of `grep` in conjunction with command substitution, as shown in the next example, provides a quick method of creating a list of files to edit based on a search for a matching string:

```
40 % vi `grep -l abracadabra *.c`
41 % _
```

This command line causes the shell to first run the grep command to search through all of the C source files in the current directory. With the -l option, this grep command returns just the list of names of the specific .c files that contained the string abracadabra within their contents. The list of filenames is then substituted into the command line, which is then supplied to the vi command (a UNIX editor). The end result is that I can then go through each of these source files and make needed changes based on the fact that they contained the *magic word!*

Summary

This chapter presented several of the C Shell's shortcut, labor-saving features. In this lesson, you learned about C Shell aliases—how to list them and how to create both simple and more complex varieties. You saw that you can use aliases to customize existing commands and to create new commands of your own design. This lesson also introduced the use of filename metacharacters to generate lists of filenames for UNIX command arguments. You were introduced to the C Shell's powerful command-substitution facility. This facility permits you to embed one or more commands in another command line for the purpose of generating filenames or other parameters for that command.

In the next chapter, you will begin to discover shell variables. You will learn the distinction between local and global, or environment, variables and how they are used by the C Shell. You also will be introduced to the first group of special shell variables, those that take values. The effects of changing the values of these shell variables will be discussed and demonstrated.

Related UNIX Topics

This chapter presented some new concepts and commands. The following is a list of some of these concepts and topics, with suggestions for sources of further information.

Metacharacters:	Consult Appendix C, "Metacharacters," as well as the pull-out reference card for listings and definitions of all the metacharacters used by the C Shell. Review Day 2 if you need to brush up on metacharacters.
Pager commands:	Look in section 1 of your UNIX manuals for the man pages for the more and pg commands. Determine which

of these commands is available on your system and learn more about the different capabilities of these versatile commands.

find *command:* Look in section 1 also for the find command and study the man page to understand this powerful file-location tool. Many of the options of this command provide versatile solutions to problems often encountered when you do shell programming.

Q&A

Q Where should aliases be placed?

A Aliases should be put in your .cshrc startup file. Because they are not passed on from one shell to the next, they need to be re-created for each shell that is started. The .cshrc file is read by each shell when it starts, so this is where you should put your aliases, letting each shell get a copy.

Q How can I find out what aliases I have defined?

A Using the alias command by itself with no arguments displays a list of all of your current aliases. You may want to pipe the output from the alias command through a pager command such as more if you have more than a few aliases defined.

Q When I define an alias, how can I include all of the arguments from the command line in my alias?

A When you create an alias that will require substituting arguments from the command line, you can place the metacharacters !* at the point in the alias where you want the parameters to be inserted. Be sure to remember to escape the exclamation character with a backslash.

Workshop

The Workshop provides sections to aid you in reviewing the topics of today's lesson. There is a quiz section to help you reinforce your understanding of the material presented for Day 3 and exercises to give you practice applying what you learned. Take the time to review these questions and exercises, so that you understand the concepts before you begin the next day's lesson. The answers are provided in Appendix F, "Answers to Quizzes and Exercises."

Quiz

1. How can you find out what aliases are currently defined for your user ID?

2. What is the difference between the semicolon and the pipe character when used to separate two commands?

3. You have defined a synonym alias for an existing command. What ways are there for you to get the command to run with its defined default behavior?

4. What is the effect of enclosing an alias that contains argument substitutions or shell variable references in double quotes rather than single quotes?

5. What are the event-designator metacharacters that you would use to substitute the last argument on the command line in an alias?

6. How do you make an alias permanent after you test it and decide to keep it?

7. What are the restrictions to remember when defining an alias?

8. What metacharacter patterns could you use to match the following filenames?

```
test
tent
talent
tempest
```

Exercises

1. Examine the dot file examples in Appendix E to see the alias definitions that are there. Experiment with these aliases until you can explain how they work. Make changes to one or more to suit your own taste and test them on your system.

2. Change directories to one such as /bin or /usr/bin and try different combinations of filename metacharacters on the ls command to see what the results are. Give yourself a group of files of which to get a directory list, and figure out how to get that list in the most concise manner with metacharacters.

Shell Variables, Part I

Introduction to Day 4

Today you will learn about shell variables. You will discover what they are, where you can use them, and how you can use them. Some of these shell variables are known only to a single process, whereas others are passed from one process to its child processes. You will learn the difference between these two types and how they can affect you when you use the C Shell.

There are special shell variables *built-in* to the C Shell that you will use in scripts and use to control your interactive environment. Some of these special variables take values; others act more like switches. Today you will be introduced to the set that take values. The remainder of these special variables will be the topic of tomorrow's lesson.

Setting Today's Goals

Today you will learn

☐ About the difference between local and environment variables

☐ How to display local and environment variables

☐ About the built-in shell variables for the C Shell

☐ The uses of each of the following special shell variables

```
$argv
$autologout
$cdpath
$child
$cwd
$fignore
$histchars
$history
$home
$mail
$path
$prompt
$savehist
$shell
$status
$time
$$
```

Local Variable and Environment Variables

What are these things called *shell variables?* You can think of them as special containers that can hold values, either numbers or strings of characters. Shell variables have many uses when you write shell scripts. They are also used by the shell itself to define and control both the user's interactive environment as well as the script's noninteractive environment.

Note: All shell variables share a common trait within UNIX shells. They are all identified to the shell by a special prefix—a dollar sign ($)—which indicates that the word that follows is the name of a variable. Throughout this book, I will always use this dollar sign prefix when referring to shell variables. This will also help you see references to shell variables in the text.

Shell variables come in two distinct varieties, local and environment. Both can hold values, string and numeric, and both have uses in scripts and in working interactively at the command prompt. The main difference between the two is in their scope. Let me explain what this means to you and how it works.

When you are working at the shell prompt, for example, you are interacting with the C Shell program, which is running on your computer system. When you give the shell a command to perform, UNIX starts a new program entity, called a *process*, which is the command that you want to run. When any new process is started by UNIX, it inherits some attributes for its environment from the process that started it, your C Shell. These attributes are passed from one process to another via *environment variables*, also called *global variables*.

The other type of variables, *local variables*, are used more as scratch pads or work areas by the shell. These are not passed from one process to another and their contents are discarded when you exit the particular shell that defined them. There are some exceptions among the built-in variables; I will discuss that next. In these cases, setting a local variable causes its contents to be stored in a corresponding environment variable as well.

> **Note:** There is a convention observed among UNIX users for naming shell variables. This convention is to use all uppercase letters when naming environment variables and to use all lowercase letters for local variable names.
>
> Because UNIX is a *case-sensitive* operating system, it matters when you use uppercase letters—as opposed to using lowercase letters—to name a variable. A variable named `$STUFF` is a different from a variable named `$stuff`.

Displaying the Contents of Shell Variables

Before you start learning the C Shell's built-in variables, it will be helpful for you to know how to display the contents of shell variables. You can use several commands to examine their contents. The syntax for these commands is shown in the following syntax box.

Syntax

The syntax for the `set` command is

```
set [var [ = value ] ]
```

```
set var[n] = word
```

The `set` command is used to display and assign values to shell *local variables*. In the syntax shown, *var* is a shell variable of the form *name*, where *name* is made up of letters, digits, and underscores (_). Variable names must start with a letter and can be up to 20 characters in length. If a variable does not exist, then reference to it in a `set` command will cause it to be created.

The `set` command can be used in several ways. Without arguments, `set` displays the values of *all* shell local variables. With a single argument *var* (a variable name), `set` assigns a null (empty) value to the variable. If arguments of the form *var* = *value* are used, then `set` assigns *value* to *var*. In this case, *value* can be one of the following:

word	A single word (or a quote-enclosed string)
(word list)	A space-separated list of words enclosed in parentheses

Before being assigned, all values are command expanded and filename expanded. Multiword variables are arrays where individual words can be accessed by specifying their subscript with square brackets (`[ ]`). When arguments of the form *var*[n] = *word* are used, then `set` uses *word* to replace the *n*th word in the multiword variable *var*.

Example: `set testvar = testing123`

```
set testarr = (testing 1 2 3)

set emptyvar

set mylist[2] = two
```

Syntax

The syntax for the setenv command is

`setenv VAR [ word ]`

The setenv command is used to display and assign values to shell *environment variables*. In the syntax shown here, *VAR* is a shell variable of the form $NAME, where *NAME* is made up of letters, digits, and underscores (_). Variable names must start with a letter and can be up to 20 characters in length. If an environment variable does not exist, then reference to it in a setenv command causes it to be created.

The setenv command, like the set command, can be used in several ways. Without arguments, setenv displays the values of *all* environment variables. With a single argument *VAR* (a variable name), setenv assigns a null (empty) value to the variable. If arguments of the form *var value* are used, then setenv assigns *value*, which can be either a single word or a quoted string, to *var*. Before being assigned, all values are command expanded and filename expanded.

> **Caution:** When shell variables are used in scripts or at the command line, you must use the dollar sign prefix ($) before the variable name. There is one notable exception to this rule. When you use the set and setenv commands to assign values to variables, the variable name that appears immediately after the command name, set or setenv, *does not* have this prefix on the name. If you do put the prefix $ on these names, you will earn an error message.

To use the set and setenv commands to display the contents of your variables, simply use either command by itself at the command line without arguments. In the following example, I have used set and then setenv to see my variable contents.

```
1 % set
argv    ()
autologout    10
cwd    /usr/dave
history    15
home    /usr/dave
ignoreeof
```

```
noclobber
path      (/bin /usr/bin /usr/lib . /usr/dave/bin)
prompt    ! %
shell     /bin/csh
status    0
term      vt100
2 % setenv
EXINIT=set ai wm=5 ts=4
HOME=/usr/dave
MAIL=/usr/spool/mail/dave
PATH=/bin:/usr/bin:/usr/lib:.:/usr/dave/bin
SHELL=/bin/csh
TERM=vt100
TZ=PST8PDT
USER=dave
3 % _
```

What you see when you type these two commands at your shell prompt will most likely be different than what my example shows. Where I show /usr/dave, for example, you will see your own home directory path. You may also have more or fewer variables set than I have shown for either local or environment variables. This is no cause for concern.

Tip: Take the time to get familiar with the variables, local and environment, that are set for you by your shell on your particular system. You might want to make a hardcopy printout of what set and setenv display and keep it for reference as you proceed through this material and the remainder of this book. To get a printout, you can use the following commands on your system.

```
3 % set ¦ lpr
4 % setenv ¦ lpr
5 % _
```

Note: In the preceding tip, I used the lpr command to print the output from the set and setenv commands. On some UNIX systems, this command might not exist and in its place you will use lp instead. If you are unsure about which of these commands you have on your system, either try one and see what happens, or ask your system administrator which you should use.

Setting Local Shell Variables

Now that you know how to display the contents of the local variables, the next question is how do you change those values or set values for new shell variables that you want to create? The answer is that you use the same set command with the optional arguments shown in the syntax box. You can create an empty variable with a null value by using the set command with no other arguments, for example:

```
5 % set myvar
6 % _
```

In event 5, I created a new local shell variable called myvar. Because I did not supply a value to be assigned to it, the shell created the variable empty with a value of null. The C Shell does not make a distinction between variables that hold strings of characters and those that hold numbers. With a variable created and initialized in this manner, you have the option to store any kind of data that you need. If you want to create a variable with an initial value, then you follow the variable name with an equals sign (=) and the value to be assigned, for example:

```
6 % set newvar = "test data"
7 % set numvar = 5
8 % set colors = (red orange yellow green blue)
9 % set colors[6] = purple
10 % _
```

In the first line of the example, event 6, I created a variable called newvar and assigned the string "test data" to the variable. Even though the string contains two words of text, the two words are treated as one (a single string) in the variable $newvar because they are enclosed in quotes. The next line sets the variable $numvar to the value of 5. You do not need to do anything different to store numeric or string data in variables; the process is that same for both.

In event 8, a multiword variable is created called colors and is initially assigned 5 values. These values are the strings for the colors red, orange, yellow, green, and blue. These values are enclosed in parentheses to indicate that you are creating a multiword variable. In the next event, a new color, purple, is added to the end of $color by directly addressing word 6 to make the assignment.

Later, on Day 8, "C Shell Built-In Commands," the set command will be covered in more detail. You will then learn more about shell variables and their more advanced features. For now you know enough to use shell variables in simple scripts.

Setting Environment Variables

Using environment variables is very similar to what you have learned for local variables. The differences between the two are these:

- ☐ For environment variables, use the command `setenv` instead of `set`. The syntax for the `setenv` command was presented earlier in today's lesson.

- ☐ In the `setenv` command, a space is used instead of an equals sign (=) between the variable name and the value to be assigned.

- ☐ The value assigned for an environment variable must be either a single word or a quoted string. You cannot create a multiword environment variable.

As you can see in the following examples, setting environment variables is as easy it was for local variables.

```
10 % setenv MYVAR 500
11 % setenv DISPLAY gandalf:0.0
12 % setenv ESTRING "multiple words"
13 % _
```

In event 10, I have set MYVAR to the numeric value of 500. The next example, event 11, sets an environment variable DISPLAY to gandalf:0.0. This string does not need to be enclosed in quotes because it has no embedded whitespace characters. In the last example, event 12, there is an embedded space so the string must be enclosed in quotes. Remember that you cannot create a multiword environment variable. On Day 8, the setenv command will be discussed in more detail along with the set command.

Note: There are several commonly used environment variables—$USER, $TERM, and $PATH—which are automatically imported or exported from the C Shell variables $user, $term, and $path. There is no need to do a setenv command for these variables. Additionally, the shell will set the $PWD environment variable from the C Shell variable $cwd whenever the local variable changes.

Built-In Shell Variables

The C Shell has a number of local variables that are specially treated, in that they are automatically assigned values by the shell each time it starts. These variables are typically used to control some aspect of the shell environment or its operation. When you set these variables or change their values, the behavior of the shell is changed. Because these are local variables, they must be set for each shell that is started.

To make the changes to these variables permanent for all of your shell sessions, the set commands should be placed in your .cshrc startup file. See the example of a typical .cshrc file in Appendix E. Day 6, "Customizing the User Environment," explains more about setting shell variables in your startup files.

The following sections explain each of the built-in shell variables. For each variable, you will learn its function, the values it can typically be assigned, and how this can affect your shell environment. These sections are intended to be an overview; many of these variables will be revisited in later parts of the book when they pertain to the current topic. At those points, you will learn more about the applied use of the particular variable.

The Argument List *$argv*

On any command line, in addition to the command name itself, you often supply arguments. These arguments can be option command flags, filenames, other parameters significant to the command, or a combination of some or all of these. Frequently, in shell scripts you want to have access to these items off of the command line. This shell variable, $argv, is used for this purpose.

This shell variable is a multiword array. Each element of this array variable corresponds to an argument word from the command line used to start the script. This permits you to use $argv to look for options or flags and to tailor the operation of the script based on their presence or absence from the command line. You can also get any parameters or filenames supplied by the user to the script and use them to operate on different files from your script.

The $argv built-in shell variable is used frequently in the examples of shells presented throughout the remainder of this book. These examples will give you more insight into the use of the $argv shell variable.

The Auto Logoff Timer *$autologout*

Many companies today have established guidelines related to system security. Typically, one of the requirements is the protection of the system from unauthorized access. Frequently, one rule dictates that an unattended terminal or workstation should be logged off or somehow locked to prevent access. The built-in variable $autologout can help in implementing this type of protection.

The $autologout variable is set to a numeric value expressed in minutes. If the terminal session is inactive for this period of time, the shell automatically logs the user off the system. This facility permits users to comply with security guidelines such as the one I've just described. It is a good habit to take precautions and protect your own files as well as the system on which they reside.

The following example sets the autologout time to 10 minutes:

```
13 % set autologout=10
14 % _
```

If there is no input activity from the terminal for more than 10 minutes, the C Shell automatically logs the user off the system. This built-in shell variable is not always implemented by all versions of the C Shell. You should check the documentation for your local system to see if the C Shell supports this feature.

Note: If you decide to use the $autologout variable as a part of your environment, you need to set it within your .cshrc startup file. In this manner, you will not need to remember to set it each time you use the system. On occasion, you might want to disable this feature for a time to avoid being logged off and losing work. To disable the autologout feature, use one of the following commands:

```
set autologout = 0
```

or

```
unset autologout
```

The first method sets the time period to zero, which signals the shell that this feature should be turned off. The second method removes the shell variable from the current environment, having the same effect. Either method can be used to inhibit the C Shell from terminating your shell session.

The Directory Stack *$cdpath*

The C Shell directory navigation commands—cd, chdir, and popd—use the special shell variable $cdpath to perform their functions. The content of $cdpath is a list of absolute pathnames, like the $path variable. It is usually set in the .cshrc startup file so that it is initialized each time the C Shell is started.

When one of the navigation commands is used with a simple filename, the current working directory is searched for the subdirectory that matches the filename. If no match is found and the $cdpath variable is not set, an error message is issued. With the $cdpath variable set to a list of directories, this behavior is modified.

```
14 % set cdpath = (/usr2/tools /usr/local/ /usr/dave/tools)
15 % pwd
/usr/dave
16 % cd myscripts
17 % pwd
/usr/dave/tools/myscripts
18 % _
```

If no match is found in the current working directory, each of the directories listed in the $cdpath is searched in turn for a match to the filename parameter. If a match is found then, that path becomes the new working directory. If no match is found after searching the entire list in the $cdpath variable, an error message is issued as before.

In the preceding example, after setting the $cdpath variable in event 14, I check my current working directory. Event 15 shows that I am in my home directory /usr/dave. With the next command, I do a simple change, using cd, to the directory myscripts, but this directory does not exist in my home directory. Instead of giving me an error, the cd command searches each of the directories in $cdpath for myscripts and eventually finds it in the subdirectory /usr/dave/tools. After the cd command, I again check my current working directory and find that I have changed to /usr/dave/tools/myscripts without having to type the entire path on the cd command in event 16.

Using the $cdpath variable permits you to use shorthand names for paths with the navigation commands. This can be a big help in reducing typing errors when you use the shell in an interactive mode. The less you need to type to resolve a path, the easier it becomes to use the system. Consider setting up this helpful facility in your startup file.

The Background Process ID *$child*

A feature of the UNIX system is the ability to run commands in a detached or background mode. You will learn more about this capability on Day 14, "Jobs." When you run a command in this manner, the shell sets this variable to the PID (process id) of the background process. When this background or child process terminates, the C Shell will unset this shell variable.

The $child variable is often useful in shell scripts where it is sometimes necessary to kill a child process. This variable permits you to write a script that can terminate a process, without going to great lengths to determine the actual PID of the background process. Without this built-in shell variable, you would need to perform some involved searching and parsing of the output from the UNIX ps command to get the PID in which you are interested.

The Current Working Directory *$cwd*

When you first log onto the system, you start positioned in your home directory. This is initially your current working directory. As you move to other directories, using one of the navigation commands of the shell, your current working directory changes to reflect the directory path of your current location. The C Shell keeps this built-in variable updated with the full pathname of your current working directory. Some versions of the C Shell also update the $PWD environment variable to reflect changes in this built-in variable.

In event 18 of the following example, the pwd command shows that I am in my home directory, /usr/dave.

```
18 % pwd
/usr/dave
19 % echo $cwd
/usr/dave
20 % cd /usr/local/bin
21 % pwd
/usr/local/bin
22 % echo $cwd
/usr/local/bin
23 % _
```

If I then examine the $cwd variable, I see that it has the same path that pwd reported. If I then use cd to change to another location, this time /usr/local/bin. When I repeat the steps of pwd and echoing $cwd, you can see that the shell variable $cwd is still in agreement with the output of the pwd command.

One typical use of the $cwd variable is in updating the C Shell prompt to contain the path of the current working directory. Rather than executing the pwd command each time you use cd to change to a new directory, you can use the $cwd variable to report your location.

The Filename Completion Suffixes
$fignore

One of the most useful features of the C Shell is file completion. In tomorrow's lesson, you will learn about the special shell variable that enables this feature for your shell sessions. This feature permits you to type part of a filename or path and have the C Shell complete the name if possible. Normally, this feature considers all files in all the directories listed in your $path shell variable when it attempts to complete a pathname.

If there are specific filename extensions that you wish to have ignored in this process, you include them in the $fignore variable. This built-in shell variable contains a list of the filename extensions that you want ignored during filename completion.

The typical contents of $fignore is the extension .o, which is used for C program object files that result from compilations. Usually, when you are issuing a command and using the filename completion feature to finish the command line, you don't want the shell to find these .o files. These files are rarely of interest to you, and they only complicate the file completion search, forcing you to resolve the extension.

For more information on the filename completion feature, look in Day 5 for the special shell variable $filec. More explanation about file completion is given when the $filec variable is explained.

The History Substitution Characters
$histchars

On Day 1, "Introducing the C Shell," you learned about history substitutions. Normally, the C Shell looks for the bang (!) character to indicate that a history substitution is being made. The carat (^) is used to bracket the *from* and *to* strings of a Quick Substitution. If you want to change either of the characters used for these purposes, you can use the special shell variable $histchars.

This variable contains a two-character string. The first character is used to replace the bang (!) as the history substitution character, and the second character is used to replace the carat (^) as the Quick Substitution delimiter. You must set both characters, even though you may be setting one or the other to the same value it currently contains.

If you were to set the $histchars variable as in the following example, you would recall events with the ampersand (&) instead of with the bang (!):

```
24 % set histchars="&:"
25 % _
```

So to recall event number 12, you would type &12 instead of !12. Likewise, you would use the colon (:) rather than the carat (^) to make Quick Substitutions. To change bon to bin, you would enter :bon:bin: rather than ^bon^bin^.

> **Caution:** Unless there is a strong reason for changing these substitution characters, I recommend that you not make any changes. Choosing a character or characters that will not be in conflict with other shell metacharacters is difficult. By making such a change, you will quite possibly cause more problems than are resolved.

The History List Size *$history*

To enable the C Shell history mechanism, you set this variable to some positive number. This number represents the number of lines kept by the shell in the history list. If this variable is not set or is set to a value of zero, then only the most recent command is saved. The following example shows the $history variable being set to 100:

```
25 % set history=100
26 % _
```

Although you want a number that will be large enough to meet your needs, keep in mind that the history list is kept in memory using C Shell resources. A number in the range of 100 to 200 is typical for experienced users, whereas novice users may want to start with around 50 and work up to a large number.

The User's Home Directory *$home*

The special $home variable always contains the full pathname of the user's home directory. When the C Shell expands the tilde (~) metacharacter to the home directory, it refers to the contents of this variable. This variable is rarely, if ever, changed. Changing the contents of this variable could have serious consequences when you run commands and scripts that depend on the value of $home to point to a user's home directory.

It is valuable to know of this variable when you write shell scripts. Using $home gives your script the flexibility to reference the home directory of a user without having to do a lookup in the password file. It is also useful in your own startup scripts. It protects you against the chance that your system administrator might change your home directory location, requiring you to make changes in your startup files and scripts that have hardcoded home directory paths.

In the following example, using $home in the path guarantees that the alias mybin will always work, even if the home directory is changed at some later date:

```
26 % alias mybin "cd $home/bin"
27 % _
```

It is a good habit to use this variable in place of hardcoded paths when at all possible.

The User's Mail Path *$mail*

If you use e-mail on your UNIX system to communicate with other users, the shell variable $mail is an important variable for you to become familiar with. This is a multiword variable that the C Shell uses for two purposes, both related to e-mail.

Regardless of which command you choose to use to read and send your mail, the C Shell can notify you when you have received new mail. In order for the shell to tell you when new mail has arrived, it needs to know where your mail files reside. You can specify one or more filenames for the shell to monitor for the receipt of new mail. The list of filenames is separated by spaces. In the following example, two filenames are monitored:

```
27 % set mail=(/usr/spool/mail/dave /usr/dave/Mail/mbox)
28 % _
```

The $mail variable can also specify the checking interval. This controls how often the shell examines the filenames in the list to see if they have changed. This interval is expressed in seconds, and, if used, the interval is the first item in the $mail variable. Here the interval is 60 seconds:

```
28 % set mail=(60 /usr/spool/mail/dave /usr/dave/Mail/mbox)
29 % _
```

The Directory Search List *$path*

You use the UNIX system by entering commands at the shell prompt. When you press Return each time, the C Shell processes your command. The first step the shell takes in processing your command is to find the program or script that you entered as the first word on the command line. To locate a program or script, the shell searches many directories on the system until a match is found or all possibilities are exhausted.

The $path shell variable contains a list of directories that the shell uses as its search list when locating commands and script files. This variable is initialized from the environment variable $PATH, which is updated by the C Shell whenever a change is made to $path. By using the environment variable to update the local variable, the shell communicates your search-path list from your login shell to each of its children.

In the following example, three new directories are added to the search path in the $path variable ahead of its current contents:

```
29 % set path=($home/bin . /usr/local/bin $path)
30 % _
```

The first directory that will be searched for command and scripts is $home/bin, my personal bin directory. It is followed by my current directory at any time and then by the /usr/local/bin directory where local commands and scripts are kept for access by all users on the system. The current contents of the $path variable are then appended to the end to form a new list, which is stored back to the $path variable.

Using this variable, the C Shell enables you to use simple filenames when running commands or scripts. The shell searches each directory path listed in the $path variable for the command or script name. The search occurs in the same order as the names appear in the $path variable. If the command or script file is not found after all of the directories in the search list are exhausted, an error message is issued.

Caution: If you have a program or script in a personal directory, with the same name as a UNIX command, it will be found by the shell only if your personal directory appears in the search list before the directory in which the UNIX command resides. You should consider placing personal directories containing scripts or programs near the front of the $path list. In this way, your personal commands will supersede like-named UNIX commands.

Note: Here are four points to consider regarding the $path shell variable.

1. If $path becomes unset or reset to a null list, then only full pathnames will permit commands and scripts to execute.

2. The default for $path is typically (. /bin /usr/ucb /usr/bin).

3. To specify that the current directory be searched for command and script files either place a null word (' ') in the $path variable or explicitly place a dot (.) in the search list.

4. A C Shell, running interactively, searches each directory in the list contained in $path after reading .cshrc at startup, and whenever $path is reset. The executable files found in these directories are kept

in an internal table. This table is called a *hash table,* named after the method used to organize and access its contents. Using this hash table greatly speeds the C Shell's search for commands and scripts. When new commands or scripts are added to any directory in the path list you should use the `rehash` command to update this hash table, because the shell does not do this automatically. /

[handwritten margin note: what specific Before/After in file directory list]

The C Shell Prompt String *$prompt*

The content and format of the prompt displayed by an interactive shell is controlled by the `$prompt` shell variable. Examples of shell commands in this book are shown with command prompts that contain the current event number followed by a percent sign. This was specified by setting the string in `$prompt` to a format that incorporated the current event number into the prompt.

In the following example, I set the `$prompt` variable to the string that produces prompts shown in this book's examples:

```
30 % set prompt='\! % '
31 % _
```

The exclamation point (!) indicates to the shell where the current event number is to be substituted. This character is escaped with a backslash (\) to keep the shell from processing it immediately. If the backslash is not used, then the event number at the time the string is set in `$prompt` will be substituted and will not change with each command. For more examples of setting the prompt string, see Appendix E, "Examples of *Dot* Files."

Note: Notice in the last example that spaces appear before and after the percent sign. The spaces are present for readability and will be displayed by the shell on each prompt. This way, the event number is set off from the command you type by a percent sign separated by spaces.

When a noninteractive shell is started, the `$prompt` variable is left unset. A test to see if `$prompt` is defined can be used within the `.cshrc` file or within shell scripts to tailor processing based on the mode in which the current shell is running. The following example shows how to test the `$prompt` variable in this manner.

```
if ($?prompt == 0) exit
```

In this example, the expression $?prompt returns 1 if the variable $prompt is set and 0 if it is not set. If $prompt is not set, the script will be exited. In the startup file .cshrc, this type of logic can be used to skip the portion of the startup script related only to interactive operation, thus reducing shell startup overhead.

> **Tip:** Here is an interesting alias to the shell's cd command. This alias changes your prompt, each time you change directories, to include your new working directory in the prompt:
>
> ```
> alias cd 'cd \!*; set prompt="$cwd % \! > "'
> ```
>
> This alias changes your prompt to display the current working directory path, followed by a percent sign, the current event number, and finally a > character. Notice the use of spaces to make the prompt more readable.
>
> ```
> /usr/dave % 31 >
> ```

The Size of the Saved History $savehist

In the first lesson of this book, you learned about the C Shell's command history facility and how to recall events. Earlier in today's lesson, you read about the $history shell variable, which controls the history feature and sets the size of the history list. I hope that by now you have had the opportunity to try out some of the examples and have found out what the shell history can do to assist you when you are using the system.

Normally, when you end your login shell session and sign off the system, the history list that you have collected is discarded. The next time you sign on to the system, the event number restarts at 1 and you have a clean history slate. You can, however, change this and have some or all of your history saved when you sign off, to be restored when you log on again to resume your work.

The $savehist shell variable, like the $history variable, is assigned a number. Just as the $history variable tells the shell how much history to retain while you are logged onto the system, the $savehist variable tells the shell how much of the history list to save until your next session.

Say, for example, that you have $history set to a value of 100:

```
31 % set history=100
32 % set savehist=50
33 % _
```

You can save all or part of that 100 lines of history by setting the $savehist variable to a number between 1 and 100. When you sign off, the shell checks to see if $savehist is set and will save that number of lines of history, counting from the most recent backwards. These lines of history are written to a file named .history in your home directory.

When you log on to the system again, the C Shell looks to see if there is a .history file in your home directory. If the shell finds such a file, it reads .history into the history list, starting the event number over at 1 again. If you saved the last 50 history lines, then you would log on to find your event number at 51 and the last 50 events from your last session appear when you use the history command.

I find this to be a big help for restoring continuity with my last session. When I return to work and say "What was I doing when I signed off yesterday?" I can find the answer simply by looking at my history list! Remember that setting large numbers for $history and for $savehist especially will slow down the startup of your C Shell. /

The Default Shell Path *$shell*

This shell variable is not usually changed by the user. The C Shell initializes the value of $shell to be its own pathname /bin/csh when the shell is started. When you run a script, or enter a command that starts another shell, the value in $shell is used for the name of the new shell.

The Command Return Status *$status*

Each time you run a command or shell script, it returns a completion status to the C Shell when it exits. This status is available to you in the shell variable $status. When you are using the shell interactively, the contents of $status are not as important to you because you see the results of running the command or script on your terminal. You know whether it ran successfully, and if it did not, you usually receive an error message.

In a shell script, however, knowing the status is not always as simple. Usually in a script, you want to test whether certain commands completed with no error before continuing on with the next steps. You can use the $status variable for this purpose, checking to see that you got the desired status, usually zero if the command ran successfully. Built-in commands, covered in this book starting with Day 8, will return zero if successful and 1 if they fail for any reason. The following code line tests the $status variable. If $status contains a non-zero value, the script is exited, returning the value of $status to its parent process.

```
if ( $status != 0 ) exit $status
```

Some commands return more involved status codes, based upon the results of the process they have completed. On the man page for each command, you can usually find a section towards the end of the document that explains any unusual error or status returns from the command. For a good example, take a look at the documentation for the UNIX grep command. /

The Command Timer Control $time

The $time built-in variable controls the C Shell's automatic command timer. Normally, this variable is not set by the shell. When it is set, the shell uses the information in the variable to control when command timings are reported and, optionally, the format of the output.

The simplest way to use the $time variable is to set it to a threshold value expressed in CPU seconds. If a command exceeds this threshold, a timing line showing the resources used is displayed by the shell. You can also supply a second value to the $time variable, which is a string of formatting tags that specify which resources to report and in what order.

The following table shows the different values for the formatting tags that the $time variable can contain. Each of these tags consists of two characters, a percent sign (%), and a single *uppercase* letter denoting the resource to be displayed. If you specify a tag value that is invalid, it will be printed as text in the resource string. You can also include your own text within the string to label resource information as desired.

Table 4.1. $time **variable resource tags.**

Tag	Description
%D	Average utilization of unshared data space, in kilobytes
%E	Elapsed (wall-clock) time for the command
%F	Page faults
%I	Number of block input operations
%K	Average utilization of unshared stack space used, in kilobytes
%M	Maximum real memory used during execution of the process
%O	Number of block output operations
%P	Total CPU time: U (user) plus S (system) expressed as a percentage of E (elapsed) time

Tag	Description
%S	Seconds of CPU time used by the kernel by request of the user's process
%U	Seconds of CPU time used by the user's process
%W	Number of times the user process was swapped from memory
%X	Average shared-memory utilization, in kilobytes

If the $time variable is set only with a threshold value, the default display includes the following tags in the order shown: %U, %S, %E, %P, %X, %D, %I, %O, %F, and %W.

In the first line of the following example, the $time variable is set with just a threshold of 3 CPU seconds:

```
33 % set $time=3
34 % set $time=(3, "Elapsed: %E CPU%: %P Kernel: %S User: %U AvgMem: %X")
35 % _
```

In the second line of the example, a string of tags is added to report elapsed time, percentage CPU use, CPU seconds used by the kernel and by the user, and finally average memory usage.

The Current Process ID $$

The $$ is a very special shell variable that returns the process ID (PID) of the current process. The most frequent use of this shell variable is within shell scripts. Often when writing a shell script, you need to create one or more work files. Usually, as a matter of good form, these files are created in the /tmp directory.

If more than one person might be using your script at one time, you need to make the files created for the first user different from those created when the second or third person is using the script. Otherwise, there will be a conflict, and the second user's process would try to write in the work files created by the first or third user's process.

To avoid such a problem, you can include this variable somewhere in the name of each work file. Each work file or set of files then will be unique for each user of the script, and there will be no conflict. The process ID contained in $$ is that of the shell running the script. It is guaranteed to be unique during the time period that the process is running.

In the following example, a variable is created that contains the name of a temporary filename:

```
35 % set workfile=/tmp/workfile1.$$
36 % echo $workfile
/tmp/workfile1.547
37 % _
```

The variable $workfile can be used as a filename argument on a command, on an if statement within a script, or anywhere else that you would normally use a filename. The second line of the example uses the UNIX echo command to display the contents of the $workfile variable. The output shows you that a string was created for the contents of the variable, which contains the template part of the name as well as the process ID of the shell, 547. This makes the filename unique, because no other process could create the same name by the use of the $$ shell variable.

Summary

Today was your introduction to shell variables. In today's lesson, you learned about shell variables. You found out that variables come in two types, local and environment, and you learned the differences between the two. You discovered how to display the contents of both types of variables by using their respective definition commands without parameters.

The remainder of the lesson was devoted to explaining each of the built-in shell variables capable of taking a value. Uses for each of the variables were demonstrated.

In the next chapter, you will continue to learn more about shell variables. Day 5 examines all of the built-in shell variables that act as switches. The last portion of Day 5 introduces you to numeric shell variables and the various kinds of operations that can be performed with them within shell scripts.

Related UNIX Topics

This chapter presented some new concepts and commands. The following is a list of some of these concepts and topics with suggestions for sources of further information:

Filename Completion: This handy feature of the C Shell is covered in more depth in tomorrow's material. When you have completed that material, combine it with today's lesson to take advantage of this facility.

Startup Files: Look at the examples in Appendix E and compare them to the startup files you are currently using. Feel free to adopt any or all parts of these examples in your own files.

Q&A

Q What is the difference between local and environment variables?

A Local variables affect only the shell in which they are defined. Environment variables are passed on to all shells, commands, and scripts that are started from the shell in which they are defined. In other words, these shells, commands, and scripts *inherit* their environment, in the form of environment variables, from their parent shell.

Q How does the shell identify variables?

A Shell variables, both local and global (environment), begin their names with a dollar sign ($). There is no way to know whether a variable is local or global, other than by seeing which command displays its name and value—set (for local variables) or setenv (for global variables). For this reason, you should follow the convention of using all uppercase letters in environment variables. Then you can visually identify whether a variable is local or global by its name.

Workshop

The Workshop provides several sections to aid you in reviewing the topics covered in today's lesson. There is a quiz section to help you reinforce your understanding of the material presented for Day 4 and exercises to give you practice applying what you learned in problem solving. Take the time to review these questions and exercises, so that you understand the concepts before you begin the next day's lesson. The answers are provided in Appendix F, "Answers to Quizzes and Exercises."

Quiz

1. How can you find out the contents of your local variables?

2. What is the difference between the variables $path and $PATH?

3. What is the relationship between $cwd and $PWD?

4. How can you set up your shell so that it will log you off after ten minutes of inactivity?

5. What shell variable is used to set the value of the tilde (~) metacharacter?

6. What is the effect of resetting $path?

7. How can you modify your shell prompt to include your username in the prompt string?

8. What three built-in shell variables affect the history mechanism's operation?

Exercises

1. Review the built-in shell variables covered in today's lesson and experiment with changing the values on some of them to find out more about their effects.

2. Look at some of the shell scripts on your system in /bin and /usr/bin to see how they use the built-in shell variables in their logic.

Shell Variables,
Part II

Introduction to Day 5

In the previous day's lesson, you were introduced to shell variables. Today you will continue with that subject and explore a different type of shell variable. Unlike the variables covered in the last lesson, these do not take values. Instead they act like switches. You use set to turn them on and unset to turn them off. These built-in *switch variables* are local variables as well, like those variables that take values.

Today you will also learn about a third type of variable, one that you can use to perform arithmetic in shell scripts. You will find out how to form expressions and to use all of the operators that are available.

Setting Today's Goals

Today you will learn

- [ ] About variables that act as switches

- [ ] About each of the following built-in switch variables

  ```
  $echo
  $filec
  $hardpaths
  $ignoreeof
  $nobeep
  $noclobber
  $noglob
  $nonomatch
  $notify
  $verbose
  ```

- [ ] About numeric shell variables

- [ ] How to form expressions with shell variables and the @ command

- [ ] About arithmetic operators

- [ ] About pattern-matching operators

- [ ] About assignment operators

- [ ] About postfix operators

- [ ] About file-inquiry operators

Variables That Act as Switches

You learned about the special built-in shell variables that take values in yesterday's lesson. Now you will learn about a different group of built-in variables that are a part of the C Shell. These variables don't take values as such, but instead can be set to one of two states, *ON* or *OFF*. As built-in variables, these switches control various aspects of the C Shell behavior or operation.

In the following sections, I will present each of these built-in switch variables. You will learn how each one affects the C Shell and your working environment. I will show you ways in which each can be used to control features of the shell and assist you in working with the C Shell.

For review, the syntax for the set and unset command is repeated here. The built-in variables that act as switches are set using the first form of the set command.

Syntax

The syntax for the set command is

```
set [var [ = value ] ]

set var[n] = word
```

The set command is used to display and assign values to local shell variables. In the syntax, *var* is a shell variable of the form $name, where *name* is made up of letters, digits, and underscores (_). Variable names must start with a letter and can be up to 20 characters in length. If a variable does not exist, using it in a set command will cause it to be created.

The set command can be used in several ways. Without arguments, set displays the values of *all* shell variables. With a single argument *var* (a variable name), set assigns a null (empty) value to the variable. If arguments of the form *var* = *value* are used, then set assigns *value* to *var*. In this case, *value* can be one of the following:

word	A single word (or a quote-enclosed string). For example, "abcd123" or "my word."
(word list)	A space-separated list of words enclosed in parentheses. For example, (red, orange, yellow, green).

Before being assigned, all values containing command and filename metacharacters are expanded. Multiword variables are arrays where individual words can be accessed by specifying their subscript in square brackets ([]). When arguments of the form *var*[*n*] = *word* are used, set uses *word* to replace the *n*th word in the multiword variable *var*.

Example   ```
set testvar = testing123

set testarr = (testing 1 2 3)

set emptyvar

set mylist[2] = two
```

Syntax

The syntax for the unset command is

`unset` *pattern*

The unset command is used to remove variables from the environment of the current shell session. All variables that match *pattern*, regular characters and filename meta-characters, are removed or "unset." In the following example, I use `set` to display my current variables. Then I define a variable name with a value `David`, and finally I remove the new name variable using the unset command.

```
1 % set
argv   ()
autologout   10
cwd   /usr/dave
history   15
home   /usr/dave
ignoreeof
noclobber
path   (/bin /usr/bin /usr/lib . /usr/dave/bin)
prompt   ! %
shell   /bin/csh
status   0
term   vt100
2 % set name=David
3 % set
argv   ()
autologout   10
cwd   /usr/dave
history   15
home   /usr/dave
ignoreeof
name   David
noclobber
path   (/bin /usr/bin /usr/lib . /usr/dave/bin)
prompt   ! %
shell   /bin/csh
status   0
term   vt100
4 % unset name
5 % set
argv   ()
autologout   10
cwd   /usr/dave
```
```

```
history    15
home    /usr/dave
ignoreeof
noclobber
path    (/bin /usr/bin /usr/lib . /usr/dave/bin)
prompt    ! %
shell    /bin/csh
status    0
term    vt100
6 % _
```

$echo

In Day 1, "Introducing the C Shell," in the section "Command Line Options," I reviewed each of the options used for starting the C Shell. Two of these options, -x and -X, cause the C Shell to set the $echo switch variable to the ON state.

When this variable is set, the shell echoes each command after *all* substitutions—history and metacharacter—have been made and just before the command is executed. The primary use for this switch is to assist in the debugging process when you write C Shell scripts. When $echo is set, you can monitor the progress as your script is executed by the shell.

In the following example script, a foreach loop sets the variable $file to each filename that matches the patterns in parentheses, * and .??*. Within the loop, for each filename, $file is tested to see if it is a directory. This is done using the -d file-inquiry operator, which is discussed at the end of today's lesson. If the filename is a directory, the echo command is executed, displaying a message that includes the contents of $file.

To illustrate the effect of setting $echo, the script is changed and run again. You can see that each line of the script is displayed for each iteration of the loop. The messages that were displayed the first time the script was run are still displayed in between the output from the $echo setting.

```
6 % cat dirtest
#!/bin/csh
foreach file ( * .??* )
    if ( -d $file ) echo $file "is a directory"
end
7 % dirtest
Mail is a directory
bin is a directory
memos is a directory
scripts is a directory
testdata is a directory
8 % cat dirtest
#!/bin/csh
set echo
```

[handwritten note: A foreach Loop?]

5

```
foreach file ( * .??* )
    if ( -d $file ) echo $file "is a directory"
end
7 % dirtest
foreach file ( * .??* )
if ( -d Mail ) echo Mail is a directory
Mail is a directory
end
if ( -d bin ) echo bin is a directory
bin is a directory
end
if ( -d memos ) echo memos is a directory
memos is a directory
end
if ( -d scripts ) echo scripts is a directory
scripts is a directory
end
if ( -d testdata ) echo testdata is a directory
testdata is a directory
end
8 % _
```

Caution: The set and unset commands expect that the first argument after the command is the name of a shell variable. Because of that, you must omit the $ from that initial variable name. If you forget and include the $ on that variable, you will get an error message from the shell. Notice in the preceding examples that the dollar sign is not included on these commands.

The options -x and -X represented different ways of setting the $echo variable. To recap briefly, the -X option sets $echo prior to the shell reading from your .cshrc startup file. The -x option sets $echo prior to the shell reading from your script file. Finally, direct use of the $echo variable gives you control over where this output is enabled from within your script.

If you are working on a lengthy or complex script, using the command-line options to debug the script can produce unwieldy amounts of output to review. Once you have narrowed down the area of the script where your problem resides, you can set the $echo variable directly, exerting more control over the debug output that is produced. Don't forget that you can use the unset command to turn off $echo when its output is of little interest.

```
8 % unset echo
9 % _
```

> **Caution:** The unset command takes an argument that is a filename substitution metacharacter pattern. This pattern is matched against each shell variable that is set for the current shell session. Each variable that matches the pattern is unset. The pattern used with unset can legally be the single metacharacter *, which would match *all* variables. If you use unset *, all of your shell variables will be removed, with undesirable side-effects. See Day 3, "Command Substitution, Aliases, and Filename Generation," for more information about filename substitution metacharacters.

$filec

There is one feature of the C Shell that I find indispensable when working interactively. This is the shell's File Completion feature. With File Completion enabled, the shell will assist you in typing filename arguments to commands. If you know the first few unique characters of the argument, the shell will supply the remaining portion of the filename for you.

To enable this feature, you turn on the `$filec` built-in variable using the `set` command. Once `$filec` is set ON, the shell will finish filename arguments for you when signaled from the keyboard. To signal that you want the shell to complete an argument, press the Escape key once (twice on some systems). The shell will supply the remaining characters up to point where more than one possibility exists among the files that match thus far. If this point is reached, the shell will beep to signal you that one or more characters need to be entered to resolve the filename further. After you have entered more characters, the Escape key can again be pressed to attempt further matching, until the filename is complete.

The `$filec` variable also controls another useful facility of the C Shell. When you have entered a portion of a filename argument on the command line, you can get a list of the files that match to that point. When you press Control-D at any point in completing a filename, the shell will display a list of files that match the preceding string.

```
9 % set $filec
10 % grep w*h testt<escape>ext
which I use in examples to display what's
inside a file with a UNIX command.
11 % _
```

In the preceding example, after I set `$filec`, I started a command line with a `grep` command. After I typed the first five letters of the filename, I pressed Escape once. The shell searched for a file that matched these letters and found an exact match. The

117

remaining characters were then appended to the command line so that all I needed to do was press the Return key to execute the command. The grep command searched testtext and found the two lines that were displayed. The first matched with the word which, and the second matched with the word with.

If you are unable to recall the exact spelling of a filename and cannot complete it on the command line, this feature can be a valuable aid. With the displayed list of potential matches to your filename, you can then complete the argument and the command line.

```
11 % set $filec
12 % more test<control-D>
testdata  testfile  testmemo.doc testtext
more testtext<Return>
This is the contents of the file testtext
which I use in examples to display what's
inside a file with a UNIX command.
13 % _
```

$hardpaths

Two C Shell built-in commands, pushd and popd, which are explained in detail later on Day 8, "C Shell Built-in Commands," use a directory stack that they modify or reorder as a part of their function. As a part of its operation, pushd places directory paths on this stack. The popd command removes a directory path from the stack. The built-in variable $hardpaths affects how the directory stack is maintained by these commands.

Normally, the directory path that is put on the stack is the same as what you entered on the command line. Even if this directory is in fact a symbolic link, the path to which it points is not placed on the stack. If $hardpaths is set ON and a symbolic link is used on a pushd or popd command, the symbolic link is resolved to a hard path. That is to say, the link is followed until an actual directory path is found. This directory is what is added or removed from the stack.

Using $hardpath will often resolve problems that can occur when symbolic links are used in certain situations. Handling the directory stack with $hardpaths set is clearer and more straightforward whenever symbolic links are in frequent use.

$ignoreeof

The built-in shell variable $ignoreeof is one of the features of the C Shell designed to save you from yourself and preserve your sanity. As you learned on Day 1, there are several ways that you can exit or end a C Shell session. One of those ways is to enter Control-D, the EOF character, at the shell prompt. When the shell sees EOF on its input file, it terminates. Another method is to type either exit or logout at the command prompt, which is the normal and preferred way to exit from the shell.

N

Unfortunately, there are some UNIX commands for which you supply interactive input terminated with the same Control-D EOF character. On occasion, you might accidentally type an additional Control-D and find that you have terminated your shell session unexpectedly! This shell variable, $ignoreeof, does exactly what its name implies. It tells that shell to ignore EOF characters on input to the command prompt.

If you set the $ignoreeof variable and type Control-D at a prompt, the shell will issue a message telling you to use logout to exit from the shell. You will then get a new command prompt and can continue with the shell if you wish. Otherwise, you can type logout or exit at the prompt to terminate your shell session.

```
13 % set ignoreeof
14 % <control-D>
You must use 'exit' to logout
15 % unset ignoreeof
16 % <control-D>

Welcome to UNIX

Login:
```

As you can see, when the $ignoreeof is set, exiting by typing Control-D is inhibited. When the variable is unset, typing Control-D at the prompt results in the shell terminating, and you get a new login prompt.

$nobeep

Earlier in today's lesson, you learned about the shell variable $filec and the C Shell's filename completion feature. When you use this facility and try to complete an ambiguous filename, the shell will beep to tell you that it is unable to furnish further characters of the filename. If you wish to suppress this notification beep when using file completion, set $nobeep, and the shell will no longer beep when it cannot complete a filename.

$noclobber

You may have already experienced the situation in which you have accidentally overwritten a file, destroying information you needed to keep. If you were using the UNIX copy command cp, you could have included the -i option to inform you that the target file existed. But if you were using file redirection or another UNIX command that writes to a file, you did not have that option to protect you.

The shell variable $noclobber is the answer to this problem. As its name implies, $noclobber keeps you from clobbering your files. When this variable is set, output redirection is restricted to new files. In addition, if you use append redirection, it is limited to existing files; when $noclobber is set and append redirection is used, the target file *must* exist. With $noclobber set, if you attempt a redirection that violates these conditions, the shell will issue an error message.

The following example shows a script that creates an empty file using the touch command. You see that the file is empty with the output from ls. Next the script sets $noclobber and attempts to copy the contents of file dirtest to the file noclob, using the cat command. Because the file noclob exists and $noclobber is set ON, the shell issues an error message. The script then unsets $noclobber and repeats the cat, which then succeeds. The last ls shows that there is now something in the file noclob.

```
17 % cat noclob.csh
#!/bin/csh -xv
touch noclob
ls -l noclob
set noclobber
cat dirtest > noclob
unset noclobber
cat dirtest > noclob
ls -l noclob
18 % noclob.csh
touch noclob
ls -l noclob
-rw-r--r--   1 dave     users          0 May 24 14:05 noclob
set noclobber
cat dirtest > noclob
noclob: File exists.
unset noclobber
cat dirtest > noclob
ls -l noclob
-rw-r--r--   1 dave     users         93 May 24 14:05 noclob
19 %
```

Table 5.1. The effects of $noclobber on file redirection.

Command	Effect
	With $noclobber set **OFF**
ls -l > newfile	Output from the ls command is written to newfile. If newfile exists, it will be overwritten.
ls -l >> oldfile	Output from the ls command is written to newfile. If newfile exists, the new output is appended to the end of the file. If newfile does not exist, it is created.
	With $noclobber set **ON**
ls -l > newfile	Output from the ls command is written to newfile. If newfile exists, the C Shell issues an error message.

Command	Effect
`ls -l >> oldfile`	Output from the `ls` command is written to `newfile`. If `newfile` exists, the new output is appended to the end of the file. If `newfile` does not exist, the C Shell issues an error message.

> **Tip:** The built-in shell variables `$ignoreeof` and `$noclobber` are extremely useful to aid you in protecting your files and UNIX sessions. I strongly recommend that you set these variables in your startup files. You should set `$noclobber` in your `.cshrc` startup file so that any shell that you start will set `$noclobber` to ON and protect you from overwriting files accidentally. You can set `$ignoreeof` in your `.login` startup file if you only want to protect your login shell from being terminated. Otherwise, set `$ignoreeof` in `.cshrc` as well, and use `exit` to leave the shell. That's a good habit to get into.

$noglob

You learned about the C Shell's collection of metacharacters on Day 2 of this book. You should recall that you can escape, or protect metacharacters from being processed by the shell, when necessary. You do this by using the backslash (\) before each character to be escaped. As you can well imagine, this can become tedious in a shell script or at the command prompt when you are doing many such commands.

If you set the built-in shell variable `$noglob` at the command prompt or within your shell script, filename substitution is inhibited. This stays in effect until you use the `unset` command to remove the `$noglob` variable from your environment. This can mean a big savings in keystrokes and can reduce typing mistakes as well.

In a shell script, after you have processed all of the filename metacharacter substitutions necessary, setting `$noglob` would allow you to use metacharacters on commands without escaping for the remainder of the script. In addition to the reduction of keystrokes and errors, setting `$noglob` helps to make the script more readable, leaving out all of the backslashes to clutter up the command lines.

> **Caution:** Be sure that you unset $noglob after you are done with it in a script and *definitely* at the shell prompt. If you forget to do this, the results of subsequent commands will be unexpected and be likely to cause the shell to issue error messages. Use this feature judiciously and with caution.

$nonomatch

On command lines, you will often use the filename metacharacters that you learned about on Day 2. These metacharacter patterns make the job of specifying filenames on commands easier. The shell finds all files that match your pattern and replaces the pattern with the list of matching files. This is also referred to expanding the metacharacters.

The pattern you typed on the command line may not match any files. In this case, the C Shell normally issues an error message that no files matched and your command is not executed. If you set the shell variable $nonomatch, this behavior of the shell is changed. Instead, when no files match the pattern, the filename substitution pattern is passed to your command, and no error is reported.

```
19 % echo ..{xx,yy,zz}[0-9]*
no files match
20 % set $nonomatch
21 % echo ..{xx,yy,zz}[0-9]*
..{xx,yy,zz}[0-9]*
22 %
```

It is the responsibility of the command receiving the match pattern to handle it properly. If the match pattern is syntactically incorrect, the C Shell will detect the error and report it, rather than pass the bad pattern to the command.

$notify

When you run a command from the shell prompt, the prompt won't return until the command completes. UNIX allows you to run commands in a batch or background mode. This frees the current shell to accept another command immediately, in foreground, while the background command runs to completion. If the background command finishes while your foreground command is running, the shell waits until the foreground command is finished before notifying you that the background command has completed. Setting $notify ON changes this behavior so the shell will give you immediate notice when a job's status changes.

Tip: In Day 14, "Jobs," you will learn about putting commands in background. This will give you more flexibility for getting more work out of your system. You can use $notify to inform you immediately when a background command has completed. If, for example, you are working in the editor, you will get notification without having to exit to the shell prompt. The more you begin to use background processing, the more you will appreciate the use of $notify.

$verbose

At the beginning of this book, the command options to the C Shell were presented. Two of these options, -v and -V you should recall, set the built-in shell variable $verbose to the ON state. When this variable is set ON—either directly using the set command, or indirectly via use of one of the options -v and -V—the shell displays commands at a point just after history substitution has been made.

In contrast, the $echo variable and its related options -x and -X display commands after all substitutions have been made. This includes history substitutions as well as filename expansion. The $verbose variable, like $echo, gives you control over where, when, and how your script displays debug output. Whereas the command-line options turn on the variable at the start of the script, using set gives you the option to turn output ON and OFF where it does the most good.

```
22 % set verbose
23 %
```

Don't forget that you can use the unset command to turn off $echo when its output is of little interest.

```
23 % unset echo
24 %
```

Tip: If you use any of the options -v, -V, -x, or -X to start a shell script, you can use unset to turn off the output later within the script. Because the effect of these options is to set one of the variables $echo or $verbose, the unset command can be used even though you did not use set to explicitly set the variable.

Numeric Shell Variables

In the lessons of today and yesterday, you learned about built-in shell variables. You found out that there are two varieties of these variables: those that take values and those that act like switches. In addition to the built-in shell variables you have learned, the C Shell supports numeric variables. You can use these numeric variables to perform all sorts of arithmetic in your shell scripts.

This section will show you how you can use numeric variables in your scripts. You will learn how you form expressions, and you'll learn about the various types of operators you can use in these expressions.

Expressions

Expressions can be formed in the C Shell in the same manner as in the C programming language. The operators available within the C Shell are similar, as well, to the C language set. Many of the shell's built-in commands—such as @, `exit`, `if`, `set`, and `while`—accept expressions that can be useful when you write shell scripts.

Syntax

The syntax for C Shell expressions is

```
@ [variable_name operator expression]
```

The @ is a special C Shell command used specifically for writing expressions and assigning their results to a shell variable. The variable can be a simple variable, or it can be a multiword variable indicated by [*n*] after the name. If a multiword variable is the destination, it must exist and have at least *n* words.

The first argument following the @ is the name of a shell variable into which the expression result will be stored. The @ command, like `set` and `unset`, expects that its first argument is a shell variable and that the variable name is given without the $.

Notice that the arguments to @ are optional (they are shown in square brackets). If the @ command is given without arguments, it behaves like the `set` command and displays the values of all shell variables.

Example: `@ count = $count + 1`

            `@ color[6] = "puce"`

In the first example, the variable `$count` is incremented by one and the results are stored back into the same variable. Note that the first variable name is without a $. In the second example, the multiword variable `$color` is updated with the color `puce`, which is stored into the sixth word of the variable.

DO separate parts of an expression with whitespace.

DON'T use a dollar sign ($) assignment variable name with @.

DO use @ for assigning expression results to a variable.

DO use the set command for assigning a constant value to a variable.

The @ command is used most frequently within scripts, although there are no restrictions to using it to form expressions at the shell command prompt. The @ command is presented later in greater detail in Day 8, "C Shell Built-in Commands." Table 5.2 shows all of the C Shell operators, grouped in the order of precedence.

Table 5.2. C Shell operators, in order of precedence.

	Parentheses
(. . .)	Grouping
	Unary Operators
~	One's complement
!	Logical negation (NOT)
	Arithmetic and Postfix Operators
* / %	Multiplication, division, remainder
+ -	Addition, subtraction
++ --	Postfix addition, postfix subtraction
	Shift Operators
<< >>	Bitwise shift left, bitwise shift right
< > <= >=	Less than, greater than, less than or equal to, greater than or equal to
	Boolean Operators
== !=	Equal to, not equal to

continues

Table 5.2. continued

	Pattern Match Operators
=~ !~	Filename-substitution pattern match, Filename-substitution pattern mismatch
	Bitwise Operators
&	Bitwise AND
^	Bitwise XOR
¦	Bitwise inclusive OR
	Logical Operators
&&	Logical AND
¦¦	Logical OR
	Assignment Operators
=	Assignment
+=	x += y is the same as x = x + y
-=	x -= y is the same as x = x - y
*=	x *= y is the same as x = x * y
/=	x /= y is the same as x = x / y
%=	x %= y is the same as x = x % y
^=	x ^= y is the same as x = x ^ y

Arithmetic Operators

The C Shell programming language supports the usual arithmetic operators for addition (+), subtraction (-), multiplication (*) and division (/). There is also a special operator (%) that returns the integer remainder which results from the division of its two operands.

```
24 % @ counter = 0
25 % echo $counter
0
26 % @ counter = ( 3 * 5 )
27 % echo $counter
```

```
15
28 % @ counter = $counter % 4
29 % echo $counter
3
30 %
```

There is an important attribute of C Shell arithmetic operators that you need to keep in mind. All of these operators are *right associative*. This can result in unexpected results. You should use parentheses to explicitly combine expressions to achieve the desired results.

Pattern Matching Operators

On Day 2, you learned about all of the different metacharacters that are available with the C Shell. These metacharacters are most often used to generate filename and other arguments on command lines. Metacharacters can also be used in conditional expressions and to perform pattern matching.

In shell scripts, you occasionally need to determine if a filename or string is a match to one of these metacharacter expressions. The C Shell provides a special set of operators, =~ and !~, for the purpose of testing the match or non-match of a metacharacter expression, to a literal string or contents of a shell variable.

```
30 % @ results = $filename =~ '.??*'
31 %
```

In the preceding example, the expression $filename =~ '.??*' returns either TRUE (1) or FALSE (0), depending on whether the contents of the variable $filename matches the metacharacter expression. If, for example, $filename contained the string '.history', which matches the metacharacter expression, the contents of $results would be 1 or TRUE. If the operator !~ is substituted for =~, then the expression would be TRUE if the contents of $filename is *not* a match for the metacharacter expression.

> **Tip:** The metacharacter expression in the preceding example, .??*, can be used to match any "dot" file. In the expression, the double question marks insure that the special files . and .. are *not* matched by this expression. Passing these special filenames to most UNIX commands as arguments typically results in error messages or other problems. Use of this expression will prevent their being included in an argument list.

Assignment Operators

The C Shell supports a number of assignment operators similar to those available in the C language. There is, of course, the simple assignment operator equals (=), which assigns the result of expressions to the right of the operator to a shell variable on the left of the equals operator.

```
32 % @ results = $value * 5
33 %
```

In addition to the equals operator, the C Shell has a whole set of assignment operators that are compact forms of a frequent expression format. These assignment operators— +=, -=, *=, /=, %=, and ^=, are used to shorten expressions where two variables are combined with an arithmetic operator, and the results assigned to the first variable.

Consider the expression @ x = $x *<operator>* $y, where *<operator>* is one of the simple arithmetic operators +, -, *, /, %, or ^. Its equivalent, using one of the preceding assignment operators, would be @ x *<operator>*= $y. Otherwise, these assignment operators are described by the function of the simple arithmetic operation they combine.

```
34 % echo $results
20
35 % echo $value
5
36 % @ results *= $value
37 % echo $results
100
38 %
```

Postfix Operators

The C Shell programming language shares two unique arithmetic operators with the C programming language. In C, there is a whole class of operators known as postfix and prefix operators. Two of these operators (the auto-increment operator ++ and the auto-decrement operator --) are also part of the C Shell operator repertoire. They are implemented only in their postfix form in the C Shell.

These operators simplify a frequent process within shell scripts, that is, incrementing or decrementing a counter.

File-Inquiry Operators

Often in a shell script you need to test a file for specific attributes. The results of the test are evaluated by a shell if conditional statement. Table 5.3 lists all of the file-inquiry operators available in the C Shell. Each of these operators tests *filename* for a specific attribute.

Table 5.3. File inquiry operators.

Operator	Description
-r *filename*	If the user has read access to *filename*, return TRUE (1). Otherwise, return FALSE (0).
-w *filename*	If the user has write access to *filename*, return TRUE (1). Otherwise, return FALSE (0).
-x *filename*	If the user has execute access to *filename* (or search permission on a directory) return TRUE (1). Otherwise, return FALSE (0).
-o *filename*	Return TRUE (1) if the user owns *filename*. Otherwise, return FALSE (0).
-d *filename*	Return TRUE (1) if *filename* is a directory. Otherwise, return FALSE (0).
-e *filename*	Return TRUE (1) if *filename* exists. Otherwise, return FALSE (0).
-f *filename*	Return TRUE (1) if *filename* is a plain file. Otherwise, return FALSE (0).
-z *filename*	If the length of *filename* is zero (empty), return TRUE (1). Otherwise, return FALSE (0).

The operators that test permissions (-r, -w, and -x) and the ownership test -o are all evaluated relative to the current user. If the user is the owner of *filename* or has read, write, or execute access to *filename*, the related operator will return TRUE (1); otherwise it will return FALSE (0).

```
38 % ls -l textfile /bin/ls
-rw-rw-r--  1  dave  staff     547   May 18 9:47   textfile
-rwxr-xr-x  1  bin   bin    @@@@@                  /bin/ls
39 % @ xaccess = -x textfile
40 % echo $xaccess
0
41 % @ xaccess = -x /bin/ls
42 % echo $xaccess
1
43 %
```

The remaining operators (-d, -e, -f and -z) test attributes of *filename* that are not specific to a user. The directory test operator, -d, returns TRUE (1) if *filename* is a directory. The existence test operator -e returns TRUE if *filename* exists.

If *filename* is a plain file, the -f operator will return TRUE. If *filename* is a directory, or a special file, or a link, the -f operator will return FALSE (0).

```
43 % ls -l textfile $home
-rw-rw-r--  1 dave  staff    547  May 18 9:47  textfile
-rwxr-xr-x  1 bin   bin      @@@@@              @@@@@
44 % @ daccess = -d textfile
45 % echo $daccess
0
46 % @ xaccess = -x /bin/ls
47 % echo $xaccess
1
48 %
```

Summary

In today's lesson, you completed your introduction to shell variables. You learned about another group of built-in shell variables that act as switches. You discovered that these variables are used to control various aspects of the C Shell's operation and behavior.

Today also taught you about the shell's numeric variables and how to use them to form expressions. The last portion of today's material introduced all of the different operators that are available in the C Shell for forming expressions.

In the next chapter, Day 6, the C Shell startup files will be introduced. You will see how to use these files to customize the C Shell to suit your own needs and style. You will learn how these files are processed by the shell and when they are processed. Day 6 will combine your knowledge of aliases and shell variables and will show you how they can be put to good use.

Related UNIX Topics

This chapter presented some new concepts and commands. Here is a list of some of these concepts and topics, with suggestions for sources of further information.

Metacharacters:	Consult Appendix C in this book as well as the pull-out reference card for listings and definitions of all the metacharacters used by the C Shell. Review Chapter 2 if you need to brush up on metacharacters.
Navigation commands:	Look in Day 8 of this book for a more detailed discussion about the C Shell's navigation commands.

Conditional commands: Look in Day 11 of this book for the section on conditional commands of the C Shell. These commands, in addition to the looping commands covered on the same day, make extensive use of the expression facilities shown in today's lesson.

Q&A

Q Do the C Shell's built-in switch variables take on values?

A The special shell variables covered today act like switches. They can't be set to different values like the variables presented on Day 4. The variables presented today are either ON if they exist or are set, or they are OFF if they are erased or unset.

Q Is there a specific command used for assigning expression results to variables in the C Shell?

A You learned about the `set` command, which can be used for assigning constant values or the contents of another variable to a shell variable. If you want or need to assign the results of an expression, you use the C Shell `@` command to make the assignment.

Q How can you protect yourself from inadvertently terminating your login shell session?

A The special built-in shell variable `$ignoreeof` acts as a switch to cancel the effect of the EOF character (Control-D) from terminating any C Shell that is running. Setting this variable in your `.login` startup file will ensure that you can terminate your login shell only with the `exit` command and not with Control-D.

5

Workshop

The Workshop provides several sections to aid you in reviewing the topics covered in today's lesson. There is a quiz section to help you reinforce your understanding of the material presented for Day 5 and exercises to give you practice applying what you learned in problem solving. The answers are provided in Appendix F, "Answers to Quizzes and Exercises."

Quiz

1. How can you find out if a specific built-in C Shell switch variable is ON or OFF?

2. What are the two shell variables that assist you when debugging shell scripts?

3. How can you find out if a background job has completed without your returning to the C Shell prompt from your current foreground command?

4. How can you turn off the beeping from the C Shell during file completion when the current string cannot be finished without further qualification?

5. What operators can you use to test a file's permissions to find out if you can write to it?

6. How can you easily increment or decrement a counter in a script?

7. What would you do to test the contents of a variable to see if they match a filename substitution pattern?

8. How can you test whether a directory exists to see if you need to create it within a script?

Exercises

1. Try out different expressions at the shell prompt and display the results. See if the results match what you would expect to see from the calculation.

2. Write a short script that would locate empty files in a directory and display their names.

```
#!/bin/csh -f
@ empty = -z *.*
echo $empty
```

Customizing the
User Environment

Introduction to Day 6

Today, on the sixth day of your C Shell adventure, you will find out how you can customize your environment when you use the C Shell. On Day 1, you were introduced to the C Shell dot files .cshrc, .login, and .logout. Today, these and several other dot files will be explored in greater detail. You will learn how you can tailor your own personal working environment on your system by making changes in these files.

Setting Today's Goals

Today, you will learn how to

☐ Know which dot file to change for customizing

☐ Add aliases to .cshrc

☐ Set up local variables in .cshrc

☐ Do additional initialization tasks in .cshrc

☐ Initialize environment variables in .login

☐ Set terminal and workstation attributes in .login

☐ Set up actions performed when you log out of the system

☐ Tips and techniques for making changes to dot files

Customizing the C Shell

On Day 1, you learned about starting and stopping the C Shell. I mentioned that there were several files that the C Shell read which controlled the startup and termination of the shell. Later in the book, you learned about shell variables, both local and environmental (or global) variables. These variables can be set within the C Shell startup files .login and .cshrc. Which of these variables you choose to set, and the values you set them to, controls to a great degree the environment you will work in with the C Shell.

Days 4 and 5 introduced the special built-in shell variables and discussed the function of each and the effect each had on the operation and behavior of the C Shell. Today's lesson takes you one step further and shows you how you can apply your knowledge of shell variables to tailor your C Shell environment. I will also present some UNIX commands that are typically used in these startup files to set up terminal and workstation attributes, window attributes if you are working with X Window and much more.

> **Note:** The C Shell has two startup dot files—.cshrc and .login—that control its operation and environment. Looking at the name of these two files, you might make the mistake of thinking that the .login file is read first when you log in to the system. In fact, this is *not* what happens. Each C Shell process reads .cshrc first when it is initiated. The shell then checks to see if it is a login shell, or a subshell started by the login shell or one of its children. If this check reveals that the shell is in fact a login shell, *then* it reads the .login file. Don't get caught putting a reference to a shell variable, set in .login, in your .cshrc file, only to find that the shell variable hasn't been set yet!

Common Points for C Shell Startup Files

First, before getting into the details of the dot files for the C Shell, I want to mention some common aspects of these files. To begin with, as you may already know, the C Shell looks for these files in your home directory. You can keep copies of them elsewhere for backup or reference, but the only ones that affect the shell are the ones in your home directory.

As you look at the examples in this lesson and at the examples in Appendix E, you will notice lines that begin with a pound sign, also called the hashmark character (#). You may also see the hashmark after the end of a command, followed by more text. The hashmark is used by general convention in all shells as a comment indicator. The C Shell takes all text that follows the hashmark (#) to be a comment and ignores this text. It is a good idea to "comment" your startup files for documentation. Doing so helps you to remember why you put certain lines in the file or to understand why someone else did if you inherited the file. Most importantly, comments can be used to indicate where something is depended upon by a particular application or environment in order to work correctly.

Linking Startup Files

Frequently, system administrators create default versions of the startup files needed by the users on their systems. When new accounts are set up for users, these files are automatically copied to the user's home directory. Occasionally, in an effort to create a more standardized environment for many users, and to aid in maintaining this environment, these files are created as links to a master set of files.

> **Caution:** You can find out whether your startup files are linked to files elsewhere on your system. If they *are* linked, you need to talk to your system administrator before making changes to these files. Making changes to a linked file, if you have the permission to do so, will affect many, or perhaps all, of the users on your system.

Symbolically Linked Files

To determine whether your startup files are linked, you can take the following steps. The first and easiest step is to see whether they are linked with symbolic links. If you do an `ls -l` listing of the dot files and they are links, your output will look something like the following example:

```
1 % ls -l .cshrc .login .logout
lrw-r--r--  1 dave    users     21 Jan 31 17:05 .cshrc->/usr/local/etc/cshrc
lrw-r--r--  1 dave    users     21 Feb 28 16:58 .login->/usr/local/etc/login
lrw-r--r--  1 dave    users     22 Mar 31 17:12 .logout->/usr/local/etc/logout
2 % _
```

You can tell that these files are symbolic links by three indications in the example. The first and most visible sign is the filename at the right side of each line of output. You asked for information about `.cshrc`, `.login`, and `.logout`, and `ls` reported the filenames with arrows (`->`), followed by another filename.

Second, if you look at the very first character of each line, you will see a lowercase `l`. On a long `ls` listing, this first position of the permissions is for the file type, and for most files the file type is a dash (`-`). Here the file type is marked with an `l` because these files are symbolic links.

Finally, you may not have noticed that the stated size of these files (indicated by the numbers `21` and `22` before the month column) is rather small. If you were to look at the contents of these files, you would see far more than the stated 21 or 22 characters of text. Why are these file sizes so small, according to the listing description? Well, the answer has to do with how UNIX handles symbolic links. Symbolic links are sometimes called *soft links*, because the relationship of one file to the other is very tenuous, as you will see shortly.

When a symbolic link is created, a special flag is set in the entry for this file. This special flag indicates that the file is symbolically linked; the flag is also what causes the l in the file-type column of the ls -l command output. Next, a file is created in your directory to represent the link, but it doesn't contain any of the contents of the file to which it points. Instead, it contains the full pathname to that file. This is the name that follows the arrow (->) on the preceding listing example. That also explains why the file size on a symbolic link is so small. The file size really represents the number of characters needed to spell out the full path to the linked file.

Caution: Earlier, I mentioned that a symbolic link is a *soft* or tenuous one. The reason is simple, one you should remember when choosing to use symbolic links. There is no provision in UNIX for handling the situation in which the target of a symbolic link is removed. When that happens, you end up with entries in your directory that point to nowhere. The preceding example would look like the following if the target files were moved or removed:

```
2 % ls -l .cshrc .login .logout
lrw-r--r--   1 dave    users      21 Jan 31 17:05 .cshrc ->
lrw-r--r--   1 dave    users      21 Feb 28 16:58 .login ->
lrw-r--r--   1 dave    users      22 Mar 31 17:12 .logout ->
3 % _
```

You can see that the arrows (->) point to nowhere. The sizes remain the same because the original pathnames are still in the link files; but because the system cannot actually see the targets, they are not reported after the arrows. Symbolic links are necessary when you need to make a link to a file that is in a different file system, but be aware of this pitfall when you do use them.

6

Hard-Linked Files

Another way that UNIX can link files is by what is known as a *hard link*. With hard links, a synonym to the file is actually created that points to the same physical file. Files linked in this manner do not have the same problem as symbolic links. If one of the hard links to a file is removed, the others remain, and the file is not deleted until the last name pointing to it is also removed.

what is the difference between hard and symbol links

137

> **Note:** Hard links relate all synonyms of a file to the physical file by something known as an *inode number*. All inode numbers are unique within a file system, which is a defined partition on the hard disk. In each directory there is a dot file (.) that contains a list of the names of each file in the directory and its inode number. The inode number relates back to an entry in a hidden area of the disk where information is kept that describes all attributes of a file.

When a file is created, part of the information that is kept to describe that file is a *link count*. This count keeps track of the number of hard links that exist for this file. You can readily see whether a file has hard links to it by again doing an `ls -l` command:

```
3 %  ls -l .cshrc .login .logout
-rw-r--r--  21 root    users    893 Jan 31 17:05 .cshrc
-rw-r--r--  21 root    users    426 Feb 28 16:58 .login
-rw-r--r--   1 dave    users    105 Mar 31 17:12 .logout
4 % _
```

Look at the output from this command and notice that the column between the permissions and the user name contains numbers, 21 and 1. These are the link counts. In the output of Event 2, the link counts were all 1 because there were no hard links to the symbolic links that were created. Here there are no links to the .logout file, but there are 21 links to .cshrc and .login. This indicates that the startup files are linked to a master set. In this case also, the files are owned by root but are readable by all users. Your output will be different from this but could well be similar in many respects. In the output of Event 3, you can look at these files but you only have read access and cannot make changes to them, with the exception of .logout, which is owned, and can be written to, by the user. To do this, you can type df . (one dot).

>
>
> **Tip:** Any time you find a file that has hard links and a link count greater than one, you can use the following commands to locate the other files to which the first file is linked. The first step is to find out in which file system the file resides. To do this, you can type df . (one dot).
>
> ```
> 4 % df .
> Filesystem      kbytes    used   avail capacity  Mounted
> /dev/dsk/hd0a    385689  306189  40931     88%   /5 % _
> ```
>
> The Mounted column shows what is known as a *mount point*, the directory where this partition on the disk can be accessed. This is

important because inodes are unique to a file system. You don't want to search all directories, because the directories may be part of another file system.

Next, you need to know the inode number of the file that has the hard link. To find out, you use the ls command again, with the options -li to get a long listing that also shows the inode number:

```
5 % ls -li /bin/ls
13478 -rw-r--r--   6 bin    bin     13893 Jan 22 1993 /bin/ls 6 % _
```

The first column of the ls output is the inode number of the file. In this case, the inode for /bin/ls is 13478. Now you want to use the mount-point directory, or one below it in the hierarchy, and the inode number in a find command like the one in the following example:

```
6 % find /bin -inum 13478 -print
/bin/ll
/bin/ls
/bin/l
/bin/lsf
/bin/lsr
/bin/lsx
7 % _
```

This output shows that there were indeed six files sharing the same inode number. The ls command uses hard links to create synonyms of itself. When you run any of these synonyms, including the original ls command, the command checks to see which name you used. If, for example, you used the lsx synonym, the -x option to ls is automatically set for you without it explicitly being on the command line.

.cshrc, the Main Startup File

The first of the shell startup files to be discussed is .cshrc. The name of this file stands for *C Shell reconfigure*. Many files within UNIX have rc in their name. Using rc in a filename is an informal convention for naming files that control the startup of applications or commands that are configurable.

Whenever you start a new C Shell process, that process looks in your home directory for the file .cshrc. The .cshrc file is the first file that is read by any C Shell process when it begins execution. The C Shell will operate if there is not a .cshrc file in your home directory. Some versions of the C Shell actually look first for a cshrc file in the /etc directory. Your system administrator can use the cshrc file in the /etc directory to establish system-wide defaults for shell variables and possibly even create some system aliases that are beneficial to a majority of the users on your system. /etc directory

Setting Shell Variables in *.cshrc*

One of the main uses for .cshrc is to set values for built-in shell variables. Because these variables are local, they must be set each time a new shell is started. Although a select few of these shell variables have corresponding environment variables, the majority need to be set if you wish to establish a consistent value for them.

In addition to setting shell variables, you often also need to set other local variables that are used within .cshrc itself. The values for these variables typically are the result of running a UNIX command that returns the desired information. For example, many UNIX systems are now part of a networked environment. You often need to go from one host to another to perform a particular task. It is not unusual to need to know the name of the host you are on at a particular point in time. The UNIX command hostname returns the name of the current system on which it is executed. Frequently in a .cshrc file, at or near the beginning you will see the following:

```
#
# Determine the local hostname
#
set host = `hostname`    unix command
```

This line includes the hostname command enclosed in backtick metacharacters. Recall that in Day 3, "Command Substitution, Aliases, and Filename Generation," you learned about command substitution using the backtick (`) metacharacter. The output of the commands enclosed in backticks, in this case hostname, is substituted for the entire expression, including the backticks. The remainder of the command line is then evaluated. Here, the results of the hostname command are assigned to the local shell variable $host. Later in today's lesson you will see that there are numerous opportunities where a variable with the current hostname as its contents comes in handy.

Updating the Search Path *$path*

The built-in shell variable $path that you learned about in Day 5, "Shell Variables, Part II," contains a list of directories that make up the search path for the C Shell. Each time you enter a command at the prompt, or the shell processes a command line in a script,

the shell searches for the command in each directory listed in $path. The search proceeds in the order that the directory names appear in the list, so the order is important.

Your system administrator most likely set a default value for $path, and equally likely it was very limited. Typically, you will want to expand the list in $path to include your home directory, $HOME or ~, and your personal bin directory if you have one, $HOME/bin or ~/bin. Usually, you will also want to include directories such as /usr/local/bin, and /usr/contrib/bin, and other directories that contain utilities and tools that are not a part of UNIX or other purchased application. If you are using X Window you might also want related directories such as /usr/bin/X11, /usr/contrib/bin/X11, and perhaps others included in your $path.

In the following example, the built-in shell variable $path is set to a list of directory pathnames. The second set command appends one more directory pathname to $path by including the variable as the first word within the parentheses. The last set command again appends to $path, this time adding *'dot'* so that the current working directory will always be searched when looking for commands:

```
# Set the default path.
#
set path = (/usr/local/bin /bin /usr/bin /usr/bin/X11 /usr/contrib/bin)

# insert any additional directories by personal preference on next line
set path = ($path $HOME/bin)

# Put the current directory last
set path = ($path .)
```

When updating the search path, as I mentioned earlier, the order of the directories is significant. You need to decide whether the directories you are going to add should be at the beginning of the list, at the end, or perhaps somewhere in the middle. The usual cases are at either the beginning or the end. Rarely is it necessary to go to the effort of inserting a directory in the middle of a search path to achieve proper effect. Occasionally, you will be adding the directory of an application you will be using, and where you position it in the search path will not affect the system's capability to find the programs.

Hash Tables, Rehash, and *$path*

When the C Shell starts, after the startup files have been read, the shell does some special processing to enhance its access to the search path. The shell looks in each directory in the list and locates all of the executable files. It takes each of those filenames and puts them in a hash table that it maintains for rapid access to the files. If your search list in $path contains the current directory, dot (.), the files there are not put into the hash table. If you are going to include dot (.) in the list, it doesn't matter whether it is first or last or in between. The C Shell gives your current working directory priority over any others on the system by searching it first when dot (.) is in $path.

When you enter a command at the prompt, the shell first checks in your current directory if you included dot (.) in the search path. If the shell finds your command there, then that is the one that is executed. If the shell does not find your command, it calculates a hash key for the command and checks to see whether the command is in the hash table created at the start of the shell. If the command is located in the hash table, the C Shell then knows where to find the command. Failing to find the command in your current directory or in the hash table, which represents the rest of your search path directories, results in an error message.

Normally, the hash table is built once and needs no further attention. But what if, during a shell session, you decide to change the contents or order of $path? In this situation, the C Shell, knowing that you have changed $path, automatically rescans all of the directories in $path and rebuilds the hash table. You do not need to take special action to have your new search order take effect.

If you were to add a new executable file, a program, or a script to one of the directories without changing $path, the shell would be unaware of this fact. If you try to run this new command, it won't be found. You will be wondering what happened. When you do an ls of the directory, there is the command, big as life. You have permission to run it and the directory is in the search path, so why can't the shell find it? Remember that the shell really is using the hash table to locate commands, and the table is built only at the start of the shell and when you change the contents of $path. Here, the table was created when you logged on, and you have not modified $path. You will have to get this new command into the hash table somehow.

The rehash command, a C Shell built-in command, is intended for just this situation. Typing rehash at the command prompt tells the shell to rebuild the hash table from the current list in $path. After the C Shell revisits these directories and rebuilds the hash table, your new command will be found when you enter it at the command prompt. Using a hash table makes the C Shell's search for commands far more efficient than having to search each directory in $path each time you run a command. If you have a long list of directories in $path, the performance of the shell would suffer greatly in locating commands.

Personalizing Your Prompt

Throughout this book, I have used a fairly boring and generic prompt in my examples. The original shell, written by Stephen Bourne, had a default prompt of $. When the C

Shell was written, in an effort to easily differentiate the two, its default prompt became %. All shells in UNIX have the capability to set the prompt string. This section shows you how you can set your prompt to your liking and give you some examples for ideas about new prompts.

One nice feature to incorporate into your prompt is the display of your current working directory. Then, just by looking at a command prompt, you know exactly in which directory you are working. If you are on a system that is part of a network, and you frequently move from host to host, it is a nice touch to include the hostname in the prompt.

In the prompts that I have used in this book, I included the history event number on each prompt. If you include the history event number on your prompt, you then have a ready reference. You can visually locate a recent command on the screen or mentally count back to determine the event number. Then it can be used to recall a prior command.

The Korn Shell implemented a testable option to determine if a particular shell process was interactive or not. In the startup scripts, this attribute can be tested to inhibit or allow portions of the setup processing. In an attempt to duplicate this capability, many have incorporated a test to see if the $prompt variable exists. Because only an interactive shell will set $prompt, this works as an effective way to figure out in which mode the shell is running. The following section of shell script can be used to set up a shell prompt that includes the hostname and current directory, as well as the event number for the next command.

```
# Set the prompt - test if prompt has been set;
#    If it has been set then redefine it to display host
#            current directory, and event; set interactive = yes
#            redefine popd, pushd and cd to update the prompt
#    If not then set interactive = no;
#
if ($?prompt) then
# note: the double backslashes at the end of the next three
# lines are important for defining a multiline alias.
# They are there to "escape" the NEWLINE so it is included in the alias
   alias prompt 'set noglob;\\
     set prompt = `dirs`;\\
     set prompt = "${host}:${prompt[1]}%\!> ";\\
     unset noglob'
   alias popd 'popd \!*; prompt'
   alias pushd 'pushd \!*; prompt'
   alias cd 'cd \!*; prompt'
   prompt                 # insure new prompt format for first prompt
   set interactive = yes
else
   set interactive = no
endif
```

6

This method is a bit more complex in order to incorporate the directory stack built-ins pushd and popd, as well as cd. It will work on all systems and provide dependable updating of the prompt if you use any of these navigation commands. A simpler method of updating the prompt is shown in the following code. It may not work on all systems if you are using the directory stack commands. A disadvantage to the following method is that it executes the hostname and pwd commands for each prompt, whereas the previous method gets the information from shell variables and built-in commands, which is more efficient.

```
if ($?prompt) then
    set prompt = "\! `hostname`:$cwd> "
    set interactive = yes
else
    set interactive = no
endif
```

X Window *$DISPLAY* Variable

If you are an X Window user, you should know that there is an important environment variable, $DISPLAY, that points to the workstation where an X client can display its output. If $DISPLAY is not set, then a client on a remote host will not execute. The following example tests to see if $DISPLAY is set, and if not, it will determine your local hostname and use that to set the variable:

```
# Set the X Display host in $DISPLAY to the name of the host the
# user logged in from. If $DISPLAY is already set, leave it alone.
#
if ( ! $?DISPLAY ) then       # if $DISPLAY is not set...
    setenv DISPLAY "${host}:0"
    tty -s
    if ("$status" == "0") then
#add -R option to the who am i command on the next line for HP UNIX systems
        set disphost = `who am i | sed -e 's/.*(//' -e 's/).*$//'`
        if ("$#disphost" == "1") then
            setenv DISPLAY $disphost\:0
        endif
        unset disphost
    endif
endif
```

This example uses the output of the who am i command with the -R option to find out the name of your login host. This output is parsed by the sed command, which extracts just the hostname from between the parentheses at the right end of the line. The results are then used to set the $DISPLAY environment variable.

The tty command, with the -s option, silently tests the current stdin file to see if it is a terminal. The tty command returns a value of 0 in $status if stdin is a terminal.

Otherwise, $status will contain a non-zero value, depending on the host and version of UNIX you are using. Without the -s option, the tty command will display the tty device name in addition to setting $status. If the current stdin is a tty, then the shell will perform the inner loop setting the $DISPLAY variable.

Setting the Environment for *man*

Many UNIX commands look for specific environment variables to be set, which then control aspects of their operation. One of these commands is the UNIX man command, which formats and displays manual pages on your terminal or workstation. The man command has two specific variables it looks for that you can set in your .cshrc file. They are $PAGER and $MANPATH. You can select which pager program man will use when displaying its output by putting the pathname of one of the pager programs—pg, more, or, if you have it on your system, less—in $pager.

You can include command-line options for the pager you select, as part of the value assigned to $PAGER. The pager command will be invoked with those options when you use man. Another method to set the default options your favorite pager will use is to set its specific environment variable with the options. Then when the pager command is used alone or with man, these options will be in effect. This is shown in the following example:

```
# Setup the man paging program defaults for $PAGER and $MANPATH
#
if (-f /usr/local/bin/less) then
   setenv PAGER '/usr/local/bin/less'
setenv MORE -cds
else
   setenv PAGER '/usr/bin/more'
setenv LESS '-ceiMqsP'
endif
setenv MANPATH "/usr/man:/usr/contrib/man:/usr/local/man"
#
# Setup environment variables for options to more and less
#
```

The $MANPATH variable, much like the $path variable, contains a search path list that man will use to find directories that contain man pages or subdirectories of man pages. When you use the man command, it will search each of the directory hierarchies listed in $MANPATH for a man page matching the one you requested. Frequently, the system administrator will set the $MANPATH variable to include the known directories on the system that include man pages.

The less command is another pager command like more and pg with many enhanced capabilities. It is a public-domain program that is readily available on the Internet and on shareware disks and CD-ROM. If you have access to one of these sources, it is well worth the effort to get a copy of less, along with other worthwhile shareware tools available from the same sources.

Selecting a Default Editor with Options

Various UNIX commands enable you to break out to an editor and also give you the option to choose which editor to use. Two environment variables, $EDITOR and $VISUAL, have come into common use to specify the editor command used by most of these programs. To select your favorite editor as the default, put its path into these variables. The vi editor, available with virtually all versions of UNIX, enables you to preset default options by using the $EXINIT environment variable. This variable contains a set command for vi, followed by the options and their values if applicable. The following example illustrates how to select a default editor and configure vi.

```
# Setup default editors and configure vi
#
setenv EDITOR '/usr/bin/vi'      # put your favorite editor path here
setenv VISUAL '/usr/bin/vi'      # and here too.
setenv EXINIT 'set ts=8 autoindent ignorecase wm=8 showmode'
#set your favorite vi defaults here.
```

The options in the $EXINIT environment variable set the tabstop to eight characters, auto indenting enabled, caseless searches enabled, set the wrap margin to eight characters from the right of the screen, and show mode enabled, in which vi will post an indicator in the bottom-right corner of the screen to show when you are in one of the modification modes.

C Shell Switch Variables

In Day 5 you were introduced to the C Shell built-in variables that act like switches. These variables can be set in .cshrc. It's a good idea to put all of these variables together in a single area of the .cshrc file. They are easier to find and maintain when grouped together, rather than spread throughout the file. Because they are all switch-like variables, none of them have values as such. You can also comment out those switches that you only use periodically so you can easily edit .cshrc and turn the option on when you desire.

In the following example, I set several of the C Shell's built-in switch variables. Because these variables act like switches, there is no need to assign them a value. Simply by including them on a set command, they are turned ON and can be turned OFF using unset. Notice that the set command for the $nobeep variable is commented out with a leading hashmark (#). I often do this for variable that I want to enable for short periods of time, commenting them out again when I am done with them.

```
# Setup switch variables that control C Shell options
#
set filec          # enable file completion with ESC
#set nobeep        # disable filec beeps when ambiguous
set notify         # enable immediate job completion notification
set noclobber      # enable overwrite protection from redirection
```

Setting Shell Variables with Values

The previous example gave you some ideas for setting some of the built-in shell switch variables. Here I will do the same for the other built-in shell variables that take values. These, too, you will likely want to keep grouped together. Other shell variables, such as $prompt and $path, were covered earlier. These built-in variables are more a matter of personal choice, whereas some of the others are set by the C Shell and modifiable by you if you so choose.

In the following example, I again set several of the C Shell's built-in variables, but this time they take values. The first three variables—$history, $savehist, $autologout—are set to numeric values. No quotes are required for these values. The last line of the example defines the built-in variable $cdpath. Because $cdpath is a multiword variable, the values assigned to it are enclosed in parentheses. The individual values do no need to be enclosed in quotes because they do no include blanks within their strings.

```
# Miscellaneous Shell Built-in Variables
#
set history = 200        # sets the size of the history buffer
set savehist = 100       # the number of commands saved for next time
set autologout = 0       # disables automatic logout timeout feature
                         # to enable set to some positive number of
                         # minutes.
#
# setup the default directory search path
set cdpath = (. .. $HOME $HOME/bin)
```

Aliases, Aliases, and More Aliases

As you saw in Day 3, the alias mechanism of the C Shell can be a powerful tool. Because aliases are not global, you have to set them again for each C Shell that you start. That is why the .cshrc is the logical place for you to put your alias definitions. This section contains one long example of different aliases that you can adopt in your own .cshrc file if you find them useful. I have collected these aliases over time, as I have moved from project to project. Some I have created on my own; some were borrowed from nameless others. A few were borrowed and were attributed; I will note them accordingly. If you choose to use these aliases, please carry the credit as well in a comment in your .cshrc file.

First are some shorthand aliases that simply create shorthand synonyms for commonly used commands. They are labor-savers, saving you keystokes, if you can remember them and use them:

```
# Shorthand Aliases
#
alias h          history
alias ht         'history ¦ tail'   # history tailed
alias hp         'history ¦ more'   # history paged
alias m          $PAGER             # alias favorite pager to 'm'
alias pd         pushd
#
# ls aliases
#
alias ls         'ls -CF'           # set YOUR favorite ls options here
alias ll         'ls -l'            # long listing of directory
alias lf         'ls -F'            # directory listing with special flags
alias lr         'ls -R'            # recursive directory listing
alias ll.        'ls -lisa .[a-z]*  # list only your 'dot' files
```

The next aliases I have seen at numerous UNIX sites where I have worked. I have tried them, liked them, and adopted them as a part of my standard alias collection. They are attributed to Robert Kaminsky, and I believe that they were found on an Internet FTP Server. The first pair enable you to bring a command from history and edit it using vi:

```
#
# The following aliases allow for editing commands given in the csh.
#   e n - visual edits command n (as numbered by history)
#   ee  - visual edits last command
# They both write to a temporary file .e_cmd in users home directory.
# By Robert Kaminsky  11/19/90
#
alias e      '( history ¦ sed -n -e "/^ *\!*[^0-9]/ s/......//p" ) >&!
 ~/.e_cmd ; \vi -w2 ~/.e_cmd ; source -h ~/.e_cmd ; source ~/.e_cmd'
alias ee     '( history 2 ¦ sed -n -e "1 s/.......//p" ) >&! ~/.e_cmd ;
 \vi -w2 ~/.e_cmd ; source -h ~/.e_cmd ; source ~/.e_cmd'
#
# The following aliases print out the command history in 2 and 3 column
# format.
# By Robert Kaminsky  11/19/90
#
alias h2     '(history 30 ¦ pr -2 -l15 -t ¦ expand ¦ cut -c1-79,80)'
alias h3     '(history 45 ¦ pr -3 -l15 -t ¦ expand ¦ cut -c1-79,80)'
```

Find It Fast with Aliases

The UNIX find command is one of the more powerful, complex, and also confusing commands available. There are a multitude of options to this command, and its syntax is a departure from that of the majority of UNIX commands. The find command, unlike many other UNIX commands, traverses down through the file hierarchy from its starting point. It looks for files that match a set of specified criteria and displays their names or performs a command with the filename as an argument. I present here a number of suggestions for aliases that you can adopt for variations on the theme of "find it" UNIX-style:

```
# find large files over 1000 blocks. delete them & make your sysadm happy
alias findbig   'find . -size +1000 -exec ls -l {} \;'

# find files older than 3 months. delete these too to please the sysadm
alias findold   'find . -atime +125 -exec ls -l {} \;'

# find files 1 day new
alias findnew   'find . \( -ctime 1 -type f \) -exec ls -l {} \;'

# find new files N days where you supply the 'N' as an argument
alias lsnew     'find . \( -ctime -\!* -type f \) -exec ls -l {} \;'

# find just directory files and list their details
alias finddirs 'find . -type d -exec ls -ld {} \;'

# the generic find by name ** MIND THE QUOTES **
alias findname  "find . -name '\!*' -print"

# find files containing given expression; ignore case; display filenames
alias findexp   'find . -type f -exec grep -il -e "\!*" {} \;'

# find files containing given expression; ignore case; display lines
alias findexps 'find . -type f -exec grep -i \!:1 {} /dev/null \;'
```

These are just a few useful ways that find can be aliased. I recommend that you study the find man page and familiarize yourself with the different options that are available. Try out a few variations of your own and see what the results are. If you find a variation you like, make it an alias.

Aliases for X Window Users

In a earlier section, I presented some examples for variable settings useful to X Window users. Here I present some aliases that I hope will also prove to be of value to the same crowd:

```
#
# Some useful X Windows aliases:
#  newsize - after resizing an xterm window
#  seltek  - convert an xterm window from vt102 to Tektronix mode
#  selvt   - convert an xterm window from Tektronix mode to vt102
# Also set "tandem" and "tostop" modes for xterms
#                       (in case ~/.login is not read).
#
if ("$?term" != "0") then
    if ("$term" == "xterm" || "$term" == "xterms" || \
      "$term" == "aixterm" || "$term" == "hpterm") then
        alias newsize '(setenv SHELL /bin/csh; eval `resize`; eval `resize`)'
```

```
      alias seltek   '(echo -n "E[?38h" ¦ tr E \\033)'
      alias selvt    '(echo -n "EC" ¦ tr EC \\033\\003)'
      tty -s
      if ("$status" == 0 && "$interactive" == "yes") then
          stty -tabs erase ^H kill ^U intr ^C susp ^Z dsusp ^Y \
              tostop ixon ixoff tandem
      endif
   endif
endif
```

Notice on the aliases for seltek and selvt the use of the tr command to circumvent a problem with echo displaying control characters. Here the E and EC, respectively, are translated to ESCAPE and ESCAPE ^C using tr. The backslashes (\) that are required to specify the octal values of the control characters are themselves escaped using backslashes to protect them from the shell during alias definition.

Developer's *.cshrc* Setup

If you are doing any development under UNIX with the C language or writing C Shell scripts, here are some lines that you might want to add to your .cshrc file. These include setting some variables and defining some aliases. If you are more of an end user and not doing programming, these suggestions will be of little or no interest to you.

When you create a new shell script using the vi editor, you first need to make the file executable before you can run it by name. To do this, you use the chmod command to turn on the execute permissions for the file. You may also want to turn on or off the ability of other users to write to your script file. The following aliases are quick shorthands for these operations.

```
# chmod aliases
#
alias +w    'chmod go+w'    # add write permission for group and other
alias -w    'chmod go-w'    # delete write ability for group and other
alias +x    'chmod +x'      # make file(s) executable for all users
```

If you are compiling C programs and using the UNIX make command with Makefile rule-definition files, you might be interested in the following environment variables. These variables are ones that the make command will examine, if set, to override or augment the default compiler and loader flags established by the system. If you regularly need to change these values, it is easier to set them once in your .cshrc file. Then, in the event you forget to put them in your Makefile for an application, your compiles will still be correct. The make command looks for an environment variable $CCOPTS to get the compiler options for cc, the UNIX C Compiler. It also looks for $LDOPTS for the options to ld, the UNIX linker and program loader. Many compilers also look for a variable $FLOAT to find any special floating-point flags and options you may wish to set.

```
setenv FLOAT     '' # clear floating point options with placeholder
# set ANSI compiling and specify X window include directories
setenv CCOPTS    '-Aa -I /usr/include/X11R5 -I /usr/include/Motif2'
# point to X and Motif window libraries plus those in /usr/local/lib
setenv LDOPTS    '-L /usr/lib/X11R5 -L /usr/lib/Motif2 -L /usr/local/lib'
```

These are just some suggestions. If you are not using X Window with Motif or you are using a different window manager, or if you are using a different version of X Window, or not using X at all, you will need to make some changes here. Check with your system administrator or project leader to determine the proper options and parameters for your local site.

.login

The .login startup file is performed once for each session by the login C Shell process. Each time a new C Shell process is started, after the shell reads and performs the contents of .cshrc, the shell looks to see if it is the login shell. If it is the login shell, the shell then reads and performs the contents of the .login startup file. Usually, this file contains commands that only need to be executed once for each login session.

> **Note:** Before networking and windows became commonplace on UNIX systems, .login was the place to put all the setenv commands to establish the values of environment variables. Because these variables are global, they get passed to all child processes, so they would last until the user logged off the system. With networking and windows, new commands have been created that run shells on other systems without the login flag being set. These new shells don't read the .login file and don't get passed the environment from the local system. Because of this behavior of remote shells, some of what used to belong in .login is now often placed in .cshrc so that the remote shells get a similar, if not exact, replica of the local environment.

This section shows you examples of what can be placed in your own .login file. Typical .login contents include commands that set the correct terminal characteristics and attributes. Other possibilities include commands to clean up work files from previous sessions, set environment variables, check for mail, and display the saying of the day.

6

> **Caution:** Don't forget these important aspects of the `.login` startup file:
>
> ☐ It is read and performed *after* the `.cshrc` file. Don't put commands in `.cshrc` that are dependant on any contained in the `.login` file.
>
> ☐ If any variables set or commands run in `.login` are important to the proper setup of a remote environment, they belong in the `.cshrc` file instead. Remember, remote shells read only `.cshrc` and not `.login`, even though they are acting much like a login shell.
>
> ☐ Local windows on a workstation behave more like remote shells and don't read the `.login` file. Frequently, it is necessary to place the setup of environment variables in .cshrc, rather than `.login`, to ensure that your windows work properly.

Proper Care and Conditioning of Your Terminal

The `.login` file is still the place to set your terminal type and establish proper characteristics and attributes. Two UNIX commands, `stty` and `tset`, are used to accomplish this task. These two commands deserve some investigation. The `stty` command can be used to set the defined control characters for a number of basic functions you use at the keyboard. Here's an example with explanation:

```
#
# set terminal characteristics
#
stty -tabs erase ^H kill ^U intr ^C susp ^Z dsusp ^Y tostop ixon ixoff
```

This command has options too numerous to mention. It is capable of setting any and all characteristics of a communication line (that is, serial port, modem, and so on). It also is used to define the keystroke bindings for the different line-editing functions, and much more. Table 6.1 explains the options shown in the preceding example and a few more commonly used ones:

Table 6.1. Options to the `stty` command.

Option	Description
tabs	Preserve tabs when printing (`-tabs` to replace with spaces when printing).

Option	Description
erase c	Set erase character to c (default is ^?).
kill c	Set kill character to c (default is ^U). This character causes the entire input line to be erased.
intr c	Set interrupt character to c (default is ^C). This character, when typed, terminates the current command.
susp c	Set suspend character to c (default is ^Z). This character causes the current command to suspend, and the command prompt to be displayed.
dsusp c	Set delayed suspend character to c (default is ^Y). This character causes delayed suspension of the current command.
werase c	Set word erase character to c (default is ^W).
lnext c	Set literal next character to c (default is ^V).
tostop	Enable stopping of background jobs that attempt terminal output (-tostop to disable).

The Unknown Dot File *.hushlogin*

Your system administrator may not appreciate my letting this one out of the bag. When you log in to the system each day, you might see a message displayed on your screen from your system administrator. This message, called the *Message of the Day*, comes from the file /etc/motd. It is updated by your system administrator and used to communicate important notices to users of the system. Not all "sys admins" take advantage of this file, and often it stays the same indefinitely. Worse yet is when it is long and boring and out of date. You can get very tired of seeing the same message, day in and day out.

I am coming to your rescue with information about a little know feature of the C Shell. There is an undocumented dot file called .hushlogin, which can remedy the problem of a monotonous message-of-the-day file. You create this file in your home directory, with nothing inside, because the contents are not important and are ignored. When you login to the system and the C Shell is going to display the contents of /etc/motd, it checks to see whether .hushlogin exists in your home directory. If it finds the file, it will skip the display of the contents of /etc/motd.

6

> **Caution:** Even as I tell you about the `.hushlogin` file, the system administrator in me has to issue a caution as well. If your local system administrator uses `/etc/motd` and is regularly changing the message to inform and perhaps even educate you, you should in good conscience not use `.hushlogin` to suppress the messages. A good sys admin will use this facility for a purpose, and suppressing it may cause you to miss an important message. This is your decision to make. You are, hopefully, informed and will make the right choice.

Parting Shots with *.logout*

The `.logout` file is, as its name implies, executed when you exit your login shell and log out of the system. Its contents, if any, are usually very simple and straightforward. You can put the `clear` command in `.logout` so that your terminal screen is cleared when you log out the system. Some choose to put the games program `fortune` in their `.logout` to leave the system with a parting word for the day. Almost anything is allowable in this file, so I leave it to you to decide what to put in your `.logout` file.

Summary

This chapter presented the ins and outs of the C Shell *dot* files. These silent configuration files—including `.cshrc`, `.login`, `.logout`, and, yes, `.hushlogin`—are used to "program" a standard configuration for your C Shell environment. You have learned, I hope, what to put where—where to put your aliases, where and how to set crucial environment variables, and how to differentiate between the noninteractive and interactive modes of the C Shell. As you learn more about the C Shell and its options, how to use aliases to your advantage, and how to set environment variables to configure your favorite commands, you should revisit this section once again for a refresher course. Then go update your startup files.

In the next chapter, Day 7, you will learn more about file redirection, pipelines, and filters. Day 7 takes you behind the scenes and shows you how the C Shell and UNIX make redirection and pipes work magic to add flexibility and adaptability to everyday commands. You will find out about filters and how, with pipes and file redirection, they can be combined to build new tools. These tools can then be applied to your daily tasks and special requirements to make your job easier to accomplish on a regular basis.

Related UNIX Topics

This chapter presented some new concepts and commands. Here is a list of some of these concepts and topics, with suggestions for sources of further information.

Symbolic and Hard Links:	Look in section 1 of your UNIX manuals for the man pages for the `ln` command, which is used to create both symbolic and hard links to files. Look around your file system for symbolic and hard links and experiment with the `find` command to track down which other files are hard-link related to one with a link count greater than one.
`find` *command:*	Look in section 1 also for the `find` command and study the man page to understand this powerful file location tool. Many of the options of this command often provide versatile solutions to problems users often encounter when doing shell programming.
Shell Variables:	Day 4 and 5 cover the built-in C Shell variables and explain what each one affects and how it can be used. A review of this material when you make changes to your startup files can contribute to the success of your efforts.
Command Aliases:	Day 2 introduces aliases, which are defined in the `.cshrc` startup file. A number of important concepts for alias definitions are discussed in this lesson.

Q&A

Q What are the names of the C Shell startup files and how are they used by the shell?

A The C Shell has two official startup files, `.cshrc` and `.login`. The `.cshrc` file is read by any new C Shell process to set the environment for that shell. It typically contains alias definitions and local variable initializations. It can also contain environment variable setups as well. The `.login` file is read and processed by the user's login shell only at the start of a session. It typically contains environment variable initializations as well as UNIX commands to set up terminal attributes.

Q Where should you put alias definitions?

A C Shell command aliases are not global by nature. They therefore must be redefined for each new shell that is started. The ideal place for this to occur is in the .cshrc file, which is read at the start of each new shell. The exception is in shell scripts where the -f option is specified on the first line. This option inhibits the reading of the .cshrc file for faster startup. Because shell scripts typically do not need or use the aliases that are defined in .cshrc, this can be a valuable option. It is recommended that environment variables be set in .login if this is to be a regular occurrence.

Q How can you change the format of your C Shell command prompt?

A The C Shell built-in variable $prompt contains the template for formatting the shell prompt. Examples in this lesson illustrate some options for the contents of this variable. Good choices for a minimum prompt include the current working directory and the current history event number.

Q How can you set a default terminal type but be prompted with the option of overriding this default at login?

A When you include the tset command in the .login startup file, it can establish a default terminal type as well as prompt the user at login to change the type. The user can press Return to accept the default or override it with a valid terminal type. Look at the examples in this lesson and in the Appendix E, "Examples of *Dot* Files," for information on how to include this in your own startup files. Look at the man page for the tset command for further options of this command.

Workshop

The Workshop provides several sections to aid you in reviewing the topics covered in today's lesson. There is a quiz section to help you reinforce your understanding of the material presented for Day 6 and exercises to give you practice applying what you learned. Take the time to review these questions and exercises, so that you understand the concepts before you begin the next lesson. The answers are in Appendix F, "Answers to Quizzes and Exercises."

Quiz

1. Where are the startup files that affect your C Shell's startup located?

2. Which startup file should contain C Shell built-in variable initializations?

3. Where and how would you change the character used to delete your current command line, so you can re-enter it?

4. If you add a command or shell script to a directory that is in your search path, what additional steps do you need to take before it will be seen by your current shell?

5. Is it acceptable to put environment variable initializations in your .cshrc file?

6. Why would you not want to put local variable initializations in your .login file?

7. Would you want to put a variable initialization in .cshrc that is dependent on one that occurs in .login? Why?

8. When is the .login startup file not read by the C Shell?

Exercises

1. To see what happens when the C Shell reads and performs your startup files, put a set echo command at the start of one or more of these files and look at the output. You may need to put in an unset echo to limit the output if you cannot scroll your display.

2. Look at the man pages for the find command. Devise at least two new useful aliases using the find command. Test them. Can you think of some different aliases for ls as well?

File Redirection,
Pipes, and Filters

Introduction to Day 7

In today's lesson you will learn more about file redirection. You will see how file redirection works and how to use it to enhance your scripts and command line capabilities. The three standard UNIX files—`stdin`, `stdout`, and `stderr`—will be explained to further enhance your understanding of how you can take advantage of I/O redirection.

Also in this lesson, pipes and filters will be examined in detail. Combined with file redirection, pipes and filters enable you to create more complex tools and commands. Today you will get a look at how UNIX manages the standard files in order to make these features all work. This lesson sets the stage for the second half of this book, where you will apply what you have learned thus far.

Setting Today's Goals

Today, you will learn how to

- ☐ Use `stdin`, `stdout`, and `stderr`
- ☐ Redirect input to commands and scripts
- ☐ Redirect output from commands and scripts
- ☐ Append output to a file
- ☐ Merge output from `stdout` and `stderr`
- ☐ Overwrite a file
- ☐ Protect a file from being overwritten
- ☐ Use a *here document* in a script
- ☐ Use pipes to combine commands
- ☐ Combine the use of file redirection with pipes
- ☐ Use pipes in aliases
- ☐ Employ filters in your scripts and command lines

stdin, *stdout*, and *stderr*

All UNIX programs have an environment associated with them in which they run. Part of this environment is the settings of the various shell environment variables. Many commands get information from these variables to decide how they will do their job. Another part of a program's environment is the files it uses (see Figure 7.1).

Figure 7.1. *Standard input and output.*

UNIX provides each running program with three standard files, which are opened automatically at the time the program starts execution. These files, one for input and two for output, are linked to the user's keyboard for input and to the terminal display for output. The input file is known by the name stdin and is called *standard in* or *standard input*. The first output file is known as stdout and likewise is called *standard out* or *standard output*. The second output file is known as stderr and is called *standard error*.

When you type at the keyboard, entering a command line at the shell prompt, the C Shell is reading from stdin and displaying the characters back to you on stdout. Many UNIX commands adopt the habit of writing diagnostic, error, and informative messages to stderr. The output from stderr is not usually the end product resulting from the processing done by the command, which is most often written to stdout.

When you are supplying input to a command via stdin using the keyboard, you need a way to inform the command that you are at the end of your input. The standard character to indicate the end of a file in UNIX is ^D, typed by holding down the Control key while typing the letter D (you don't need to hold down the Shift key too, because the lowercase *d* with the Control key works to generate ^D). This is referred to as the EOF character, for *end-of-file*. Recall that in Day 4, "Shell Variables," you learned about $ignoreeof, which causes the C Shell to ignore the ^D EOF character, thus inhibiting the capability of EOF to terminate the current shell. If you don't set $ignoreeof, the C Shell sees the EOF character on its input. The shell assumes then that it has reached the end of its command input and that it has no more to do, so it terminates.

A Look Behind the Scenes at Command Execution

You have run many commands from the shell prompt without knowing what happens after you press Enter to start the command. The C Shell goes through several steps to process your command before it actually starts the command. Understanding what these steps are, and how they affect the execution of your command, will help you make better use of the options available to you when running programs under UNIX.

Expansion of Metacharacters on the Command Line

The first of these steps actually is made up of a number of related operations, all grouped under the heading *Metacharacter Expansion*. On previous days, you learned about the different groups of metacharacters used by the C Shell. To recap, Table 7.1 describes the different metacharacter groups.

Table 7.1. C Shell metacharacter groups.

Metacharacter Group	Description
Syntactic	Used as special punctuation characters between and around commands. They are used to combine multiple UNIX commands to make a single logical command. They provide a means to effect conditional execution of a command or commands, based on the outcome of a previous command.
Filename	Used on command lines to form match patterns for filename substitution. They are also used to identify or form abbreviations.
Quotation	Used to selectively control when metacharacters from other groups are protected from expansion or interpretation by the C Shell.
Input/Output	Used for file redirection and to form command pipelines.

Metacharacter Group	Description
Expansion/Substitution	Act as special indicators to the C Shell for shell variables and history substitutions.
Other	Used to identify commands to be run in the background and to indicate the start of comments on a command line.

When you press Enter after typing in your command, the C Shell scans the command line, analyzing it to determine how to process your request. The shell looks for any syntactic metacharacters to see if more than one command is involved. The command line is checked for ampersands (&) to see if any background processing is required. The command line is examined for the presence of input/output metacharacters indicating file redirection. Also, filename and expansion/substitution metacharacters are processed.

The result of all this analysis and processing is that your command line ultimately has all of its metacharacters removed. If more than one command is involved, each is handled separately to resolve and expand filenames and shell variables. If file redirection is involved, the C Shell takes steps to provide the proper environment for each command so that its input and output are directed as requested.

Command Execution with *fork()* and *exec()*

In order to understand how your command begins execution, you need to know a bit about how UNIX creates new processes. There are two system functions, `fork()` and `exec()`, that are the foundation of the UNIX system. I'll begin to discuss their definitions through this illustrative example. Assume that you are going to enter the following command line at the C Shell prompt:

```
% cat < infile > outfile
```

The `fork()` function in UNIX is used to create a new process to execute the `cat` command. This new process, shown as Box b2 in Figure 7.2, is referred to as the *child process*. The original process that issued the `fork()`, shown as Box a, is known as the parent process. When `fork()` is called, an exact copy of the parent process is created in memory. This copy becomes the child process. When the child process begins, execution starts immediately after the call to `fork()` that created it in the C Shell program. The parent process resumes execution just after the `fork()` as well, shown as Box b1.

7

>
>
> **Note:** In Figure 7.2, each of the boxes contains text to indicate which files stdin, stdout, and stderr are pointing to at that stage in the process. Starting out, they are all open on the user's terminal (*term*). After the fork() call, the child process, Box b2, reopens stdin to infile and stdout to outfile. Finally, in Box c, the cat command has retained the files, pointing as indicated to infile, outfile, and the user's terminal.

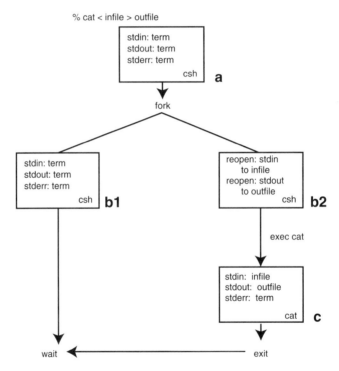

Figure 7.2. *Input and output file redirection.*

When the fork() function completes, it returns a value to the calling program. In the parent process, fork() returns a number that is the *process ID*, or *PID*, of the child process just initiated. In the child process, fork() returns the value of zero, which indicates to the process that it is the child process. If for some reason the fork() call fails, a value of -1 is returned to the parent process. Typically, any program that uses the fork() function tests the returned value to determine the success of the call and whether it is the parent or child process.

When the parent C Shell process continues after the fork(), it checks to see whether the command it just started was to be run in background. If so, then the parent continues execution and eventually displays another shell prompt on your display. If the child was not to be run in background, as in the previous example, the parent shell waits until it gets notification that the child has terminated. At that time, it continues and displays a shell prompt for your next command.

When the child process resumes execution after the fork() call, it has the same files opened as the parent process, the same values in variables, the same registers, and so on. It is an exact clone of its parent C Shell process. At this point, the child tests the return from the call to fork() and finds that it is a child process. It then looks at the processed command line to see whether file redirection metacharacters are present. If there are, then either stdin or stdout or both are reopened to the appropriate file specified on the command line. This is indicated by the text in Box b2.

Once the required file reopening is completed, the child process is ready to start the command you requested to be executed. To do this, the child uses another system function called exec(). The command line that was processed and expanded by the C Shell is passed to the exec() function, complete with options and arguments. The first parameter to exec() is the name of the program to be run. The actual executable file for the program may not be in one of the directories that make up the shell's search path. In this case, the program name must be a fully qualified pathname in order for the program to be located by the system. /

The exec() function searches for the program and, if it does not find the program, it issues an error message. Once the program file is located, exec() replaces the current process's program space with the new program. It doesn't start a new process but instead overwrites the current program with the new one. Everything else about the environment stays the same, so the new program inherits what the original child set up. This is illustrated by the line leading from Box b2 to Box c in Figure 7.2.

Ultimately, the cat command is started. When it reads from stdin, or so it thinks, it is really reading from infile. When it writes to what it assumes is stdout, it is really writing to outfile. Handling file redirection in this manner gives UNIX a great deal of flexibility. It means that commands can be written to read from stdin and write to stdout, and without any changes, their input or output can be redirected on the command line. The following sections will go into more detail about how to use input and output redirection with most UNIX commands and programs.

Input Redirection

Input redirection, you may recall, allows you to supply information to a command from a file, rather than having to type it manually from the keyboard. The input redirection metacharacter (<) indicates to the C Shell that a filename that contains input for the command follows. In the previous section, you saw how the shell reopens stdin before the command to be run is actually started. The command does not know that it is reading from a file and not the keyboard. This works, in part, because UNIX treats devices as if they were files. Thus, the command cannot tell the difference between input direct from the keyboard or read from a file. The same call is used in UNIX to read input from both sources.

In the following example of using input redirection, the contents of the file chapter7.doc are read by the wc command:

```
1 % wc < chapter7.doc
278 1886 13994
2 % _
```

This command counts the lines, words, and characters contained in its input. You can remember it because wc stands for "word count". The three numbers that follow on the line below the command tell you that the file contained 278 lines, 1886 words, and 13,994 characters.

The wc command, like many UNIX commands, can take its input from more than one source. In this example, the input came from stdin, which really was a file, but wc can also accept one or more filenames on the command line and will examine and report the counts from each file individually. If you want to use input redirection with a command, look at its manual page to see if it can take its input from stdin. If it can, then you can use input redirection to supply the input.

Output Redirection

There are several varieties of output redirection metacharacters, as you learned in Day 2, "Metacharacters." Table 7.2 summarizes these for your reference here.

Table 7.2. Output redirection metacharacters.

Metacharacter	Description of Function
>name	Output from command is redirected to *name*. If *name* exists, it is overwritten.

Metacharacter	Description of Function
>&*name*	Output from stderr is combined with stdout and written to *name*.
>! *name*	Output from command is redirected to *name*. If *name* exists, it is overwritten. This form is used when $noclobber is set and you want to override its effect.
>&! *name*	Output from stderr is combined with stdout and redirected to *name*. If *name* exists, it is overwritten. This form is used when $noclobber is set and you want to override its effect.

All four of these metacharacter combinations perform output redirection. This section discusses only the standard output redirection metacharacter, >. The other variations of output redirection are covered later on in today's material.

Think back to what you learned about the behind-the-scenes processing that the C Shell does to make redirection work. Remember that input and output redirection are handled in an identical fashion, by reopening either stdin or stdout to the redirection file.

Here, an example from earlier is changed by adding output redirection to it:

```
3 % wc < chapter7.doc > chap7.wc
4 % cat < chap7.wc
278 1886 13994
5 % _
```

Again, wc is used to count the lines, words, and characters in chapter7.doc, but this time the output from wc is redirected to the file chap7.wc. In Event 4, chap7.wc is displayed using cat, and you see the same results as in the earlier example.

Using output redirection, you can capture the output resulting from a process, or series of processes, and have it available as a source of input for use by other commands. If you need to reuse the output from a command or job, it often saves time and computer resources to use output redirection and capture the output. The output can then be reused without the overhead involved in re-creating it each time it is needed. In the preceding example, very little processing was required to create the output, but in another situation creating output could involve a considerable amount of resources.

Appending to a File

As with output redirection, there are several varieties of metacharacters used to append command output to a file. Table 7.3 summarizes these for your reference.

Table 7.3. Metacharacters for appending to a file.

Metacharacter	Description of Function
>>*name*	Output from command is appended to the end of *name*. If $noclobber is set and *name* does not exist, an error message is issued.
>>&*name*	Appends output from stderr, combined with stdout, and appended to the end of *name*.
>>! *name*	The same as >>, used when $noclobber is set. When *name* does not exist, it is created without an error being issued.
>>&! *name*	Appends output from stderr combined with stdout and appended to the end of *name*. The same as >>&, used when $noclobber is set. When *name* does not exist, it is created without an error being issued.

All four of these metacharacter combinations append command output to a file. This section discusses only the standard metacharacter for appending, >>. The other variations for appending output to a file are covered in a later section of today's material. With the >> and >>& cases, the file *name* must exist prior to the start of the command. Otherwise, the shell will issue an error message.

Appending output to a file using >> is accomplished in a manner similar to regular output redirection using >. The difference between normal and appending redirection is in the mode that the Shell uses to *reopen* the output file. For normal output redirection, the file is opened in standard output mode, and it is opened in append mode when the >> redirection operator is used. Opening a file in append mode signals the system to position the file pointer to the end of the file. The *file pointer* is a special indicator that maintains the location where the next I/O operation will occur. When your command writes to stdout, its output is added to the end of the redirection file.

Note: The system maintains information about each file that is opened by a process running under UNIX. This information is kept in an area within the process referred to as the *file control block*, or *FCB*. One of the items of information kept in the FCB is a pointer used by the system to determine the next location where I/O will be done on that particular file. This pointer, the *file pointer*, is initially set to point to the first byte in a file that is opened for input. If the file is opened for normal input, this pointer is set to point to the first byte in the first empty block of the new file. When a file is opened in append mode, however, the file pointer is set to point just after the last byte in the file.

The following example illustrates how to use the >> redirection operator to append output to an existing file. In this example, the shell script myscript is executed and its output appended to the file mylog.

```
5 % myscript >> mylog
6 % _
```

Merging Output

You read earlier about the two files that the system provides for output, stdout and stderr. At times, it is necessary or convenient for you to combine both of these output streams to write to a single file or to provide both as input to another process. The C Shell provides a means for accomplishing this when you do output redirection.

In Tables 7.1 and 7.2, where the output and append redirection metacharacters were shown, you saw several combinations that included the ampersand metacharacter (&). Although this metacharacter has a special meaning of its own at the end of a command line, when combined with file redirection metacharacters it has a different meaning. In the latter case, it tells the C Shell that you want to merge stderr with stdout, writing both outputs to the single file whose name follows the redirection metacharacters.

To capture both stdin and stderr and write them to a file named mylog, you would use >& mylog, as in this example:

```
6 % myscript >& mylog
7 % _
```

If mylog did not exist, it would be created in your current directory. If it did exist in your current directory, it would be overwritten (the exception to this is discussed in the next section). If you want to append `stdin` and `stderr` to `mylog`, you would use `>>& mylog`. Remember that the target filename of appending redirection must exist to avoid an error message from the shell.

Overwriting a File

On Day 4, you learned about the special shell variable `$noclobber`. With `$noclobber` set ON, you protect existing files from being overwritten by file redirection. If an existing file is the target of output or appending redirection with `>` or `>>`, an error is issued by the shell and the operation does not proceed. To override the effect of `$noclobber` and avoid getting an error for a pre-existing file, you can add an exclamation point (`!`) to any of the output or appending redirection metacharacters. This includes the combinations with and without the file-merge ampersand character (`&`). To avoid an error with `myscript >> mylog`, add an exclamation point, thus:

```
7 % myscript >> mylog
8 % _

8 % myscript >>! mylog
9 % _
```

If `mylog` exists, it will be overwritten if `$noclobber` is set. If `mylog` doesn't exist, it will be created without error as well. If you want to merge `stdout` and `stderr` and avoid an error when the output file exists, change the command to this:

```
9 % myscript >>&! mylog
10 % _
```

Here Document

You will recall from Day 2, "Metacharacters," that the input metacharacters `<<` enable you to redirect lines from a script to the input of a UNIX command within the script. Input redirection in this manner is known as a *here document*.

Think back to the earlier description of the shell's behind-the-scenes activities that make redirection work. Remember that after the fork, the child process reopens one of the standard I/O files on the specified redirection file. For the here document the same thing occurs, but in this case `stdin` is reopened. With input and output redirection, a filename follows the metacharacters that indicate the type of redirection to be done. With a here document, no filename is supplied because it is implied to be the file `stdin` points to in the current shell.

The << metacharacters are followed by *word*, which is a unique set of characters marking the end of input to the here document. Each input line read by the << metacharacters is examined for a match to *word* before any other substitutions or metacharacter expansions are performed. Because variable substitution and metacharacter expansion are performed on the here document text, shell variables can be included in the text to dynamically customize the message text or commands.

Consider the following example:

```
10 % cat <<STOP_HERE
Welcome to the System $USER
Your current working directory is: $PWD
And the current date and time are: `date`
STOP_HERE
Welcome to the System dave
Your current working directory is: /usr/dave
And the current date and time are: Mon  Jul 4 14:04:27 PDT 1994
11 % _
```

Notice that the variables and command substitution included in the here document were expanded and replaced with the contents of the variables and the results of the command execution. The result is a personalized message that is different for each person who uses your script. The << can also be used to output multiline messages from a script without the need to use multiple echo commands.

```
11 % cat <<END_of_MESSAGE
You can use this method in a script to display multi-
line messages to the user. Without the here document
you would have to use many echo commands. Another
alternative is to use a single echo command with escaped
newlines. You would do that by placing backslashes (\)
at the end of each line, to protect the newline and keep
it as part of the message. Otherwise, the shell would
take the newline to indicate the end of the echo command.
Using this method is very cumbersome. The here document
is an easy as well as esthetic solution to this problem.
END_of_MESSAGE
You can use this method in a script to display multi-
line messages to the user. Without the here document
you would have to use many echo commands. Another
alternative is to use a single echo command with escaped
newlines. You would do that by placing backslashes (\)
at the end of each line, to protect the newline and keep
it as part of the message. Otherwise, the shell would
take the newline to indicate the end of the echo command.
Using this method is very cumbersome. The here document
is an easy as well as esthetic solution to this problem.
12 % _
```

And << can also be used to supply repeatable multiline command input to many different UNIX commands and utilities. This makes automating frequently performed tasks involving these commands very easy.

171

The following example illustrates the use of the here document. In event 12, I use the cat command to display a script that I wrote, named `instoday.csh`. This script gets today's date and uses it to replace the string %today% wherever it occurs in a text file. The `instoday.csh` script expects an argument that is the name of the file to be used as input for the substitutions. The script sets a local variable, $today, to the value of the current time and date using the date command in backticks. Next, the ed command, a line editor, is used to search the file given on the command line. This is indicated by the $1 on the ed command line. This command line also contains the here document metacharacters, <<, followed by the match word ++.

The here document contains commands to ed. These commands instruct ed to globally substitute the contents of $today for each occurrence of %today% on all lines containing %today%. After all lines in the file are processed, they will be rewritten to the file and ed will then quit. Remember that the line containing ++ marks the end of the here document and is not provided as input to ed. The last line of my script displays a message to my terminal to tell me that it has completed running. This message includes the name of the file I included on the original command line.

After the output from cat, I then invoke my `instoday.csh` script with the filename `today.txt`. When the script completes it displays the message "Done inserting today's date in today.txt" on my terminal. To prove that my script ran successfully, I again use cat, this time to show the contents of `today.txt` updated with today's date.

```
12 % cat instoday.csh
#!/bin/csh
set today=(`date`)
ed $1 <<++
g/%today/s//$today/g
w
q
++
echo "Done inserting today's date in $1"
13 % cat today.txt
Wherever the word today delimited with percent
signs appears it will be replaced with today's
date. Here -> %today% <-
Even if it appears twice!
%today% [ %today% ]
14 % instoday.csh today.txt
Done inserting today's date in today.txt
15 % cat today.txt
Wherever the word today delimited with percent
signs appears it will be replaced with today's
date. Here -> Mon  Jul 4 14:05:32 PDT 1994 <-
Even if it appears twice!
Mon  Jul 4 14:05:32 PDT 1994 [ Mon  Jul 4 14:05:32 PDT 1994 ]
16 % _
```

here documents read up to word

Pipes

The C Shell pipe facility provides a mechanism by which you connect the standard output of one program directly to the standard input of another program. This connection is indicated to the shell using one of the metacharacters shown Table 7.4. The second entry in Table 7.4 shows a pair of metacharacters that are used when you need to merge both `stdout` and `stderr` of the first program into `stdin` of the second.

Table 7.4. Metacharacters for creating pipelines.

Metacharacter	Description of Function
¦	Creates a pipeline between two commands. The output of the command to the left of the pipe (¦) is connected to the input of the command to the right of the pipe.
¦&	Creates a pipeline between two commands, with the output from both `stderr` and `stdout` of the command to the left of the pipe (¦) combined and connected to the input of the command to the right of the pipe.

Figure 7.3 is a flowchart that illustrates the steps the C Shell performs to execute the simple pipeline of who ¦ wc -1. The following sections explain the figure in detail and show you more examples of how pipes can be used with UNIX and the C Shell.

Pipes Defined

The steps and processes that the C Shell performs with pipes are very much like those for simple file redirection. They still involve calls to the UNIX `fork()` and `exec()` functions to create new processes and to start execution of commands. The major difference is that output is directed to a pipe rather than to a file, and input is read from the pipe rather than a file.

What is a pipe anyway? If you think of the image of your plumbing, with the pipes connected from one place to another, you will have a good sense of what UNIX does. You already know that UNIX treats *everything* as a file; pipes are not excluded from this treatment. Treating pipes as files makes creating pipes easy. Again, as with file redirection, it eliminates the need to re-write programs to allow them to be used with pipes.

The Differences and Similarities of Pipes

There are two differences between I/O with pipes and I/O with regular files. One is the special UNIX function used to open a pipe file. Once the pipe is open for reading or writing, it is indistinguishable from any other file, to the program that is reading or writing it. The second is that, because pipes are unidirectional, they can be opened only for reading or for writing, but not for both—as you *can* do with a regular file.

For two programs to use pipes to communicate with each other, back and forth, they need to open two pipes. One is written by program A and read by program B. The other goes in the opposite direction, written by program B and read by program A. Communication between two programs or processes in this manner is known as *interprocess communication*, or *IPC* for short.

Variations on IPC are used throughout the UNIX world to implement all sorts of applications, facilities, and features. It is just this kind of simple building-block construction to create more sophisticated capabilities that has propelled UNIX to the forefront of the computer industry today.

A Peek at Pipes and What Makes Them Work

Look at Figure 7.3 to see what happens when the C Shell processes the command line `who ¦ wc -l`.

Similar to file redirection, the shell forks to create a child process that will do all the work to accomplish the execution of the command line. The child examines the command line to be executed. Finding one or more pipe metacharacters, it first opens input and output pipes. Then the child forks accordingly to create enough new processes to execute all the commands in the pipeline.

Looking at Figure 7.3, you can see that the child must fork once to create the additional process. Then these two process, the original child and its child, close `stdin` and `stdout`, reopening them as input and output pipes, similar to the example of file redirection shown in Figure 7.2. Because command line pipes are unidirectional, each process also needs to close one of its pipes. The process that will become the `who` command closes its read pipe, because it is only producing output to the pipeline. The other process, which will become the `wc` command, closes its write pipe, because it needs only to read from the pipeline and does not write back to the other command.

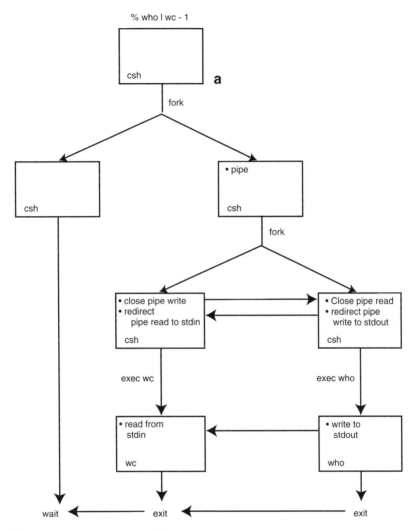

Figure 7.3. *stdin and stdout with pipes.*

Now that the pipes are properly opened, both processes call exec to start their respective commands. Now when the who command writes to stdout, it is really writing to the pipe. Likewise, when the wc command reads its input from stdin, it is actually getting the characters from the pipe connected to the who command.

Pipelines and *stderr*

In Table 7.4, you saw an entry for pipelines, namely, the metacharacter pair ¦&. Even before you read the description that went with it, you may have figured out that it involved merging stderr. Just as with file redirection, the ampersand (&) metacharacter signifies that the output from stderr is to be merged with that of stdout.

Unlike the Bourne and Korn shells, the C Shell does not provide a nice mechanism for separate capture of stderr output. You have two alternatives for dealing with stderr:

☐ You can leave stderr to default and output to the users terminal or display device.

☐ You can merge it with stdout to a file with >&, >&!, >>&, or >>&! file redirection metacharacters. Alternatively, you can merge it with stdout through a pipeline with the ¦& metacharacters.

> **Note:** Using the standard pipe metacharacter (¦) only affects stdin and stdout of the commands in the pipeline. Output that any of the commands would normally write to stderr still goes to the user's terminal or display device. This has built-in benefits. First, it ensures that any errors or informative messages from the commands get to the user. Second, it also keeps the information passing through the pipes limited to the production output of the commands.

The pipe merge metacharacters (¦&) are rarely used. When they are used, it is usually in a script where the output from some or all of the commands is captured in one or more log files. Controlled portions of the output are allowed to go to stdout for the user's benefit.

Mixing File Redirection and Pipes

Today's material to this point has been devoted to two topics, file redirection and pipelines. These two facilities of UNIX give you a great deal of power and flexibility in creating new commands and tools to get your job done. Unfortunately, these two aspects of UNIX—file redirection and pipelines—don't mix well within the C Shell.

The only place that file redirection can be accommodated with pipelines is at the end of the last command. There you can use output redirection to capture the final output to a file. If you attempt to redirect the output of a command in the beginning or middle of

the pipeline, all of the data will go to the file and nothing will be left to pass through the pipe to the next command.

> **Tip:** There is a work-around to this situation, when it is required that output be captured from a command which is part of a pipeline. The UNIX command called tee is specifically designed to solve this problem. Just like a plumber who is fitting water pipes together uses a T-shaped piece to split a flow to two destinations, you can use the tee command to split out the flow through your pipeline. Using tee, you specify a filename following the command. The input that tee reads from stdin is written to stdout and also to the filename you specified. The -a option to tee causes the output to be appended to the file. Otherwise, the default behavior of tee is to overwrite the file with the new data.

This tee ?? Other ? (handwritten note)

Pipelines and input redirection suffer a similar fate as pipes and output redirection. You can use input redirection only on a command that is the first in a pipeline. Using input redirection on a command in the middle or at the end of a pipeline typically causes it to ignore the input coming to it through the pipe itself. This is not usually the desired effect. I cannot think of any UNIX commands that even support input from both stdin and files, let alone input from stdin *and* a pipeline.

Pipes and Aliases

Unlike pipes and file redirection, pipes and aliases are a match made in heaven! Day 3, "Command Substitution, Aliases, and Filename Generation," introduced the C Shell aliasing facility. You learned how you can create

☐ Aliases that are synonyms for commands

☐ Aliases that redefine existing commands in some way

☐ Aliases that define new commands

It is the last item that is important here. UNIX today, in its various forms, has a robust command set, numbering more than 450 for some versions. Many of these commands you will never have occasion to use, whereas others you will use frequently every day. UNIX is not a perfect operating system; the perfect operating system doesn't exist. You can, however, take steps towards making UNIX more perfect for your needs by using aliases, with pipes and file redirection if needed, to create your own new commands.

Say, for example, that you find yourself frequently looking in a particular directory for a set of files, and occasionally that listing gets long and runs off the screen. Your first thought should be to combine that particular ls command with one of the UNIX pager commands, more or pg, to create a new tool tailored to your need, for example:

```
alias ltxt 'cd ~/textfiles; ls -ltr *.txt ¦ more'
```

This new alias, ltxt (short for ls textfiles), uses a few of the metacharacters you have already learned, including the pipeline character. It is a labor-saver, reducing your keystrokes and combining multiple commands into one. It helps you by getting the command-line options just right for this particular situation.

Text Processing UNIX-Style with Pipes

Here is another example of the use of pipes where an alias can be an aid. UNIX has a group of related commands that perform text processing. These commands were added to the UNIX command set before PCs and the word processors that we have today were even available. These commands assume that the user has a only simple display terminal, not even windows. Each of these commands performs a different functional role in the total task of preparing a document for publication. Table 7.5 shows the commonly used commands in this group, with a description of the function each performs.

Table 7.5. UNIX text-processing commands.

Command	Description
troff	This command was originally written as a formatter to generate output for a phototypesetter. In recent years, with laser printers becoming commonplace, troff has been updated to output in a format they require. This is usually the last command in a pipeline or script.
ditroff	A newer version of troff that is device-independent. The *di* added to the front represents this new functionality.
nroff	Because troff output cannot be directly viewed on character-based devices, such as display terminals and even today's X Stations, this command was created. It accepts the same input as troff but formats the input as best as possible so that it can be viewed on the user's terminal. Some or all graphics that might be in the document are lost.

Command	Description
eqn	A preprocessor specifically designed to format complex equations, such as differentials or statistical summations, which have their own special character set.
neqn	For the same reasons that nroff exists, neqn exists, that is, to make the best of the input that normally would be formatted by eqn, but in this case, for display on a terminal rather than a troff compatible-output device.
pic	A preprocessor for drawing pictures that are included in a document. It uses simple geometric shapes as building blocks to create its line drawings.
tbl	A preprocessor for formatting tabular data. It provides for formatting complex table formats with the capability to draw lines and boxes around selected portions of the table.

These powerful text processing commands are usually used together in a pipeline. One of the applicable preprocessors is selected at the start of the pipeline, and it has the name of the document file on its command line. The output of this first command is piped to a second, which processes the input further and creates output to the next in the series. Each of these preprocessors takes its own commands and macros, and converts them to the necessary troff commands. This proceeds until the end of the pipeline, typically one of the 'roff' commands, which does the final formatting and output to either the terminal or the printer device.

In this example, pic starts off the pipeline and reads from the presentation.doc file, which contains the entire document with all the formatting commands embedded:

```
16 % pic presentation.doc ¦ eqn ¦ tbl ¦ ditroff -me
```

The data and commands are read by pic, which processes and expands the commands and macros for which it has responsibility, writing them to stdout. Any text, data, commands, or macros that it does not process are simply written to stdout untouched. Next, eqn takes input from stdin, looking for its commands and macros. In the same manner as pic, eqn processes and expands its macros and commands, writing the output to stdout, along with the information that it skipped over.

7

The information on the pipeline grows as it proceeds through each preprocessor until it reaches `ditroff` at the end of the pipeline. The `ditroff` command takes the input and expands any remaining commands and macros, in this case using the `me` macro package. When `ditroff` is done expanding macros, there should be only 'roff' commands and text remaining. The last step is then taken, in which the `ditroff` (this could be replaced with `nroff` or `troff`, if desired) command formats the commands and text into a finished form for output.

Filters

The text-formatting commands presented in the previous section, along with many other UNIX commands, are members in a large class known as *filters*. This section explains more about what filters are and how you can use them to best advantage.

Filters Defined

With all that build-up, you probably expect some great and grand revelation at this point. Actually, there is no real magic or complexity to filters; you have been using them all along not knowing what they were and not really needing to know. A filter, simply put, is a program or command that processes an input and produces an output. Most all programs take some input and produce some output.

In the case of true filters, though, the definition is refined a bit to include those commands that take input from `stdin` and write output to `stdout` as their default operation. Filters are usually not interactive. By that, I mean that they do not issue prompts for input. Instead, they just read `stdin` continually until they reach EOF.

Examples of Filters

Very few UNIX commands expect their input solely from files whose names are supplied on the command line or in response to an input prompt. Most UNIX commands write their output to `stdout` as a default, instead of writing to a file, again supplied as a command line argument or option. Many commands that are filters have been used in this book up to this point. Table 7.6 has a list of a few UNIX filters that you will find to be extremely useful as you learn more about using the C Shell and UNIX. These commands are worth further study to learn more about their capabilities and limitations.

Table 7.6. Common UNIX filters.

Filter Name	Description
awk	Programming language that can search one or more files or data on `stdin` for matches to complex text patterns. The `awk` command can also do limited text formatting and perform simple arithmetic.
grep	Command used to search one or more files or data on `stdin` for matches to patterns expressed as simple strings or as regular expressions.
head	Command used to display the first part (head) of a file or `stdin`.
pr	Command used to paginate files or data on `stdin` in preparation for printing. Each page is formatted with a header listing the name of the file, date, time, and page number. For `stdin` input, a command-line option can be used to supply header information in lieu of a filename.
sed	Batch stream editor that can accept commands from either the command line or a separate program-file. This command can perform a fairly complex series of operations on each line of input from either `stdin` or filenames on the command line.
sort	Command used to sort data from either `stdin` or filenames from the command line. Input data can be sorted by keys on fields delimited by whitespace or a specified delimiter character. The default is to treat the entire record as a single key.
tail	Command used to display the last part (tail) of a file or `stdin`.
tee	Command that copies `stdin` to `stdout` *and* one or more files from the command line.

Summary

This chapter presented three important features of UNIX and the C Shell: file redirection, pipes, and filters. You will use them regularly as you become more comfortable with UNIX and the shell. In fact, you'll reach a point where you will wonder

what you did before you learned about them! File redirection extends the capability of many commands by permitting you to specify an alternative output destination or an alternative input source.

Pipes allow you to combine multiple commands in a form that joins the output of one command to the input of the next. Information flows through the pipeline, from one command to the next, with each processing the data a bit more until the finished product emerges from the end of the pipe. Filters are a large subset of the UNIX command set with a standard behavior of reading from `stdin` and writing to `stdout`. They are the typical constituents of pipelines.

In the next chapter, Day 8, you will begin to discover the shell's many built-in commands. These are commands that actually are a part of the C Shell rather than separate programs. Because they are built-in, they can take advantage of the shell's intimate knowledge of your environment. Also, because they are built-in, you can depend on them being available regardless of which UNIX version you are using. These built-in commands provide a basic command set that will become an important part of your everyday use of UNIX.

Related UNIX Topics

This chapter presented some new concepts and commands. Here is a list of some of these concepts and topics, with suggestions for sources of further information.

Metacharacters:	Consult Appendix C in this book, as well as the tear-out reference card for listings and definitions of all the metacharacters used by the C Shell. Review Day 2 if you need to brush up on metacharacters.
filters:	Look in section 1 of your UNIX manuals or the man pages for more information on these commands listed in Table 7.6. Determine which of these commands is available on your system and learn more about the different capabilities of these versatile commands.
text-processing commands:	Look in section 1 for these commands and study the man pages to understand this powerful set of text processing tool. On some versions of UNIX, these commands are bundled separately, so you may find that some or all are unavailable on your system.

Q&A

Q What do you do to indicate that you want file redirection?

A For the simplest form, you can use the metacharacters < and > to indicate input and output file redirection, respectively. Each of these metacharacters is followed by a filename that will be used for the source of input or destination of output, depending on the metacharacter used.

Q How would you append output to a file rather than overwrite it with file redirection?

A The special metacharacter pair >> is used to append output to a file. The file must exist before the redirection operation, or an error will result.

Q If you have set the `$noclobber` shell variable, how do you override it to redirect output to a file without an error?

A By adding an exclamation point metacharacter (!) to any output file-redirection operator, you can specify that you want to override the effect of the `$noclobber` variable (that is, use >! or >>!).

Q Can any command be used as part of a pipeline?

A There is not a simple answer to this question. The answer is *no*, in that not *all* UNIX commands act as filters, so you cannot depend on being able to put any command anywhere in a pipeline. A good example is the `ls` command. It outputs to `stdout`, so it can start a pipeline; but it doesn't take any input from `stdin`, so if you place it in the middle of a pipe or at the end, it will 'clog' the pipe by not accepting the output of the previous commands. In general, you need to consult the man page for any command you are unfamiliar with to see if it both reads from `stdin` and writes to `stdout`.

Workshop

The Workshop provides several sections to aid you in reviewing the topics covered in today's lesson. There is a quiz section to help you reinforce your understanding of the material presented for Day 7 and exercises to give you practice applying what you have learned. Take the time to review these questions and exercises, so that you understand the concepts before you begin the next day's lesson. The answers are provided in Appendix F, "Answers to Quizzes and Exercises."

Quiz

1. How would you use file redirection to merge the stdout and stderr output from a command into a single file?

2. As in question 1 above, how would you merge the same two streams but use a pipeline rather than file redirection?

3. What happens to the output going to stderr when a command is part of a pipeline?

4. If you wanted to save the output of a command that is part of a pipeline, without removing it from the pipeline, what filter would you need to insert into the pipeline?

5. If you wanted to look at the ten most recently created files in a directory, how would you do this with pipes and filters?

Exercises

1. Think of several new aliases that you can create using pipes and filters to automate a repetitive process you now perform manually.

2. Look in the man pages for your system and find three more commands that are filters and that are not listed in Table 7.6.

You have completed your first week of learning about the UNIX C Shell. Here is a list summarizing the topics covered in the first seven days of this book. Use the list as a tool to refresh your knowledge of these subjects.

Day 1: Introducing the C Shell

You should now be able to

☐ Display the C Shell command history list

☐ Recall history events by event number

☐ Recall history events using a search string

☐ Modify a history event line and execute it

Day 2: Metacharacters

You should now be able to

☐ Use syntactic metacharacters to

1. Separate multiple sequentially executed commands on a single command line (;)

2. Form a pipeline joining the output of one command to the input of a second command (¦)

3. Isolate commands separated by semicolons or pipelines, so that they are treated as a single unit (( ))

4. Place a command in background (&)

5. Conditionally execute a command depending on the results of a prior command's execution (¦¦) (&&)

☐ Use filename metacharacters to

1. Form a match pattern to match a single character in a specific position of a filename (?)

2. Form a match pattern to match zero or more characters from a specific point in a filename (*)

3. Form a match pattern that designates a class of characters that are matched against a specific character in a filename ([ ])

4. Form an abbreviation using sets of words that share common parts (these abbreviations can be used to match against specific characters in a filename) ({})

5. Abbreviate the path to the home directory of the current user or of a specific user on the system (~)

☐ Use quotation metacharacters to

1. Prevent a specific metacharacter from being interpreted by the shell as a metacharacter (\)

2. Prevent a string of characters from being interpreted by the shell as metacharacters, without preventing command or variable substitution from occurring (")

3. Prevent a string of characters from being interpreted by the shell as metacharacters, and prevent command and variable substitution from occurring (')

☐ Use input/output metacharacters to

1. Redirect input to a command from a specified filename (<)

2. Redirect output from a command to a specified filename (>)

3. Redirect output from a command to a specified filename, merging the output of stderr with stdout (>&)

4. Redirect output from a command to a specified filename, overwriting the file if it exists and $noclobber is set ON (>!)

5. Redirect output from a command to a specified filename, merging the output of stderr with stdout and overwriting the file if it exists and $noclobber is set ON (>&!)

6. Append output from a command to a specified filename (>>)

7. Append output from a command to a specified filename, merging the output of stderr with stdout (>>&)

8. Append output from a command to a specified filename, overwriting the file if it exists and $noclobber is set ON (>>!)

9. Append output from a command to a specified filename, merging the output of stderr with stdout and overwriting the file, if it exists and $noclobber is set ON (>>&!)

10. Create a here document, where command input is read from `stdin` of the shell, up to a line that contains only the match word specified (`<<`)

11. Form a pipeline joining the output of one command to the input of a second command (`¦`)

12. Form a pipeline, joining the output of one command to the input of a second command, with the output of both `stderr` and `stdout` combined and passed to the input of the second command (`¦&`)

☐ Use expansion/substitution metacharacters to

1. Indicate to the C Shell that the word following is the name of a shell variable (`$`)

2. Indicate to the C Shell that the word following is a history event number (`!`)

3. Indicate to the shell that the word following is a history event match string (`!?`)

4. Indicate to the C Shell that the word following is a modifier for a history event or shell variable (`:`)

Day 3: Command Substitution, Aliases, and Filename Generation

In this chapter, you learned how to

☐ Use the `alias` command to

1. List all current alias definitions

2. Create command synonyms

3. Redefine existing commands

4. Create new commands

☐ Include command line arguments in an alias

☐ Remove an existing alias definition

☐ Generate filename arguments with metacharacters

☐ Use regular expressions on a command line

☐ Use command substitution to create command line arguments from the output of other commands

Day 4: Shell Variables, Part I

Now you should be able to

☐ Distinguish between local and global or environment variables

☐ Display local variables using the set command

☐ Display global variables using the setenv command

☐ Use the following C Shell built-in variables

1.	$argv	Command line argument list
2.	$autologout	Automatic logout timer
3.	$cdpath	Directory stack
4.	$child	Background process ID
5.	$cwd	Current working directory
6.	$fignore	Filename completion suffixes
7.	$histchars	History substitution characters
8.	$history	History list size
9.	$home	User's home directory
10.	$mail	User's mail path
11.	$path	User's directory search path
12.	$prompt	C Shell prompt string
13.	$savehist	Saved history size
14.	$shell	Default shell path
15.	$status	Command return status
16.	$time	Command timer control
17.	$$	Current process ID

Day 5: Shell Variables, Part II

In this chapter, you learned how to

☐ Use the following C Shell built-in variables

1. `$echo`   Echo commands before execution after all substitutions have been made

2. `$filec`   Enable filename completion facility

3. `$hardpaths`   Resolve symbolic links to hard path for `pushd` and `popd` commands

4. `$ignoreeof`   Disable EOF (`^D`) capability to terminate the C Shell

5. `$nobeep`   Disable file completion beep when unable to complete current filename

6. `$noclobber`   Prevent overwriting of files with redirection

7. `$noglob`   Disable expansion of filename metacharacters

8. `$nonomatch`   Enable passing of unmatched pattern to a command and inhibit "no match" error message

9. `$notify`   Enable immediate notification of background job status changes

10. `$verbose`   Echo commands before execution after history substitutions have been made

☐ Create and use numeric shell variables

☐ Form expressions with shell variables using the `@` command

☐ Use C Shell arithmetic operators

☐ Use C Shell pattern-matching operators

☐ Use C Shell assignment operators

☐ Use C Shell postfix operators

☐ Use C Shell file-inquiry operators

Day 6: Customizing the User Environment

After studying this chapter, you should know

- ☐ Which dot files to make changes in for customizing
- ☐ How to add aliases to the `.cshrc` file
- ☐ How to initialize local variables in the `.cshrc` file
- ☐ How to do additional initialization tasks in the `.cshrc` file
- ☐ How to initialize environment variables in the `.login` file
- ☐ How to set up terminal and workstation attributes in the `.login` file
- ☐ Setup of actions to be performed when logging out of the system
- ☐ Tips and techniques for making changes to the dot files

Day 7: File Redirection, Pipes, and Filters

Here you learned how to

- ☐ Use `stdin`, `stdout`, and `stderr`
- ☐ Redirect input to commands and scripts
- ☐ Redirect output from commands and scripts
- ☐ Append output to a file
- ☐ Merge output from `stdout` and `stderr`
- ☐ Overwrite a file
- ☐ Protect a file from being overwritten
- ☐ Use a here document in a script

□ Use pipes to combine commands

□ Combine the use of file redirection with pipes

□ Use pipes in aliases

□ Employ filters in your scripts and command lines

Now that you have completed the first week, you should be ready to move on and begin the remaining half of your studies to learn the C Shell in 14 days. This first week has prepared you with a solid foundation in the C Shell. The expansion of your knowledge continues with the turn of a page, where the next week begins.

This second week takes you from being a novice user of the C Shell to becoming a power user. You will learn what each of the C Shell built-in commands are and why they are useful. After that, you will see the real power of using the C Shell as a programming language. As a part of the task of learning programming, you will need to take on a complicated project, a programming tool to correct spelling mistakes in a document.

Finally, you will learn about jobs. You will learn how to identify jobs, start and stop them, and kill them. After you have accomplished these tasks, you will be ready to use the C Shell for any eventuality.

Here is a list of the topics for the week and a brief overview of the lesson for each day.

Day	Overview
8	This is the first day for learning built-in commands. The commands covered here are those used to navigate the file tree and move from directory to directory. Also, the commands used to manipulate shell variables will be covered, and some miscellaneous commands for aliases and history will be included.
9	The tour of built-in commands will continue, with a look at the job control commands. Although the details of job control will have to wait until Day 14, the basics are presented today. Also included are the commands used to terminate the C Shell and the various reasons why you may use them.
10	The tour of built-in commands finishes today, with a look at the hash table commands, the resource control commands, and a few difficult-to-classify stragglers. An introduction to signals is also presented for those of you who want to know more about UNIX.
11	This day introduces you to the basic programming structures. The commands to create loops and to execute commands conditionally are presented here. Some other commands restricted to shell programming also are presented, such as `onintr` and `shift`. A good understanding of loops and conditionals is required to understand good programs.
12	Day 12 begins the programming of the C Shell. Six short shell scripts (Say that fast 10 times!) are presented to help familiarize you with how to program the shell. Each script introduces a problem and has a suggested solution that exercises different shell constructs. After you experiment with these programs and understand the decisions made, you will be ready to move to the next day.
13	This day introduces you to using the C Shell to solve a big problem. The program for the day is a spelling checker and corrector; you will learn how this program is developed and put together. The job is broken into individual pieces, each easier to think about and easier to solve, before the different pieces are integrated into a cohesive solution.
14	The last day covers job control and job manipulation. One of the more powerful aspects of the C Shell is how it can act like a batch processor, setting up different tasks to run in the background and

manipulating those tasks as needed. On this day, you will learn how to start and stop jobs, and how to move them from the background to the foreground, and back.

C Shell Built-In
Commands, Part I

Introduction to Day 8

This chapter starts an in-depth tour of commands that are built into the C Shell. You will first learn how to navigate the UNIX file system, and you will learn to recognize why some commands are built-in. Then you will learn how to modify your execution environment by setting and unsetting environment variables. At the same time, you will learn how to perform simple mathematics. In the last part of the chapter, you will find out how to see what your previous commands were, see how long commands lasted, and create simple handles to complex commands. You will also get some pointers to tricks that will make your use of the C Shell easier.

Setting Today's Goals

Today, you will learn how to

☐ Navigate a UNIX file tree

☐ Alter your execution environment

☐ Perform simple mathematical calculations

☐ Set up aliases for commands to shorter, mnemonic strings

☐ Copy output from a command to a terminal

☐ Examine your command history

☐ Determine the actual amount of time a command used

☐ Execute a command multiple times from a single command

☐ Alter file creation permissions

Navigation and Directory Stack Commands

The UNIX file structure is often compared to that of a tree, with a simple root and then multiple directories creating the branches of the tree. Finally, the individual files can be considered the leaves of the tree. Considered from the top downwards, each leaf has its own unique branch, and each branch joins the trunk, down to the root of the tree.

Unfortunately, this simple analogy breaks down quickly, as links and symbolic links can create the impression that a single leaf is attached to multiple branches and that even a branch can be attached to multiple lower branches. If we want to keep this analogy alive, we can view symbolic links as "magic" leaves: when we access a magic leaf, we are instantly transported to a different location on the tree.

> **Note:** When one examines how UNIX implements a file system, this analogy holds up rather well. Everything in UNIX is a file, even the root. Directories are a special type of file used to organize files. Each directory entry has a name and an *inode* associated with it. This inode points to a specific location on the hard disk where the file is located, along with some file-specific information, such as the access permissions. When multiple directory entries point to the same inode, these files are considered linked to each other.
>
> A symbolic link works in the same way as does the "magic" leaf. It is another special type of file used to point to other files. Inside the symbolic link is simply a path to another file, the magical transportation to another location on a tree. Symbolic links are useful in that they allow linking of files across different hard disks (something not possible with regular links), but they do have some risks. The parent directory of a linked directory is not the directory where the link is located but is the actual parent of the original directory. Moreover, although hard links can be removed without harming the file, if the actual file is removed, any symbolic links pointing to the file end up pointing to nowhere.

cd and *chdir*

The cd and chdir commands are used to change the actual working directory for the C Shell. The working directory is the current tree branch in which you are located. Your current working directory determines the form you may use to access files.

The syntax for cd and chdir is

```
cd [dir]
```

```
chdir [dir]
```

The two commands are synonymous. The *dir* is an optional argument; without the argument, you return to your home directory. Otherwise, your current directory is changed to the directory specified by the argument.

Example: `cd /usr/james/Docs`

If an argument is present, the actions of `cd` are determined by the form of the argument. If the first character is slash (/), this is considered to be a full path (also called *absolute path* or *absolute addressing*), and if the directory exists, it becomes your current directory. If not, the command first examines the current directory to see if it can find the destination from there. Then, it checks the `cdpath` environment variable and sees whether it can build a valid path from that environment variable. Finally, if no valid path exists and the argument is a shell variable that points to a valid full path, that full path will be used as the destination directory.

Note: The `cdpath` variable, discussed in Day 4, "Shell Variables, Part I," is actually a very useful variable. It takes the same form as the `path` variable, but it specifies a set of normal home directories from which you may base your searches. I currently keep my `cdpath` pointing to my home directory, my documents directory, and my current project's home directory. That way, I can more easily move to my desired directory.

pushd

The `pushd` command, with its siblings `popd` and `dirs`, manages a directory stack. By using `pushd` and `popd`, you can create a trail through the tree that you can also follow back. The `pushd` command is also useful for quickly jumping to a directory to solve a problem. Then `popd` command then moves you back to the previous directory.

Note: If there has been a need in file system navigation, it has been for an "oops" command, one that returns you to your previous directory. The Korn Shell has the syntax `cd -`, which is a good approach. The Bourne Shell offers nothing. The C Shell requires you to use `pushd` and `popd` to effect this recovery.

Syntax

The syntax for `pushd` is

```
pushd [ +n ¦ dir ]
```

With no arguments, this command adds the current directory to the stack and changes the working directory to the previous top of the stack, swapping the top two elements. If there is only one element on the directory stack, an error message is generated.

With a single, numerical argument *n*, the stack is rotated *n* places, and the new current directory becomes the new top element.

With a directory as an argument, that directory—if it is a valid location—will be added to the top of the stack and will become the new, current directory. It will follow all the conventions of `cd` for determining a directory.

It is a misnomer to call the listing of directories a "directory stack," because it is a more powerful data structure than that. A stack is really just a simple data structure where you can access only the top-most item, and everything you add is to that top. It is like a discard pile in a game of rummy; to reach any older discarded card, you've got to go through those discarded after it.

Instead, the directory list is related to a stack. In its simplest form, you add elements with `pushd`, then remove them with `popd`. You might see the following sequence:

```
1 % pushd workarea
~/workarea ~
2 % pushd xls
~/workarea/xls ~workarea ~
3 % popd
~workarea ~
4 % popd
~
5 % _
```

Here, I first used `pushd` to change my working directory to `workarea`, but I wanted to save the reference to my home directory. Then, after a while, I needed to access the `xls` subdirectory and did some work there. Two calls to `popd` returned me back to where I started.

The real power of `pushd` comes in its capability to manipulate the directory stack. If you need to work in just two directories, you can easily use `pushd` to keep swapping back and forth between them, like so:

```
5 % pushd dir1
~/dir1 ~
6 % pushd dir2
```

```
~/dir2 ~/dir1 ~
7 % pushd
~/dir1 ~/dir2 ~
8 % pushd
~/dir2 ~/dir1 ~
9 % _
```

After pushing the two desired directories on top of the stack, pushd with no arguments acts as a toggle to move between the two directories.

Moving between multiple working directories is easy when you use the pushd +n syntax. The following illustrates the technique for setting up and moving between directories:

```
9 % pushd dir1
~/dir1 ~
10 % pushd dir2
~/dir2 ~/dir1 ~
11 % pushd dir3
~/dir3 ~/dir2 ~/dir1 ~
12 % pushd dir4
~/dir4 ~/dir3 ~/dir2 ~/dir1 ~
13 % pushd +2
~/dir2 ~/dir1 ~ ~/dir4 ~/dir3
14 % pushd +1
~/dir1 ~ ~/dir4 ~/dir3 ~/dir2
15 % pushd
~ ~/dir1 ~/dir4 ~/dir3 ~/dir2
16 % pushd +3
~/dir3 ~/dir2 ~ ~/dir1 ~/dir4
17 % _
```

After the four directories are pushed onto the stack, repeated calls to pushd illustrate the rotation of the directory stack, with a swap thrown in.

Caution: Notice that pushd and pushd +1 are not the same! The first, pushd, just swaps the two elements, leaving everything after that in the same order. The second, pushd +1, takes the top element and moves it to the bottom of the list.

popd

This command is used to remove elements from the directory stack.

8

Syntax

This is the syntax for `popd`:

```
popd [ +n ]
```

With no arguments, `popd` removes the top element from the directory stack and changes directories to the new top element.

With an argument, the *n*th element of the directory stack is eliminated.

Given the previous example, I have five directories on the stack, but I only need four of them. So, if I then typed `popd +2`, I'd have eliminated the unneeded directory:

```
17 % popd +2
~/dir3 ~/dir2 ~/dir1 ~/dir4
18 % _
```

Now, by using the combination of `pushd` and `popd`, I can create a list of all the directories I need, and merrily hop my way through the tree as needed.

> **Caution:** One potential error using `pushd` and `popd` could occur when you also use the `cd` command. All the directory commands are tied in with each other, so using `cd` will silently change the top directory on your stack. The subsequent results may not be what you expected.

dirs

Once you've become familiar with `pushd` and `popd`, you may find yourself getting confused with the state of the directory stack. Sure, you see it after each call to `pushd` and `popd`, but suppose you've done a lot of work, and the last listing of the directory stack has scrolled off the top of the screen?

The `dirs` command provides you with an exact snapshot of your directory stack.

The syntax for `dirs` is

```
dirs [ -l ]
```

With no argument, a listing of the stack is provided, in order. With the `-l` flag, the ~ notation is replaced with full paths.

After some moving about using `pushd` and `popd`, you may have remained in a directory for a while. You want to move back to `dir1` but don't know where it is on the list. You could keep using `pushd +1` until you get to where you want to be, but this could be time-consuming.

So, you first run `dirs`:

```
18 % dirs
~/dir3 ~/dir2 ~/dir1 ~/dir4
19 % _
```

You can see that `dir1` is the third element on the list. So, a quick move to there would yield the results shown here:

```
19 % pushd +2
~/dir1 ~/dir4 ~/dir3 ~/dir2
20 % _
```

This places you in `dir1`, where you want to be, and rotates the stack accordingly.

Shell Variable Commands

Like a programming language, the C Shell supports a limited set of variables. These variables can affect the performance of the shell and any programs invoked by the shell.

These variables were discussed at length in Days 4 and 5, but it may be helpful to remember the differences between a shell variable and an environment variable. Environment variables are passed on to child processes. Common environment variables include PATH, PWD, TERM, and so on. These are used by child processes as a means of conveying information about the invocation environment. Although they may occasionally have spaces in the value, they are single scalar values.

Shell variables are different. Although they are not passed to child processes, some variables do affect how the shell responds. Others can be used to store data needed by the C Shell or any programs. Some of the variables are created by the shell when it starts from existing environment variables, such as how PATH becomes the path variable.

One big difference between the environment variables and the shell variables is that C Shell variables can consist of multiple elements. A shell variable can actually contain an array of values.

When the C Shell is started, it converts the scalar PATH variable into an array of directory paths, and this becomes the path variable. Arrays are indicated by a grouping of strings surrounded by parentheses. Each value is separated by a space. If spaces are important to the value of an element, then that element must be enclosed with quotes. Individual elements of an array may also be addressed with a C-like syntax.

set

The set command is used to create shell variables and assign them values. It is also used to examine the shell variables. With the exception of evaluating numerical expressions, no shell variable can have a value modified, except through set.

Note: The syntax for set is described on Day 4.

Let's assume I want to keep track of the opponents of the United States in the recent World Cup soccer tournament. I might want to set a variable of opponents:

```
20 % set opponent = ( Switzerland Colombia Romanya )
```

I've created a shell variable—opponent—and assigned it three values, the names of the first three opponents. But, as you can see, I misspelled the name of the third opponent, Romania. I can correct this easily:

```
21 % set opponent[3]=Romania
22 % echo $opponent
Switzerland Colombia Romania
23 % _
```

As the Cup competition goes along, I want to add the scores of the games:

```
23 % set opponent[1]="Switzerland, 1-1"
24 % echo $opponent
Switzerland, 1-1 Colombia Romania
25 % _
```

This is actually correct, but it does indicate a weakness in the C Shell's display of variables. I would have been better off if I included quotes in the variable's value or perhaps offset the score with a colon. This is easily corrected:

```
25 % set opponent[1]=Switzerland:1-1
26 % echo $opponent
Switzerland:1-1 Colombia Romania
27 % _
```

That looks a little bit better. After the first three games of the World Cup, I ended up with an array that looked like the following:

```
27 % echo $opponent
Switzerland:1-1 Colombia:2-1 Romania:0-1
28 % _
```

These results meant that the United States qualified for the second round; that is, the United States had another game. It turns out that the opponent was Brazil. I first tried to just add it to the array:

```
28 % set opponent[4]=Brazil
set: Subscript out of range
29 % _
```

This is not good! Do I need to retype the whole array to add the value? Fortunately, no. I can include the array as part of the value of the new assignment:

```
29 % set opponent=($opponent Brazil)
30 % echo $opponent
Switzerland:1-1 Colombia:2-1 Romania:0-1 Brazil
31 % _
```

This has added Brazil as the fourth value.

Caution: It is important to consider the effect a space in a variable name might have. If I had kept the first value as `"Switzerland, 1-1"` and assigned a new value to the whole array as shown previously, everything would have looked OK, but it really wouldn't be.

```
31 % set opponent=($opponent Brazil)
32 % echo $opponent
Switzerland, 1-1 Colombia:2-1 Romania:0-1 Brazil
33 % _
```

It looks fine until I try to access the different values. When I add the Brazil score, I expect to add it like so:

```
% set opponent[4]=Brazil:0-1
```

But when I use the `echo` command, I see this:

```
Switzerland, 1-1 Colombia:2-1 Brazil:0-1 Brazil
```

When the shell expanded the opponent variable when I assigned a new entry for Brazil, it expanded the first element properly as `"Switzerland, 1-1"`, but it did not include the quotations. This made the assignment statement read:

```
set opponent = ( Switzerland, 1-1 Colombia:2-1 Romania:0-1 Brazil )
```

Without the quotes, the shell interpreted the "Switzerland," and the "1-1" as separate words in the list. Even if I had included the quotes in the name the first time, it would have removed the quotes this time, and an additional add would have created the same problem.

The way to avoid this problem is to use the :q modifier. This causes each entry to be treated as a separate entry, even if there is a space present.

Finally, I can easily show the variables I have set.

```
34 % set
argv    ()
bad     1
cdpath  (/usr/james /usr/james/Docs )
cwd     /usr/james/dir1
history 100
home    /usr/james
opponent        (Switzerland:1-1 Colombia:2-1 Romania:0-1 Brazil)
path    (/usr/bin/X11 /usr/ucb /usr/james/bin /usr/lang /opt2/pure /usr/bin .
 /utilities/netnews /usr/openwin/bin /usr/progressive/bin /usr/5bin ./bin
 /usr/local /usr/local/bin /usr/hub/bin /usr/hub/newsprint/bin
 /opt2/sentinel/bin /opt2/insight/bin.solar!
is /usr/lib/uucp /usr/ccs/bin /utilities/netnews)
prompt  %
shell   /bin/csh
status  0
term    xterm
tty     /dev/pts/6
user    james
```

Along with some standard variables, you can see the opponent variable on the list.

setenv

The set command only works with shell variables. To create or alter the values of environment variables, setenv must be used.

The syntax for setenv is

```
setenv [ VAR [ word ] ]
```

With no arguments, setenv displays a list of all the environment variables and their values. It is a built-in equivalent to the printenv command found on some systems, but as a built-in command it will be faster than an external program. With a single argument, a variable is created and assigned a null value. With two arguments, the second argument is the value assigned to the variable named by the first argument.

The assignment of environment variables is a bit different from shell variables. There are no arrays, for starters, and an effort to assign an array will generate the message `Badly placed ()'s`. Spaces can be included in environment variables, if the string is quoted:

```
35 % setenv STRING "A string"
36 % echo $STRING
A string
37 % _
```

Furthermore, later assignments of this variable can be easily accomplished using quotes:

```
37 % setenv STRING2 "$STRING"
38 % echo $STRING2
A string
39 % _
```

Environment variables are passed to child processes and can be a means of passing important information. A good example comes from efforts to compile a program. For example, you may want to use the compiler gcc, whereas the default compiler is cc. You can get around this by using the following example:

```
39 % setenv CC gcc
40 % make
gcc -o program program.c
41 % _
```

Here, you want the make process to understand that you want a different compiler than the default. The make process will understand that if a CC environment variable is present, its value should be used as a compiler instead of the default.

Another good example comes from X Windows. All X clients need a DISPLAY variable defined to identify which X server to use and basically which machine to display the program. When X is invoked, the DISPLAY environment variable is set to the host machine, but if you then log in to a remote machine, you'll need to set the DISPLAY variable yourself to get the output on your screen. I do this as follows:

```
41 % setenv DISPLAY sagarmatha:0.0
42 % xterm
43 % _
```

Any xterm and any subsequent X application will display on my sagarmatha display, assuming I have given it permission to do so.

Note: It is a common convention in UNIX to use all capital letters for environment variables. This will help distinguish them from shell variables.

unset

The unset command is used to remove shell variables from the current environment. We first saw this command on Day 5, but we will look at it a bit more here.

Syntax

The syntax for unset is

```
unset pattern
```

The pattern is a normal UNIX file-matching pattern, and any variables that match the pattern are deleted.

To continue with the previous example, the World Cup is finally over, so I no longer need to follow the opponents with the opponent variable. I can easily delete it, as follows:

```
43 % unset o*
```

Note that this matches opponent, and only opponent. After this command is run, the command set produces the following output:

```
argv    ()
bad     1
cdpath  (/usr/james /usr/james/Docs )
cwd     /usr/james/dir1
history 100
home    /usr/james
path    (/usr/bin/X11 /usr/ucb /usr/james/bin /usr/lang /opt2/pure /usr/bin .
 /utilities/netnews /usr/openwin/bin /usr/progressive/bin /usr/5bin ./bin
 /usr/local /usr/local/bin /usr/hub/bin /usr/hub/newsprint/bin
 /opt2/sentinel/bin /opt2/insight/bin.solar!
is /usr/lib/uucp /usr/ccs/bin /utilities/netnews)
prompt  %
shell   /bin/csh
status  0
term    xterm
tty     /dev/pts/6
user    james
```

The opponent variable is gone.

DO	DON'T
DO be careful with pattern matches. In this author's opinion, pattern matching for unset is a bad thing. The user is better off just typing in the whole variable name. **DON'T** use the pattern * if you must use patterns. This will remove every shell variable, including those essential to the continued functioning of the shell	

> program. The path would be gone, history would be elided, and you'd no longer have a home. You wouldn't even have a prompt to indicate when the command terminated. The only way to really correct this situation would be to immediately terminate the shell process and start again.

unsetenv

The companion to unset for environment variables is unsetenv.

Syntax

The syntax for unsetenv is

```
unsetenv variable
```

There is no pattern matching; the variable specified is removed from the environment.

Sometimes, environment variables are useful only for a short period of time. A good example is the CCFLAGS variable for makefiles. You may need to set it for debugging, but when you've completed that task, you no longer need it. Indeed, its continued existence is unnecessary. The following removes the variable:

```
44 % unsetenv CCFLAGS
```

The unsetenv command is nice, in that it doesn't have the pattern-matching capabilities of unset. Although you still can accidentally remove the wrong variable, you've got to explicitly do it with unsetenv, rather than by an accidental pattern match in unset.

@

The @ command is a bit unusual. For one thing, other commands discussed so far have all been made of alphabetic characters. Also, this command will perform arithmetic on a variable. It is very powerful and much needed for most real shell applications.

Syntax

The syntax for @ is

```
@ [ var = expr ]

@ [ var[n] = expr ]
```

With no arguments, @ will display a list of all shell variables and their values. With arguments, @ will set the variable or the *n*th word of a variable to the value of the specified expression.

Expressions can be tricky things in the C Shell. Because many of the operators for expressions also duplicate significant characters for the C Shell, care should be taken when you create expressions.

The only hard-and-fast rules are that if something could be interpreted as a word, use spaces. The command @q=$a/$b, where a is 10 and b is 5, will just return @q=$a/$b: Command not found. Proper syntax requires a space after the @ character, and it is advised for clarity to include spaces between each operator. The command @ q = $a / $b will set the value of q to 2. The best way to learn what is and isn't acceptable is to experiment. However, I've found you can't go wrong if you use spaces to separate every value.

There are many supported expressions. Just as in any other mathematical endeavor, there is a set of precedences for resolving expressions. These are listed in Table 8.1.

Table 8.1. Expression operator precedence.

Operator	Action
(...)	Grouping
~	One's complement
!	Logical negation
* / %	Multiplication, division, remainder[*]
+ -	Addition and subtraction[*]
<< >>	Bitwise left shift, right shift
< > <= >=	Less than, greater than, less than or equal to, greater than or equal to
== != =~ !~	Equal to, not equal to, file substitution pattern, file mismatch
&	Bitwise AND
^	Bitwise XOR
¦	Bitwise OR
&&	Logical AND
¦¦	Logical OR

* These operations are right associative.

Command groupings are the highest level of precedence. When the expression is evaluated, the contents of any parentheses are evaluated completely before other results are calculated. This is the same in as the C programming language and is used to group expressions. The value of @ q = 2 + 3 * 5 is different than @ q = (2 + 3) * 5. The first will yield the value 17 (2+15); the second will yield 25 (5*5).

One's complement is a bitwise operation. This will go through the variable's value and change every bit that is set to 0 to 1, and every bit that is set to 1 to 0. It isn't strictly negation, as the bit pattern for 1 and -1 are not directly opposite. Mathematical negation is best accomplished with a minus sign, or subtraction from zero. One's complement does have some specific uses, most notably for setting bit patterns for later bitwise operations.

Logical negation is used to change true and false values. In UNIX, any time a bit is set in a variable, it will also equate to TRUE in comparisons. Likewise, any 0 value is considered FALSE. So, a logical negation of any non-zero number becomes 0, and a logical negation of 0 becomes 1.

The first set of common arithmetic operations set multiplication, division, and remainder. Because all mathematics in the C Shell is integer-based, there can be no fractional results to division, so a remainder operator is provided. It is vital to note, though, that arithmetic in the C Shell is right associative. This is different from the C language, where arithmetic expressions are left associative.

Note: Right and left associativity are important concepts in mathematics. They determine the order of evaluation of operations of equal precedence. In school, we are taught that these operations are all left associative. When we see something like 4*5%3, we automatically think to evaluate 4*5 first, getting 20, then divide by 3 to get a remainder value, which is 2. This is left associative. For right associativity, we'd evaluate 5%3 first, getting a remainder of 2, and multiply that by 4, for the value 8. The C Shell approach is counterintuitive.

Another approach is post-fix operators. In these cases, the two values would be listed, then the operation performed. This uses the concept of the stack, as values are pushed and popped for operations. Hewlett-Packard calculators work using this technique. It eliminates the need for command groupings and command precedence, but how many of you know what 4 5 * 3 % really means?

To get around the problems of right associativity in the C Shell, the use of parentheses for groupings will ensure the proper evaluation order. The expression should become (4 * 5) % 3. This expression will be evaluated in the same way regardless of the associativity order.

Below multiplication, division, and remainder operations are the addition and subtraction operations. This order replicates the common practice in mathematics. If one needs to have an addition completed before multiplication, then a grouping is required. These are also right-associative operations, so groupings may be recommended anyway.

The bitwise shifts are used to change bit patterns for masks and the like. Because the characters used to identify the operation are also important characters for file I/O redirection, any time these characters appear in an expression, they must be placed in a grouping.

The logical operators for greater than, and so on, are also the same as command separation characters, so the same caution about parentheses applies. These operations will return 1 or 0, based on whether the expression is true or false. These are regular integer values as well and can be used in any arithmetic expression.

The equals (==) and not-equals (!=) operators are used to compare strings. This sets them apart from the above operators, which work on integer values. These operators still work with integers, because any number can be represented by a string.

The pattern-matching operators are interesting. They take two operands. The left operand is a string, and the right operand is a file-matching pattern. They are useful when attempting to determine if a value fits a specific need, and they are easier than using a switch statement.

Note: The ~ operation in the C Shell is different from the ~ operation in awk. Both have the same basic concept, except that the C Shell uses the file-matching conventions, and awk uses a regular expression for matching. Regular expressions in UNIX are powerful pattern-matching tools, but they can become very complicated to read and difficult to understand from a cursory glance. File expansion is comparatively easier and is the basis for all C Shell pattern matching.

The next three operations, in terms of precedence, are all bitwise operations. They all go back to basic logic. Each bit in one operand is compared to the same positional bit in the second operand. The results of the comparison are listed in Table 8.2.

Table 8.2. Bitwise operations.

Bit Values	AND (&)	XOR (^)	OR (¦)
0 0	0	0	0
0 1	0	1	1
1 0	0	1	1
1 1	1	0	1

Bitwise operations are useful for matching masks and the like. The last two operators in the table are logical operations. These are the same as the C language operations, which can be used to build complex conditional statements.

Operations and expressions are also useful in writing C Shell programs, as described on Day 11, "Programming with the C Shell."

There are some additional operators that originated in the C language and have found their way into the C Shell. They are the single operand operators, +=, *=, and so on. A command @ q *= expr is expanded to @ q = $q * (expr). This is a convenient shorthand when you need to modify a variable.

Finally, the postfix increment and decrement command are also available. These are @ q++ and @ q--. These provide a very handy shorthand for writing loops and other operations to step through a series of numbers.

Note: Expressions, which are absent in the Bourne Shell, are a very powerful addition to the C Shell. To perform any arithmetic calculation in the Bourne Shell, the command expr must be called. It can only perform simple operations. To perform 4 * 5 % 3, you'd need two separate calls to expr.

Miscellaneous Commands

Several commands are difficult to categorize. In a sense, each stands alone as its own category. Some of the more common ones are alias, echo, history, time, repeat, and umask. These are described here.

alias and *unalias*

The capability to create aliases for commands is one of the biggest benefits of the C Shell. Day 3, "Command Substitution, Aliases, and Filename Generation," covered some of the mechanisms to create aliases and why you would want to create them.

Syntax

The syntax for alias and unalias is

```
alias [ name [ def ] ]

unalias pattern
```

With both arguments, alias assigns the value of *def* to the alias name. The *def* is a word list that may contain escaped history substitution syntax. The name cannot be alias or unalias. If only the name is provided, the current definition for that alias is provided. If no arguments are present, all aliases will be displayed.

The unalias command accepts a C Shell file-matching pattern and deletes all aliases that match that pattern.

There are many different reasons to use aliases. Some of the best targets for aliases are frequently used commands and also commands that are frequently mistyped. Setting up an alias is simple:

```
45 % alias q /usr/lib/sendmail -bp
```

Now, whenever q is typed at the command prompt, the command /usr/lib/sendmail -bp is executed. (This command is used to examine the mail queue, so q is an apt alias.) Some simple aliases are

```
46 % alias ls ls -F
47 % alias env setenv
48 % alias cls clear \; ls
```

Event 48 above illustrates an important consideration for aliasing: remember to escape characters relevant to the shell. The semicolon is a command separator, so without the escape, the shell would see the command alias cls clear followed by the command ls. The intent of the alias is to clear the screen, then provide an ls listing. To do this, you need to put two commands in the alias and separate them. The backslash (\) tells the command parser that you really want the semicolon as part of the current command. Then, in the alias, the presence of the semicolon indicates there are two commands to be run sequentially.

There are several characters that need backslashes to be properly understood. They include any characters that pertain to history expansion, any that pertain to file matching, any that pertain to I/O redirection, and any others that have special meaning to the shell. One interesting example is the alias `rmcore`:

```
49 % alias rmcore find . -name core -print -exec rm {} \\\;
```

The `find` command is used to search down a file tree for files that match a certain pattern. This `find` command looks for files named `core`, prints out the file name, and executes the `rm` command. The syntax of `find` is unusual; the arguments to an executed command are included in curly braces, and there must be a semicolon. But because the semicolon is important to the C Shell, it must normally be escaped with backslashes. Because this command is setting an alias to the `find` command, both the backslash and semicolon must be escaped again. Make sense?

> **Note:** On a UNIX system, a file named `core` is often one with some special importance. When a program fails catastrophically, a `core` file is generated. It is just a dump of the current program state in memory when the error occurred. These errors can be division by zero, accessing illegal memory, and the like. There are several tools that can be used to debug programs; they will interpret the `core` and allow the user to attempt to determine why a program failed.

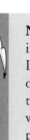

Arguments can be passed to aliases. They follow the pattern of history substitution. To swap the names of two files, you might set up an alias like this:

```
50 % alias swap mv \!:1 /tmp/$$swap \; mv \!:2 \!:1 \; mv /tmp/$$swap \!:2
```

This alias calls three move commands. To swap the files, you want to move one to a temporary location, then move the other file to replace the first, and finally move the first from the temporary location to the original location of the second. The preceding alias does this.

The notation `!:1` comes from history substitution. This says take the first word of the history of the command, that is, the first argument. The zero word exists, and it is the actual command or alias name. Because the `!` character is significant, it must be escaped.

Another sample alias is one that will execute a vi command in an xterm.

```
51 % alias vi "xterm -T 'vi \!*' -g 80x62 -e vi \!*&"
```

This means whenever vi is typed, an xterm command will be called. The arguments to xterm indicate that the title of the window is the vi command and that vi is executed in a window. You don't escape the ampersand, because you want to run the vi in the background.

To remove aliases, use the unalias command. The same cautions apply for the use of unalias as for unset, in that unalias removes aliases that match a pattern.

Caution: Be careful with unalias to make sure you don't remove any aliases you might later need. Though the results are not as catastrophic as those generated by unset, you may find yourself needing to restart the C Shell session, anyway.

A good procedure before calling unalias is to list the existing aliases with alias and then determine if the pattern you plan to use is the best.

Event 52 illustrates a listing of all the aliases you've created so far this session.

```
% 52 alias
cls clear; ls
env setenv
ls ls -F
rmcore find -name core -print exec rm {} \;
swap mv !:¦ /tmp/736swap ; mv !:¦ ; mv /tmp/736swap !:z
vi xterm -T 'vi !*' -g80x62 -e vi !+&
```

echo

This command is used to print a line of output.

Syntax

The syntax for echo is

```
echo [ -n ] [ text ]
```

The value of text is printed on standard output. If -n is present, no newline is appended; otherwise, a newline is appended.

This echo should not be confused with the UNIX command /bin/echo. C Shell's echo is less powerful, in that it doesn't handle any of the escape sequences, but as a built-in command it will be much faster. The echo command is most useful in shell scripts for providing output to the user or for debugging. In the interactive shell, using echo is another way to examine the value of the environment.

```
53 % echo $cwd
/usr/james/Docs/Sams/Csh
54 % echo -n "What is your name:   "
What is your name:   %
```

Event 53 illustrates one of the many ways to determine the current working directory (the command pwd is another). The shell variable is expanded and echoed. The second echo statement shows the lack of a new line; note that the C Shell prompt appeared right after the statement was echoed. This is a good technique for prompting for any input in a shell script.

> **Note:** When you use the -n option, C Shell's echo truncates the output at the end of the last character of the last word on the command line, even if you type some spaces after that. The only way to force a space at the end is to quote the text string.

history

Perhaps the biggest advantage to the C Shell is its capability to remember what you have done and to present that information back to you. C Shell introduced the history mechanism many years before AT&T introduced the Korn Shell, which also includes history.

The syntax for history is

```
history [ -hr ] [ n ]
```

This displays the history list. If an integer *n* is given, only the *n*th most recent events will be displayed. With the -r option, the order of events is reversed, with the most recent first. If -h is given, then the history list is produced without the event numbers, in a file suitable for sourcing.

Day 1, "Introducing the C Shell," discussed how to use the history feature. A simple listing of a command history allows the user to repeat long commands without retyping the entire contents of the command.

Here, you see the last twenty commands executed, each associated with an event number:

```
55 % history
    47  cat FUTRES4
    48  awk '{ NAM=$1" "$2;printf "%-20s %d\n",NAM,$9 }' FUTRES4
    49  awk '{ NAM=$1" "$2;printf "%-20s %d\n",NAM,$9 }' FUTRES4 > FUTRES5
    50  vi FUTRES5
    51  cd .mailbox
    52  ls
    53  mail -f soccer
    54  mv soccer real.soccer
    55  cat 9407*/soccer > soccer
    56  mail -f soccer
    57  rm soccer
    58  ls
    59  mv real.soccer soccer
    60  cd 940704
    61  mail -f ross
    62  cd
    63  mail scottish-discussion@netcom.com < FUTRES5
    64  popd
    65  rn ca.earthquakes
    66  history
56 % _
```

The shell variable `history`, discussed on Day 4, determines how much history is available. Here, the variable is set to 20, so you see the 20 most recently executed commands. If only the last five were of interest, `history 5` would have shown this:

```
56 % history 5
    63  mail scottish-discussion@netcom.com < FUTRES5
    64  popd
    65  rn ca.earthquakes
    66  history
    67  history 5
57 % _
```

Because `history` is also a command, it appears as one of the history events.

Caution: The memory of `history` is not perfect. Multiline commands, such as those when a shell program is written interactively, are not fully remembered. Only the first line of the command is kept in the history list.

If I'd set the history variable to 100, the oldest events would scroll past my view. I could pipe the output through `more`, but if I knew that the event required was old, `history -r` would show the event:

```
57 % history -r
(deleted)
     6  pushd /usr/spool/uucp/.Log/uuxqt
     5  man csh
     4  rm core
     3  what core
     2  file core
     1  ls -l core
58 % _
```

I started a login session by looking at a core file but decided to just scrap it. Finally, I may just want to see what I've done. The history -h command will give me the history without the event numbers. This can be used to generate history files for later loading with the source command.

```
58 % history -h
vi FUTRES5
cd .mailbox
ls
mail -f soccer
mv soccer real.soccer
cat 9407*/soccer > soccer
mail -f soccer
rm soccer
ls
mv real.soccer soccer
cd 940704
mail -f ross
cd
mail scottish-discussion@netcom.com < FUTRES5
popd
rn ca.earthquakes
history
history 5
history -r
history -h
59 % _
```

If this were saved into a file, this could be loaded into a later invocation of C Shell as a preset history. Between login sessions, such a file can keep a memory of important commands. The command options can be used in any combination to generate output.

Note: One technique for writing simple scripts is to execute the commands at the C Shell prompt, and when you are satisfied, run history -h with the appropriate number of recent commands, with output redirected to a file. With some quick editing to add the magic cookie #!/bin/csh -f to the top and to delete the history command from the bottom, you have a simple C Shell program written directly from history.

Once users are familiar with the C Shell, `history` becomes one of the heaviest used features. If the interactive session of a C Shell expert were to be transcribed, it would not look like a series of recognized commands. Instead, it would be filled with cryptic access to the history list. Commands such as `!-2` or `mv !$ !-2:$` are the mark of a C Shell expert.

time

The `time` command is one that helps provide some information on how the system is using its resources. The `time` command will give you the amount of system time and user time used to complete a command.

Syntax

The syntax for `time` is

```
time [ command ]
```

If a command is present, `time` reports on the elapsed time for the command. If there is no command, then `time` reports the elapsed time for the C Shell.

By default, `time` reports the number of seconds of CPU time consumed by the user for the process, the number of seconds used by the kernel, the total elapsed time, the fraction of CPU time of the elapsed time, the average amount of shared memory used, the average amount of data space used, the number of block input operations, the number of block output operations, the number of page faults, and the number of swaps. On some systems, only the first four values are implemented.

> **Note:** The `time` command brings up several UNIX-specific terms.
>
> The *kernel* is the main program driving the UNIX system. It is responsible for the allocation of resources and the execution of commands.
>
> The CPU, central processing unit, is the part of a computer that performs the actual work. *User CPU time* is that which performs calculations and manipulations of data in the program's memory. *System CPU time* is that used to access system resources, such as disk I/O and other system calls.
>
> *Shared memory* is system memory that can be accessed by more than one process at any given time. Normally, when memory is allocated, it is dedicated to a single process.
>
> UNIX operates on a paging system, where a process consists of one or more pages in memory. These pages are swapped in and out of main memory as

> needed, ideally to optimize the speed of a process. A *page fault* occurs when
> an attempt is made to access a page that has been swapped out of main
> memory.
>
> UNIX memory management is based on *swapping*. When a process has a
> page that needs to be in main memory and there is a page of memory that
> has not been accessed for a while, the unaccessed page is swapped with the
> needed page.

Running `time` is simple. Just type `time` at the command line:

```
58 % time
689.0u 297.0s 203:11:33 0% 0+0k 0+0io 0pf+0w
59 % _
```

The output indicates that the current invocation of the C Shell has been running for 203
hours, 11 minutes, and 33 seconds. In that time, 689 CPU seconds have been used by
the process, and 297 CPU seconds of system time, probably `forks` and `execs`, have been
required.

The `time` command can also be used to determine how system resources are employed
by a process. All that the user needs to do is prepend the command with `time` to generate
the report:

```
60 % time ./amfoot < a3
65.0u 40.0s 3:29 50% 0+0k 0+0io 0pf+0w
61 % time ./statcalc < /usr/games/Foot/solo/statdat
8.0u 1.0s 0:15 58% 0+0k 0+0io 0pf+0w
62 % _
```

Here, I run the program `amfoot`, which runs for about three and a half minutes, of which
about half the time is spent in the CPU. When not in the CPU, the process is either
preempted or waiting for I/O. More than a minute of CPU time was spent on user
operations.

Next, the program `statcalc` runs in fifteen seconds. It spends a little over half the time
in the CPU and is heavily user oriented. This makes sense, because `statcalc` was written
to manipulate a large array of values.

The output of `time` can be customized. Day 4 discussed the `time` variable, used to
customize the output of `time`. The `time` variable takes two values; the first is a threshold
in CPU seconds for reporting time, and the second is a format string. The format
parameters are in Table 8.3.

Table 8.3. Time format parameters.

Parameter	Explanation
%D	Average amount of unshared dataspace (Kbytes)
%E	Elapsed time
%F	Page Faults
%I	Block input operations
%K	Unshared stack size
%M	Maximum memory used
%O	Block output operations
%P	Percentage of elapsed time used by the CPU
%S	System CPU time
%U	User CPU time
%W	Number of swaps
%X	Shared memory use

If I want to see only the elapsed time, percentage of CPU time, and maximum memory, I'd set the variable and run `time`:

```
62 % set time=(0, "Elapsed time %E, CPU time %P, Maximum memory %M" )
63 % time
Elapsed time 203:29:21, CPU time 0%, Maximum memory 0
64 % _
```

Text included in the string can be used to help make the output less cryptic.

Note: Many systems do not implement the resource modifiers beyond CPU time and elapsed time, or only implement those requests if system accounting is turned on. If you need that data and it isn't produced, check with your system administrator or contact the support line for your operating system provider.

There are also non-built-in variants of `time`. The `/usr/bin/time` provides the same CPU usage numbers but is a separate process. On some systems, `timex` is also a provided command. Because these are actual programs, they use more resources than do the C Shell built-in commands.

repeat

The `repeat` command is used to repetitively execute the same command.

Syntax

The `repeat` syntax is

```
repeat count command
```

The command is run *count* number of times. The command must be a simple command, not a grouping in parentheses.

The `repeat` command is a good way to catch the attention of a user from a shell program:

```
64 % repeat 2 echo No space left on the device
No space left on the device
No space left on the device
65 % _
```

umask

The umask command is used to provide some extra security on a system by "masking" permissions when a file is created.

Syntax

The umask syntax is

```
umask [ value ]
```

With no argument, umask displays the file-creation mask. With an argument, which must be octal, the file creation mask is set. The default is 0.

When a file is first created, permissions for accessing the file must be set. This is usually represented as a three-digit octal number, where the digits represent permissions for the owner, the owner's group, and all the system users. The meanings of each permission digit are listed in Table 8.4.

Table 8.4. File permissions.

Digit	Meaning
0	No access
1	Execute access only (directory search permission)
2	Write access only (directory write only)
3	Write and execute access (search and write directory only)
4	Read only access (read contents only)
5	Read and execute access (read and search only)
6	Read and write access (read and write files)
7	Unlimited access

The meanings for directories are slightly different. Read permission says that you can list the contents of the directory. Write means that you can change the directory's contents by adding or removing files. Execute should be considered use permissions; it means you can use the contents of the directory. When a file is created, normally it is created with 666 permissions, giving everybody read and write access. Directories are normally created with 777 permissions. Executable files, created by compilers, are normally given 777 permissions. The value of the umask is subtracted from these creation permissions to determine the actual creation permission. Some normal umasks are 2, 22, and 27. Table 8.5 shows the file creation permissions with those umasks. The umask does not effect the operation of the chmod command.

Table 8.5. Umask effects.

Umask	File	Directory/Executable
0	666	777
2	664	775
22	644	755
27	640	750
77	600	700

Summary

Today, you've learned about several categories of built-in commands. You've covered the commands needed to navigate the file tree, and some of the tricks for navigating through symbolic links. You learned about the commands that change the shell's execution environment and the environment for the commands you execute. Finally, you wrapped up with some commands that make the job easier, `alias` and `history`, along with some other minor commands.

The directory navigation commands can be used to create a stack of directories, which can be accessed in some easy shorthands. The `pushd` command adds to this stack and allows you to move through it easily. The `popd` command removes directories from the stack, and `dirs` shows you the stack. Along with the basic `cd` command, you can now navigate the tree with ease.

The shell commands `set`, `unset`, `setenv`, and `unsetenv` are all used to create, change, and remove shell and environment variables. Some are useful for shell programs; other variables may change how other commands perform. The special `@` command is used to perform simple and complex expressions.

Finally, `alias` and `unalias` showed you how to create simple commands, and `history` showed you how to observe your past work and re-create it. The `echo` command taught simple output. The `time` command gave you a glimpse into how the system resources are allocated. The `repeat` command demonstrated a simple way to perform repetitive tasks, and `umask` showed how to change file permissions at creation time.

Related UNIX Topics

There are several reasons why commands are built into shells, as opposed to being separate programs. One set of commands must be built in, and for others it is a matter of convenience. To understand more about why this is so, you need to understand how the UNIX operating system handles processes.

> **Note:** Although C Shell and C Shell-like command execution environments may exist on many different operating systems, the C Shell was originally developed to be an easier-to-use shell for the Berkeley UNIX Operating System, BSD. It is that parentage that leads to some of the decisions for which commands were built-in.

UNIX is a multiprocessing operating system—many different programs are run simultaneously on UNIX machines. The exact number depends on the size of the machine, the number of CPUs, and the number of users. The number is usually set by a kernel parameter and is included when a new kernel is generated.

The kernel is a process that tracks system resources, including the processes currently running. The kernel does this by creating a process table when the kernel is started, with one available entry for each possible process. There is a one-to-one relationship between processes and process-table entries. Each process-table entry includes many pieces of information about the process, including process ownership, open file pointers, signal masks, process ID, parent process ID, and where the program resides in memory.

The memory of each process has several components. Among these is the "text" area of the process, where the actual code is stored. There is also a "data" area and a "stack" area. Additional memory can be accessed from a "heap." The data area includes constants and global variables. The stack is where automatically allocated variables are stored. Any variable declared inside a procedure is stored on the stack. Anything declared global to the process is in the data area.

Among those variables is a pointer to the environment structure, which is an array of strings of the form NAME=VALUE. The NAME is the identifier of the environment variable, and VALUE is the value. The last value in the array is always NULL.

To start a new process, the system first must create a new process entry. The UNIX system call for this is fork. The fork will copy all the existing process information into the next available process slot, except it will allocate a new process ID and change the parent process ID to reflect the old process ID. It also copies the existing memory for the process, including the entire text, data, stack, and heap. These consume a good bit of CPU time; fork is one of the most expensive calls in UNIX.

You should note that this includes copying the environment pointer and the entire environment. The new process has its own environment, inherited from the parent.

Now a new process exists, but it is a copy of the old process. The next task in starting a new command is to overlay the existing process with a new process. The UNIX system call for this is exec. With exec, all the old memory is freed, and a new memory image is created. The code for the new process is placed in the text area, the global variables and other data are initialized, and the stack is created. A segment of memory for the heap is assigned but is not accessible to the program until it is called. The first variables on the stack are a count of command-line arguments, a pointer to the array of those arguments, and a pointer to the environment. These two arrays are kept in the data area. Some entries in the process table are also changed; file pointers can be set to close on exec, and the signals are reset. The exec system call is also an expensive call in terms of resource and time consumption.

> **Note:** There is not a single system call named exec. Instead, exec refers to a family of system calls. There are six different forms of exec:
>
> execl: This takes a variable number of arguments. The first is always the path to the new process, then a list of arguments as a separate string followed by a NULL for the last argument. The second argument to execl is usually just the filename component of the path.
>
> execv: This takes two arguments—the path to the command and an array of strings for the command-line arguments.
>
> execle: This is the same as execl, except that after the NULL argument, an array of strings is passed for the environment.
>
> execve: This is the same as execv, except that a third argument is passed. This is an array of strings that describes the environment.
>
> execlp: This is the same as execl, except instead of a path that points to the new process file, the first argument is a file, and the PATH environment variable is searched to find a file that matches the filename. If the file is not executable, it is considered to be standard input to the Bourne Shell.
>
> execvp: This is the same as execv, except instead of a path that points to the new process file, the first argument is a file, and the PATH environment variable is searched to find a file that matches the filename. If the file is not executable, it is considered to be standard input to the Bourne Shell.

So, a new process now has its own environment. It begins as a copy of the parent process's environment, but it is independent of the parent process. No changes made here are reflected back to the parent. Instead, the changes are made in the child process's data area.

This is why commands that alter the environment must be built into the shell. If setenv, for example, were not built-in, the shell would fork and exec the new command, and then setenv would change the value of the variable in the new command, not touching the current shell. After setting the value, setenv would exit and the change would be lost. Commands discussed in this chapter that fall into this category are @, alias, cd, chdir, history, popd, pushd, set, setenv, umask, unalias, unset, and unsetenv. Although the

environment could be stored in temporary files on the hard disk, this would involve repeated disk accesses, which are even slower than calls to fork and exec. By caching these in memory, the C Shell operates at an acceptable speed.

Other commands, which are quick commands, are built-in, even though there is no requirement to do so. Because the fork and exec calls perform a lot of work, it is helpful in some cases to just build those small commands into the shell. The commands discussed in this chapter that fall into this category are echo and time. In both of these cases, programs already exist that perform the same task, in slightly different ways. The repeat command is a slightly different case. Because the command for repeat can include the built-in functions, for repeat to be a separate process, those built-ins would have to be included in repeat. This would create a larger than necessary process. In discussions of subsequent built-in commands, the reason the command is built-in will be discussed with the command.

Q&A

Q I want to change my directory to one with a symbolic link. How do I do that so I can return to my current directory?

A Your current directory is already on the directory stack. By using pushd to add the symbolic link, you can return to the previous directory in three different ways. The pushd command without an argument swaps the top two directories on the stack, taking you back to your previous directory but keeping the link as next on the stack. The pushd +1 command cycles the link to the bottom of the stack and makes your previous directory the top and current directory. Finally, popd removes the link from the stack and restores you to the previous directory.

Q The documentation for a program says I must set the variable LM_LICENSE_FILE to /usr/local/license.dat. I tried set, but the program still failed. What should I do?

The problem is that set only creates the variable for the local C Shell, and the variable will not be passed to the program. You need to set LM_LICENSE_FILE as an environment variable. The proper command is

```
setenv LM_LICENSE_FILE /usr/local/license.dat
```

Q I'm a clumsy typist, and I keep mistyping commands. Is there a way to chnage the keyboard?

A Although the C Shell can't help correct typos in command arguments, the alias capability will help correct mistyping some commands. First, use the history command to see if there are any frequent command typos. Then, use `alias` to set an alias for each typo to the proper command. Three that I find I use often are

```
alias xs cd
alias vf cd
alias gerp grep
```

Q **I'd like to rerun a command I executed a while back, but I don't remember the history event number.**

A By using `history`, you can get a complete listing of all your commands, up to the value of your history variable. Because it is an older command, `history -r`, which lists the history in reverse order, may be more useful. The event number is to the left of the command.

Workshop

This workshop will allow you to practice using some of the built-in commands presented today. The answers are provided in Appendix F, "Answers to Quizzes and Exercises."

Quiz

1. How do you move to the third directory on the directory stack?

2. How do you delete the third directory on the directory stack?

3. What is the fastest way to remove the C Shell variables `element` and `nelement`?

4. How do you check to see if a command is an alias?

5. What does `umask 027` mean?

Exercises

1. Experiment with aliasing commands.

2. On Day 1, you saw how to include the event number in the prompt. Often it is useful to also include the current working directory, but just setting prompt `set prompt="\!: $cwd` will not keep it up-to-date. Figure out a technique that will update the prompt with every directory change.

C Shell Built-In Commands, Part II

Introduction to Day 9

This chapter continues the in-depth tour of C Shell built-in commands. You will first learn about the commands that terminate the C Shell, how they are different, and why you would use them. After that, you will learn about the commands associated with job control, including the capability to move jobs to the background and to the foreground. You will learn which jobs can be placed in the background and why the background is a good option. You will also learn why some jobs must be run in the foreground. At the end of the chapter, you will learn about signal processing in the UNIX operating system and how it relates to job control.

Setting Today's Goals

Today, you will learn how to

☐ Terminate the C Shell by starting other commands

☐ Terminate the C Shell with a new login

☐ Terminate the C Shell—with extreme prejudice

☐ Place a program in the background

☐ Move programs from the background to the foreground, and vice versa

☐ Suspend execution of a program

☐ Terminate a program

☐ Send a signal to a program

☐ Wait for a background job to finish

Shell Termination Commands

There are four separate commands that terminate a C Shell. Two are commands that will replace the C Shell with another program, and two will just terminate the shell. It is important for you to know which command to use and how to use it.

exit

The exit command terminates the C Shell and can provide information to the process that invoked the shell.

Syntax

The syntax for `exit` is

```
exit [ expr ]
```

This command will terminate the shell and optionally return the value of the expression to the invocation environment.

The expression for `exit` must be formed to generate a single, integer value. If it is more than just an integer, the value must be enclosed in parentheses. The following are some examples of poorly formed `exit` commands:

```
1 % exit howitat
exit: Expression syntax
2 % exit 4+2
exit: Badly formed number
```

In both cases, because of the syntax error, `exit` failed to terminate the shell. The following are three examples of valid `exit` commands:

```
3 % exit
4 % exit 4
5 % exit ( 4 + 2 )
```

In the first case, `exit` is called with no value. This will be evaluated to zero. In the two subsequent examples, there are numerical returns. The second example returns the value 4 to the parent process, and in the last case, the expression (4 + 2) must be evaluated, and that value is returned.

The main use for `exit` is to return a value to the parent process, because this is the only way to directly send information to the parent. If the parent is another C Shell process, this return value will be found in the status variable. If the parent is other than the C Shell, then it will need to have a call to the `wait` system call to determine the return value. This system call has different formats on different flavors of UNIX. The value returned by `wait` will often have other components, including one to determine the signal that terminated the process, if relevant.

As a result, `exit` is most commonly found in C Shell programs. The return value is used to communicate to the parent process whether or not the shell program successfully accomplished its task. You will learn more about writing C Shell programs beginning on Day 11, "Programming with the C Shell."

The `exit` command must be a built-in command, because it terminates the shell and communicates to the parent.

exec

The `exec` command is one of two commands used to replace the C Shell with a new process.

The syntax for `exec` is

```
exec command
```

The C Shell is terminated and the new command is run in its place.

Yesterday, you learned a bit about how the UNIX system starts new processes—first with a call to `fork`, which creates a new process entry, then with a call to `exec`, which starts the new process. Every external command run by the C Shell is started in this fashion.

There is a reason why these are two different system calls. Although they are intimately tied together and they do perform two important, interrelated tasks, there are circumstances in which you might want to run one and not the other. Fork system calls may be made when two processes are necessary to handle different, but related, tasks. The UNIX command `cu` is one of these programs. One `cu` process will wait on the user's terminal to get input and transmit it to the appropriate communications channel, and the other will wait on that channel for input to send to the terminal. Because the two processes are essentially identical, apart from the specific I/O ports, the program will `fork` a copy of itself when the communications are established and alter the I/O ports.

Exec system calls may be made when a process has finished all of its requirements and a new process must be started. One process that uses `exec` without a `fork` is `/usr/bin/login`. Once a user has completed the login sequence correctly, his or her login shell is `exec`'ed by the login process. This technique exemplifies the concept where one program can perform a preparatory task, such as verifying a user, and then execute a different task.

The C Shell `exec` command is analogous to the `exec` system call. The current C Shell process is overwritten with a new process. It inherits the process ID, parent process ID, and entire environment, but the text, data, and stack segments of memory are overlaid with new information.

The C Shell `exec` command is not often used in interactive C Shell programming, except to perhaps change to another shell. In writing scripts, though, `exec` is occasionally used to run a final command after the script prepares to run the command.

In the interactive shell, `exec` is used to change from the C Shell to the Bourne Shell. In the following example, the C Shell is terminated, and the Bourne Shell is started:

```
6 % exec /bin/sh
$
```

The exec command must be built into the C Shell, because it actively alters the C Shell environment by terminating it.

When the exec'ed command is terminated, its return value is the value returned to the C Shell's parent. The same can be accomplished with the following code:

```
7 % command
8 % exit $status
```

The command exec command would be a shorthand for events 7 and 8.

9

login

The login command is used to terminate the C Shell and start a new login session.

The syntax for login is

```
login [ username ¦ -p ]
```

You use this syntax to terminate the login session and invoke the login command. Do not execute the .logout file. If no user is specified, login will prompt for a user. If -p is specified, the current environment is preserved.

When used simply, the login command is another shorthand for exec login. The C Shell's process slot is overwritten with the login process, and that process continues as if it were invoked by the init daemon.

> **Note:** At the top of all processes is the *init daemon*. It is usually process ID 1, and all processes can trace back their parents to this one process. Init is responsible for maintaining the machine's run state, cleaning up any orphaned processes, and making sure that certain processes are running at all times. Among these processes is the getty process. On each available terminal, getty prompts for a user ID, and when there is input, triggers the login process.

The login built-in will immediately spawn the /usr/bin/login command. (To differentiate the two, the built-in is called login and the UNIX command is called /usr/bin/login.) The /usr/bin/login command is used to begin a terminal session and to identify the user to the system. If no name is present, it will prompt for a username, and if there is a password required, it will prompt for the password. Terminal echoing is turned off while the password is typed so there won't be a written record.

If there are no lowercase letters in the first input line, /usr/bin/login assumes that it is connected to an uppercase-only terminal and sets the terminal I/O options accordingly. The /usr/bin/login is also fairly forgiving. If you make any mistakes in the login procedure, you are informed, and a new login prompt will appears. Only when you reach five consecutive failures is an entry logged in an admin file, and /usr/bin/login drops the line.

The /usr/bin/login command also has a timer included. If no one successfully logs into the system in that period of time, /usr/bin/login will silently terminate. In this case, the terminal will act as if the C Shell had been disconnected normally. When the login is successful, the appropriate accounting files are updated, and a new device owner, group, and permissions are set accordingly. The time of your last login is also displayed.

For a login to be valid, the user ID must exist in the /etc/passwd file, and the password must be matched from an encrypted string in either /etc/passwd or /etc/shadow. From that /etc/passwd entry, the new user ID and group ID are found, and these become the new user and group IDs of the process. The new working directory is also set from the /etc/passwd file, and finally, the "command interpreter," or login shell, is executed. This is not necessarily the C Shell but is whatever shell you have specified.

The command interpreter need not even be an interactive process. Commands such as /usr/bin/who can be the default shells. When their execution is completed, the session is over. With C Shell's login command, the current environment can be passed on to the new terminal session. This is not possible with exit or logout. If there is a specific environment variable that is needed by the next login session, the -p option is very handy.

The diagnostics for /usr/bin/login are

Login incorrect: The user name and/or the password are not correct.

Not on system console: This system requires that root may log in to only the system console, for security reasons. This prevents root logins on remote lines, requiring an administrator to log in as a regular user.

No directory! Logging in with home=/: The directory specified in /etc/passwd as the new working directory either doesn't exist or the user does not have permission to access it.

No shell: The command interpreter specified in the /etc/passwd file cannot be executed by that user.

C Shell's `login` is smart enough to recognize when the shell is the login shell. If it isn't, `login` will fail; `login` can be run only from the login shell.

logout

The `logout` command is another technique for terminating the C Shell process.

Syntax

The syntax for `logout` is

```
logout
```

It takes no arguments, and it terminates the shell.

The `logout` command is the fourth technique for terminating the C Shell. Like `login`, `logout` first checks that this session is the original login shell. If not, it will not allow the session to end and will report the message, `Not login shell`. In this case, `exit` should be used.

The `logout` command will not report a status value to the parent process. It will run the commands in the `.logout` file in the home directory before terminating. (These are the commands usually used to "clean up" after the user, such as clearing the screen.) The `.logout` file is also run by `exit`, but it is not run by `exec` or `login`.

EOF

There is a fifth way to terminate a C Shell, but it is not a command. The EOF character, usually set to Control+D on UNIX machines, tells the C Shell that there is no further input. The EOF character must be the only character on that line of input. When the C Shell sees this, it runs the `.logout` script and terminates.

The capability to terminate a C Shell session with EOF is disabled if the `ignoreeof` variable is set.

Job Control Commands

One of the powerful features of the C Shell is the capability to control the tasks run from the command line. These tasks are called *jobs*, and they can be run from the background or the foreground. The specifics of jobs and job control will be discussed on Day 14, "Jobs," but as a preview, the commands related to job control will be presented here.

jobs

The `jobs` command is used to show the jobs currently associated with a C Shell session.

Syntax

The syntax for `jobs` is

```
jobs [ -l ]
```

This lists the active jobs under the user's control. With the `-l` option, the process IDs of the jobs will also be listed.

The `jobs` command presents three pieces of information: a job number, which is used by other job control commands; job status; and the actual command. To determine this information, enter `jobs` on the command line:

```
9 % jobs
[2]  + Running                xterm -T vi c9 -g 80x62 -e vi c9
```

This example shows that job number 2 (job number 1 has already terminated) is currently running, and it is an `xterm` running `vi`. It is the command that I am using to type in this document at this very moment. If you trigger a command that requires input in the background, you get

```
10 % jobs
[2]  - Running                xterm -T vi c9 -g 80x62 -e vi c9
[3]  + Stopped (tty input)    amfoot
```

This tells you that the job `amfoot` is waiting for some input, but because it is in the background, it cannot be accessed. Bringing the job to the foreground requires the `fg` command, discussed next.

In each job listing, there will be a job marked with a + sign. This is the most recent job started or signaled. The job marked with the - sign is the previous + job. For the subsequent `bg` and `fg` commands, this + job does not need a job argument; otherwise, an argument must be specified.

fg

This command is used to bring jobs to the foreground.

Syntax

The syntax for `fg` is

```
fg [ % [ job ] ]
```

With no arguments, or with just `%`, `fg` brings the current job to the foreground. With a job number, it brings the specified job to the foreground.

When a jobs listing indicates that jobs are being run in the background, you have the option to pull those jobs back into the foreground for immediate processing. Sometimes, when a job is waiting for input or waiting to display output, it is necessary to bring the job back. At other times, it may be desired by the user.

Consider the case in which you have two processes running in the background, an xclock and an xterm. The jobs listing may look like the following:

```
11 % jobs
[1]  + Stopped (user)        xterm
[2]  - Running               xclock
12 %  _
```

You want to put the xterm in the foreground, because it is currently suspended. You can use either fg or fg %1 to bring it forward:

```
12 % fg %1
xterm
```

Now, the shell will not respond to commands until you either complete the xterm process or return the xterm process to the background. By allowing you to transfer a background job to the foreground, you can kick off a program that may need a lot of initial processing—such as setting up a database—in the background, and perform other tasks while it gets started. Meanwhile, the background process will continue until it completes or until it needs to interact with the user.

bg

Analogous to fg is the bg command, which places programs in the background.

Syntax

The syntax for bg is

```
bg [ %job ]
```

This runs the current, or specified, job in the background.

Jobs can exist in three states—foreground, background, and suspended. A foreground job overrides the user's ability to access the C Shell. A background job is hidden from I/O, and a suspended job is also hidden but not executing. Placing these suspended jobs in the background is the task of the bg command.

The following jobs output shows two commands, an xterm and an xclock.

```
13 % jobs
[1]  + Stopped (user)        xterm
[2]  - Running               xclock
14 %  _
```

The xclock is already running successfully in the background, but the status of the xterm is Stopped (user). It is a process that has been suspended by the user. Details on how to stop and start jobs are described in Day 14.

In the last chapter, I opted to move the xterm process to the foreground and waited until it finished before entering other C Shell commands. In this case, I can move the process to the background and use the C Shell to run more commands, including more xterms.

```
14 % bg %1
[1]     xterm &
15 % xterm&
[3] 17330
16 %
```

You will note a number next to the job number on the second xterm, which is started in the background. This is the process ID, a unique identifier for each process in UNIX.

> **Note:** The xterm process brings up a shell in a window on a UNIX system. As such, xterm processes are often run in the background and give you an opportunity to have multiple shell processes running at the same time. The xterms can also run other processes, such as event 51 in yesterday's lesson.

Jobs can be started in the background by appending an ampersand to the end of the command. These jobs print a process ID, as above, and will appear on listings by the jobs command.

The % Command

The % command is used to change the status of a job.

Syntax

The syntax for % is

%[*job*] [&]

This will bring either the current or indicated job to the foreground. If the ampersand is present, it will send the job to the background.

With no arguments, the most recently signaled job is brought to the foreground with this command. The %- command can be used to specify the previous job. Otherwise, a job number can be specified.

The % command is really just a shorthand for fg and bg. In the two previous examples, the fg and bg commands could have been substituted for the % command. Event 14 could

have been replaced with events 17 or 18 below. Event 17 will bring the xterm command to the foreground, and event 18 runs the xterm in the background.

```
16 % jobs
[1]  + Stopped (user)        xterm
[2]  - Running               xclock
17 % %
xterm
```

or

```
18 % % &
[1]      xterm &
19 %
```

For some of you, this shorthand may be convenient, but others of you may be confused by the cryptic nature of this command. If so, it is nothing to worry about; it just duplicates the function of other commands.

> **Caution:** If you plan to be a frequent user of the % command, you may want to consider changing your prompt from the default prompt. This can be done by setting the prompt variable, as was discussed on Day 4.

notify

The notify command is used to identify the processes for which the user expects to see status changes asynchronously.

The syntax for notify is

```
notify [ %job ]
```

This will set notification for the specified job or, if no argument is present, the most recently signaled job.

By default, the C Shell will not notify you of any changes in a process's status until it is required to print a new command prompt. This means that your current command, such as editing a file, running a more command, or examining output, is not interrupted. Instead, the shell waits until this task is finished.

You can change this default behavior globally by setting the notify shell variable. When the notify variable is set, the shell interrupts your process with status change information. This may be too intrusive for some users.

The notify command provides a simple way to selectively pick which commands need immediate attention and which do not. By specifying notify, your task will be interrupted by a message when the other job changes state.

You might be building a software package using make, but you don't want to wait for it to finish before doing some other editing. However, you do keep several other commands in the background and don't really care about them as much as the make. By using notify, you can run important tasks in the background that don't need user input, and in the foreground finish that status report for your boss, or even play a game. You might perform the following sequence of steps.

```
19 % make &
[3] 17723
20 % jobs
[1]  + Running             xclock
[2]  - Running             xbiff
[3]    Running             make
21 % notify %3
22 %
```

Then, you run another command, such as checking the man page for one of the functions needed by the software. Normally, when the make finishes, the shell will remain silent. Instead, you get the following output:

```
--More--(32%)
[2]    Done                make
```

This tells you that the make is already finished. You can exit your man page and determine either if the make was correct and you can test your program, or if you need to edit the code some more to allow it to compile.

kill

The kill command is used to send a signal to a process.

The syntax for kill is

```
kill [ -sig ] [ pid ] [ %job ] ...
kill -l
```

The kill command's default will send the terminate signal to the indicated process ID or job. Signals are given either by number or by name. There is no default process to receive the signal. Multiple processes and jobs can be sent a signal with the same kill command.

The kill -l command will list the signal names that can be sent.

The simplest form of communicating between processes is with signals, the details of which are discussed later in this chapter. Signals are the primary means of notifying processes of a change of state or of entering an illegal situation.

The default signal sent by `kill` is the terminate signal, `SIGTERM`. A process receiving this signal is being told to terminate execution, regardless of the current state of the process. The process is given an opportunity to perform any cleanup work necessary, and then it exits.

Most signals have specific default actions. Usually, these involve dumping a core and terminating execution, although some are set to be ignored. The programmer has the option to catch any signal, except `SIGKILL`, and perform any action desired. Two signals—`SIGUSR1` and `SIGUSR2`—are even provided to the programmer for interprocess communications.

> **Note:** A *core dump* is an image of an executable file from the system's memory at the moment a program failed. These core dumps are used by software developers to determine why a program failed and to remove bugs from programs using debugging tools such as `sdb`. To people who are not involved in software development, the core file is just a large file that they can't read. Tomorrow you will learn how to prevent core files from being generated.

> **Note:** `SIGKILL` cannot be caught for a simple reason; for any system there must be a way to stop runaway processes. `SIGKILL` is the technique for eliminating processes that cannot be otherwise stopped.

For example, you might have started the `xclock` program and have tired of watching the clock. First, you can get a listing of all your background jobs with `list` and then use `kill` to terminate the clock program.

```
22 % jobs
[1]  + Running               xterm
[2]  - Running               xclock
[3]    Running               xbiff
23 % kill %2
24 %
[2]    Terminated            xclock
24 %
```

Note that the extra carriage return was needed to see the termination notice; I did not have a `notify` variable set, nor did I run the `notify` command for that process.

Most of these job control commands are just sending signals. Stopping and starting jobs are done with `SIGSTOP` and `SIGCONT`.

The character sequence Control+C will also send a terminate signal to a process running in the foreground. This character sequence is fairly standard, but the sequence may be different on different systems, so if Control+C doesn't work, check with your system administrator.

stop

The `stop` command is used to halt jobs in their tracks.

Syntax

The syntax for `stop` is

```
stop [ %job ]
```

This stops the current or specified job.

The `stop` command is simply a shorthand for `kill -STOP %`. The stop signal is used to interrupt processing without terminating the job. This allows you to move a job between background and foreground, and it allows you to halt a job to prepare a modified input file.

Using the preceding example, I have

```
24 % jobs
[1]  + Running           xterm
[2]  - Running           xclock
[3]    Running           xbiff
25 % stop %2
[2]  + Stopped (signal)  xclock
26 % jobs
[1]  - Running           xterm
[2]  + Stopped (signal)  xclock
[3]    Running           xbiff
27 %
```

The `xclock` will remain frozen at that time until the job is restarted by moving it into a background or foreground position or by sending the continue signal.

> **Note:** The C Shell does not behave as you might expect when a stopped
> process is sent the SIGCONT with the kill command. The process will resume
> execution, as expected, but the jobs listing will still indicate that the job is
> stopped with a signal. To make matters worse, the stop command will not
> re-stop the job, as the C Shell thinks the job is already stopped. Following
> the preceding example, I have
>
> ```
> 27 % kill -CONT %2
> 28 % jobs
> [1]  - Running                 xterm
> [2]  + Stopped (signal)        xclock
> [3]    Running                 xbiff
> 29 % stop %2
> %2: Already stopped
> 30 %
> ```
>
> Meanwhile, the xclock is actually running.

For a job running in the foreground, the Control+Z sequence will usually send the stop
signal to the process and return you to the C Shell prompt. If you can not suspend a few
processes with Control+Z, check with your system administrator to determine the
correct sequence.

suspend

The suspend command is used to suspend the current C Shell.

Syntax

The syntax for suspend is

suspend

It will suspend the current C Shell process as if the process had been sent the SIGSTOP
signal.

There are some occasions on which you may wish to stop the current shell immediately,
without terminating execution. The most common situation is when you have used the
su command to change your effective user ID to somebody else, and you need to keep
switching between the two user IDs.

A good example is one of someone needing root access to modify files for a process to run:

```
30 % myproc
Error, cannot write to /tmp/foo
31 % su
Password:
# chmod 0666 /tmp/foo
# suspend

Stopped (signal)
32 % jobs
[1]  + Stopped (signal)      su
33 % myproc
OK, we ran
34 % fg
su
# exit
35 % _
```

The preceding sequence shows a process that attempts to create a temporary file, foo. The file already exists, however, and I cannot write to it. So, I use su to gain root permissions and change the permissions on the file. Then, I suspend the root shell (in case there are other problems) and run the process as my regular user ID. When the process completes successfully, I resume the root shell to exit.

> **Note:** The suspend command is smart enough to recognize the login shell and does not permit you to stop the login shell. If it were possible to suspend the login shell, you would be frozen out of performing any commands until either you logged into another terminal and sent the initial login the SIGCONT signal, or the superuser sends the same signal to your login process.

Suspended shells are treated like other suspended processes and can be moved to the foreground as needed.

The *wait* Command

The wait command is used to wait for all background processes to terminate.

The syntax for wait is

wait

The command waits for background jobs to finish or for the command to be interrupted by a signal.

When you run a group of background jobs, it is sometimes convenient to know when they have all finished. When there is a single job running, you can put it in foreground, and that will be adequate. You will be able to see when it is finished. But when there are multiple jobs running, `wait` is the only real alternative.

```
35 % jobs
[1]   + Running          xterm
[2]   - Running          xclock
[3]     Running          xbiff
36 % set notify
```

Here I have set the `notify` variable so I know when each job completes.

```
37 % wait
[2]     Terminated        xclock

[3]     Terminated        xbiff

[1]     Done              xterm

38 %
```

It is only after each of the three background processes is terminated that the `wait` process returns you to a command prompt.

If one or more of the processes is time-consuming or if a problem occurs with a process, such as the need to send output to the terminal or receive user input, the `wait` process can be terminated with Control+C. The `wait` command cannot be stopped with Control+Z. This key sequence is silently ignored.

Because `wait` directly affects the user environment, it must be a built-in command.

Summary

In this chapter, you have learned about two classes of commands: the commands to terminate the C Shell, and the commands to control the jobs running in a C Shell.

You should know the differences between the commands `exit`, `logout`, `login`, and `exec`, and when to use them. You have learned that both `exit` and `logout` will run the `.logout` script from your home directory, but `login` and `exec` will not.

The details of job control are discussed on Day 14, but you have already learned the basic commands for manipulating jobs invoked from your C Shell. You have learned how to stop and start jobs, how to move them from background to foreground, and how to suspend a child shell process.

Related UNIX Topics

One subject touched on briefly in the section on job control commands is that of signal processing. One key feature of any operating system is to provide some technique for processes to communicate. This Interprocess Communication (IPC) can range from something quite simple, such as writing a piece of data to a file and having a second process read that file, to using highly complicated data structures, such as semaphores.

The first true form of IPC in UNIX was the signal, and it remains one of the more common and more powerful techniques. Initially, the kernel was the sender of a signal, indicating that the program was performing an illegal operation. The signal list has since expanded to over 30 signals. Some are common to all flavors of UNIX, and others are specific to certain vendors. The POSIX standard for defining UNIX allows vendors to add any signals necessary for their new features, so long as the standard signals are present. Table 9.1 shows the current signals on Solaris 2, a System V Release 4 compliant UNIX operating system.

Table 9.1. UNIX Signals.

Name	Value	C Shell (int)	System Condition
SIGHUP	1	HUP	Hangup, the terminal is disconnected.
SIGINT	2	INT	Interrupt the process.
SIGQUIT	3	QUIT	Quit the process.
SIGILL	4	ILL	Illegal instruction.
SIGTRAP	5	TRAP	Trace trap.
SIGIOT	6	(none)	IOT instruction.
SIGABRT	6	ABRT	Abort process.
SIGEMT	7	EMT	EMT instruction.
SIGFPE	8	FPE	Floating point exception.
SIGKILL	9	KILL	Kill the process.
SIGBUS	10	BUS	Bus error.
SIGSEGV	11	SEGV	Segmentation violation.
SIGSYS	12	SYS	Bad argument to a system call.

Name	Value	C Shell (int)	System Condition
SIGPIPE	13	PIPE	Bad write to a pipe.
SIGALRM	14	ALRM	Alarm clock.
SIGTERM	15	TERM	Software termination signal.
SIGUSR1	16	USR1	User defined signal 1.
SIGUSR2	17	USR2	User defined signal 2.
SIGCHLD	18	CLD	Death of child signal.
SIGPWR	19	PWR	Power-failure restart.
SIGWINCH	20	WINCH	Window size change.
SIGURG	21	URG	Urgent socket condition.
SIGPOLL	22	POLL	Pollable event occurred.
SIGIO	22	(none)	Socket I/O possible.
SIGSTOP	23	STOP	Stop the process.
SIGTSTP	24	TSTP	User stop request from tty.
SIGCONT	25	CONT	Stopped process can be continued.
SIGTTIN	26	TTIN	Background process needs input.
SIGTTOU	27	TTOU	Background process needs output.
SIGVTALRM	28	VTALRM	Virtual timer expired.
SIGPROF	29	PROF	Profiling timer expired.
SIGXCPU	30	XCPU	CPU limit exceeded.
SIGXFSZ	31	XFSZ	File size limit exceeded.
SIGWAITING	32	WAITING	Process wait returns are blocked.
SIGLWP	33	LWP	Special signal used by threads library.
SIGFREEZE	34	FREEZE	Special signal used by CPU.
SIGTHAW	35	THAW	Special signal used by CPU.

9

Signals up to 31 are standard for POSIX. The signals above 31 are specific to Solaris 2 and are related to process threads.

Each signal has a default action associated with catching the signal. These actions can normally be changed or overridden by the programmer. The SIGKILL and SIGSTOP signals cannot be changed by the programmer. When the process catches these signals, the default action always occurs.

Each signal has a special meaning and a special default. SIGHUP is the hangup signal. It is received by a process when a modem connected to the computer drops its carrier. SIGHUP is then sent to all processes associated with that terminal line. The default action is for the process to exit.

SIGINT is an interrupt signal. It is sent from the keyboard using Control+C, and it tells the process to stop execution. The default action is for the process to exit.

SIGQUIT is the quit signal. It is related to SIGINT, except that when the process exits, it will generate a core dump. The key sequence Control+¦ (vertical bar) will send the quit signal to a foreground process. After generating the core, the program will exit.

SIGILL indicates that an illegal instruction has been sent to the CPU. This may occur from an illegal branch instruction in the assembly code of a process. The default action is to dump a core and exit.

SIGTRAP is sent to a process when the process breakpoint trap is triggered. These traps are controlled by the ptrace() system call and are useful for process debugging. The default action is to dump a core and exit.

SIGABRT is sent when the process aborts. This signal is created by a call to abort() in the program. A core is dumped, and the program exits.

SIGEMT happens when the emulator fails. The default action is to dump a core and exit.

SIGFPE happens when an illegal arithmetical instruction is attempted, such as division by zero. The CPU generates this signal when the math error occurs, and the default action is to dump a core and exit.

SIGKILL is not catchable. The program will terminate immediately, with no process cleanup or core file generated. This is the "kill with extreme prejudice" signal.

SIGBUS is an I/O bus error. Attempts to read or write beyond the boundaries of a program's memory will result in a bus error. When caught, the process will dump a core and exit.

SIGSEGV is the segmentation violation. This will occur when a process attempts to access a different segment of memory illegally. An example might be trying to assign a variable's value to an address in the text segment. When caught, a core is dumped and the process terminates.

SIGSYS indicates that a bad system call has been attempted. These signals are rare, but when they occur, a core dump is generated and the program exits.

SIGPIPE indicates that an attempt has been made to write to a pipe where the receiving end has already exited. The program will not dump a core, but it will exit. Usually, this occurs when a child command has already terminated abnormally.

SIGALRM is sent to the process when the "alarm clock" goes off. The process can set the clock to send the signal with the alarm() system call. This is usually used when there are some time constraints for the system to complete a specific task. Alarm signals are normally caught with special handlers, but the default is to exit the program without a core dump.

SIGTERM is the software termination signal. Although it seems to have the same meaning as SIGINT, the interrupt is driven from the keyboard, and the termination signal comes in from another process. The default is to exit, although it can be caught, and cleanup performed.

SIGUSR1 and SIGUSR2 are user-defined signals. Any software engineer can use them to trigger a specific response in another process. These responses are defined by the designer of the receiving process, but if no provisions are made, the process will terminate.

SIGCHLD (or SIGCLD) is often called the "death of child" signal. Historically, it affected whether dead processes would remain as zombies in the process table until the parent cleaned them up. Now, it indicates to the receiving process that the status of a child has changed. By default, it is ignored.

SIGPWR indicates that there was a power failure, but the system was able to restart without a reboot. Catching this signal is useful if you are working on a system prone to crashing, as it may allow time to clean up. The default is to ignore this signal.

SIGWINCH indicates that the window for a process has changed size. This can be ignored, although catching it may allow the program to adjust its I/O parameters.

SIGURG indicates that an urgent situation exists on a socket. A *socket* is another type of IPC that allows the transfer of data. SIGURG occurs when some data is transferred out of the bandwidth of the socket, indicating that there may be some data loss. The default is to ignore this signal.

SIGPOLL indicates that there is a readable event on an I/O stream. The default is to exit the program.

SIGSTOP and SIGTSTP are signals to stop a process. The process will remain active, but no instructions will be executed. SIGSTOP cannot be caught, although SIGTSTP can be caught and ignored.

SIGCONT will tell a stopped process to resume execution.

SIGTTIN and SIGTTOU indicate that a process needs access to a tty for input or output. These signals will occur when a C Shell process is in the background. The default is to stop the process and wait for the problem to be corrected by the user.

SIGVTALRM and SIGPROF are triggered when the virtual timer and the profiling timer expire. The default is to exit the program.

SIGXCPU and SIGXFSZ are triggered when C Shell resource limits are exceeded. These limits can be set with the limit command, discussed in the next chapter. When the limits are exceeded, a core is dumped and the process exits.

The signal function sets what to do when a signal is received. There are two default functions available for signals, SIG_IGN and SIG_DFL. SIG_IGN is used to set a signal's action to be ignored. When that signal is received, the process will do nothing differently. SIG_DFL is used to restore a signal's actions to the default, described previously. Otherwise, the programmer needs to create a process to perform the actions required when a signal arrives. These actions range from corrective behavior to just cleaning up temporary files and exiting.

Q&A

Q What are the differences between exit and logout?

A The exit command will pass a return value back to the calling process, as specified by the expression on the command line. The exit command will always end a shell process, while logout is only valid for a login shell. Furthermore, logout only works with the login shell.

Q Why have a separate command login when exec /usr/bin/login will do the same thing?

A The login command is shorter to type, and login also allows you to pass your current environment to the new login environment with the -p option.

Q I've started a long command, and I meant to put it in the background. How do I do that?

A First, type Control+Z at the terminal. This will suspend execution of the process without deleting the work done. Then, type bg to place the process in the background.

Q How will I know when the process is complete?

A When you finish a command and a prompt is about to be issued, the C Shell will check to see if any jobs have changed their status. If so, you will be notified. If you need immediate feedback, you can either set the notify variable or use the notify command to indicate that a process should notify you on status changes asynchronously.

Workshop

This workshop tests your knowledge of C Shell termination and job control commands. You can check your answers in Appendix F, "Answers to Quizzes and Exercises."

Quiz

1. How do you send the value 3 back from the shell to its parent process?

2. What is the .logout script?

3. How do you determine what jobs are running? How do you determine their status?

4. How do you move a background job that is waiting for input to the foreground?

5. How do you terminate a background job?

6. How do you put a C Shell process in the background?

Exercise

1. Experiment with moving jobs between the background and the foreground. Notice that interactive programs will quickly stop to wait for input while in the background, yet noninteractive programs will keep running.

WEEK
2

C Shell Built-In
Commands,
Part III

Introduction to Day 10

Today you will finish the in-depth tour of C Shell built-in commands. The commands today are in three groups: one for the hash table, one for resource limitation, and one for miscellaneous commands. You will learn what the hash table is about and how it is used in the C Shell. You will also learn how to manipulate the hash table. Next, you will learn about how the C Shell watches certain system resources and about how your use of those resources can be limited. The last grouping of commands are those that defied categorization. These commands are used to evaluate commands and to run commands in the current shell. At the end of the chapter is a more detailed discussion of the UNIX operating system, particularly about how it manages system resources for all users.

Setting Today's Goals

Today, you will learn how to

- ☐ Examine statistics on the performance of the hash table
- ☐ Create a new hash table
- ☐ Disable the hash table
- ☐ Limit your use of UNIX resources
- ☐ Change the priority of your commands
- ☐ Disable the hang-up signal, SIGHUP
- ☐ Evaluate a command
- ☐ Load a command history
- ☐ Check global file expansion

Hash Table Commands

At the heart of C Shell command execution is the hash table. If a command is not built into the shell, it must be found somewhere on the path before it can be executed. For the Bourne Shell, this means each element of the path is checked to determine whether a file with the same name as the command exists, and then that file is exec'ed after a fork. The C Shell builds a hash table of all possible commands and keeps the hash table in memory. The C Shell uses this hash table to eliminate from the path directories that have no

applicable files. This way, when the shell searches down the list of directories in the path, it will skip unnecessary checks.

Three commands are used with the hash table. The `hashstat` command determines the effectiveness of the hash table, and consequently, of your path. The `rehash` command rebuilds the hash table, and the `unhash` command removes the hash table from consideration.

Note: A hash table is one of the fastest ways to access data using a keyword. In the past, data access came via a straight, flat file. The file could be ordered, and you'd step down each entry until you found the entry you desired. A dictionary is designed like this, with the words in alphabetical order. For a computer program, though, this isn't very efficient, because any number of lookups could be required to reach a given entry, and if the entry were near the end of the list, the number of lookups could be huge. For a randomly selected word, the number of entries checked will average half the total entries in the table. For a large table, this is unacceptable.

The next historical step was the binary tree. In this case, each entry has two pointers: one to an entry before and one to an entry after the current entry. Given that the tree is properly balanced, it will never be more than $\log_2 n$ deep, where n is the number of entries, rounded up to the next integer. That is the maximum number of checks to find the desired entry.

An example of the "binary tree" is a guessing game. I've picked a number between 1 and 100, and you have to guess what it is. If I've picked 82 and if you guess sequentially (starting at 1), you will make 82 guesses until you get it right. With a binary search, you'd start at 50, then guess 75, then 87, then 81, then 84, and finally 82—six guesses, a lot fewer than 82.

However, if the table is large, with over 1,000,000 entries, this approach becomes too slow also. So, a new approach is needed. That approach is a hash table.

The difference between a hash table and a regular table is that the key is used not only as a comparator, but also as an operator. A procedure is performed with the key to generate a number value, and that slot in the tree is checked. Other operations are used if this is not an exact hit. Ideally, there will be very few collisions, and the first access will be the correct access. This approach is

> fast and clean. The downside is that a hash table needs to be larger than the actual table, usually by at least 50 percent. The larger the ratio between hash table size and actual table size, the fewer the number of "collisions" when searching for an entry, and the faster the table.
>
> There is more to hash table theory. Any number of good computer science texts will provide a more detailed explanation.

hashstat

The hashstat command generates statistics on the performance of your hash table.

Syntax

The syntax for hashstat is

```
hashstat
```

No arguments are available.

The hashstat command provides information on the effectiveness of your path and your hash table. It will provide you with the "hit" rate of your path, and the number of misses, or collisions.

```
% hashstat
106 hits, 479 misses, 18%
% _
```

My path is large, so I expect many misses. With a simpler path, you'll see different results. I changed my path to the basic path (/usr/bin /usr/ucb /usr/local/bin .), ran a series of commands, and generated the following:

```
% hashstat
30 hits, 18 misses, 62%
% _
```

Because most commands I ran were located in /usr/bin, I generated a very high hit rate. If you are making your own programs, you may want to put the *dot* (.) directory first. If you use a specific package of programs, such as FrameMaker, you may want to put that directory near the front of your path.

How Do I Improve My Hit Rate?

You may run the hashstat command and feel that your hit rate is too low. A low hit rate suggests that the shell is spending more time than needed to find and run your

commands. You need to do two things. First, take a look at your command history, using
history. To get a good sample, you may need to set your history variable to a large
number and run your normal commands until you've filled the history list. This history
will show you the commands you normally run.

Next, examine your path with echo $path. You will get a space-separated list of
directories. Assume you have this rather large path:

```
% echo $path
/usr/ucb /usr/bin /usr/james/bin /usr/bin/X11 /usr/lang /opt2/pure .
/utilities/netnews /usr/openwin/bin /usr/progressive/bin /usr/5bin
./bin /usr/local /usr/local/bin /usr/hub/bin /usr/hub/newsprint/bin
/opt2/sentinel/bin /opt2/insight/bin.solaris /usr/lib/uucp /usr/ccs/bin
/utilities/netnews
% _
```

And your command history (set to 50 events) is varied:

```
% history
 87  ls -ld /usr/bin
 88  ls -ld /bin
 89  wc c10
 90  rn
 91  pushd News
 92  xv *
 93  xsetroot -solid black
 94  xv *
 95  cu netcom
 96  su
 97  uustat -a ; uustat -q
 98  Uutry netcomsv
 99  cd
100  grep elm .newsrc
101  rn
102  vi SUBFILTER
103  grep pine .newsrc
104  mail news-server@netcom.com < SUBFILTER
105  rn
106  cu netcom
107  su
108  clear
109  bc
110  cd /usr/games/Foot/solo
111  vi week27
112  Uutry netcomsv
113  cd
114  cd .mailbox/940722
115  mail -f russ
116  uustat -a ; uustat -q
117  cd
118  rn
119  rn
120  cd News
121  xv *.gif *.jpg
```

```
122   at 10:30AM Thursday
123   rn
124   ls
125   xv *.jpg *.gif & xv Hole &
126   ls *.gif *.jpg
127   mkdir /usr/james/images/.old/940721
128   mv 94*.gif cencal.gif sfbay.gif lvc.gif usa.gif world.gif
      /usr/james/images/.old/940721
129   ls *.gif *.jpg
130   mv *.gif *.jpg /usr/james/images/.nature
131   rn
132   rn
133   hashstat
134   man csh
135   csh -f
136   history
```

Nine of these commands are C Shell built-ins. By eliminating them, you have a list of 41 commands, with several repeats. Three of the commands were really multiple commands, so you ended up with a list of 44 different commands. Because the arguments are unimportant, you may remove them and sort the list to generate a count of the commands. The sorted list, in the order of the most frequent commands, is shown in Table 10.1.

Table 10.1. Command rates.

Command	Number of Calls	Directory
rn	8	/usr/local/bin
ls	5	/usr/ucb
xv	5	/usr/james/bin
uustat	4	/usr/bin
Uutry	2	/usr/lib/uucp
cu	2	/usr/bin
grep	2	/usr/bin
mail	2	/usr/ucb
mv	2	/usr/bin
su	2	/usr/bin
vi	2	/usr/ucb
at	1	/usr/bin

Command	Number of Calls	Directory
bc	1	/usr/bin
clear	1	/usr/ucb
csh	1	/usr/bin
man	1	/usr/bin
mkdir	1	/usr/bin
wc	1	/usr/ucb
xsetroot	1	/usr/bin/X11

So, the most frequently used commands here are rn, a news reader; ls, to list the files; and xv, an image viewer. To improve the hit rate, it would help to know where those files are located and to put them closer to the front of the path. Using the which command, you find that rn is in /usr/local/bin, ls is in /usr/ucb, and xv is in /usr/james/bin. Most of the path is good for these commands, but /usr/local/bin is well down on the list. To improve the hit rate, you need to move /usr/local/bin closer to the front of the path. To confirm the improvement of this path setting, you start a new C Shell (to remove the older hash data, and start fresh) and run each command the requisite number of times. Even after running these 44 commands, you end up with a poor percentage:

```
% hashstat
44 hits, 172 misses, 20%
% _
```

Still, this result represents an improvement on the 18 percent shown earlier. A further examination of the commands indicates that you need to look at the directories for all of them. These directories are listed in Table 10.1, and a summary is listed in Table 10.2.

Table 10.2. Directory access frequencies.

Directory	Number of Accesses
/usr/bin	17
/usr/ucb	11
/usr/local/bin	8

continues

Table 10.2. continued

Directory	Number of Accesses
/usr/james/bin	5
/usr/lib/uucp	2
/usr/bin/X11	1

So, /usr/bin and /usr/ucb need to be at the front of your path, not /usr/local/bin. Based on examining the path, any call to /usr/bin will have six misses before any hits! Because /usr/ucb overrides some commands in /usr/bin, to have the same functionality, you need to keep /usr/ucb ahead of /usr/bin in the path. To make the path as efficient as you can, you make the following changes:

```
% set path = ( /usr/ucb /usr/bin /usr/local/bin /usr/james/bin \
/usr/lib/uucp /usr/bin/X11 $path )
%
```

Rerunning the 44 commands now gives the following output to hashstat:

```
% hashstat
44 hits, 61 misses, 41%
%
```

This is a definite improvement over 18 percent and 20 percent. If you were willing to sacrifice the UCB behavior for certain commands, and eliminate /usr/ucb from the path, you'd reach a hit rate of 61 percent, with only 28 misses for 44 hits.

After determining your best path, you will want to change your .cshrc file to reflect this path in future invocations of the shell.

rehash

The rehash command is used to reset the hash table.

Syntax

The syntax for rehash is

rehash

There are no arguments.

The rehash command recomputes a hash table to account for new commands. When a command is added to a directory, the C Shell will not see it immediately. You need to rebuild the hash table in order for the C Shell to find the new command. The hash table is rebuilt using rehash.

The command hash table will also be rebuilt whenever you change directories or whenever you change your path variable. Both are acceptable alternatives, including the seemingly no-op command cd ..

unhash

To turn off hashing, use the unhash command.

Syntax

The syntax for unhash is

unhash

There are no arguments.

To disable the hash table, use the unhash command. The real-world effect of this is that the C Shell is prevented from eliminating unnecessary directories from the path variable. If a directory does not exist or if it has no executable files, the C Shell normally removes it from its internal path. When hashing is disabled and a command is executed, that directory will still be checked if the command is not found.

The unhash command is useful once you have settled on a fixed path, and you do not intend to change the path or add commands to your path.

Resource Control Commands

The single most important function of an operating system is to fairly allocate resources between processes. These resources include CPU time, disk space allowed, and memory usage. Normally, UNIX is very liberal in how much of a given resource a user may use. CPU time is unlimited, and files are restricted only by the size of the disk.

Available C Shell Resources

The C Shell provides some means of restricting the limits to an even greater extent. Seven specific resources can be limited through the C Shell; they are listed in Table 10.3.

Table 10.3. C Shell limitable resources.

Resource	Description
cputime	Processor usage time.
filesize	Largest single file in blocks.
datasize	Largest allowable data size in a program.
stacksize	Largest allowable stack size in a program.
coredumpsize	Maximum size of a core dump file.
descriptors	Maximum number of open file descriptors.
memorysize	Maximum size of memory allowed to a process.

Each limit is set to a specific value, and each limit serves a specific purpose.

cputime

The cputime variable is designed to prevent a single process, or multiple processes, from "hogging" all the CPU time. This can happen inadvertently when a program being developed has a CPU-intensive infinite loop. The process will remain active in the CPU, eating time and preventing other processes from accessing the CPU as readily, slowing the whole system.

When cputime is limited, a signal is sent to the process when the CPU time limit is exceeded, and the process terminates. This signal, SIGXCPU, can be caught, but by default a core is dumped, which can be used to help identify the loop. A sample output is the following:

```
% a.out
Cpu Limit Exceeded (core dumped)
%
```

filesize

The filesize resource limits the files created to a given size, usually measured in kilobytes. This limit is useful for systems with limited hard disk space or for smaller accounts. Large files may be desired, but if the large file is just extraneous output, then limiting file size will force an early termination.

If a program is exceeding the maximum file size allowed, a signal is generated, and the process terminates. The SIGXFSZ signal can be caught, but the default is to dump a core. Sample output is this:

```
% a.out > outputfile
File Size Limit Exceeded (core dumped)
% _
```

datasize

The datasize resource limits the maximum size of the data segment of a program. This segment is responsible for the statistically allocated variables, and it is best set on machines with limited memory. If too much data is used by a program, the machine could start swapping, which slows the system for all users, or if swap space fills, the system could fail.

If this limit is exceeded, the program will fail. No signal is generated; it is incumbent on the program to provide adequate information describing the failure. An example of this failure is this:

```
% gcc tartar.c
cc1: virtual memory exhausted
% _
```

stacksize

The stacksize resource limits the amount of program memory that can be used for the stack. The effective result of this limit is to restrict infinite recursion. Each call to a routine recursively increases the stack size, and when the limit is reached, an error is generated.

When the limit is reached, the program can no longer increase the memory size for the stack. This results in a segmentation violation, SIGSEGV. This signal defaults to a core dump, but it can be caught. An example of this limit is the following:

```
% a.out
Segmentation Fault (core dumped)
% _
```

coredumpsize

The core dump is an important file for a software developer, but it just doesn't matter for end users. Setting the core dump size to zero prevents core files from being produced when a program fails. On systems with limited hard disk space, or where there are other restrictions on disk usage, setting coredumpsize to 0 is useful.

There are no signals generated by breaching this limit. Instead, the code to produce a core is aborted at the limit, and any debugging information after that limit is lost.

descriptors

The number of open files for the C Shell can also be limited. The system limit is 64 (this number may vary from system to system), but a smaller number is sometimes useful. One common mistake for a software developer is to fail to close a file once it is open. In a small program, this error may go uncaught, but as programs increase in size, the limit may be reached. Setting a lower limit may help to debug the open file issue, as the error is reached faster.

This error does not generate a signal. Instead, a call to create a new file descriptor will fail. A good program will notice the failure and produce an error message. A bad program may result in a SIGBUS or a SIGSEGV error when the system attempts to use a bad file pointer.

memorysize

The last limit that can be set is for total memory size for the process. Another common programming mistake is the allocation of memory from the heap without a subsequent call to free. This is called a memory leak. Several commercial products are designed to catch the leaks. Still, an unwary program could result in a significant decrease in machine performance before this error is caught. By setting a smaller memory size, the program will fail before the system does.

Again, this failure does not result in a signal, but instead a request to increase the amount of available memory fails. A good program will catch this error and produce a message. A bad program will fail when it attempts to access the memory, generating a segmentation violation, SIGSEGV.

limit

The limit command is used to check and set C Shell resource limits.

Syntax

The syntax for limit is

```
limit [ -h ] [ resource ] [ max-use ]
```

With no arguments, the current limits are displayed. With the -h option, limit checks the hard system limits. With a resource, that resource is checked or is set with max-use.

The `limit` command directly sets and checks the limits of the current C Shell and all processes spawned by that shell. To first check the actual limits and the hard limits, use `limit` without specifying a resource.

```
% limit
cputime         unlimited
filesize        unlimited
datasize        2097148 kbytes
stacksize       8192 kbytes
coredumpsize    unlimited
descriptors     64
memorysize      unlimited
% limit -h
cputime         unlimited
filesize        unlimited
datasize        2097148 kbytes
stacksize       2097148 kbytes
coredumpsize    unlimited
descriptors     1024
memorysize      unlimited
% _
```

For five resources, the C Shell defaults to the system maximums, but for two, `stacksize` and `descriptors`, there are smaller limits. You can increase those to the maximum with a call to `limit`, specifying the resource and the limit.

```
% limit descriptors 128
% limit descriptors
descriptors     128
% _
```

Now you can have 128 files open from the C Shell. If you attempt to exceed the legal maximum, an error message is generated.

```
% limit descriptors 1280
limit: descriptors: Can't set limit
% _
```

The limit remains the same.

Some limits can be modified with values. The size limits can be in either kilobytes or megabytes. Kilobytes is the default; kilobytes can be indicated with a k after the number. Megabytes is signified with an m after the size. This m also marks minutes of CPU time allowed. The `cputime` defaults to seconds. Hours can be marked with h, and a specific number of minutes and seconds can be marked with mm:ss.

Only the root user can change a hard limit up, but anyone can change it down. This downward change is permanent. An example of the problem is this:

```
% limit -h descriptors 528
% limit descriptors 700
```

```
limit: descriptors: Can't set limit
% limit -h
cputime          unlimited
filesize         unlimited
datasize         2097148 kbytes
stacksize        2097148 kbytes
coredumpsize     unlimited
descriptors      528
memorysize       unlimited
% limit -h descriptors 1024
limit: descriptors: Can't set hard limit
```

In this example, you can see the hard limit for file descriptors set to 528, then an attempt is made to raise the soft limit to 700. Upon that failure, a listing of all the hard limits is made, and an effort to increase the hard limit for descriptors is attempted and fails.

> **Caution:** Playing with hard limits for your C Shell resources should not be attempted. Instead, use the hard limit solely as a reference, and you won't be caught lowering your limits permanently.

unlimit

The unlimit command is used to remove C Shell resource limits.

Syntax

The syntax for unlimit is

unlimit [-h] [*resource*]

This removes limitations on resources. If a resource is specified, that resource is unlimited. Otherwise, all resources are unlimited. If -h is specified, and the user is the root user, then all limits no longer have hard upper boundaries.

The unlimit command is often used after a temporary lower limit is set. Either a specific resource is freed for the user to exploit, or the entire set of resources is freed.

An example is when a cputime is set to 2 minutes to debug an infinite loop:

```
% limit cputime 2m
% limit cputime
cputime          2:00
% a.out
Cpu Limit Exceeded (core dumped)
% unlimit cputime
% limit cputime
cputime          unlimited
%
```

With a limit set for cputime, the infinite loop eventually ran out of time and dumped a core. Use of a debugging tool, such as sdb, may help isolate where the loop occurs, and thus allow the programmer to correct that error.

Attempts by anyone other than the root user to increase hard limits will fail. If a resource is already unlimited, then the request will be ignored; otherwise, an error is generated:

```
% unlimit -h
unlimit: datasize: Can't remove hard limit
unlimit: stacksize: Can't remove hard limit
unlimit: descriptors: Can't remove hard limit
% limit -h
cputime         unlimited
filesize        unlimited
datasize        2097148 kbytes
stacksize       2097148 kbytes
coredumpsize    unlimited
descriptors     1024
memorysize      unlimited
% _
```

Running unlimit brings the limits up to the maximum specified. The unlimit command never allows you to exceed the hard resource limits.

nice

The nice command is used for changing process priorities.

The syntax for nice is

```
nice [ +n ¦ -n ] [ command ]
```

The nice command changes the process priority (lower is better) for a command or for the shell. Only the root user can lower the priority for any process.

Priorities in UNIX are not what they seem. The kernel allocates CPU time to the process with the lowest priority, until the process needs a system resource or until its slice of time is finished. The time slices are usually one one-hundredth of a second, but this length of time is dependent on the implementation. Process priorities and CPU allocation are discussed in greater detail in Day 14, "Jobs."

Process priorities can be changed with the nice command. An ordinary user may only increase the priority (effectively lowering the chance that a priority will run). Because this helps other users, as well as other processes you run yourself, you are considered to be "nice" to other users.

Here we will examine the time taken by two processes, one run with `nice +20` and the other run with no change in priority, and see how long each takes to complete. The process is a simple loop to call a function one million times:

```
% a.out & nice +20 a.out&
[1] 19570
[2] 19571
% _

[2]  + Exit 1              a.out
Elapsed time 0:15, CPU time 31%, Maximum memory 0
[1]  + Exit 1              a.out
Elapsed time 0:17, CPU time 29%, Maximum memory 0
% _
```

Because of how the shell parses the line, the `nice`'d job is Job 1 and the regular job is Job 2. As you can see, despite the fact that the two jobs are performing exactly the same task, the `nice`'d job finished two seconds after the regular job. For a more realistic test, you can compare the times to compile the public domain mailer, `elm`. When compiled on a SPARCstation 10, the `nice`'d version took 10 minutes, and the regular version took 8 minutes. The heavier the load on the system, the greater the worth of `nice`.

The range of priority changes is 20. Each increment up decreases the chance that the process will get a slice of CPU time. You can examine the `nice` value for any process with the `ps` command using the `-l` option:

```
% ps -l
 F S UID   PID  PPID  C PRI NI ADDR       SZ   WCHAN   TTY   TIME  COMMAND
 8 S  69  9180  9175 80   1 20 fe55f000  225 fe55f1c8 pts/5  0:06  csh
 8 O  69 13237  9180 11   1 20 fe36d800  152 175      pts/5  0:00  ps
% _
```

The NI column gives the current nice value, and the PRI column gives the current priority value. The other fields are discussed on Day 14.

You will note that the `nice` value for each process is 20, not 0. This is because "niceness" can be decreased as well as increased. Only the root user can lower the niceness of processes; and in doing so, the root user enables those processes to get a better chance at grabbing CPU time. The `nice` values can go down to -20, speeding a process.

Note: Setting a higher `nice` value doesn't automatically lock out a process, just as setting a lower `nice` value doesn't force the process to stay in the CPU. The `nice` value is just one of several factors used to figure out a process's overall priority.

You can change the `nice` value for your C Shell by running `nice` without any commands. This will change the priority for all commands run from your shell, and if you are not the root user, you may not decrease the nice value to return to the previous state.

The `nice` command needs its numerical argument prepended with a plus (+) or minus (-) sign; otherwise, it will attempt to interpret the number as a command. In this case, the default `nice` increment is 4.

nohup

The `nohup` command is used to disable the `SIGHUP` signal.

Syntax

The syntax for `nohup` is

```
nohup [ command ]
```

If a command is present, it is run in a subshell and will ignore the `SIGHUP` signal. If no command is present, the shell and child processes will ignore `SIGHUP`.

The `SIGHUP` signal is usually sent to processes when a modem line is dropped and the line hangs. It is used to clean up after this occurrence. `SIGHUP`s can also be generated when a shell exits and there are background jobs.

By default, `SIGHUP` is ignored when a process is started in the background with the `&` terminator. Otherwise, the default action is for the program to exit. Ignoring `SIGHUP` indicates that a process is to continue running after the shell terminates or that the shell should continue running if the modem line drops.

Commands run via `nohup` need to be "simple" single-line commands. No pipes, command lists, or parenthesized command lists are permitted.

> **Note:** Pipes and command lists can be run with `nohup`, but only by running a C shell `-c` and passing the list as an argument:
>
> ```
> nohup csh -c "command | command | command"
> ```

More Miscellaneous Commands

The last three built-in commands defy easy classification. The eval command is used to run a command that results from command or variable substitution. The source command is used to run a set of commands within the current shell, and glob is a different, specialized form of echo.

eval

The eval command is used to run a command as standard input to the shell.

The syntax for eval is

```
eval arguments
```

The arguments are read as standard input to the shell.

The eval command is used when the output of a command is another series of commands that can run in the current shell. Although the command can be executed by using back quotes, using eval ensures that the variable substitution occurs properly. The standard example for eval is the tset command:

```
% eval `tset -s options`
% _
```

The tset command sets up a terminal and often is run at login time. The output of tset is treated as standard input to the shell: the tset output is just some commands that need to be run.

source

The source command is used to run a command or series of commands from a file in the current shell.

The syntax for source is

```
source [ -h ] name
```

A series of commands are read from the named file. If the -h option is specified, the commands are added to the history list without being executed.

The source command is one of the more powerful commands in the C Shell. It is used to read commands from a file and execute them in the current environment. If you've

decided to modify your .cshrc file, and you want to use that environment immediately, you need to run source .cshrc.

When you specify the -h option, commands are added directly to the command history list and can be accessed accordingly.

Source requests can be nested. If you have a file with commands that need another file, it is perfectly acceptable to source that second file within the first. The only risk is that you might run out of file descriptors if the sources are nested too deeply or if there is a loop in the source requests. If there is an error in a sourced file, then all sourcing is terminated immediately.

An example of sourcing a file is the patrunc command. This is a set of C Shell commands to eliminate duplicate entries from a user's path. On Day 12, you will see how this program is created and how it works:

```
% set path = ( /bin /usr/ucb /bin . )
***Analysis***
The second /bin entry is clearly superfluous.
***End Analysis***
% source patrunc
% echo $path
/bin /usr/ucb .
% _
```

The patrunc command must be sourced to effect the path in the current shell. Another option might have been to end patrunc with the line echo set path = ($path) and then use eval to evaluate patrunc, but this approach is a bit clumsier.

Adding items to the history is also a useful trick. You may be working on several projects, with different commands. Using the savehist variable helps establish a command history, but only if you return to the same project. By keeping a small set of frequently used commands in a file, you may add these to your history when you move to that project.

Note: Clever use of aliases will perform create local history lists automatically for you. Just create two aliases, dhist and lhist, as follows:

```
alias dhist 'history -h > .dhist'
alias lhist 'if ( -f .dhist ) source -h .dhist'
```

The dhist alias dumps the current command history into a file, .dhist. When you use the -h option on history, the file is set up to allow the source

command to read the commands. The `lhist` alias checks to see whether a `.dhist` file exists, and if it exists, the `lhist` alias will use `source` to read the commands into the history list.

To use these aliases properly, you need to change the `cd` alias to use the `dhist` and `lhist` aliases:

```
alias cd dhist\;chdir \!\*\;pathprompt\;lhist
```

You need to use `chdir` instead of `cd`; otherwise, an alias loop is created. Now when you use `cd`, you will save the current history into a file, change your working directory, change your prompt (see Day 8 for the `pathprompt` alias), and load any history that might be present.

Although not an official C Shell function, creation of local histories in directories is easily accomplished and helps users on multiple projects.

glob

The `glob` command performs filename expansion.

Syntax

The syntax for `glob` is

```
glob wordlist
```

Filename expansion is performed on the *wordlist* and written to standard output.

The `glob` command is similar to `echo`, except that no escape sequences are permitted in the filename expansion, and the resultant words are separated by the null character, not spaces.

Consider the following as the contents of a directory:

```
% ls
doda1r   doda2r   doda3r   doda4r   doda5r   doda6r   doda7r   doda8r
doda1t   doda2t   doda3t   doda4t   doda5t   doda6t   doda7t   doda8t
doda1u   doda2u   doda3u   doda4u   doda5u   doda6u   doda7u   doda8u
doda1y   doda2y   doda3y   doda4y   doda5y   doda6y   doda7y   doda8y
%  _
```

The `glob` command can be used to isolate names that end in `y`:

```
% glob *y
doda1ydoda2ydoda3ydoda4ydoda5ydoda6ydoda7ydoda8y%
```

The uses for `glob` are discussed in detail in Day 3.

Summary

Today, you have learned about the C Shell hash table and how it can be used to improve the performance of your path variable. You also learned how to recreate the hash table and how to disable the hash table.

You learned about how the C Shell controls UNIX resources and how limits on these resources are set. These resources are governed by the `limit` and `unlimit` commands, although only the root user can expand the hard limits of the system. You learned a simple command to ignore the `SIGHUP` signal, and you learned how to change the priority of your commands.

Finally, you wrapped up the day with an examination of three commands that defied classification. The `eval` command is used to send the output of one command to the standard input of the shell. The `source` command is used to run commands in the current shell or to load those commands into the history list. The `glob` command is used to perform file expansion based on a list of arguments.

Now, you are ready to approach the topic of C Shell programming. Tomorrow you will examine the building blocks of a C Shell program, the control structures that allow looping through commands and the commands that allow for conditional execution of other commands.

Related UNIX Topics—UNIX Resource Management

The entire purpose for an operating system on a computer is resource management. From the simplest computer to the most complex, the task of allocating resources to processes has been tricky to implement and tricky to manage.

What is a resource? To a computer, everything. The keyboard you use for typing in commands is a resource, as is a mouse. They each generate interrupts for every action, and each keystroke or mouse movement requires some processing, or the data is lost. The screen is a resource, as is the printer, the modem, and the hard disks. If you have a tape drive, a floppy drive, or a CD ROM drive, those are resources that also require some form of management.

Within the computer are resources that need to be managed as well. The CPU needs careful management, as does the internal RAM. Different chips within the computer serve different purposes, and each requires some form of oversight.

The most common form of management—and one that everybody recognizes—is management of the CPU. Only one program can run at any given moment per CPU, so something must decide who gets access and when. This scheduling capability separates UNIX as an operating system from lesser systems, such as DOS. Through a series of algorithms, each process is assigned a priority, and the lowest priority process not waiting on an event is given a slice of the CPU.

This scheduler is driven with regular interrupts from the system clock (another resource!). These interrupts come at regular intervals, and they force the system to recompute priorities and assign a new process to the CPU. If a process in the CPU is forced to wait for I/O, or is otherwise put to sleep, then the scheduler kicks in again, and a new process gets its crack at the CPU. More details of process scheduling are discussed on Day 14.

Another resource requiring management is the internal memory of the computer, RAM. This memory is broken into "pages" of memory, each one kilobyte in size. (The specific page sizes are implementation-dependent.) These pages include all the memory used by the process, including the text area, stack, data segment, and memory heap. The swapper will follow how often each page is accessed, and it will apply a heuristic to determine when a page needs to be swapped in and out.

Paging is a process whereby a page of internal memory is freed for use by moving the current contents to a location on the hard disk. This area of the hard disk is called the swap space. Because swapping can be an expensive process, good heuristics are needed to minimize the paging performed.

Note: The term *swapping* comes from the older days when an entire process was either in memory or in the swap space. The more appropriate term at present is *paging*, because the memory is now broken into pages, but swapping is still heard.

When a process is not using the CPU, it is not necessarily paged out of the RAM. That way, when a process is restored to the CPU, the memory pages for the process are already available. Calls to the swapper to restore a page of memory are one I/O interrupt that will result in the loss of access to the CPU.

Certain pages cannot be removed from the RAM, including the commands that make up the operating system. If the swapper were paged out of memory, how could it swap itself back into memory to restore itself? These pages are called *preemptive pages*, and the pager knows not to swap them out to the swap space.

A machine that is spending much of its time swapping pages is considered to be *thrashing*. If this is a regular situation for your machine, you need either to reduce the load or to increase the memory in the machine.

Another important resource is the hard disks. Most current UNIX systems use the SCSI interface for accessing remote disks, tapes, and other peripherals. Each device still needs its own device driver.

You might be surprised to know that when you write out data to a disk, your data doesn't immediately go to the disk. Instead, the operating system buffers the I/O calls to the remote peripherals. The data is stored in an area of the kernel's memory until it can get a slice of time to transmit the data to the medium. Similarly, input is also buffered. A request to read a file from the disk is just a request to the operating system to give you the data. The operating system must then ask the device driver if that piece of data is already in the buffer. If it is there, the operating system gives it to the process. Otherwise, the device driver must find the data on the hard disk, read it into the buffer, and give the request piece to the operating system to pass on to the process. All this time, your process is denied access to the CPU, until the operation is complete. This is "system time" in the output of the `time` command.

Devices such as the keyboard and mouse also have buffers. Each keystroke generates an interrupt and adds the character to the end of the buffer. Each character is then processed by sending it on to the program requesting the data. Typing this section into the document using `vi` uses the buffer to read my input; then my input also needs to be displayed on the screen.

Without a doubt, the operating system is the most complicated piece of software you will run on your machine. Without it, you'd need to write your programs to watch for interrupts for input and output, you'd need to design some form of input and output buffering, and you'd need to know the details of every piece of hardware associated with your machine. If the machine was multiprocessing, you'd also need to contend with other processes attempting to use the same resources.

Q&A

Q What is the hash table, and how is it used?

A The hash table is a tool used by the C Shell to help speed command execution. It sheds from the path any directories that aren't accessed to run commands. It also keeps statistics to determine the efficiency of your path.

Q Why use rehash?

A Rehash provides a quick and easy way to change the contents of the hash table, based on the addition of a new file to the path.

Q Why restrict resources?

A There are several good reasons why resources may be restricted. On a multiuser system, resource limits are good for preventing a user from hogging too much of a system, harming the performance for other users. On single-user systems, resource limits can be used as a debugging tool for correcting processes and to prevent a runaway process from impacting system performance.

Workshop

This workshop provides you with an aid for understanding the concepts presented in today's lesson. To make sure you understand the material, work through this quiz and exercise before proceeding to the next day's lesson. Answers are provided in Appendix F, "Answers to Quizzes and Exercises."

Quiz

1. What does unhash do?

2. How do you improve hash table performance?

3. What is the datasize resource?

4. How do you eliminate core files?

5. How do you add commands to the history list without running them?

Exercises

Look at the dhist and lhist aliases presented earlier in the chapter, in the note on changing history by directory. Currently, the aliases are valid only for the cd command. How would you change them for chdir, pushd, and popd?

Also, suppose there were ten basic commands that you would use, regardless of your directory. How would you change dhist and lhist to include them in your history list?

11

Programming with the C Shell

Introduction to Day 11

Yesterday, you finished learning about the built-in commands for the C Shell. So far, you should have a good grasp of all the tools needed to run a C Shell as a command interface. Starting today, and for the next two days, you will learn about how to program the C Shell, how to use the programming tools at the command line to increase your power, and how to write complex shell scripts to solve programming problems.

Today, you will concentrate on learning the building blocks of a shell program. These are the commands for looping through a block of code and executing it as many times as you like. You'll also learn how to terminate the execution of a block of code.

Next, you will learn how to execute code conditionally, including circumstances where there are multiple options. Using conditional commands, you will be able to tailor the commands you execute without needing to know in advance the specific data being used.

Finally, you will learn two specialized commands, `shift` and `onintr`, for processing data that is needed for C Shell programs. Lastly, you will finish the lesson with a quick rundown of some Bourne shell equivalents to the C Shell control structures.

Setting Today's Goals

Today, you will learn

- [ ] How to loop a predetermined number of times
- [ ] How to loop until a condition is met
- [ ] How to break out of a loop
- [ ] How to move to an arbitrary line of C Shell code
- [ ] How to execute a command on a given condition
- [ ] How to execute a command based on a matched condition
- [ ] How to catch interrupt signals
- [ ] How to shift command-line arguments

Looping Commands

In C Shell programming, there are two types of loops. One is a loop that is executed a fixed number of times, based on an argument within the loop. This is the `foreach` loop, which executes once for each item on the line. The second type of loop is indeterminate, executing code while a condition is met. This is the `while` loop.

> **Note:** A loop is a set of code that can be executed a multiple number of times in the fixed order in which it appears. Most languages, even assemblers, support some form of looping.
>
> The code executed is called a *block of code* or a *command block*. Syntactically, it can be either a command or a set of commands followed by a command block; these recursive definitions frequently occur when defining a grammar. What a command block really means is that these are one or more commands.
>
> A few other terms will be used today. One is a pipeline. A *pipeline* is a set of commands that has its output piped to the standard input of a later command. The command `ls ¦ more` is a simple example.
>
> A *parenthesized list* is a grouping of commands, separated by semicolons or ampersands (&), grouped within parentheses. This means the commands should be run in a subshell. The list `(ls;clear;echo done)` runs the `ls` command, clears the screen, and echoes `done`.
>
> A *simple* command consists of a single command and its arguments—no pipelines, no parenthesized lists, and no command blocks. Some commands already discussed, such as `nice` and `nohup`, take simple commands only. Where a simple command is required, that will be noted.

foreach

The `foreach` loop is a determinate loop. When you expect to run the loop for a certain number of values, use `foreach`.

The syntax for `foreach` is

```
foreach var (wordlist)
    command block
end
```

The variable *var* is set to each successive item in the *wordlist*, and the command block is executed. The `foreach` and the `end` commands must appear at the start of their respective lines. Also, the `foreach` arguments must be on the same line with the command. The `end` must be alone on the line.

The `foreach` command is used to step through a series of values. Suppose you want to e-mail a couple of `tar` files to a friend. You could write a simple `foreach` loop to send each file separately:

```
% foreach i ( *.tar )
? uuencode $i $i ¦ mailx -s $i friend
? end
% _
```

In this case, for every file with the `.tar` suffix, you will execute the command `uuencode` and pipe it to `mail`. The uuencode is used to encode non-ASCII files into an ASCII format for transmission via `mail` and news. You encode the file and then pipe that output to `mail`. By using `$i`, you set the encoded filename to the same as the `.tar` file, and you also set the subject of the mail to that file. That way, your friend will know what has been sent.

Note that the C Shell is smart enough to know that more information is coming after the `foreach` line. Instead of giving you the regular prompt, C Shell prompts you with a question mark, telling you that the command isn't finished. The C Shell will keep reading commands into the block until it encounters a solitary `end` on a line. Then it will run the loop as many times as necessary to cover each file given in the *wordlist*.

Also, you should note that file and variable expansion are accomplished before the loop is run. That way, the file expansion of `*.tar` is performed before the loop is started, allowing one iteration for each file. If this were not the case, you'd have ended up running the command `uuencode *.tar *.tar ¦ mail -s *.tar friend` once, with unpredictable results.

In addition, if there is no match for file expansion, the attempt at expansion before the loop is started allows the C Shell to flag the error before you've typed in all the commands of the command block—no problem for a script, but when running a `foreach` loop from the command line, this is no small blessing!

Variable expansion is a real benefit. When you place a single variable as the `wordlist` (if the variable is an array), the loop will be iterated once per array item. An example is this:

```
% foreach i ( $cdpath )
? echo Valid Cd destination: $i
? echo " "
? ls $i
? echo " "
? end
Valid Cd destination: /usr/james

Docs/                   USMNTS                  parsem*
FAQ                     addem*                  procII/
HGE-Table               crons                   testdata
Install*                dbm/                    usmnts
JCAR.exp                dir2/                   xds/

Valid Cd destination: /usr/james/Docs

Canada/        Sams/           a.out*          photo/          reviews/

%
```

Because the cdpath has two entries, /usr/james and /usr/james/Docs, this little loop will print the directory name, followed by a blank line and a listing of the directory, followed by a second blank line.

Note: If you have a space in a variable name, you need to use the variable modifier :q to insure that the variable is taken as a single entry.

Failure to use :q may have unexpected results:

```
% set tmpvar=( This "is my" variable )
% foreach i ( $tmpvar )
? echo $i
? end
This
is
my
variable
% foreach i ( $tmpvar:q )
? echo $i
? end
This
is my
variable
% _
```

The :q modifier is not present in some older versions of the C Shell. You will need to test your shell to determine whether it works.

If you start to enter a `foreach` loop but realize you don't need the loop, the interrupt key, Control+C, will discard the command and return you to the C Shell prompt.

The `foreach` command is smart enough to recognize when there are no entries in the *wordlist*. In that case, the loop is "valid," but the command block is never executed. A simple example is this:

```
% foreach i ( )
? echo $i
? end
% _
```

Although creating a loop with no entries may not make sense from a command line, doing so in a C Shell script is perfectly valid.

There is no requirement that you even use the variable for the command block. Although this is a bit simplistic, this `foreach` loop is perfectly valid:

```
0% foreach i ( 1 2 3 4 )
? echo Duke rules.
? end
Duke rules.
Duke rules.
Duke rules.
Duke rules.
% _
```

This is better performed with the built-in command, `repeat`; or, if that command block is dependent on a variable, `repeat $#var` will do the trick. On the other hand, because `repeat` takes only a simple command, if a number of commands or a pipeline is required, the simple `foreach` loop will do the job adequately.

A `foreach` loop executes each command successively, even if one should fail. An error message will be generated each time:

```
% foreach i ( $cdpath )
? do
? echo $i
? end
do: Command not found
/usr/james
do: Command not found
/usr/james/Docs
% _
```

Although the repetitious error message may be annoying, it is reassuring to note that the echo command is executed properly.

> **Note:** The variable used for the foreach command is not just local to the command block, but is still in scope after the foreach command finishes. The only sure way to eliminate the variable is with unset after the loop terminates.

while

The alternative to a determinate number of iterations is the while command, which provides an indeterminate number of iterations through the loop.

The syntax for while is

```
while (expr)
        command block
end
```

While the expression is true, the command block is executed.

The while (expr) and the end must remain alone on their input lines.

The while loop is used to execute a block of code repeatedly while a condition is true. Suppose you wanted to check the status of a process while a file existed. You could write a simple while loop:

```
% while ( -f file )
? ps ax
? sleep 10
? end
# ps output
% _
```

In this case, while the file exists, the block of code containing the ps command and the sleep command will be executed. The ps command gives a listing of all commands running on the system, and the sleep command forces the block to wait 10 seconds between iterations.

The C Shell is again smart enough to recognize when it is building a `while` command, and it will prompt for more input. Again, the question mark is used as a prompt. Lines of input are read to form a command block until the C Shell encounters a solitary `end` on a line. Then, the loop will be run while the condition is true.

Caution: One weakness of the C Shell is that the history will not remember the command block; the history will remember only the first line of the command. If you attempt to use history substitution to replay the loop, you'll get only the first `while` line and a question mark prompting for more input.

As with the `foreach` command, file expansion and variable substitution are completed before the C Shell prompts for input. That way, if a loop is based on a variable, the full variable is tested for the loop. This is not as important for the `while` loop, as there is no internal loop variable set for the command block. Again, if file expansion fails, the `while` loop signals the error before you are required to type in the command block.

While loops are ideally designed to step through a sequence of numbers. So long as the command block has some form of numerical increment (or decrement), the `while` loop will terminate at some point:

```
% @ i=1
% while ( $i < 10 )
? echo $path[$i]
? @ i++
? end
/usr/ucb
/usr/bin
/usr/local/bin
/usr/james/bin
/usr/lib/uucp
/usr/bin/X11
/usr/lang
/opt2/pure
 .
% _
```

This loop steps through the first nine entries in the `path` variable and prints them on a separate line. This technique is also useful for older C Shells that do not have the `:q` modifier. By starting at 1, you can step through the variable and test each element separately:

```
% set myvar=( This "is my" variable )
% @ i=1
% while ( $i <= $#myvar )
? set tv = "$myvar[$i]"
```

```
? # command block
? echo $tv
? @ i++
? end
This
is my
variable
% _
```

In terms of action, this is identical to the following:

```
% foreach tv ( $myvar:q )
? # command block
? echo $tv
? end
This
is my
variable
% _
```

The former example shows a more complicated approach to stepping through a variable. It also illustrates the similarity of the two types of loops. Unlike the C language, in which loops can be easily substituted for one another, the C Shell does not always allow easy substitution. The `foreach` loop will step through the *wordlist* and will not allow more or less repetitions of the loop, except though the `break` command.

Conditional Expressions

The `while` loop uses a conditional expression to determine whether or not to execute a loop. Arithmetic conditional expressions were discussed during Day 8, but the conditional expressions for the C Shell go beyond simple arithmetic. There are also file inquiries, as listed in Table 11.1.

Table 11.1. File inquiries.

Inquiry	Meaning
-r	Can you read the file?
-w	Can you write the file?
-e	Does the file exit?
-o	Do you own the file?
-z	Is the file empty?
-f	Is the file a plain file?
-d	Is this file a directory?

The file query can appear directly after the `while`, but for readability, placing the inquiry in parentheses looks cleaner and has no effect on the shell.

Commands can also be tested in a `while` loop. By when you place curly braces `{}` around the command, the return is evaluated, and if successful, the expression evaluates to 1 and the conditional is considered true. This is the opposite of how the command really works. Usually successful commands return 0, and unsuccessful commands have non-zero return values. If the actual return is important, use `$status` instead of curly braces.

Commands that are run will still generate output to the terminal, unless the output is redirected to a file. These conditions can be negated:

```
% while ! { file baddir }
? echo baddir does not exit
? ...
? end
baddir:         cannot open: No such file or directory
baddir does not exist
(etc...)
```

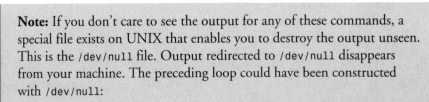

> **Note:** If you don't care to see the output for any of these commands, a special file exists on UNIX that enables you to destroy the output unseen. This is the `/dev/null` file. Output redirected to `/dev/null` disappears from your machine. The preceding loop could have been constructed with `/dev/null`:
>
> ```
> % while ! { (file baddir >& /dev/null) }
> ```
>
> With `/dev/null`, the only thing you'll see is the repeated line `baddir does not exist`. The redirection needs to occur from a subshell.

Suppose you have a friend `dave`, and you are waiting for him to log into the system. A `while` loop can be written that will wait for him to log in, and when he does, the loop terminates and you will be notified:

```
% while ! { ( who ¦ grep dave ) }
? sleep 30
? end
dave      pts/0      Jul 25 07:30
% _
```

The `grep` command looks for any occurrences of the string `dave` in its input, the `who` command. When `dave` appears, the line is written to the screen, and the loop terminates. Each iteration of the loop is just a request to sleep for 30 seconds; this prevents you from hogging system resources by repeatedly executing `who` and `grep`.

break

The break is one technique for terminating a loop. Break commands are used to exit a command block and proceed beyond the block.

Syntax

The syntax for break is

```
break
```

It takes no arguments.

The break command is used when you no longer wish to continue with the loop, even though more loop iterations are still possible. A good example is this short routine to check that a directory is in your path:

```
% set needed=/usr/local/bin
% foreach i ( $path )
? if ($needed == $i ) then
? echo The directory is found
? break
? endif
? end
The directory is found
% _
```

This command scans down the path variable to find the given directory. After you know it is in the path, you don't need to search any longer, so you notify the user that the directory was found, and end the search. If there were no break command and a second occurrence of the needed directory were present, the statement The directory is found would be echoed twice.

Breaks can also be nested, just like loops can be nested. Suppose you have an array of directories to be checked—you need to see if you have the same directories in your path and cdpath. You only want to know if any are the same. You can loop through both, and if you find a match, break out of both:

```
% set cdpath = ( /usr/james /usr/james/Docs /usr/james/bin )
% set path = ( /usr/ucb /usr/bin /usr/local/bin /usr/james/bin . )
% foreach i ( $cdpath )
? foreach j ( $path )
? if ( $i == $j ) then
? echo found a match: $i
? break;break
? endif
? end
? end
found a match: /usr/james/bin
% _
```

To break out of two loops, there must be two break commands, separated by semicolons. One break for each level of loop is required, and they must all be on the same single line to be processed properly.

In the example, you stop all processing once you find the first match. If you wanted to see all the matches, you would use only a single break and start at the next element of the cdpath variable.

continue

The continue command is used to restart an iteration of the loop at the next value.

Syntax

The syntax for continue is

continue

It takes no arguments.

Unlike the break command, the continue command stays in the loop, but starts at the next iteration. If the loop is a foreach loop, the next item in the *wordlist* is used. If the loop is a while loop, the condition is retested, and if still true, the command block is executed again.

Suppose that, in the path-checking loop, you don't want to process the /usr/bin entry from the path variable, but you do want to process everything else. One approach would be this:

```
% set needed=/usr/local/bin
% foreach i ( $path )
? if ( $i == "/usr/bin") continue
? echo checking $i
? if ($needed == $i ) then
? echo The directory is found
? break
? endif
? end
/usr/ucb
/usr/local/bin
The directory is found
% echo $path
/usr/ucb /usr/bin /usr/local/bin /usr/james/bin
% _
```

As you can see, when the foreach loop reached its second word, /usr/bin, the continue command was run. This returned straight to the top of the loop to run the command

block with the third word, /usr/local/bin.

An undocumented feature of C Shell is that a string of breaks, separated by semicolons, can terminate with a continue. In this case, the lower loops are broken with the break, and the next loop starts again at the beginning of the block with the next test. In the last break example, you observed the effect of two breaks. In this example, you change the second break to a continue:

```
% set cdpath = ( /usr/james /usr/james/Docs /usr/james/bin /usr/local/lib )
% set path = ( /usr/ucb /usr/bin /usr/local/bin /usr/james/bin . )
% foreach i ( $cdpath )
? echo Outer loop tests $i
? foreach j ( $path )
? if ( $i == $j ) then
? echo found a match: $i
? break;continue
? endif
? echo testing $j
? end
? echo Outer test for $i is complete
? end
Outer loop tests /usr/james
testing /usr/ucb
testing /usr/bin
testing /usr/local/bin
testing /usr/james/bin
testing .
Outer test for /usr/james is complete
Outer loop tests /usr/james/Docs
testing /usr/ucb
testing /usr/bin
testing /usr/local/bin
testing /usr/james/bin
testing .
Outer test for /usr/james/Docs is complete
Outer loop tests /usr/james/bin
testing /usr/ucb
testing /usr/bin
testing /usr/local/bin
found a match: /usr/james/bin
Outer loop tests /usr/local/lib
testing /usr/ucb
testing /usr/bin
testing /usr/local/bin
testing /usr/james/bin
testing .
Outer test for /usr/local/lib is complete
```

You should note that when the loops found a matching pair with /usr/james/bin, they broke the inner loop (no printing of testing /usr/james/bin or testing .) and started the outer loop at the top (no printing of Outer test for /usr/james/bin is complete).

This increases the power to move from locations within loops.

The function of the `continue` command could easily be duplicated with an `if` command, grouping remaining commands into a command block, but `continue` provides a convenient shorthand for restarting the loop. Multiple `continue` commands have an advantage over multiple `if` commands: They are easier to read and understand.

goto

The `goto` command allows the C Shell user to repeat commands from within a script.

The syntax for `goto` is

```
goto label
```

Labels are placed on lines with the form

```
label: command
```

The C Shell will jump to the labelled line and resume execution from there.

The `goto` command works only in a C Shell program, not in an interactive session. After a command is labelled, a `goto` command can be used to resume execution from that command. These are sometimes useful for error handling:

```
if ( error condition ) goto fail
...
fail: echo we failed
exit 1
```

> **Note:** `goto` commands in any high-level programming language are a matter of controversy. Some scholars believe that `goto` commands are unnecessary; the same code can be generated in a cleaner fashion using existing control flow structures and conditional commands. Other scholars feel that `goto` commands are perfectly acceptable tools in a programming language.
>
> Personally, I've never used `goto` commands in any shell language, although I could see circumstances where they could be useful. I just believe that the widespread use of `goto` commands makes a program harder to read and understand; the larger the program, the worse the problem. This shouldn't prevent you from using a `goto` command, however, if you feel it makes sense.

Goto commands can jump in either direction in a shell script. Once a label has been reached, the shell will remember the location, and if a goto command requests that label, the input will be rewound to that point, and execution resumed. Similarly, if the label is after the current line, input is read until the label is found, and execution resumes from there.

There are some restrictions on label placement. It is illegal to place a label on a command within either a foreach loop or a while loop. The shell would not understand the situation within the loop: What iteration should it be for a foreach loop?

If a label is not found, the goto command produces an error, Label not found. Execution of the script terminates at that point.

The break and continue commands are special cases of a goto command. There is an implicit label at the start and finish of each loop; break is just a "goto" to the label at the end of the loop, and continue is just a "goto" to the beginning label. The switch command, described later, is another, more complicated variant of a goto command.

Conditional Commands

Conditional commands allow for execution of a command block based on the value of an expression. You have already seen some simple if commands illustrated in examples of break and continue today, and yesterday, you saw an if included in the aliases for the local history commands.

Today, you will explore the if command and the switch command, along with their related pieces.

The *if* Command

The if command is used to execute a block of code if a certain condition is true.

Syntax

The syntax for if is

```
if (expr) simple command
if (expr) then
command block
[ else if (expr2) then
command block2 ]
[ else
command block3 ]
endif
```

There are two forms to the `if` command. The first is the simple execution of a command on a condition. The second is the execution of a series of commands on a condition, with an optional set of commands for other conditions, and a set of commands if no conditions are met.

The `if` commands you saw yesterday were the simple form of the `if` command, where a condition is tested, and if the return code is 1, a command is run. Let's look at it again:

```
alias lhist 'if ( -f .dhist ) source -h .dhist'
```

The alias `lhist` is just an `if` command. It uses the file inquiry `-f` to see whether a file exists. Should there be a `.dhist` file in the current directory, the inquiry returns 1, and the command is executed. This is a simple sourcing of the file.

Normally, during the interactive running of the shell, you won't find much reason for using an `if` command, because you'll already know, or easily determine, if the condition is true, and need only to execute the command. The `if` commands are usually found in aliases and scripts.

One common script where you might find an `if` command is your `.cshrc` file. Some aliases may not make sense under different circumstances, and in other circumstances, you may want to have different values for your `path` variable. This example illustrates an `if` command to add an element to a path:

```
if ( -x /usr/local/bin/rn ) set path = ( $path /usr/local/bin )
```

In this case, if the system has a copy of the `rn` program in `/usr/local/bin`, you want to add that directory to your path. If `rn` is not on the system, you have no need for the directory.

Note: `rn` is a common newsreader program, available on many architectures. On some systems, it may be installed in a different location. For more information on `netnews` and `rn`, see *Teach Yourself the Internet in 21 Days*.

Conditional aliasing is illustrated with this command:

```
if ( $?DISPLAY ) alias vi "xterm -e /bin/vi \!* &"
```

In this case, if the `DISPLAY` environment variable exists, you want to alias the `vi` command to invoke an `xterm` process and run `vi` in the `xterm`. `DISPLAY` is a variable that should be present when running X Windows, and `xterm` is the program to bring up a new window. By default, it will run a shell, but with the `-e` option, you can specify a command. If you are running X Windows, whenever you decide to edit a file with `vi`, the editing session

will appear in its own window, allowing you to continue to use your session for other purposes. Otherwise, vi remains unaliased and will appear on your screen normally.

The second form of the if command is more powerful and more complicated. It allows for the execution of a block of commands if the condition is true, and the execution of an alternate block of commands if the condition is false.

You saw a simple example earlier in this lesson:

```
? if ($needed == $i ) then
? echo The directory is found
? break
? endif
```

Here, two commands are executed if a condition is true. This cannot be formed in the simple if, because the simple command forbids parenthesized commands. These two commands force the if to the multiple line format.

Another example comes from an installation script hacked together to place X11R5 files in the correct locations:

```
if ( -e /usr/bin/X11 ) then
    echo /usr/bin/X11 exists, will not link.
else
    ln -s /opt2/X11R5/bin/X11 /usr/bin/X11
endif
```

Here, the shell first checks to see if there is a directory entry for /usr/bin/X11. If this exists, the user might need to clean up something before establishing the link, or the link may already be there, so the script issues a brief message that the file exists. If there is no entry, a symbolic link can be created with no problem, and the else option allows for this.

A more complicated example comes from a script to refuse mail. After creating a count of messages to be refused and a list of the refusals, you need to delete the messages from the file:

```
if ( $count > 0 ) then
    foreach j ( $returns )
        echo message $j is bounced back.
    end
    /usr/ucb/mail << EOF
    d $returns
EOF
endif
```

This conditional is rather complicated. You check to see whether the count is greater than zero. This could have been done implicitly with just if ($count) then, but the comparison makes it clear to the reader. If it's true that the count is more than zero, you enter the block. The first command is a foreach loop that lists each message to be deleted. Then a call to the mail command deletes the messages.

Programming with the C Shell

> **Note:** The full development of these scripts will be discussed in detail
> tomorrow.

A more complicated use is extracted from a script to load bitmaps on the root window
for a background:

```
if ( $#woof == 6 ) then
    shift woof
    set argv[1] = $woof[1]
else if ( $#woof != 5 ) then
    echo No such root: $1
    exit
endif
```

Here, you check the count of elements of the woof variable. If there are six elements, you
want to shift the arguments down a notch, and replace the first element of argv with the
first element of the woof variable. If woof doesn't have six elements, you check to make
sure it has five elements. If it doesn't, you know you've selected a bad root background,
so you produce an error message and exit.

> **Note:** The C Shell also supports a form of an online conditional execution.
> If a command is followed by && and another command, then the second
> command is executed only if the first command was successful, which is
> defined as having a return code of 0. If the first command is followed by ¦¦,
> then the second command will be executed only if the first one fails. These
> are shorthands inherited from the Bourne shell. You do not need to use
> them; however, a quick examination of their equivalents shows their worth:
>
> ```
> if ( { file testfile } ) echo testfile is there
> file testfile && echo testfile is there
> if ( ! { grep sammy /etc/passwd } ) echo Sammy is not in the password file
> grep sammy /etc/passwd ¦¦ echo Sammy is not in the password file
> ```
>
> The shorthand is an easier way to write an if command; however, the if
> command may be clearer to someone maintaining a script.

These else if clauses can be strung together any number of times in an if command.
Although this may make sense to the novice programmer, the switch command also
provides a good means to make this kind of code.

switch

The `switch` command is used to differentiate between several different options. Although often these options can also be expressed with an `if` command, the `switch` command is a clearer approach to the problem.

Syntax

The syntax for `switch` is

```
switch (string)
case label:
command block
endsw
```

Any number of cases can be present in a `switch` command.

The `switch` commands, and their additional pieces (`case`, `default`, and `breaksw`, described later) are useful for executing code based on a variety of options. Unlike the previous conditional `if` and unlike the `while` loop, the `switch` command isn't controlled by an expression. Instead the `switch` takes a string and searches through the `case` commands until a matching string is found, and then subsequent commands are executed. If no matching cases are found and there exists a default case, the commands associated with the default case are executed. If there is no default, execution resumes after the `endsw` command.

The string for the `switch` command undergoes both filename expansion and variable substitution. The case labels do not have this luxury and can only be exact strings.

An example of a `switch` command is this code to bring up an X Windows command based on an argument:

```
switch ($wintype)      this    matches
case upper:  this
    xterm -g =80x28+0+93&      or
    breaksw
case lower:  this
    xterm -g =80x28+0-0&      or
    breaksw
case right:  this
    xterm -g =80x59-0-0&
endsw
```

In this example, depending on the value of `wintype`, a new shell window will be produced on the screen. If `wintype` is `upper`, the window will be located against the left side of the screen, 93 pixels from the top (in the top-left quadrant). If `wintype` is `lower`, the window will appear in the bottom-left quadrant, and if `wintype` is `right`, the window will appear on the right side of the screen.

Another example occurs in a standard login script. If you have access to multiple machines, you may need different setting for each type of machine. The `switch` command is ideal for handling this situation:

```
switch ( `hostname` )
case duke:
case krzyzewski:
     source .cshrc.solaris2.3
     breaksw
case gaudet:
     source .cshrc.sunos4
     breaksw
case brey:
     source .cshrc.hp.addon
case amaker:
     source .cshrc.hp
     breaksw
default:
     source .cshrc.other
     breaksw
endsw
```

This example assumes a network of five different machines. If you access the machines `duke` or `krzyzewski`, then you will source the `.cshrc.solaris2.3` file. If you've logged into `gaudet`, you source `.cshrc.sunos4`. If you log into `brey`, you source `.cshrc.hp.addon` and the `.cshrc.hp` files. If you log into `amaker`, you source just the `.cshrc.hp` file. Presumably, these files configure your environment for the correct machine.

This `switch` example illustrates a couple of important considerations. You can have multiple labels for the same command block. Both the `duke` and the `krzyzewski` machines require the same file, so having that command block identified with both labels allows the same commands to be run. Also, this example illustrates the principle that once execution resumes, it continues regardless of labels. Because the case for `brey` did not come with a `breaksw`, after the block for `brey` is finished, execution continues immediately onto the block for `amaker` and continues on until it reaches a `breaksw`. Finally, this example shows a default case. If a new machine is added onto the network, when you log in, you want some default environment until you configure a special environment for that machine. The default case handles this situation.

Caution: The default case includes a `breaksw` command, even though it is not necessary. Including the `breaksw` is a good procedure for any command block in a `switch` command, unless you've specifically decided that you want to fall through to the next command block. This way, when you add a case, you don't need to worry about falling through accidentally, with unexpected results.

Switch commands can also be used to handle input and output. In this example, a user is prompted for a disposition to a file, and the result is a `switch` command:

```
echo "r- read, d- delete, f- forward, q- quit"
set io=$<
set io=`echo $io ¦ cut -c1 ¦ tr "[A-Z]" "[a-z]"`
switch ( "$io" )
case "r":
    cat file
    breaksw
case "d":
    rm file
    breaksw
case "f":
    mail $user < file
    breaksw
case "q":
    exit
default:
    echo Illegal input
    breaksw
endsw
```

Here, you've prompted the user for one of four commands. The second command reads standard input to get the user's response. Because you only need one letter and wish to keep it lowercase, you use the command pipeline in the third command to convert the user's input to a form you can use.

The `switch` command examines the value of the `io` variable, set just above. It then examines each case, until it finds a match and performs the actions of the command block. If no match is found, the user has given a bad command; you notify the user of the error and proceed beyond the `switch`.

Note: The quit option does not include a `breaksw`. This is because here the user can exit the program. After the `exit` command, no further commands can be executed.

Another example of a `switch` command is this version of `getopt`, a tool to parse a command line:

```
while ($#argv > 0 )
    switch ($argv[1])
    case "-g":
        set gflag
        breaksw
    case "-O":
        set oflag
        set oarg=$argv[2]
```

11

```
        shift
        breaksw
    case "-r":
        set rflag
        breaksw
    default:
        echo unrecognized option: $argv[0]
    endsw
    shift
end
```

This script has an outer `while` loop, which continues while the argv variable has elements. The loop consists of a `switch` command and `shift` command. The `shift` command will be examined later in the chapter. The `switch` command looks at the first element of argv; you know there will be an element because the loop would not execute without one. Below the `switch`, you are looking for three cases of three valid command options. If the value of the switch string is -g, -o, or -r, then you set a variable with no value to indicate that the option is present. If -o is the string, you also assign the variable oarg with the second element of argv, and shift argv one place.

If the value of `$argv[1]` is not recognized, you report the error and continue with the loop.

Fully exploiting the power of `switch` and `case` require understanding the different related pieces of the command—`case`, `default`, and `breaksw`—as described below.

case

The `case` command is a flag to notify a `switch` command of a label.

The syntax for case is

`case label:`

The `label` must appear on the same line as the `case`. The word `case` must appear at the beginning of the line.

There can be any number of case labels in a `switch` command; if encountered in the flow of code, they are treated as regular labels and are ignored.

default

The `default` command is a special type of label for a case.

11

Syntax

The syntax for `default` is

```
default:
```

The word `default` must start the line.

The `default` condition is run only if there are no case labels that match a string for a `switch` command. It must be the last option for the `switch`, and only one can be present in a `switch` command.

breaksw

The `breaksw` command is used to terminate a condition in a `switch` command.

Syntax

The syntax for `breaksw` is

```
breaksw
```

It takes no arguments.

When a `breaksw` is encountered, the next command executed is the one immediately following the next `endsw`. The `breaksw` is used to terminate execution for a case option. Outside a `switch` command, `breaksw` has no meaning.

> **Caution:** Using `breaksw` interactively produces an unexpected result. In one test, the C Shell produced a question mark prompt, expecting more input. After providing a `case` command, the prompt was still a question mark. Only after termination with a Control+C was the error message `breaksw: endsw not found` produced. If a single `endsw` is produced, the request terminates, and no commands are run. This is contrary to the expected performance of the shell and constitutes a bug.

Interrupt Handling

One aspect of writing a C Shell program is interrupt handling. There are times when a C Shell script may need to catch an interrupt signal, `SIGINT`, to clean up before exiting. The command to catch the interrupts is `onintr`.

The syntax for `onintr` is

```
onintr [ - ¦ label ]
```

This controls the actions of the shell when it receives SIGINT. With no arguments, the default action is restored. With a minus sign (-), SIGINT is ignored, and if a label is provided, when SIGINT is caught, control will jump to that label and the commands present will be executed.

The default actions for SIGINT are for all shell scripts to be terminated, and control is restored to the terminal command input level, the login shell. Effectively, all commands being run in the foreground are ended, and the login shell resumes.

The `onintr` enables you, the script writer, to change the actions when a SIGINT is caught. You can ignore the signal or proceed to some action. A simple example is this one showing the three different effects.

```
onintr badone
echo step one
sleep 5
onintr -
echo step one
sleep 5
onintr
echo step one
sleep 5
exit
badone:
echo outta here
```

You should copy this script into a file, and run it with csh. You will note that it prints step one three times and terminates. To show the effects of `onintr`, run the program and press Control+C after each step one.

Pressing Control+C after the first step one should produce the output outta here and terminate immediately. In this case, the SIGINT generated by Control+C is caught, and the script immediately executes a goto badone. At this label is the echo command, and the script ends. The echo is executed before termination. If this does not happen, your interrupt key is set to something other than Control+C. You should consult with your system administrator to determine which is the correct key, and then proceed with the lesson.

Pressing Control+C after the second step one should have no effect. In this case, the command `onintr -` means that SIGINT should be ignored. No commands are terminated, and execution proceeds as if nothing happened.

Pressing Control+C after the third step one should immediately terminate the program with no output. This is the default action for the C Shell when it catches SIGINT, to terminate all shell scripts and return to the terminal command input level.

There are some locations where catching SIGINT is mandatory. As a system administrator, you may want to prevent a user from consuming too many resources, so you may want to limit the user with the limit command. However, a crafty user could attempt to get around this by interrupting the default login script. You can prevent this by using onintr to ignore the interrupt signal while the script is executing:

```
onintr -
limit -h cputime 1h
onintr
```

While the limit command is running, the user cannot interrupt the command, effectively preventing the user from abusing system limits. These onintr commands can be placed around the entire script, not only around the relevant pieces.

> **Note:** Unfortunately, the C Shell can trap only the SIGINT signal. If it receives any other signal, even if sent from the keyboard, the signal will cause a failure of the program.

11

The most common form for using onintr is to catch the signal and clean up a process. If your script creates temporary files, use onintr to trap the interrupt signal, and then clean up:

```
onintr cleanup
echo data > /tmp/tempfile
# Other commands that create temporary files, t1 and t2.
echo Finished!
cleanup:
rm -f /tmp/tempfile t1 t2
exit
```

The preceding code sets a trap to send control to the cleanup label if an interrupt is caught. After cleanup are the last two lines of the script, which remove the temporary files quietly and exit the program. This way, if a user feels bogged down by your script and terminates it early, you don't leave files around that might mess up other users.

> **Note:** It is a common practice to use the process ID, $$, to create unique filenames for temporary files.

shift

The shift command is used to move the elements of a variable to the virtual left.

Syntax

The syntax for shift is

```
shift [ variable ]
```

The values of the variable are shifted to the left one position, and the first value is discarded. If no variable is specified, the shift command operates on argv.

The shift is most useful for the destructive examination of a variable's elements. The most common usage is when examining the command-line arguments to a script; after the argument's actions are completed, it is no longer necessary for the value to remain. Earlier, you saw an example of shift:

```
set oflag
set oarg=$argv[2]
shift
breaksw
```

These commands are extracted from the command block of the switch example where command-line arguments are verified. In this case, the -o option was specified. Because this option takes an argument, the value is assigned to a variable, and the argv variable is shifted. The same could also have been accomplished with a while loop:

```
@ i=1
@ j=2
while ( $i < $#argv )
    set argv[$i] = "$argv[$j]"
    @ i++
    @ j++
end
set argv[$i] = ""
set argv = ( $argv:q )
```

This command loops through the different elements of argv and assigns them to the previous element. Then, when the loop is complete, the last element is assigned a null value. Then, to insure the removal of the last element, the variable is reassigned the variable.

If argv were set to (1 2 3 4), then the loop would convert the value to (2 3 4 4). The assignment would make the value (2 3 4 ""), but when this undergoes variable replacement, the value will be seen as (2 3 4). Even with spaces in element values, this will reduce the size of the variable.

Of course, shift does not apply to just the argv variable. Earlier, you saw a situation

where shift was used on a variable named woof. Here, the variable is shifted one to the left if woof has six elements. This adjusts the number of elements to the expected five. That first element for a six-element variable is used to replace the first element of argv.

One weakness of shift is that it can only shift one place at a time. If you wish to shift a variable two or more places, you'll need to specify a separate shift command for each place desired. Tomorrow you will examine a script that will make this multiplaced shift for you.

The shift command will generate some error messages. If there are no values in the array, shift will produce the error message shift: No more words. If the variable doesn't exit, the standard message name: Undefined variable will be written to the output.

Summary

Today you have covered extensively the different control structures required for C Shell programming. First, you learned about the two types of looping commands, the foreach loop and the while loop. The foreach loop is determinate in the number of iterations; a *wordlist* is included and the command block is executed once for each word in the list. The while loop is indeterminate, executing repeatedly while a condition is true. The differences between the two loops are significant. A foreach loop can be represented as a while loop, but it is not always possible to do the reverse.

You also examined two techniques to halt the execution of a command block for a loop. The break command will terminate the loop and resume execution on the next possible command. The continue command will return to the top of the loop, taking the next word of the *wordlist* in a foreach loop and retesting the condition for a while loop. These commands can be stacked to break multiple loops.

Next, you learned about the conditional execution of commands. The if structures provided two techniques for executing a conditional command. The simple if tests a condition and executes a simple command if true, and the more complicated if can have a number of different branches based on the evaluation of a condition or conditions. Also, you learned about the switch command and its additional features, case, default, and breaksw. These commands allow for a block of commands to be run based on a string comparison.

To end the day, you learned about two special commands for shell programming. The first, onintr, traps the SIGINT signal and enables you to determine a course of action when the signal is caught. This is particularly useful for cleaning up scripts. The last command of the day was shift, which alters the value of a variable by deleting the first member and shifting every element down one position.

Tomorrow, you will start to put these concepts together and write some simple shell scripts. You will see how to write a script to bounce mail, a script to assign a root window from an index, a script to shift a variable a multiple number of places, and other scripts to perform simple tasks.

After that, on Day 13 you will learn how to create a large C Shell script. This script will be a spelling checker and corrector that you can use to verify that you have used correct spelling in your documents. The script will keep its own lexicon for words you add that are not in the dictionary, and it will correct the spelling of words automatically in the document. It will even keep a listing of frequently misspelled words for you, with your corrections. Finally, it will produce an updated document for you. After you have finished these two lessons, you will be able to write C Shell programs at any level.

Related UNIX Topics—Bourne Shell Equivalents

The Bourne shell is, like the C Shell, a programmable shell, and it is also present on many UNIX systems. For each of the C Shell control structures, there is an equivalent Bourne shell structure. Knowledge of the differences may be useful, if you should need to translate a script from one shell to the other.

foreach and *for*

The Bourne shell equivalent for a `foreach` command is `for`. In the first example in this chapter, you used `foreach` to step through a list of `tar` files to be uuencoded and mailed. Your script looked like this:

```
foreach i ( *.tar )
uuencode $i $i ¦ mail -s $i friend
end
```

Bourne shell will also handle this simple loop, in the following form:

```
for i in *.tar
do
uuencode $i $i ¦ mail -s $i friend
done
```

The commands look very similar, and in this case, they do exactly the same job. The C Shell variant is a bit more compact, however, and it does not need a starting word to indicate where the command block begins.

In contrast, the `for` command does not need a list of words. If no words are present, the Bourne shell equivalent of `$argv` is used, instead.

while and *while*

The Bourne shell and the C Shell use the same command name for a `while` loop, but the syntax is very different. In this chapter, the first example of a C Shell `while` loop was to wait on the existence of a file:

```
while ( -f file )
ps ax
sleep 10
end
```

The Bourne shell version would look similar, but the real differences are surprising:

```
while test -f file
do
ps ax
sleep 10
done
```

You will note that the conditional is actually a command, `test`. This is because the Bourne shell does not include a series of file inquiries. Instead it uses the `test` built-in command, and one of the `test` arguments is `-f`, for file existence. The `test` command is both more and less powerful than the expression handlers for C Shell. It has more options for testing, but it does not use the commonly recognized arithmetical symbols for numerical comparisons, and it does not handle empty strings quite as gracefully.

Another C Shell `while` example shows another real strength for the C Shell:

```
@ i=1
while ( $i < 10 )
echo $path[$i]
@ i++
end
```

The preceding code steps through the first 10 elements of the path. In the Bourne shell, the code for that task looks like this:

```
i=1
set `echo $PATH | sed 's/:/ /g'`
while [ $i -lt 10 ]
do
echo $1
shift
i=`expr "$i" + 1`
done
```

Confused?

The Bourne shell does not support variable arrays, so you don't even have a `path` variable to test. Instead, you must start with the PATH environment variable and convert the separating colons into spaces with the command `sed`. Then, you use the Bourne shell `set`

command to make these positional parameters. The actual loop prints the first positional parameter, then shifts those parameters to the left, similar to the C Shell's `shift` command. The last command of the loop is even more confusing.

The Bourne shell does not have built-in arithmetical operations. So, to perform even simple arithmetic, such as adding 1 to a number, you would need to use the `expr` command. This is not a built-in command, so executing it requires a separate `fork` and `exec` for each arithmetical operation! This makes arithmetic a slow proposition for the Bourne Shell.

One strength of the Bourne shell is that you can specify multiple commands in the condition easily. A Bourne shell `while` loop may look like this:

```
while
     v=`echo $1 ¦ cut -c1`
     [ X$v = X- ]
do
     targ="$targ $1"
     shift
done
```

In this one, a command is executed to get the first character of an argument, and that single character is tested.

break and *continue*

These C Shell commands are the same in the Bourne shell, except that instead of requiring a series of breaks to exit multiple loops, a numerical argument can be given in the Bourne shell commands to break or continue to break a number of enclosing loops.

if-then-else-endif and *if-then-else-fi*

The first `if` example in this chapter was to add a directory to the path if a certain file existed. In the C Shell, that command looked like this:

```
if ( -x /usr/local/bin/rn ) set path = ( $path /usr/local/bin )
```

The Bourne shell does not have this simple `if` format, so the Bourne shell command would look like this:

```
if [ -x /usr/local/bin/rn ]
then
PATH=$PATH:/usr/local/bin
fi
```

The commands are fairly similar, except that the Bourne shell requires a `then` and `fi` around the command block. This can also be a accomplished in Bourne shell with

```
[ -x /usr/local/bin/rn ] && PATH=$PATH:/usr/local/bin
```

For more complicated `if` commands, the Bourne shell contracts the `else if` to `elif`. Consider the following code.

```
if ( $woof == 6 ) then
    echo woof is six
else if ( $woof != 5 ) then
    echo woof is not five
    exit
endif
```

When the preceding C Shell code is translated to the Bourne shell, it looks like this:

```
if  [ "$woof" -eq 6 ]
then
    echo woof is six
elif [ "$woof" -ne 5 ]
then
    echo woof is not five
    exit
fi
```

The Bourne shell's use of non-English words can be confusing to a novice programmer. Just remember that `fi` is `endif` and `elif` is `else if`.

switch and *case*

The `switch` command in C Shell is similar to the Bourne shell's `case` command. Both perform string comparisons, but in the `case` command of the Bourne shell, the labels get file expansion. In the Bourne shell's command it is not possible to explicitly execute multiple command blocks; after each block, control exits to beyond the `case` command. You saw this C Shell example earlier in the chapter:

```
switch ($wintype)
case upper:
    xterm -g =80x28+0+93&
    breaksw
case lower:
    xterm -g =80x28+0-0&
    breaksw
case right:
    xterm -g =80x59-0-0&
endsw
```

To do this in Bourne shell, you'd need the following code:

```
case "$wintype" in
upper) xterm -g =80x28+0+93& ;;
lower) xterm -g =80x28+0-0& ;;
right) xterm -g =80x59-0-0& ;;
esac
```

The Bourne shell code is more compact and a bit clearer, but it lacks the functionality of the C Shell `switch` command.

Bourne Shell Versus C Shell

As with any language, there are advantages and disadvantages to any choice. Selecting a shell is a matter of making a choice of the best tool to solve a problem. Through the next two lessons, you will learn some of the more explicit advantages to the Bourne and C shells, and you will also learn when it is best to choose one instead of the other. As always, this decision is not one of absolutes and not about one shell being better than the other, but it is instead a choice of a tool to do the job.

Q&A

Q What is the difference between a `foreach` loop and a `while` loop?

A A `foreach` loop is used when a program needs to loop through a list of values and will be manipulating those values in the command block. This type of loop is determinate, in that the program will know in advance how many iterations through the loop are needed to solve a problem. The `while` loop, however, executes repeatedly while a condition is true. In advance, the program will not know how often to execute the loop. This type of looping is indeterminate.

Q How does a user terminate a loop early?

A When you use the `break` command, the loop will be terminated early. If `continue` is used, the loop restarts at the top, with the next `foreach` value or with a retest of a `while` condition. Multiple loops can be broken with multiple `break` commands, all on the same line, separated by semicolons.

Q What file inquiry would I use to see whether a file was writeable?

A The `-w` inquiry is used to determine whether the user can write to a file. The other inquiries are `-r`, to determine whether the user can read a file; `-e`, to determine whether the file exists; `-o`, to determine whether you own the file; `-z`, to determine whether the file is empty (that is, whether it has a length of zero); `-f`, to determine whether it is a plain file; and `-d`, to determine whether it is a directory.

Q Why should I use a `switch` command when a series of `if` commands will do the same job?

A Using the correct tool for a given problem is always a challenge. Yes, you can get by with never learning about `switch`, but there are times when using `switch` is clearer to understand. The `switch` doesn't force the program to execute alternative blocks of code, such as an `if` command would do. Also, it can be

difficult to track all the conditions for a multiline `if` command, particularly when the command spans several pages of output. A `switch` command would be a lot clearer.

Workshop

The workshop provides two sections to aid you in understanding the topics covered in today's lesson. The quiz section provides a quick review of today's topics, and the exercises enable you to apply your knowledge to solving some problems. Make sure you understand these answers before you proceed to tomorrow's lesson. The answers are in Appendix F, "Answers to Quizzes and Exercises."

Quiz

1. What is the difference between a label for `goto` and a label for a `switch` statement?

2. What does `shift` do?

3. How do you trap `SIGTERM`? `SIGINT`? `SIGHUP`? `SIGKILL`?

4. How do you execute a block of code if a directory exists and is readable?

5. You need to break out of two loops and restart the third. What command do you use?

Exercises

1. Convert the following `if` command into a `switch` command:

```
if ( $j == blue ) then
    echo Now it is green
else if ( $j == cat ) then
    echo Now it is mouse
else if ( $j == hot ) then
    echo Now it is cold
else
    echo No match
endif
```

2. Write an `if` command to indicate whether a number is odd or even.

Applied C Shell Programming, Part I

Introduction to Day 12

Yesterday, you learned about the basic control structures required to make C Shell programs. You should now understand the two different looping commands, `foreach` and `while`, and the differences between them. You also learned how to stop the execution of loops. Finally, you learned about the conditional commands `if` and `switch`.

Today, you will first see how C Shell programs are written. You will work through six examples of simple C Shell programs and understand them step-by-step. This should help you learn more about how to program the shell.

The first example is a simple script used to clean up your path. Often, particularly on complex systems, your path may grow out of control, to the point that not even you can understand it. This script is designed to be used with the `source` command to remove duplicate and nonexistent entries from your path.

The second example is a script used to delete unwanted mail, based on the information presented in the mail screen. It illustrates some different concepts of I/O redirection in a script.

The third example is a command to implement a multiplaced shift command. In this command's case, the output of the command is used just like the return value of a function.

The fourth example paints root windows in X Windows with a certain pattern. This script is slightly longer than the others and shows a table-driven script.

The fifth and sixth examples are the standard UNIX commands `uuto` and `uupick` illustrated in C Shell. Both already exist, but as Bourne Shell programs.

Setting Today's Goals

Today, you will learn

☐ How to piece together C Shell commands to make meaningful scripts

☐ How to use C Shell scripts as functions

☐ The elements of a C Shell script

☐ When to use C Shell scripts as with the `source` command or a regular command

☐ How to make a table-driven application

Tackling Small Programs to Solve Problems

A C Shell program is just a script of C Shell commands in a file. Your .cshrc file, discussed on Day 6, is one example of a C Shell program. The .login and .logout are also programs run by the C Shell at their respective times.

As a result, there are some common features of all C Shell programs. They are all pure ASCII text files, and they can be examined with standard UNIX tools. Once written, they don't need any special tools to make them usable—just a change of permission to allow execution, and even that isn't always necessary. They all contain C Shell commands as written in an interactive session; they still perform variable substitution and file expansion.

There are two ways to execute a C Shell program. The most common way is to include the line #!/bin/csh -f as the first line of the file. This tells the exec system call to execute the /bin/csh program with the -f option and to include this file as the standard input to that program. A new C Shell process is created to run these commands. The -f option is used for a fast start, meaning your .cshrc file is ignored. This is strongly recommended for C Shell programs, because you cannot know what other users may have done to their environment. What if another user had aliased ls to rm, for whatever reason, and you attempted an ls *? That user wouldn't be happy to find all his files removed. To run a program this way, the file must have execute permission.

The second way to run a C Shell program is to explicitly execute a C Shell command with the program name as an argument. The C Shell recognizes this as an effort to run this program in the C Shell, and it will use this file as standard input. In this case, the file does not need execute permissions set.

Note: Another name for a C Shell program is a *script*. On manual pages, script is used to mean a file with a list of commands. The two terms are used synonymously here.

Each of the following examples solves a specific problem. You should already have the skills needed to address each problem given. The best way to learn is by doing, so read each problem carefully, and before you look at how I solved it, think up a solution yourself. Then read over my solution carefully to see how I addressed the problem. Who knows, perhaps your solution is better than mine!

Path Cleaner

Problem: On large systems, frequently many different directories are added to a path, and often directories are duplicated or non-existent. Write a C Shell script, to be used with the `source` command, that will eliminate duplicates and non-existent directories from your path.

Solution: The solution is to step through the path variable and to build a new path. This definitely looks like a job for a `foreach` loop, so you will start with that.

```
foreach element ( $path )
```

You also need to create a new path variable. At first, it should have no elements. A `set` command alone (or by itself) will create a variable:

```
set newpath
foreach element ( $path )
```

> **Note:** You know that there are no spaces in the names of any directories in the path variable, so you don't need to worry about the `:q` modifier.

There are two conditions for keeping a path entry. One is that it must be a directory. You should use the file inquiry `-d` to determine whether the current element is a directory. You can make this the first test:

```
set newpath
foreach element ( $path )
    if ( -d $element ) then
    endif
end
```

> **Note:** You will see that I've indented the loop. This is not a requirement, and when you are programming interactively you won't see the indents. I include the indentation simply because it makes the script easier to read.

The other condition for a directory to be a part of the path is that the directory must not be a duplicate. To check that, the best approach would be to step through the `newpath` variable. If the element is the same as an element of `newpath`, you have a duplicate, so you don't want to add that element. This step is another `foreach` loop, within the `if` command:

```
set newpath
foreach element ( $path )
    if ( -d $element ) then
        foreach newelement ( $newpath )
        end
    endif
end
```

The program is already getting rather complex, compared to previous examples. You also need a comparison to show when you don't want to add the directory. In this comparison, you can set a flag to indicate that you don't need the directory:

```
set newpath
foreach element ( $path )
    if ( -d $element ) then
        foreach newelement ( $newpath )
            if ( $element == $newelement ) set notneeded
        end
    endif
end
```

The problem with the preceding setup is that once an element matches, notneeded is always set. You are better off setting a flag before the foreach loop, telling you to add the element, and when the match is found, unsetting that flag. When this is done, the script becomes

```
set newpath
foreach element ( $path )
    if ( -d $element ) then
        set needed
        foreach newelement ( $newpath )
            if ( $element == $newelement ) unset needed
        end
    endif
end
```

Now, when you see needed after the foreach loop, you should append the element to the newpath variable. The script will now look like the following:

```
set newpath
foreach element ( $path )
    if ( -d $element ) then
        set needed
        foreach newelement ( $newpath )
            if ( $element == $newelement ) unset needed
        end
        if ( $?needed ) set newpath = ( $newpath $element )
    endif
end
```

Check to see whether needed is still set, and if so, add the element to the newpath with the set command.

> **Note:** The element is added at the end of the `newpath` variable to preserve the order of the elements of the original path.

If you want to speed execution, after you've found that the element is no longer needed, you could use a `break` command after the `unset` command. This changes the shape of the `if` command:

```
set newpath
foreach element ( $path )
    if ( -d $element ) then
        set needed
        foreach newelement ( $newpath )
            if ( $element == $newelement ) then
                unset needed
                break
            endif
        end
        if ( $?needed ) set newpath = ( $newpath $element )
    endif
end
```

This change is optional. Finally, you need to set the path variable to the new value. A simple `set` command will do so:

```
set newpath
foreach element ( $path )
    if ( -d $element ) then
        set needed
        foreach newelement ( $newpath )
            if ( $element == $newelement ) then
                unset needed
                break
            endif
        end
        if ( $?needed ) set newpath = ( $newpath $element )
    endif
end
set path = ( $newpath )
```

This is all that is needed for a script to reduce the path. If you have a path that looks like (`/usr/bin /usr/james/bin /usr/local/bin /etc /usr/bin`), the following is an annotated description of what will happen with the script. Each command that the C Shell executes is listed, with my comments marked with #. If you use this script yourself, you won't see my comments.

```
set newpath
# A newpath variable is set
foreach element ( /usr/bin /usr/james/bin /usr/local/bin /etc /usr/bin )
```

```
# The path variable is expanded and the loop is entered.  element is
# assigned the value /usr/bin
    if ( -d /usr/bin ) then
# Does this directory exist?  You know it does.
        set needed
# The needed variable is set since the directory exists
        foreach newelement ()
# Newpath has no members, so the loop isn't executed
        end
        if ( $?needed ) set newpath = ( /usr/bin )
# Needed still exists, so newpath is assigned its first member
    endif
end
# The foreach loop is finished with its first element, so now element
# is assigned the value /usr/james/bin
    if ( -d /usr/james/bin ) then
# This directory also exists
        set needed
        foreach newelement ( /usr/bin )
# Newpath has one element, and you set newelement to that value.
            if ( /usr/james/bin == /usr/bin ) then
# You make a comparison, but it is false.
            endif
        end
        if ( $?needed ) set newpath = ( /usr/bin /usr/james/bin )
# Again, needed remains, so newpath adds a new element
    endif
end
# The third iteration, element is /usr/local/bin.
    if ( -d /usr/local/bin ) then
# There is no /usr/local/bin on the system now, so, this time the
# in statement block is not executed.
    endif
end
# A fourth iteration looks at /etc.
    if ( -d /etc ) then
        set needed
        foreach newelement ( /usr/bin /usr/james/bin )
            if ( /etc == /usr/bin ) then
            endif
            if ( /etc == /usr/james/bin ) then
            endif
        end
        if ( $?needed ) set newpath = ( /usr/bin /usr/james/bin \
            /etc )
# In stepping through the loop, you find that /etc exists as a
# directory, and is not already part of the newpath, so it is added.
    endif
end
# The fifth iteration looks at /usr/bin
    if ( -d /usr/bin )
        set needed
        foreach newelement ( /usr/bin /usr/james/bin /etc )
            if ( /usr/bin == /usr/bin ) then
# You have a duplicate.
                unset needed
```

```
# This element of the original path is not needed.
                    break
# You don't need to perform any more comparisons.
            endif
        end
        if ( $?needed ) set newpath = ( /usr/bin /usr/james/bin \
            /etc /usr/bin )
# Needed is not set, so the set command for newpath is not executed.
    endif
end
set path = ( /usr/bin /usr/james/bin /etc )
# Now that you've looked at all the elements, you've eliminated two
# parts of the path, the /usr/local/bin entry, because it doesn't
# exist, and the second /usr/bin, since it is a duplicate.
```

A listing of the commands run can be easily generated by running the program with csh -x. To help keep this output clear, I've slightly modified the output to retain the indents and to show the $?needed test explicitly.

> **Note:** This script actually contains nothing but built-in commands for the C Shell, and it will execute without calling fork and exec.

If you choose, you can save this script in the file clean_path. The way to use clean_path is with the command source clean_path, and you can include it near the end of your .cshrc file to help you keep your path variable as simple as required to perform the job.

Mail Bouncer

Problem: You get a lot of extraneous mail that you'd rather not see. This may include mail from MAILER_DAEMON, indicating that mail has failed, or from a user badguy@badsite who has been sending you annoying mail.

Solution: Clearly, you need a script that can examine the incoming mail and delete mail from undesired senders before you even see it.

There are two users you want to omit from your mail file. This again calls for a foreach loop:

```
foreach user ( MAILER_DAEMON badguy@badsite )
end
```

You may want to put this list in a file and then do the loop on the contents of the file, because your list of possible bad users may change. Assuming that you name the file .bounce in your home directory, this makes a small change to the program:

```
foreach user ( `cat ~/.bounce` )
end
```

This now executes the cat command to create a list of bounced users. You add the two names to this file. If the file doesn't exist, though, this prints the error message cat: cannot open /usr/james/.bounce and will run no tests. Although receiving this message is not catastrophic, you should first test the file, and if it doesn't exist, you can exit:

```
if ( ! -f ~/.bounce ) exit
foreach user ( `cat ~/.bounce` )
end
```

You need to get a listing of the people who have sent you mail. The Berkeley Mailer does this easily with the -H option, so you can use /usr/ucb/mail -H to get a listing.

This will produce output that looks like the following:

```
1 chill%star3@concer Fri Jul 29 19:11   79/2639  Re: UNC Schedule
2 MAILER_DAEMON      Fri Jul 29 19:11   83/3620  Mail failed
3 marv@netcom.com    Sat Jul 30 01:32   11/733   Hi ya!
4 badguy@badsite.bad Sat Jul 30 09:55 8677/98562 I hate you
```

Already you know you don't want to see the second and fourth message, but how do you delete those messages programmatically? This calls for the grep and the cut commands.

Note: The grep command is a standard UNIX utility that searches for lines of a file that include a regular expression. Regular expressions are complicated UNIX strings for pattern matching. Fortunately, the simplest regular expression is a string, so you can use grep for a string.

The name grep comes from the original UNIX editor, ed. The command in the editor to print a line that matched a pattern was g/re/p, where re was the regular expression. Removing the slashes yielded *grep*.

There are some modified grep commands, too. The egrep command is an extended grep command. The fgrep command is "fast grep." For more information on these commands, you can look at the manual pages, or read about these commands in Dave Taylor's excellent book, *Teach Yourself UNIX in a Week*.

The cut command is another UNIX command, designed to remove data from a file. The cut command can work with fields of data, with a selectable separator, or with columns. This is also explained in Dave Taylor's book and in manual pages.

12

First, you can use `grep` to get the specific line that matches the pattern:

```
/usr/ucb/mail -H ¦ grep MAILER_DAEMON
     2 MAILER_DAEMON      Fri Jul 29 19:11   83/3620  Mail failed
```

So, you've isolated one of the lines. Next, by using `cut`, you can get the message number:

```
/usr/ucb/mail -H ¦ grep MAILER_DAEMON ¦ cut -c1-5
     2
```

This is the number needed to delete a command using Berkeley mail, so you need to set a variable to that number.

```
if ( ! -f ~/.bounce ) exit
foreach user ( `cat ~/.bounce` )
    set returns=`/usr/ucb/mail -H ¦ grep "$user" ¦ cut -c1-5 `
end
```

> **Note:** You include $user in quotes in case there is a space in the name of the account to be eliminated. Otherwise, `grep` takes the second argument as the name of a file and ignores the input of `/usr/ucb/mail`.

You now have the list of returns, and you can use a form of I/O redirection to feed this request to the `mail` command:

```
 if ( ! -f ~/.bounce ) exit
foreach user ( `cat ~/.bounce` )
    set returns=`/usr/ucb/mail -H ¦ grep "$user" ¦ cut -c1-5`
    /usr/ucb/mail << EOF
    d $returns
EOF
end
```

Place the input to `mail` directly in the script, with the I/O redirection metacharacters <<. Now, when the script executes, it will delete messages two and four, but what happens if you execute the script a second time? There will be no matches to the `grep`, so `return` will be set to a zero length string. When a zero length return is used to delete mail, it will delete the first mail entry in the file, removing the first two pieces of mail. To prevent this, you need to see if there is a value for the `return` variable.

Clearly, the test $?return will not work, because the variable does exist. A count of the elements of `return` also will not work, so what can be done?

Again, you need to look at the pipeline that generated the message number. There is another UNIX utility, `wc`, that can count the number of lines of a file. This provides you with your solution.

Note: The wc command is short for "word count," but it also has flags for a count of lines and a count of characters. The manual page or Dave Taylor's book provides more details.

```
/usr/ucb/mail -H ¦ grep MAILER_DAEMON ¦ wc -l
      1
```

There is a single piece of mail for MAILER_DAEMON. You can set this to another variable and test it before running the mail command to delete the mail.

```
if ( ! -f ~/.bounce ) exit
foreach user ( `cat ~/.bounce` )
    set returns=`/usr/ucb/mail -H ¦ grep "$user" ¦ cut -c1-5`
    set count=`/usr/ucb/mail -H ¦ grep MAILER_DAEMON ¦ wc -l`
    if ( $count > 0 ) then
        /usr/ucb/mail << EOF
        d $returns
EOF
    endif
end
```

This is a complete script to delete mail messages.

When you run this, here are the results, annotated by the comments marked with #:

```
if ( -f ~/.bounce ) exit
# The file exists, so you keep going.
foreach user ( `cat ~/.bounce` )
# This requires the execution of the cat command:
cat ~/.bounce
MAILER_DAEMON
badguy@badsite
# This foreach becomes:
foreach user ( MAILER_DAEMON badguy@badsite )
# For the first iteration of the loop, user is set to MAILER_DAEMON
    set returns=`/usr/ucb/mail -H ¦ grep "$user" ¦ cut -c1-5`
# This pipeline sets returns to a value, based on the pipe's
# execution.  First, /usr/ucb/mail -H produces output:
/usr/ucb/mail -H
    1 chill%star3@concer Fri Jul 29 19:11    79/2639   Re: UNC Schedule
    2 MAILER_DAEMON      Fri Jul 29 19:11    83/3620   Mail failed
    3 marv@netcom.com    Sat Jul 30 01:32    11/733    Hi ya!
    4 badguy@badsite.bad Sat Jul 30 09:55 8677/98562 I hate you
# Then, this is piped through "grep MAILER_DAEMON":
grep "MAILER_DAEMON"
    2 MAILER_DAEMON      Fri Jul 29 19:11    83/3620   Mail failed
# And finally, the cut command is used:
cut -c1-5
    2
# and this value is assigned to return:
    set returns=    2
# The next command is also a pipe:
```

```
     set count=`/usr/ucb/mail -H ¦ grep "$user" ¦ wc -l`
# You know the output through the grep, and just pipe it into wc:
wc -l
     1
# This is used to set the count variable:
     set count=     1
# The next command checked is the comparison command:
     if ( $count > 0 ) then
# Since $count is 1, this is really:
     if ( 1 > 0 ) then
# You execute the if block of commands.
          /usr/ucb/mail << EOF
          d 2
EOF
# This runs the mail command, and deletes the second mail message.
# Now, you hit the end of the endif and the loop, and start again.
     endif
end
# For the second iteration, you set user to "badguy@badsite".
# Again, you test the pipeline:
/usr/ucb/mail -H
     1 chill%star3@concer Fri Jul 29 19:11   79/2639  Re: UNC Schedule
     2 marv@netcom.com    Sat Jul 30 01:32   11/733   Hi ya!
     3 badguy@badsite.bad Sat Jul 30 09:55 8677/98562 I hate you
# Since you deleted the second message previously, there are only
# messages.
grep "badguy@badsite"
     3 badguy@badsite.bad Sat Jul 30 09:55 8677/98562 I hate you
# There is still a message for deletion.
cut -c1-5
     3
# This is used to set returns.
     set returns=     3
# The pipeline with the wc sets count to 1.
     set count=       1
# Then, you hit the if command again, and execute the mail command
     if ( 1 > 0 )
          /usr/ucb/mail << EOF
          d 3
EOF
# The mail from badguy@badsite is now gone.
     endif
end
# This terminates this program.
```

This script shows several different types of I/O redirection and how they can be incorporated into a C Shell program. If you save this script in a file mailbouncer, you can create an alias for mail like the following:

```
alias mymail mailbouncer\;/usr/ucb/mail
```

Then, when you execute mymail, you get the following:

```
mailx version 5.0 Mon Sep 27 07:25:51 PDT 1993  Type ? for help.
"/var/mail/james": 2 messages
```

```
     1 chill%star3@concer  Fri Jul 29 19:11    79/2639   Re: UNC Schedule
     2 marv@netcom.com     Sat Jul 30 01:32    11/733    Hi ya!
?
```

The mail you don't want to see has been quietly removed.

> **Note:** Several mail tools already have techniques to remove unwanted messages. Elm, the most popular UNIX mail tool, includes a system of filters that allow for very complicated parsing of mail headers and for specific actions as a result.

Multiplace *shift*

Problem: In yesterday's lesson, you learned about the `shift` command, and that you could shift only one place. How do you write a script that will shift a multiple number of places, based on the first argument?

Solution: At first glance, you might think a simple list of shifts would do the trick. Any attempt to do this as an alias is bound to fail. Instead, the value of the array needs to be passed as an argument, and a `while` loop needs to be created.

Because the first argument is the number of shifts and the rest are the values from the variable, you need to save that value, and to shift the rest of the arguments.

```
set count=$1
shift
```

Now, the main loop looks like it should be a `while` loop. You can address this as "while the count is a positive number," and decrement the count:

```
set count=$1
shift
while ( $count > 0 )
    @ count--
end
```

The other action of the loop is simple. You just need to shift the values one space:

```
set count=$1
shift
while ( $count > 0 )
    shift
    @ count--
end
```

Now, the `argv` value is the proper value for the array after shifting. So, all that is now needed is to echo $argv and allow the receiving process to handle it properly:

```
set count=$1
shift
while ( $count > 0 )
    shift
    @ count--
end
echo $argv
```

Running this script is non-trivial. After you've saved it to a file, called `mshift`, it needs to be invoked as in the following:

```
set var = ( `mshift num $var` )
```

> **Note:** This script work only if there are no spaces in the arguments to be shifted. This is because any spaces would be treated as word separators. However, if the arguments are enclosed in quotes, the effect would still not be the desired effect, as the quotes would be evaluated as part of the words.
>
> One possible work-around would be for `mshift` to write a temporary file; then the parent process would source that file. The problem is non-trivial.

So, if you have a variable seuss = (the cat in the hat) and you need to shift it three spaces, you'd need to do the following:

```
set seuss = ( `mshift 3 $seuss` )
```

This expands to

```
set seuss = ( `mshift 3 the cat in the hat` )
```

The execution path of `mshift` would be

```
set count=$1
# This sets the count to 3
shift
# The new argv is ( the cat in the hat ), the same as the $seuss
# variable.
while ( $count > 0 )
# This is really while ( 3 > 0 )
    shift
# Argv becomes ( cat in the hat ).
    @ count --
# Count becomes 2
end
while ( 2 > 0 )
    shift
```

```
# Argv becomes ( in the hat )
     @ count --
# count becomes 1
end
while ( 1 > 0 )
     shift
# Argv becomes ( the hat )
     @ count --
# Count is now 0
end
while ( 0 > 0 )
# the loop is finished
echo $argv
the hat
# and the command is finished.
```

The parent process now becomes

```
set seuss = ( the hat )
```

The shift is complete.

Root Window

Problem: You have a file that lists root window patterns and colors, and you need an easy way to build an xsetroot command to paint the root window. The format of the file is `pattern: foreground background cursor_foreground cursor_background`. This file and the root bitmaps are all in the same directory, `/usr/share/roots`. The bitmap has the same name as the pattern, and the cursor files are the same as the pattern, but with `_cur` and `_mask` appended.

Solution: This command needs to take an argument, so you will start there:

```
if ( $#argv < 1 ) then
     echo an argument is expected.
endif
```

Next, you need to move to the correct directory:

```
if ( $#argv < 1 ) then
     echo an argument is expected.
endif
cd /usr/share/roots
```

You can then use grep to pull the pattern out of the file, and set a variable to that pattern:

```
if ( $#argv < 1 ) then
     echo an argument is expected.
endif
cd /usr/share/roots
set args = ( `grep "${1}:" index` )
```

Now, the args variable has the patterns and colors you want. It is easy to set up the xsetroot command now:

```
if ( $#argv < 1 ) then
    echo an argument is expected.
endif
cd /usr/share/roots
set args = ( `grep "${1}:" index` )
xsetroot -bitmap $1 -fg $args[2] -bg $args[3]
xsetroot -cursor ${1}_cur ${1}_mask -fg $args[4] -bg $args[5]
```

> **Note:** The xsetroot is an X Windows utility for painting the root window of an X session. X Windows is the default windowing system for UNIX, so if you have a windowing machine, odds are good that xsetroot is present. To test it, try xsetroot -solid, followed by any color you'd like.

It is easy to run this script. If you save it to a file setroot, and you have patterns for startrek, kitten, and face, then the command is just setroot startrek, setroot kitten, or setroot face. The execution path is also simple. If you type setroot face, the following occurs:

```
if ( $#argv < 1 ) then
# argv is ( face ), so the command is
if ( 1 < 1 ) then
endif
cd /usr/share/roots
# You can safely cd, as this is a child environment; your parent
# working directory is not affected.
set args = ( `grep "${1}:" index` )
# This command has a builtin command that needs to be executed first:
grep "face:" index
face: pink brown red blue
# There is a line for face, so the command is now
set args = ( face: pink brown red blue )
xsetroot -bitmap $1 -fg $args[2] -bg $args[3]
# After variable substitution this is
xsetroot -bitmap face -fg pink -bg brown
# This puts a pink and brown face on the root window.
xsetroot -cursor face_cur face_mask -fg red -bg blue
# This creates a red and blue cursor for the window.
```

This is a simpler C Shell script than some of the earlier examples. Instead of looping, it just pulls data from a file and runs a command.

uuto and *uupick* in C Shell

Problem: UUCP is an ugly command; you need two utilities to build the proper UUCP command. To send a file, you want only to type the filenames and the remote machine name and user (like an e-mail path). To receive a file, you want to type in only a single command, and the script will prompt you with filenames and offer you a menu to select options for a file. The options should be these: skip this file, delete this file, move this file to the current or specified directory, quit, and print the menu.

> **Note:** UUCP is a utility to transmit files from one UNIX machine to another.

Files should be received on the remote machine in the uucppublic directory (the default for sending files) in a subdirectory for the recipient, further divided by directories that indicate the sending machine. Both commands, uuto and uupick, need to understand how to use this directory structure. A file data from machine duke sent to user simon should be in /var/spool/uucppublic/receive/simon/duke/data.

uuto

Solution: This is a complicated problem. First, you should tackle uuto. It seems fairly easy: just use a foreach loop through the arguments. You need a minimum of two arguments. Otherwise, the command will not have the data it needs to succeed. So test the count first. Then you need to save the last argument as a destination name:

```
if ( $#argv < 2 ) then
    echo usage: uuto file [ file ] destination
    exit
endif
set dest=$argv[$#argv]
```

> **Note:** The usage line given for the error condition is not a requirement of the solution. However, providing the usage line does remind users who mistype the program how to use the command.

The destination address actually needs to be a machine and a username, separated by an exclamation point. So, to split the address properly, you use cut:

```
if ( $#argv < 2 ) then
    echo usage: uuto file [ file ] destination
    exit
endif
set dest=$argv[$#argv]
set remotemachine=`echo $dest ¦ cut -d\! -f1`
set remoteuser=`echo $dest ¦ cut -d\! -f2`
```

> **Note:** Before the advent of domain addressing, remote machine addresses
> followed the format of machine!machine!machine!user. The mail sender had
> to know the names of every machine between his and his recipient's mail
> machine. When I was a graduate student at the University of St. Andrews in
> Scotland, in order to send mail to my father at AT&T, I needed to send to
> csastand!west44!ukc!mcvax!research!panther!jca and he needed to send
> to research!mcvax!ukc!west44!csastand!csbstand!james. Now it is much
> easier to address mail to a user@domain. My father is now retired, but
> if he were still at AT&T, his address would be something like
> jca@panther.att.com—much faster, and easier to remember.

This program does no error checking on the destination. Two simple comparisons with
a null string can change that:

```
if ( $#argv < 2 ) then
    echo usage: uuto file [ file ] destination
    exit
endif
set dest=$argv[$#argv]
set remotemachine=`echo $dest ¦ cut -d\! -f1`
set remoteuser=`echo $dest ¦ cut -d\! -f2`
if ( $remoteuser == "" ) then
    echo You must supply a user
    exit
endif
if ( $remotemachine == "" ) then
    echo you must supply a machine
    exit
endif
```

These two conditions supply a simple error message and an exit. You need to put your
hostname into a variable for the remote directory:

```
if ( $#argv < 2 ) then
    echo usage: uuto file [ file ] destination
    exit
endif
set dest=$argv[$#argv]
set remotemachine=`echo $dest ¦ cut -d\! -f1`
set remoteuser=`echo $dest ¦ cut -d\! -f2`
```

```
if ( $remoteuser == "" ) then
    echo You must supply a user
    exit
endif
if ( $remotemachine == "" ) then
    echo you must supply a machine
    exit
endif
set hn=`hostname`
```

Also, because the last argument is not a file to be transferred, it can be removed by setting it to the null string.

```
if ( $#argv < 2 ) then
    echo usage: uuto file [ file ] destination
    exit
endif
set dest=$argv[$#argv]
set remotemachine=`echo $dest ¦ cut -d\! -f1`
set remoteuser=`echo $dest ¦ cut -d\! -f2`
if ( $remoteuser == "" ) then
    echo You must supply a user
    exit
endif
if ( $remotemachine == "" ) then
    echo you must supply a machine
    exit
endif
set hn=`hostname`
set argv[$#argv] = ""
```

Now, you must build a UUCP command. UUCP is a complicated command, so you should look at the manual page to determine the needed options. Your requirements are fairly simple—copy the file to a given directory. To do this, you need to loop through the files and run a uucp command on each file.

```
if ( $#argv < 2 ) then
    echo usage: uuto file [ file ] destination
    exit
endif
set dest=$argv[$#argv]
set remotemachine=`echo $dest ¦ cut -d\! -f1`
set remoteuser=`echo $dest ¦ cut -d\! -f2`
if ( $remoteuser == "" ) then
    echo You must supply a user
    exit
endif
if ( $remotemachine == "" ) then
    echo you must supply a machine
    exit
endif
set hn=`hostname`
set argv[$#argv] = ""
foreach i ( $argv )
    uucp -n$remoteuser $i $remotemachine\!~/receive/$remoteuser/$hn
end
```

12

This uucp command notifies the remote user when the file arrives, and it places the file in the correct directory. If you save this to a file uuto and set the appropriate permissions, you can now send a set of files to a remote machine using the uuto command:

```
uuto data1 data2 data3 amaker\!tom
```

This command sends the three data files to the user tom on the machine amaker.

> **Note:** The backslash (\) is needed before the exclamation point to prevent the history replacement for !tom.

The course of execution is simple:

```
if ( 4 < 2 ) then
# The count of arguments is four, so you don't execute the error
# condition.
endif
set dest=amaker!tom
# the last element of argv is this string.
set remotemachine=`echo $dest | cut -d\! -f1`
# You execute the pipeline:
set remotemachine=amaker
set remoteuser=`echo $dest | cut -d\! -f2`
# And the pipeline gives:
set remoteuser=tom
if ( tom == "" ) then
# The remoteuser variable is OK.
endif
if ( amaker == "" ) then
# The remote machine is also valid.
endif
set hn=`hostname`
# Another command replacement
set hn=krzyzewski
set argv[4]=""
# This eliminates the last entry, the destination.
foreach i ( data1 data2 data3 )
# This foreach loop starts with i set to data1
    uuto -ntom data1 amaker\!~/receive/tom/krzyzewski
# This sends the first file
end
# The second iteration is for data2
    uuto -ntom data2 amaker\!~/receive/tom/krzyzewski
end
# And the third is for data3.
    uuto -ntom data3 amaker\!~/receive/tom/krzyzewski
end
# All three files are sent.
```

uupick

The uupick program is a bit more complicated than uuto. At the heart, it would seem to be a series of loops with a switch statement. First, though, it needs to see if anything is present for the user. The C Shell provides you with the username in the variable user. So you first need to test whether the directory is present:

```
if ( ! -d /var/spool/uucppublic/receive/$user ) exit
```

You don't need to generate an error message, because there is no error. For simplicity's sake, you may want to set this to a variable, simply because the directory will be used several times:

```
set pubdir=/var/spool/uucppublic/receive/$user
if ( ! -d $pubdir ) exit
```

If the directory exists, you first want to loop on the directories present. Those are the machines from which you have received files:

```
set pubdir=/var/spool/uucppublic/receive/$user
if ( ! -d $pubdir ) exit
foreach rem ( `ls $pubdir` )
end
```

The rem variable is the remote machine sending the file. If there are no files, this loop is not run. Within the loop, you want to check on files from that machine. Again, this is a foreach loop:

```
set pubdir=/var/spool/uucppublic/receive/$user
if ( ! -d $pubdir ) exit
foreach rem ( `ls $pubdir` )
    foreach file ( `ls $pubdir/$rem` )
    end
end
```

The two loops enable you to inspect each file for each machine. The job for each file is to prompt with the menu and to perform the specified action. The menu needs to be designed. You can use a space, no input, or a plus to skip a file. The letter d can indicate a delete. You can use m for move, q for quit, and p to reprint the menu.

This menu is easily printed with echo commands.

```
set pubdir=/var/spool/uucppublic/receive/$user
if ( ! -d $pubdir ) exit
foreach rem ( `ls $pubdir` )
    foreach file ( `ls $pubdir/$rem` )
        echo You must select an action:
        echo " "
        echo d delete the file
        echo m move the file to an optional directory
        echo p print the menu
        echo + skip the file
```

12

```
            echo q quit
            echo " "
        end
end
```

The `print` option is an interesting option. Every other option moves on to the next file, but `print` just repeats the menu. This can happen any number of times, suggesting that the printing of the menu is enclosed in a `while` loop.

```
set pubdir=/var/spool/uucppublic/receive/$user
if ( ! -d $pubdir ) exit
foreach rem ( `ls $pubdir` )
    foreach file ( `ls $pubdir/$rem` )
        while ( 1 )
            echo You must select an action:
            echo " "
            echo d delete the file
            echo m move the file to an optional directory
            echo p print the menu
            echo + skip the file
            echo q quit
            echo " "
        end
    end
end
```

Saying `while (1)` makes the script an infinite loop, but you can use `break` to leave the loop. Next, you should prompt with the filename and originating system:

```
set pubdir=/var/spool/uucppublic/receive/$user
if ( ! -d $pubdir ) exit
foreach rem ( `ls $pubdir` )
    foreach file ( `ls $pubdir/$rem` )
        while ( 1 )
            echo You must select an action:
            echo " "
            echo d delete the file
            echo m move the file to an optional directory
            echo p print the menu
            echo + skip the file
            echo q quit
            echo " "
            echo -n "file $file from $rem"
            echo -n ": "
        end
    end
end
```

You prompt and expect the input on the same line, so the next job is to read the input:

```
set pubdir=/var/spool/uucppublic/receive/$user
if ( ! -d $pubdir ) exit
foreach rem ( `ls $pubdir` )
    foreach file ( `ls $pubdir/$rem` )
```

```
            while ( 1 )
                echo You must select an action:
                echo " "
                echo d delete the file
                echo m move the file to an optional directory
                echo p print the menu
                echo + skip the file
                echo q quit
                echo " "
                echo -n "file $file from $rem"
                echo -n ": "
                set inp=$<
            end
    end
end
```

Input is read into the `inp` variable. To process it, you need only the first character, which you can convert to lowercase. Then, a `switch` statement processes the input:

```
set pubdir=/var/spool/uucppublic/receive/$user
if ( ! -d $pubdir ) exit
foreach rem ( `ls $pubdir` )
    foreach file ( `ls $pubdir/$rem` )
        while ( 1 )
            echo You must select an action:
            echo " "
            echo d delete the file
            echo m move the file to an optional directory
            echo p print the menu
            echo + skip the file
            echo q quit
            echo " "
            echo -n "file $file from $rem"
            echo -n ": "
            set inp=$<
            set inpc=`echo $inp | cut -c1 | tr 'DMPQ' 'dmpq'`
            switch ( $inpc )
            endsw
        end
    end
end
```

There needs to be five cases for the `switch`: one for each option, and one for the default. The action for d is a simple `rm` command; m will use `mv`; + will do nothing; q will exit; and p will print the menu again. The default will repeat the input, indicate that the input is invalid, and rerun the menu.

```
set pubdir=/var/spool/uucppublic/receive/$user
if ( ! -d $pubdir ) exit
foreach rem ( `ls $pubdir` )
    foreach file ( `ls $pubdir/$rem` )
        while ( 1 )
            echo You must select an action:
            echo " "
            echo d delete the file
```

12

```
echo m move the file to an optional directory
echo p print the menu
echo + skip the file
echo q quit
echo " "
echo -n "file $file from $rem"
echo -n ": "
set inp=$<
set inpc=`echo $inp ¦ cut -c1 ¦ tr 'DMPQ' 'dmpq'`
switch ( $inpc )
case p:
    continue
case d:
    rm -f $pubdir/$rem/$file
    breaksw
case m:
    set mvcom= ($inp)
    if ($#mvcom > 1 ) then
        set rmdir=$mvcom[2]
    else
        set rmdir="."
    endif
    mv $pubdir/$rem/$file $rmdir
    breaksw
case q:
    exit
case "":
case " ":
case +:
    breaksw
default:
    echo Invalid command: $inp
    continue
endsw
break
    end
end
end
```

The switch statement is the real engine of this program. Here, the user's input is processed. For the p and default options, continue is specified at the end of the block. This returns control to the next enclosing loop, the while (1). The other options use breaksw to jump to the endsw, where the next statement is the break. This ends the while loop and acts on the next foreach.

The m option has a special set of commands. If the user has specified a directory, you want to get the directory name. The set command will break inp into multiple words, enabling you to count the words. If there's more than one, a directory is specified. Set the rmdir to that directory or to *dot* (.), the current directory.

This is, by far, the largest script you've written yet. Because of its size, some shortcuts are taken in the execution flow sample. Namely, I will not illustrate how the menu is printed.

```
set pubdir=/var/spool/uucppublic/receive/$user
# This sets the pubdir to the user's specific area for receiving uuto.
if ( ! -d $pubdir ) exit
# The user may have nothing waiting, if not, just exit.
foreach rem ( `ls $pubdir` )
# You need to expand the pubdir.  In this case, there is one entry,
# krzyzewski, so rem is assigned krzyzewski.
    foreach file ( `ls $pubdir/$rem` )
# Now, you need to look at the files under that directory, to see what
# files have been sent from that machine.  There are three, data1, data2,
# and data3.  The first file will be data1.
        while (1)
            (menu)
            set inp=$<
# After examining the options, you need to decide what to do.  In this
# case, suppose you want data1 in your current directory, data2 in
# your home directory, and you don't want data3.  So, the input in
# this case might be "Move"
            set inpc=`echo $inp | cut -c1 | tr 'DMPQ' 'dmpq'`
# Here, you use the pipeline to trim the input to a single character,
# and force correct answers to lower case.  Piecewise, this is:
echo Move
Move
cut -c1
M
tr 'DMPQ' 'dmpq'
m
set inpc=m
# Now that inpc is set, you are ready to enter the switch.
            switch(m)
            case p:
            case d:
# m does not match p or d
            case m:
# There is a match.
                set mvcom = ( Move )
                if ( 1 > 1 ) then
                else
                    set rmdir="."
                endif
# m can take an argument, so you need to see if there is one.  Since
# there isn't you take the else branch, and assign rmdir the value "."
        mv /var/spool/uucppublic/receive/tom/krzyzewski/data1 .
# This command moves the file to the current directory, .
                breaksw
# Break to the endsw
            endsw
            break
# Break the enclosing while or foreach loop, in this case, while (1)
        end
    end
# End this iteration of foreach, and set file to the second value,
# data2
        while (1)
            (menu)
            set inp=$<
```

```
# This time, the user inputs "move ~"  The input is treated as a single
# element of inp, in spite of the space in the text.
                set inpc=`echo $inp ¦ cut -c1 ¦ tr 'DMPQ' 'dmpq'`
# In this case, the text is trimmed to m.
                switch (m)
                case p:
                case d:
                case m:
# Into the appropriate case.
                        set mvcom = ( move ~ )
                        if ( 2 > 1 ) then
                            set rmdir=~
                        else
                        endif
# The assignment without :q or quotes allows the input to be broken into
# two words at the space.  So, mvcom[1] is "move" and mvcom[2] is "~".
# This allows the execution of the if branch, assigning "~" to rmdir.
                mv /var/spool/uucppublic/receive/tom/krzyzewski/data2 ~
# The ~ is expanded to tom's home directory, and data2 is moved there.
                        breaksw
                    endsw
                    break
            end
    end
# The next file to be tested is data3.
            while (1)
                (menu)
                set inp=$<
# This time, the input is just d
                set inpc=`echo $inp ¦ cut -c1 ¦ tr 'DMPQ' 'dmpq'`
# inpc is also d.
                switch (d)
                case p:
                case d:
# The match is earlier.
            rm -f /var/spool/uucppublic/receive/tom/krzyzewski/data3
# The file is removed if you have the correct permissions.
                        breaksw
                    endsw
                    break
# Terminate the while loop
            end
    end
# There are no longer any files to check
end
# There are no other remote systems sending files.
# The program is finished.
```

On the screen, this command would look like the following:

```
% uupick
You must select an action:

d delete the file
m move the file to an optional directory
p print the menu
```

```
+ skip the file
q quit

file data1 from krzyzewski: Move
You must select an action:

d delete the file
m move the file to an optional directory
p print the menu
+ skip the file
q quit

file data2 from krzyzewski: move ~
You must select an action:

d delete the file
m move the file to an optional directory
p print the menu
+ skip the file
q quit

file data3 from krzyzewski: d
% _
```

A subsequent run of uupick returns immediately, confirming that the command has done its work.

> **Note:** The C Shell uuto and uupick commands already exist on many UNIX systems as the Bourne Shell's uuto and uupick. These Bourne Shell commands actually have more options than the examples above. If they are on your system, take a look at them. Compare the added complexity of those commands and the added features, and see which you think is easier to use and maintain.

12

Summary

Today, you have learned by example how to build a C Shell script. The six examples showed how to build a script for sourcing, how to place command input into the text of a shell, and how to use each of the major control blocks—if, switch, foreach, and while.

The first example, the path cleaner, was a script designed to be sourced because it changes the working environment of the shell. It illustrated a foreach loop as a major component of the script, and it showed that the loops can be nested. It also illustrated how a variable can be set and unset for use as a flag.

The second example, the simple mail bouncer, was a regular command that is best used as part of an alias to read mail. It illustrated how a command's input can be included as part of a script, and how that input can include C Shell variables. The script also illustrated the inclusion of pipelines for assigning values to variables.

The third example, the multiplace shifter, was intended to be part of a command pipeline to assign a variable. It illustrated a simple `while` loop.

The fourth example, the root window painter, illustrated a table-driven command. This was the first (and only) script example that did not require looping. The complexity of the problem, though, still required a script, as opposed to an alias.

The fifth and sixth examples were the most complex. They were designed to provide an easier interface to `UUCP`, and the problem definition was rather explicit in its requirements. The `uuto` command illustrated a larger amount of error checking than previous examples, and it showed how to write a script to requirements. The `uupick` command illustrated a `switch` statement and the use of an infinite loop in a shell program. The `uupick` command also illustrated an interactive shell program that prompts the user for input during execution.

Each of these examples was actually rather small. Tomorrow, you will see the building of a major shell script. That program will check and correct spelling within a document, maintain a lexicon of new words, and will also maintain a list of frequently misspelled words.

Related UNIX Topics—C Shell Weaknesses

As mentioned yesterday, the C Shell is not perfect. The real key to becoming a power user of any tool is not only to master the features of a tool, but also to know when the tool is the right tool to use and when it is not. Without question, the C Shell is a very friendly command interface to use interactively. It has many useful features for programming, but there are also some weaknesses.

If you need to write a portable application, there are some caveats. Although the C Shell should behave the same way on all systems, there are still some older systems on which the C Shell is not present. The shell originated at Berkeley, where computer scientists developed their own flavor of UNIX, BSD. System V, as developed by AT&T, moved down parallel lines, and it has its own alternative to the Bourne Shell, the Korn Shell. It was only with the merger between System V and BSD, called System V Release 4, or SVR4, that the C Shell made its appearance in the AT&T UNIX line. If your script needs to run on older UNIXs, then you may want to use the Bourne Shell.

I/O redirection also has some weaknesses. C Shell does not permit stdout and stderr to be easily separated to different files. The only redirection option for stderr is >&, which merges stdout and stderr into a single file. Although a work-around exists, it is not pretty, as the following illustrates:

```
( command > file ) >& file2
```

The command is run in a subshell. The command's standard output is redirected, and the subshell's stdout and stderr is redirected to a second file. Because the command's standard output is already redirected, the subshell will have no output there, just the standard error output. Although this can be done, it has the added cost of "forking" and "execing" an additional process.

Similarly, the C Shell does not permit files and additional file descriptors to be opened. The Bourne Shell permits this. The only way for the C Shell to receive input is from an associated terminal, standard input. Although the third example—the table-driven command to set a root pattern—could have been faster by reading in the table, this is not possible within the shell.

With the C Shell, you can only catch the SIGHUP and SIGINT signals. Every other signal sent to a C Shell program will result in the default action, usually a core dump and termination. Although it is difficult to know when you will be writing a process that may receive an unexpected signal, if that possibility exists, you may want to write your script in the Bourne Shell, or even as a C program, instead.

Another weakness of the C Shell is the lack of subroutines. The Bourne Shell provides a way to create subroutines for frequent command groups. Although C Shell does support aliases, there are many restrictions to them. The C Shell can fake subroutines by having multiple programs. This solution is less than optimal.

There are also some bugs in the C Shell, as there are in most software. If you expect an argument list longer than 1,048,576 characters or with more elements than 1,706, the C Shell will fail. Because the control structures for C Shell programming are built-in commands and not parsing structures, piping and command termination characters do not work with them.

The evaluation of a command line is not always intuitive. For example, the following command will generate an error if var is not set:

```
if ($?var) echo $var
```

The entire line receives substitution before the test case is evaluated.

Instead, this structure should be used:

12

```
if ( $?var) then
     echo $var
endif
```

By being aware of these weaknesses, you are better equipped to choose the right tool to solve a problem. Tomorrow I will discuss some of the strengths of the C Shell for shell programming, and why the C Shell can be the right choice.

Q&A

Q How do I run a C Shell script?

A The script can be provided as an argument to the C Shell command, `csh`.

Q I want to see the commands as they are run. Can I do that?

A Yes, with the `-v` option. Run the script like this: `csh -v script`. Each command is printed after variable expansion, but before it is executed.

Workshop

The workshop is designed to help you understand the day's lesson, programming the C Shell. Because this lesson is a more active lesson, the quiz will be shorter to allow for more exercises. The answers are in Appendix F, "Answers to Quizzes and Exercises."

Quiz

1. What is the meaning of the `-f` option for the C Shell, and why is it a common feature of C Shell scripts?

2. Identify the correct looping commands for each situation:

   a) For looking at each file in a directory

   b) For looking at the first ten elements of a variable

   c) For creating an infinite loop

   d) For looking at three values

Exercises

1. There is a problem with the first example, `clean_path`. If it is sourced, it creates several new variables, and if those variables already exist, it overwrites their values. What do you need to do to prevent this from happening?

2. The second script, `mailbouncer`, could be sped up by using the `egrep` command. How would the script change?

3. Change the fourth example, the root mapper, to allow the user to specify a flag `-r` for reversing the colors of the image.

12

Applied C Shell Programming, Part II

Introduction to Day 13

Yesterday, you saw how the C Shell can be used to solve simple problems with C Shell scripts. You saw scripts to clean a user's path, to bounce unwanted mail, to implement a multiplaced shift, to paint a root background via a table, and to implement UUCP commands in a cleaner format.

These examples illustrated different aspects of C Shell programming, and they used several of the tools you learned in previous days.

Today, you will tackle a major project. You will learn how to break a project into separate, manageable tasks, and you will learn how to integrate these pieces into a single script. This will illustrate an organized approach to problem solving.

The task at hand is to write a C Shell script that not only will catch spelling errors, but also will create its own lexicon of new words, correct the mistakes, and produce a document without errors. Clearly, this is a complicated task.

Setting Today's Goals

Today, you will learn about

☐ How to break a task into pieces

☐ How to solve the individual pieces

☐ How to integrate the solutions into a single whole

☐ Management of a large-scale project

Tackling a Large Problem with C Shell

Creating the spelling checker and corrector is a complicated task. The first step to solving the problem is to design what the program will do.

Overall Design

Clearly, if a new lexicon is going to be built, this project is going to be interactive. So, some rules for what will be written to the screen, and what will be received back, must be developed. Every word misspelled must be presented to the user in a method that

identifies the misspelled word easily. It would probably be best to do this sequentially. After each unrecognized word is presented to the user, some option needs to be input by the user. The user need to know the menu, but the regular printing of the menu may not be necessary.

So, you can develop a flow chart similar to this:

☐ Find misspelled words

☐ Prompt for each word, and ask for the correction

☐ Update the user's lexicon, and correct spelling mistakes

The tasks are simple enough, or so they would seem. Because there are permanent files associated with this problem, you also need to determine what they are and how to use them. One on-going file will be the user's lexicon. This is a list of words that are correctly spelled but are not in the system's list of words. Often, this will include names and acronyms. Because this is the user's lexicon for all applications, it should remain in the home directory. To keep things simple, you should call it `.lexicon`. You will also be saving a list of commonly misspelled words and their corrections. You should call this `.corrections`, and it should also remain in the user's home directory. There will also be some temporary files. You will be building a list of corrections to be applied. This is use-specific, so it should be either in the current directory or in `/tmp`, with the PID appended. UNIX guidelines suggest that temporary files should be in `/tmp`, so you should make `/tmp/fix.$$`. The `$$` variable is the process ID, a unique identifier. You can keep a list of misspelled words in a temporary file.

The determination of these files and the documentation is an important step in designing the program. So far, the files are listed in Table 13.1.

Table 13.1. Files for the Speller program.

File	Purpose
`~/.lexicon`	A permanent file for the correct words that are not present in the system lexicon.
`~/.corrections`	A listing of frequently misspelled words and their corrected spellings.
`/tmp/fix.$$`	A list of commands to correct the spellings of words in the document.
`/tmp/spl.$$`	A list of the misspelled words in the document.

The next step in the development of this program is to divide the tasks and develop each piece of the code. You broke the task up earlier with the simple flow chart, so now you can break the tasks up more easily.

Developing the Pieces

There are three pieces to be developed. The first determines a list of spelling errors, the second processes the list of errors, and the third corrects the document.

Finding the Errors

You can describe this piece of the project simply: Find all the spelling errors in the document, and write a file of these errors to /tmp/spl.$$. You should begin by examining the tools available.

The spelling tool for UNIX is `spell`. It can take several options, including an additional file for the user's lexicon. There is also an option to specify British or American spelling, a useful flag to remember.

The `spell` command makes the project a lot easier. Because the file to be corrected is on the command line, you can use the first argument as the document. This makes the creation of the misspelled list easy:

```
if ( -f ~/.lexicon ) then
    spell +~/.lexicon $1 > /tmp/spl.$$
else
    spell $1 > /tmp/spl.$$
endif
```

Another approach would be one to allow the user to pass the options to `spell` as command-line arguments. In this case, you'd need to examine the arguments and build your own command line for `spell`. Although this could be done with a `foreach` loop, a `while` loop may be the better choice. In this `while` loop, you want to check against the valid `spell` options and build your own option list. The valid options for `spell` are listed in Table 13.2.

Table 13.2. Options to spell.

Option	Purpose
-b	Use British spelling.
-l	Follow chains of all include files.
-v	All words not in the list are printed with plausible derivations.

Option	Purpose
-x	Every plausible stem is displayed, one per line.
-d hlist	Use hlist as the hashed spelling list.
-s hstop	Use hstop as the hashed stop list.
+file	Include this file in the lexicon.

Examining the options, you should clearly see that you should not support the -v and the -x options, even though they are valid spell options, because they would introduce other words into the output that are not specified in your problem description.

Each option starts with one of two characters, a hyphen (-) or a plus (+). The plus (+) option starts a filename, so it should be copied intact. The hyphen (-) options all depend on a second letter, so the hyphen should be compared, as well. This suggests a pair of switch commands, one for each letter. With the while loop, you end up with an argument parser that looks something like this:

```
set arglist
set files
@ i=1
while ( $i <= $#argv )
    set optc=`echo $argv[$i] ¦ cut -c1`
    switch (optc)
    case +:
        set arglist = ( $arglist $argv[$i] )
        shift
        breaksw
    case -:
        set opt2c=`echo $argv[$i] ¦ cut -c1-2`
        switch (opt2c)
        case -b:
        case -l:
            set arglist = ( $arglist $argv[$i] )
            shift
            breaksw
        case -v:
        case -x:
            echo -n $argv[$i] is supported by spell,
            echo but not supported by $argv[0]
            shift
            breaksw
        case -d:
        case -s:
            set arglist = ( $arglist $argv[$i] )
            @ i++
            set arglist = ( $arglist $argv[$i] )
            @ i --
            shift
```

13

```
                 shift
                 breaksw
           default:
                 echo $argv[$i] is not supported.
                 shift
           endsw
           breaksw
     default:
           set files=($files $argv[$i])
           shift
     endsw
end
```

The preceding code parses the command line. If an option is identified, it is added to the arglist variable and removed from the command line. Where an option takes a second argument, both are added to arglist and removed from argv.

There are several repetitive steps in the preceding code. Those steps can be simplified with a couple of aliases:

```
alias addarg      set arglist = \( \$arglist \!\* \)
alias procarg     addarg \!\*\; shift
```

Adding these two aliases to the code produces a simpler loop:

```
alias addarg set arglist = \( \$arglist \!\* \)
alias procarg      addarg \!\*\; shift
set arglist
set files
@ i=1
while ( $i <= $#argv )
     set optc=`echo $argv[$i] ¦ cut -c1`
     switch (optc)
     case +:
           procarg $argv[$i]
           breaksw
     case -:
           set opt2c=`echo $argv[$i] ¦ cut -c1-2`
           switch (opt2c)
           case -b:
           case -l:
                 procarg $argv[$i]
                 breaksw
           case -v:
           case -x:
                 echo -n $argv[$i] is supported by spell,
                 echo but not supported by $argv[0]
                 shift
                 breaksw
           case -d:
           case -s:
                 addarg $argv[$i]
                 @ i++
                 addarg $argv[$i]
                 @ i --
```

```
                shift
                shift
                breaksw
        default:
                echo $argv[$i] is not supported.
                shift
        endsw
        breaksw
    default:
            set files=($files $argv[$i])
            shift
    endsw
end
```

You can also add a simple `if` statement to add your own lexicon to the argument list:

```
if ( -f $home/.lexicon ) then
    addarg +$home/.lexicon
endif
```

Then, running the `spell` command is easy:

```
spell $arglist $file
```

Note that `spell` can take any number of files. Because you plan to process these files interactively, you should consider using a `foreach` loop to pass over the remaining arguments. Before running `spell`, you should also make sure the file exists; otherwise, there may be some other errors down the road. This loop becomes the following:

```
foreach file ( $files )
    if ( ! -f $file ) then
        echo $file does not exist
        break
    endif
    spell $arglist $file > /tmp/spl.$$
end
```

This code establishes the first part of the shell script. To make reviewing the code easier on other users and developers, you should comment this script to say what you are doing in the code, and you should communicate any changes you have made to the other development teams. (Ideally, in a large development project, there is a project leader, and some of the changes you have made will need to be approved. I have glossed over these steps.)

So, the first piece of code is finished, and it may end up looking like this:

```
 #!/bin/csh -f
# First create two aliases for adding arguments to the argument list
# for spell.  The first, addarg, just adds the argument.  The second,
# procarg, adds the argument and alters argv for the loop.
alias addarg set arglist = \( \$arglist \!\* \)
alias procarg   addarg \!\*\; shift
set arglist
```

13

```
set files
@ i=1
while ( $i <= $#argv )            # Look at each argument
        set optc=`echo $argv[$i] ¦ cut -c1`
                                 # Since arguments start with either `-'
                                 # or '+', you chop the argument to check
                                 # this character
        switch (optc)
        case +:
                procarg $argv[$i]        # '+' is always added.
                breaksw
        case -:
                set opt2c=`echo $argv[$i] ¦ cut -c1-2`
                switch (opt2c)           # '-' takes a second letter
                                         # to indicate the option.
                case -b:
                case -l:
                                # Both -b and -l take the same processing
                        procarg $argv[$i]
                        breaksw
                case -v:
                case -x:
                                # Both -v and -x are ignored.
                        echo -n $argv[$i] is supported by spell,
                        echo but not supported by $argv[0]
                        shift
                        breaksw
                case -d:
                case -s:
                                # Both -d and -s need a second argument,
                                # and take the same processing.
                        addarg $argv[$i]
                        @ i++
                        addarg $argv[$i]
                        @ i --
                        shift
                        shift
                        breaksw
                default:
                        echo $argv[$i] is not supported.
                        shift
                endsw
                breaksw
        default:
                set files = ( $files $argv[$i] )
                shift
                                # Default on the outerloop is a file
                                # to be checked.
        endsw
end
if ( -f $home/.lexicon ) then
     addarg +$home/.lexicon
endif
        # Add the user's lexicon here.
foreach file ( $files )
        # Each file needs to be run separately, for interactive processing.
        if ( ! -f $file ) then
```

```
            echo $file does not exist
            break
    endif
            # Run spell and gather the output
    spell $arglist $file > /tmp/spl.$$
            # Here the project integrator will include the other two
            # pieces.
end
```

Processing the Error List

The second task is to process the error list. The specifications for this job have changed a bit due to the changes in the preceding section. You want to perform a systematic task:

- ☐ For each error in the document, prompt the user with the error and ask for a disposition.

- ☐ Process each disposition.

- ☐ Prepare a list of corrections to be passed to the next phase of the project.

The next question is, What do you want to do with each misspelling? Three courses of action are apparent. You could add the word to the user's lexicon, indicating that the spelling is actually correct. Alternatively, you could get a corrected spelling from the user and pass that to the next phase for the project. Then again, you could ignore the error.

Another requirement is to maintain a list of commonly misspelled words, and apply those corrections. There is no specification for the format of this file. Here is a good place to start.

The obvious format is to keep each entry on a separate line that can be grepped. So, each line should start with the misspelled word, anchored to the first column and terminated with a space. Then, the correction can follow. You must be prepared to handle a space (such as changing *cannot* to *can not*) in a correction, so some extra processing is required here.

Because you will be examining the list of words, a `foreach` loop is required. If you start with that, your code looks like this:

```
foreach word ( `cat /tmp/spl.$$` )
end
```

Remember, though, that there are limitations for this loop. The C Shell restricts argument lists to 1,709 words and 1,048,576 characters. If the user's spelling is really bad and the document is really long, these limits may be reached. It is always a good idea to check this:

```
set wordcount = ( `wc /tmp/spl.$$` )
```

The output of wordcount is a count of lines, words, and characters. So, you need to check the second and third values to see if they are within the allowable limits, and break the loop otherwise:

```
set wordcount = ( `wc /tmp/spl.$$` )
if ( $wordcount[2] > 1709 ) then
    echo Too many misspelled words in $file
    break
endif
if ( $wordcount[3] > 1048576 ) then
    echo Too many misspelled words in $file
    break
endif
foreach word ( `cat /tmp/spl.$$` )
end
```

Within the foreach loop, the first job should be to check the frequent-misspellings list for the word, and if the word is there, add the correction to the corrections file.

Note: Some of the code lines in this chapter are too long to be represented as a single line, given the width of this book. When the ➡ character appears at the beginning of a line, it means that the "line" is really a continuation of the preceding line. The two should be typed in and regarded as a single line.

```
foreach word ( `cat /tmp/spl.$$` )
 set tcor=(` grep "^$word " ~/.corrections ¦ sed 1q` )
  if ( $#tcor ) then
    set cor = $tcor[1]
    shift tcor
    set correct = ( $cor "$tcor" )
    echo s/\\\(\[^a-zA-Z\]\\\)$correct[1]\\\(\[^a-zA-Z]\\\)/\\1$correct[2]\\2/g
      ➡ >> /tmp/fix.$$
    echo s/^$correct[1]\\\(\[^a-zA-Z]\\\)/$correct[2]\\1/g >> /tmp/fix.$$
    echo s/\\\(\[^a-zA-Z]\\\)$correct[1]\$/\\1$correct[2]/g >> /tmp/fix.$$
    echo s/^$correct[1]\$/$correct[2]/g >> /tmp/fix.$$
    continue
  endif
end
```

This is ugly, but this is how you set up a file for the sed command, which is the best choice for changing the file.

Note: The strings are being set up for the sed command, which is a stream editor. This command provides the user with the ability to modify the text in a file, based on specific patterns called "regular expressions." This is not all

the command can do, though, as you may see the sed command on the second line of the example. In this case, it is being used to quit output after a single line. For a fuller description of sed, check your manual page.

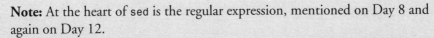

Note: At the heart of sed is the regular expression, mentioned on Day 8 and again on Day 12.

The description of the regular expression is simple. If the expression is a string, sed will find a string that matches the expression exactly. Consider the following poem:

> My candle burns at both ends
> It will not last the night
> But ah my foes and oh my friends
> It gives a lovely light!

If you set the regular expression to be love, the expression will only match the fourth line. But suppose instead you wanted to match all words that start with l and that have four letters? For a file-matching pattern, that is easy: l???. With a regular expression, it is also easy: either l.\{3\} or l... will do the trick. The ed manual page gives an introductory explanation of regular expressions, and Dave Taylor's *Teach Yourself UNIX in a Week* provides some samples.

A quick description of the regular expression matching conventions are in Table 13.3.

13

Table 13.3. Regular expression metacharacters.

Characters	Meaning
.	Match any single character except newline.
*	Match any number of the single preceding character, including zero matches.

continues

Table 13.3. continued

Characters	Meaning
[. . .]	Match any single character of those enclosed in brackets. Ranges, such as a-z, are acceptable.
[^ . . .]	Match any one single character not enclosed in brackets.
^	As the first character of a regular expression, it matches the beginning of a line.
$	As the last character of a regular expression, it matches the end of a line.
\	Escape the meaning of the next character.
(. . .)	Groups the regular expression (for below).
+	Match one or more copies of the preceding regular expression.
?	Matches exactly one or zero of the preceding regular expression.
¦	Specifies either the preceding or the following regular expression should be matched.
\{m,n\}	Matches a range of special expressions; m and n must be non-negative integers less than 256. If only one is present, \{m\} matches exactly m occurrences of the preceding regular expression, \{m,\} matches m or more occurrences, and \{m,n\} matches the range.

The four echo commands will produce output that looks like this:

```
s/\([^a-zA-Z]\)the\([^a-zA-Z]\)/\1your\2/g
s/^the\([^a-zA-Z]\)/your\1/g
s/\([^a-zA-Z]\)the$/\1your/g
s/^the$/your/g
```

What this code means is simple. The first line says match the, unless the is preceded or followed by a letter, and replace the with your, with the same characters before and after. Unfortunately, the regular expression does not match at the start or end of a line, so you need three more explicit tests for the conditions where the begins a line, ends a line, and is alone on a line. These four tests are being added to a file, /tmp/fix.$$, that will be used by sed to correct the spelling errors.

This handles the situation where the misspelled word is already in a corrections list. If the word isn't in the corrections list, you need to prompt the user with the word and ask what to do. Because it is nice to highlight the word, you can surround it with plus signs; again, this change will need a sed command.

You can use sed to find the misspelled words and highlight them. Thus, the next step is to prepare this temporary sed script:

```
foreach word ( `cat /tmp/spl.$$` )
  set tcor=(` grep "^$word " ~/.corrections ¦ sed 1q` )
  if ( $#tcor ) then
    set cor = $tcor[1]
    shift tcor
    set correct = ( $cor "$tcor" )
    echo s/\\\(\[^a-zA-Z\]\\\)$correct[1]\\\(\[^a-zA-Z\]\\\)/\\1$correct[2]\\2/g
      ➥ >> /tmp/fix.$$
    echo s/^$correct[1]\\\(\[^a-zA-Z\]\\\)/$correct[2]\\1/g >> /tmp/fix.$$
    echo s/\\\(\[^a-zA-Z\]\\\)$correct[1]\$/\\1$correct[2]/g >> /tmp/fix.$$
    echo s/^$correct[1]\$/$correct[2]/g >> /tmp/fix.$$
    continue
  endif
  echo $word is not recognized in this context:
  echo " "
  echo s/\\\(\[^a-zA-Z\]\\\)$word\\\(\[^a-zA-Z\]\\\)/\\1+$word+\\2/g
    ➥ > /tmp/und.$$
  echo s/^$word\\\(\[^a-zA-Z\]\\\)/+$word+\\1/g >> /tmp/und.$$
  echo s/\\\(\[^a-zA-Z\]\\\)$word\$/\\1+$word+/g >> /tmp/und.$$
  echo s/^$word\$/+$word+/g >> /tmp/und.$$
  grep $word $file ¦ sed -f /tmp/und.$$
  rm /tmp/und.$$
  echo " "
end
```

So far, the loop now checks for words already corrected, and it presents the misspelled words with a highlight. The next step is to prompt for a user's action. The while loop illustrated yesterday for uupick makes a good prototype. You need to determine what commands you will use to determine the responses. A suggested set is in Table 13.4.

Table 13.4. Commands for the Spelling Corrector.

Command	Action
i,I	Ignore this error.
l,L	Add this to the lexicon as a valid word.
c,C	Supply a correction.
p,P	Print these options.

Adding the `while` loop, with the modifications for the commands, makes the program as follows:

```
foreach word ( `cat /tmp/spl.$$` )
  set tcor=(` grep "^$word " ~/.corrections ¦ sed 1q` )
  if ( $#tcor ) then
    set cor = $tcor[1]
    shift tcor
    set correct = ( $cor "$tcor" )
    echo s/\\\(\[^a-zA-Z\]\\\)$correct[1]\\\(\[^a-zA-Z\]\\\)/\\1$correct[2]\\2/g
        ➥ >> /tmp/fix.$$
    echo s/^$correct[1]\\\(\[^a-zA-Z\]\\\)/$correct[2]\\1/g >> /tmp/fix.$$
    echo s/\\\(\[^a-zA-Z\]\\\)$correct[1]\$/\\1$correct[2]/g >> /tmp/fix.$$
    echo s/^$correct[1]\$/$correct[2]/g >> /tmp/fix.$$
    continue
  endif
  echo $word is not recognized in this context:
  echo " "
  echo s/\\\(\[^a-zA-Z\]\\\)$word\\\(\[^a-zA-Z\]\\\)/\\1+$word+\\2/g
      ➥ > /tmp/und.$$
  echo s/^$word\\\(\[^a-zA-Z\]\\\)/+$word+\\1/g >> /tmp/und.$$
  echo s/\\\(\[^a-zA-Z\]\\\)$word\$/\\1+$word+/g >> /tmp/und.$$
  echo s/^$word\$/+$word+/g >> /tmp/und.$$
  grep $word $file ¦ sed -f /tmp/und.$$
  rm /tmp/und.$$
  echo " "
  while ( 1 )
      echo -n "Please enter the disposition of this error:   "
      set inp=$<
      set inpc=`echo $inp ¦ cut -c1 ¦ tr 'ILCP' 'ilcp'`
      switch ($inpc)
      case i:
      case l:
      case c:
      case p:
          break
      default:
          echo -n "$inp is not a valid command.  Use 'p' to "
          echo see the list of commands
      endsw
  end
end
```

The last thing you need to do is to add the code for each command. Three are easy: p should just print a table, l should add the word to the lexicon unchanged, and i should do nothing. The l, i, and c should break the `while` loop; however, p should remain in the loop.

For the c command, first you should check and see if the correction is supplied on the command line. Otherwise, you should prompt the user for the correction. You also need to prompt the user to add the correction to the corrections list. Then, you need to build

the sed command to add to the `/tmp/fix.$$` file. This is the most complex command, and it should be developed separately. Starting there, the first thing to check is the command line, just as for the move case for uupick.

> **Tip:** This also illustrates a good coding practice: *Theft!* ;-)
>
> Seriously, any time you have coded something before, you should use the code again if it works, or use it as a prototype to make something that solves a problem. There is no need to re-invent the wheel with every project.

The code for the c command now looks like this:

```
set ccom=($inp)
if ($#ccom > 1 ) then
    shift ccom
    set answer="$ccom"
else
    set answer
    set anscnt=0
    while ( $anscnt==0 )
        echo -n "Please enter the correction:  "
        set answer=$<
        set anscnt=`echo $answer ¦ wc -c`
    end
endif
```

This code fragment gives you a correction for the misspelling found earlier. Now, you can prompt the user to add this to the common misspellings list:

```
echo Do you want to add this correction to the list of
echo -n "your common spelling errors\?  "
set inp=$<
```

Note that the question mark is escaped; otherwise, the shell would attempt to expand `"errors?"` into a filename. After you get the input, if it is y, just append this to the corrections file. Last, you need to set up the sed command:

```
set inp=`echo $inp ¦ cut -c1 ¦ tr Y y`
if ( $inp == y ) echo $word $answer >> $home/.corrections
echo s/\\\(\[^a-zA-Z\]\\\)$word\\\(\[^a-zA-Z]\\\)/\\1$answer\\2/g
    ➥ >> /tmp/fix.$$
echo s/^$word\\\(\[^a-zA-Z]\\\)/$answer\\1/g >> /tmp/fix.$$
echo s/\\\(\[^a-zA-Z\]\\\)$word\$/\\1$answer/g >> /tmp/fix.$$
echo s/^$word\$/$answer/g >> /tmp/fix.$$
break
```

This is all that is needed for the c command. With the code for the other commands, and after comments are inserted, this makes the complete spell correction loop:

```
set wordcount = ( `wc /tmp/spl.$$` )
        # Check the limiting conditions, make sure you won't bomb.
if ( $wordcount[2] > 1709 ) then
    echo Too many misspelled words in $file
    break
endif
if ( $wordcount[3] > 1048576 ) then
    echo Too many misspelled words in $file
    break
endif
foreach word ( `cat /tmp/spl.$$` )
        # Examine each word spell reports as incorrect.
    set tcor=(` grep "^$word " ~/.corrections | sed 1q` )
        # Check to see if the user has misspelled this word
        # before, and if so, add the correction silently.
    if ( $#tcor ) then
        set cor = $tcor[1]
        shift tcor
        # Here, the correction is added.  It is not pretty,
        # but sed is the most efficient corrector.
        set correct = ( $cor "$tcor" )
        echo s/\\\(\[^a-zA-Z\]\\\)$correct[1]\\\(\[^a-zA-Z]\\\)/\\1$correct[2]\\2/g
            ➥>> /tmp/fix.$$
        echo s/^$correct[1]\\\(\[^a-zA-Z]\\\)/$correct[2]\\1/g >> /tmp/fix.$$
        echo s/\\\(\[^a-zA-Z\]\\\)$correct[1]\$/\\1$correct[2]/g >> /tmp/fix.$$
        echo s/^$correct[1]\$/$correct[2]/g >> /tmp/fix.$$
        continue
    endif
        # If not caught, prompt the user with the misspelled
        # word highlighted.
    echo $word is not recognized in this context:
    echo " "
    echo s/\\\(\[^a-zA-Z\]\\\)$word\\\(\[^a-zA-Z]\\\)/\\1+$word+\\2/g > /tmp/und.$$
    echo s/^$word\\\(\[^a-zA-Z]\\\)/+$word+\\1/g >> /tmp/und.$$
    echo s/\\\(\[^a-zA-Z]\\\)$word\$/\\1+$word+/g >> /tmp/und.$$
    echo s/^$word\$/+$word+/g >> /tmp/und.$$
    grep $word $file | sed -f /tmp/und.$$
    rm /tmp/und.$$
    echo " "
    while ( 1 )
        echo -n "Please enter the disposition of this error:  "
        # Ask for the correction
        set inp=$<
        set inpc=`echo $inp | cut -c1 | tr 'ILCP' 'ilcp'`
        switch ($inpc)
        case i:
                # Ignore is easy, go on to the next word.
            break
        case l:
                # Add it to the lexicon, and move on.
            echo $word >> $home/.lexicon
            break
```

```
        case c:
                # Here's the sticky bit.  How to make
                # the correction.
            set ccom=($inp)
            if ($#ccom > 1 ) then
                shift ccom
                # Maybe the user supplied it on the
                # command line.
                set answer="$ccom"
            else
                # Otherwise, you'll need to prompt for it.
                set answer
                @ anscnt=0
                while ( $anscnt == 0 )
                    # And don't take no for an answer!
                    echo -n "Please enter the correction:   "
                    set answer=$<
                    set anscnt=`echo $answer ¦ wc -c`
                end
            endif
                # You've got the correction in $answer.
            echo Do you want to add this correction to the list of
            echo -n "your common spelling errors\?   "
            set inp=$<
            set inp=`echo $inp ¦ cut -c1 ¦ tr Y y`
            if ( $inp == y ) echo $word $answer >> $home/.corrections
                # May as well keep that list up to date.
            echo s/\\\(\[^a-zA-Z\]\\\)$word\\\(\[^a-zA-Z]\\\)/\\1$answer\\2/g
                    ➥>> /tmp/fix.$$
            echo s/^$word\\\(\[^a-zA-Z]\\\)/$answer\\1/g >> /tmp/fix.$$
            echo s/\\\(\[^a-zA-Z\]\\\)$word\$/\\1$answer/g >> /tmp/fix.$$
            echo s/^$word\$/$answer/g >> /tmp/fix.$$
            break
                # Some more ugly sed commands, then
                # go on to the next word.
        case p:
            echo Command Action
                # Print a pretty table.
            echo " "
            echo i       Ignore this error
            echo l       Add this word to your lexicon
            echo c       Correct this error
            echo p       Print this table
            echo " "
            breaksw
        default:
                # This is not a valid command.
            echo -n "$inp is not a valid command.  Use 'p' to "
            echo see the list of commands
        endsw
    end
        # And, here is the end of this loop.
end
```

13

361

Now, you have completed the second piece of the project: finding all the misspelled words and getting corrections. The last part of the project—correcting the document and updating the files—is easy.

Changing the Document

The last major piece of the program is the one that changes the document and maintains the files. You know that the file /tmp/fix.$$ will contain a series of sed commands to change the contents of the file. You also know that there is some data in .lexicon and .corrections.

The correction process is easy. Running sed with the file created is one command. The only issue is to see whether the file is there, and it would be friendly to provide a backup copy.

The spell manual page specifies that the entries must be in "sort" order, so the file should be sorted.

> **Note:** The sort is another UNIX tool. It has many options, but the two of interest are -u and -o. These enable you to sort the file in place (-o *filename* sends the output of sort to that file) and remove duplicate entries.

If you start with the lexicon, the commands are these:

```
if ( -f $home/.lexicon ) sort -u -o$home/.lexicon $home/.lexicon
```

Then, adding the file change and backup is also easy:

```
if ( -f /tmp/fix.$$ ) then
    cp $file $file.orig
    sed -f /tmp/fix.$$ $file.orig > $file
endif
```

Because the .corrections file is maintained entirely within the second piece of this program, the third part is already complete. It has become this:

```
if ( -f $home/.lexicon ) sort -u -o$home/.lexicon $home/.lexicon
    # If the user has a lexicon, sort it to be used properly.
if ( -f /tmp/fix.$$ ) then
    # If there are fixes, save the file and run the sed script
    cp $file $file.orig
    sed -f /tmp/fix.$$ $file.orig > $file
endif
```

This completes the coding required for the spell checker and corrector. The next job is integrating the pieces so that they all work together.

Integrating the Pieces

This program was initially designed to work with each piece running sequentially into the next piece, but because the first part was redesigned to accommodate multiple files, this is no longer the case. The last two pieces of the program need to be incorporated into the loop, and the whole process must be tested to make sure that it works in unison.

For testing these pieces, the simplest approach would be to first test the first piece. Run this piece several times and generate some spelling-error lists. These will be in /tmp, and they can be examined with any text editor. After you are satisfied that the command line is processed cleanly and that the proper spell command is run, you are ready to integrate the second piece.

Because these are tests and not the final copy, you may want to include the second piece with sort. If you've named the file sccpart2, you can include this in the foreach loop after the spell command is run:

```
foreach file ( $files )
        # Each file needs to be run separately, for interactive processing.
        if ( ! -f $file ) then
                echo $file does not exist
                break
        endif
                # Run spell and gather the output
        spell $arglist $file > /tmp/spl.$$
                # Here the project integrator will include the other two
                # pieces.
    source sccpart2
end
```

Now, the program will run the spell command and then enter the loop to process each spelling mistake. The output of this command should now be in /tmp/fix.$$ and in /tmp/spl.$$. Both are text files and can be examined with an editor. Also, you should make sure you check the ~/.lexicon and ~/.corrections files. Here, you should be able to add misspelled words and keep a running corrections list.

After you are satisfied, you can add the last part, again with the source command:

```
foreach file ( $files )
        # Each file needs to be run separately, for interactive processing.
        if ( ! -f $file ) then
                echo $file does not exist
                break
        endif
```

13

Applied C Shell Programming, Part II

```
                    # Run spell and gather the output
          spell $arglist $file > /tmp/spl.$$
                    # Here the project integrator will include the other two
                    # pieces.
        source sccpart2
        source sccpart3
    end
```

This time, a run of the program will actually correct any files. This time, the only output that matters is the original file, and a good way to compare the file with the original is by using `diff`:

```
diff file file.orig
```

> **Note:** The `diff` command gives you a listing of the lines that are different between two files. The listing is compact and, as such, will allow you to see that the spelling corrections have been made correctly.

During your testing, you may have noticed a number of files building up in /tmp. At no time is your process cleaning up these temporary files, and it should. Because the files are re-used during iterations of the outermost loop, they should be cleaned at the end of each iteration. The `rm` command is used for this:

```
foreach file ( $files )
        # Each file needs to be run separately, for interactive processing.
        if ( ! -f $file ) then
                echo $file does not exist
                break
        endif
                # Run spell and gather the output
        spell $arglist $file > /tmp/spl.$$
                # Here the project integrator will include the other two
                # pieces.
    source sccpart2
    source sccpart3
    rm -f /tmp/fix.$$ /tmp/spl.$$
end
```

The `-f` option suppressed all warning messages, including the message if a file doesn't exist. Also, you may want to consider the case where a person has made no spelling mistakes. Before the source sccpart2, you may want to check the length of the spell file, and if it is zero, congratulate the user and move to the next file.

```
foreach file ( $files )
        # Each file needs to be run separately, for interactive processing.
        if ( ! -f $file ) then
                echo $file does not exist
```

```
                break
        endif
                # Run spell and gather the output
        spell $arglist $file > /tmp/spl.$$
                # Here the project integrator will include the other two
                # pieces.
    if ( -z /tmp/spl.$$ ) then
        echo No spelling mistakes found in $file
        rm -f /tmp/spl.$$
        break
    endif
    source sccpart2
    source sccpart3
    rm -f /tmp/fix.$$ /tmp/spl.$$
end
```

Lastly, the process should probably catch the SIGINT signal and clean up any temporary files. At the start of the process, you should include the line `onintr cleanup` and at the bottom include this:

```
exit
cleanup:
rm -f /tmp/fix.$$ /tmp/spl.$$
exit
```

With this code, there are no temporary files left.

Finally, you can copy the code into the mail procedure with your editor. All told, with comments, your file is now 193 lines long and should look something like this:

Note: Some of the echo commands went beyond 80 characters on a line, so for cleanliness sake, I've cut them into two echo commands, each less than 72 characters. This makes the program easier to read.

13

```
#!/bin/csh -f
# First create two aliases for adding arguments to the argument list
# for spell.  The first, addarg, just adds the argument.  The second,
# procarg, adds the argument and alters argv for the loop.
onintr cleanup
alias addarg set arglist = \( \$arglist \!\* \)
alias procarg   addarg \!\*\; shift
set arglist
set files
@ i=1
while ( $i <= $#argv )       # Look at each argument
    set optc=`echo $argv[$i] | cut -c1`
            # Since arguments start with either '-'
            # or '+', you chop the argument to check
            # this character
```

```
        switch (optc)
        case +:
         procarg $argv[$i]        # '+' is always added.
         breaksw
        case -:
         set opt2c=`echo $argv[$i] ¦ cut -c1-2`
         switch (opt2c)        # '-' takes a second letter
                # to indicate the option.
         case -b:
         case -l:
             # Both -b and -l take the same processing
             procarg $argv[$i]
             breaksw
         case -v:
         case -x:
             # Both -v and -x are ignored.
             echo -n $argv[$i] is supported by spell,
             echo but not supported by $argv[0]
             shift
             breaksw
         case -d:
         case -s:
             # Both -d and -s need a second argument,
             # and take the same processing.
             addarg $argv[$i]
             @ i++
             addarg $argv[$i]
             @ i --
             shift
             shift
             breaksw
        default:
             echo $argv[$i] is not supported.
             shift
        endsw
        breaksw
        default:
         set files = ( $files $argv[$i] )
         shift
             # Default on the outerloop is a file
             # to be checked.
        endsw
    end
if ( -f $home/.lexicon ) then
        addarg +$home/.lexicon
endif
    # Add the user's lexicon here.
foreach file ( $files )
    # Each file needs to be run separately, for interactive processing.
    if ( ! -f $file ) then
     echo $file does not exist
     break
    endif
    # Run spell and gather the output
    spell $arglist $file > /tmp/spl.$$
    # Here the project integrator will include the other two
```

```
     # pieces.
if ( -z /tmp/spl.$$ ) then
 echo No spelling mistakes found in $file
 rm -f /tmp/spl.$$
 break
endif
set wordcount = ( `wc /tmp/spl.$$` )
     # Check the limiting conditions, make sure you won't bomb.
if ( $wordcount[2] > 1709 ) then
 echo Too many misspelled words in $file
 break
endif
if ( $wordcount[3] > 1048576 ) then
 echo Too many misspelled words in $file
 break
endif
foreach word ( `cat /tmp/spl.$$` )
     # Examine each word spell reports as incorrect.
 set tcor=(` grep "^$word " ~/.corrections | sed 1q` )
     # Check to see if the user has misspelled this word
     # before, and if so, add the correction silently.
 if ( $#tcor ) then
     set cor = $tcor[1]
     shift tcor
     # Here, the correction is added.  It is not pretty,
     # but sed is the most efficient corrector.
     set correct = ( $cor "$tcor" )
     echo -n s/\\\(\[^a-zA-Z\]\\\)$correct[1]\\\ >> /tmp/fix.$$
     echo (\[^a-zA-Z\]\\\)/\\1$correct[2]\\2/g >> /tmp/fix.$$
     echo -n s/^$correct[1]\\\(\[^a-zA-Z\]\\\)/ >> /tmp/fix.$$
     echo $correct[2]\\1/g >> /tmp/fix.$$
     echo -n s/\\\(\[^a-zA-Z\]\\\)$correct[1]\$/ >> /tmp/fix.$$
     echo \\1$correct[2]/g >> /tmp/fix.$$
     echo s/^$correct[1]\$/$correct[2]/g >> /tmp/fix.$$
     continue
 endif
     # If not caught, prompt the user with the misspelled
     # word highlighted.
 echo $word is not recognized in this context:
 echo " "
 echo -n s/\\\(\[^a-zA-Z\]\\\)$word\\\(\[^a-zA-Z\] > /tmp/und.$$
 echo \\\)/\\1+$word+\\2/g >> /tmp/und.$$
 echo s/^$word\\\(\[^a-zA-Z\]\\\)/+$word+\\1/g >> /tmp/und.$$
 echo s/\\\(\[^a-zA-Z\]\\\)$word\$/\\1+$word+/g >> /tmp/und.$$
 echo s/^$word\$/+$word+/g >> /tmp/und.$$
 grep $word $file | sed -f /tmp/und.$$
 rm /tmp/und.$$
 echo " "
 while ( 1 )
     echo -n "Please enter the disposition of this error:  "
     # Ask for the correction
     set inp=$<
     set inpc=`echo $inp | cut -c1 | tr 'ILCP' 'ilcp'`
     switch ($inpc)
     case i:
         # Ignore is easy, go on to the next word.
```

13

367

```
        break
case l:
        # Add it to the lexicon, and move on.
    echo $word >> $home/.lexicon
    break
case c:
        # Here's the sticky bit.  How to make
        # the correction.
    set ccom=($inp)
    if ($#ccom > 1 ) then
        shift ccom
        # Maybe the user supplied it on the
        # command line.
        set answer="$ccom"
    else
        # Otherwise, you'll need to prompt for it.
        set answer
        @ anscnt=0
        while ( $anscnt == 0 )
          # And don't take no for an answer!
          echo -n "Please enter the correction:  "
          set answer=$<
          set anscnt=`echo $answer ¦ wc -c`
        end
    endif
        # You've got the correction in $answer.
    echo Do you want to add this correction to the list of
    echo -n "your common spelling errors\?  "
    set inp=$<
    set inp=`echo $inp ¦ cut -c1 ¦ tr Y y`
      if ( $inp == y ) echo $word $answer >> $home/.corrections
        # May as well keep that list up to date.
    echo -n s/\\\(\[^a-zA-Z\]\\\)$word\\\(\[ >> /tmp/fix.$$
    echo ^a-zA-Z]\\\)/\\1$answer\\2/g >> /tmp/fix.$$
    echo -n s/^$word\\\(\[^a-zA-Z]\\\)/ >> /tmp/fix.$$
    echo $answer\\1/g >> /tmp/fix.$$
    echo -n s/\\\(\[^a-zA-Z\]\\\)$word\$/ >> /tmp/fix.$$
    echo \\1$answer/g >> /tmp/fix.$$
    echo s/^$word\$/$answer/g >> /tmp/fix.$$
    break
        # Some more ugly sed commands, then
        # go on to the next word.
case p:
    echo Command Action
        # Print a pretty table.
    echo " "
    echo i        Ignore this error
    echo l        Add this word to your lexicon
    echo c        Correct this error
    echo p        Print this table
    echo " "
    breaksw
default:
        # This is not a valid command.
    echo -n "$inp is not a valid command.  Use 'p' to "
    echo see the list of commands
```

```
        endsw
    end
        # And, here is the end of this loop.
    end
    if ( -f $home/.lexicon ) sort -u -o$home/.lexicon $home/.lexicon
        # If the user has a lexicon, sort it to be used properly.
    if ( -f /tmp/fix.$$ ) then
        # If there are fixes, save the file and run the sed script
        cp $file $file.orig
        sed -f /tmp/fix.$$ $file.orig > $file
    endif
    rm -f /tmp/fix.$$ /tmp/spl.$$
end
exit
cleanup:
rm -f /tmp/fix.$$ /tmp/spl.$$
exit
```

Running the Process

If you save the program to the file scc and add that directory to your path, then it is easy to run this script. The script takes a subset of the arguments for spell and will bounce bad arguments without terminating the command.

I ran the command on a document that I wrote describing the Brazil-versus-U.S.A. World Cup game. The following is a listing of the output generated.

Listing 13.1. scc session.

```
% scc worldcup
74th is not recognized in this context:

the game and the attack.  They were rewarded with a goal in the +74th+

Please enter the disposition of this error:  help
help is not a valid command.  Use 'p' to see the list of commands
Please enter the disposition of this error:  p
Command Action

i Ignore this error
l Add this word to your lexicon
c Correct this error
p Print this table

Please enter the disposition of this error:  i
Chapin is not recognized in this context:

While heading out, I had a pleasant surprise.  My friend Steve +Chapin+,

Please enter the disposition of this error:  l
Halftime is not recognized in this context:
```

13

continues

Listing 13.1. continued

```
+Halftime+ was 0-0.  Playing with a man advantage, I expected the US to

Please enter the disposition of this error:  l
Jang is not recognized in this context:

at Jing +Jang+ in Palo Alto.
traffic lights.)  Jing +Jang+, when we finally reached it, was its usual

Please enter the disposition of this error:  i
Jing is not recognized in this context:

at +Jing+ Jang in Palo Alto.
traffic lights.)  +Jing+ Jang, when we finally reached it, was its usual

Please enter the disposition of this error:  i
Juventus is not recognized in this context:

+Juventus+, Ireland, Ajax, and Rangers.  There were no Celtic jerseys

Please enter the disposition of this error:  l
Meola is not recognized in this context:

had one threatening shot, and Tony +Meola+ was not tested.  I was

Please enter the disposition of this error:  l
SF is not recognized in this context:

pick up my sister in San Francisco, we left +SF+ at 8:35, and arrived on
hope the USSF can exploit to form a strong league and a national side

Please enter the disposition of this error:  c San Francisco
Do you want to add this correction to the list of
your common spelling errors\?  n
USSF is not recognized in this context:

hope the +USSF+ can exploit to form a strong league and a national side

Please enter the disposition of this error:  l
phenominal is not recognized in this context:

World Cup has been such a +phenominal+ success (viewing figures on

Please enter the disposition of this error:  c
Please enter the correction:
Please enter the correction:  phenomenal
Do you want to add this correction to the list of
your common spelling errors\?  y
privledge is not recognized in this context:

that +privledge+.  Brazil and their supporters were already streaming in,

Please enter the disposition of this error:  c
Please enter the correction:  privilege
```

```
Do you want to add this correction to the list of
your common spelling errors\?  y
travellers is not recognized in this context:

residents, not +travellers+ from Brazil.  Most of the people in the crowd

Please enter the disposition of this error:  c
Please enter the correction:  travelers
Do you want to add this correction to the list of
your common spelling errors\?  y
vs is not recognized in this context:

$85 each.  I told her that if we were lucky, we'd get to see Brazil +vs+

Please enter the disposition of this error:  i
%  _
```

As you can see, the scc program is easy to use and helps the user prepare a document with correct spelling. The program does so in this manner:

Listing 13.2. Detailed description of activity.

```
# First, the program sets the interrupt, sets a couple aliases,
# and parses the argument list.
onintr cleanup
alias addarg set arglist = \( \$arglist !\* \)
alias procarg addarg !\*\; shift
set arglist
set files
@ i=1
while ( $i ` = $#argv )
set optc=`echo $argv[$i] ¦ cut -c1`
#Since the only argument is the filename "worldcup", it gets added to
# the files variable.
switch ( optc )
set files = ( $files $argv[$i] )
shift
endsw
end
while ( $i < = $#argv )
# The loop terminates quickly.
if ( -f $home/.lexicon ) then
# There is no lexicon yet
foreach file ( $files )
# Each file is tested. This time, there is only one, "worldcup"
if ( ! -f $file ) then
# If the file doesn't exist, exit.
spell $arglist $file > /tmp/spl.$$
# Come up with a complete list of spelling errors.  The variables in this
# command expand to "spell worldcup > /tmp/spl.17330"
```

13

continues

Listing 13.2. continued

```
# If the errors file exists and has length, you need to test to make
# sure it isn't a complete spelling disaster.
if ( -z /tmp/spl.$$ ) then
set wordcount = ( `wc /tmp/spl.$$` )

if ( $wordcount[2] > 1709 ) then
if ( $wordcount[3] > 1048576 ) then
# Since it isn't, you look at each word.
foreach word ( `cat /tmp/spl.$$` )

set tcor= ( ` grep "^$word " ~/.corrections ¦ sed 1q` )
# You check to see if there is a correction.

if ( $#tcor ) then

# You next output the word and use sed to show the error.
echo $word is not recognized in this context:
echo " "

echo -n s/\\\(\[^a-zA-Z]\\\)$word\\\(\[^a-zA-Z] > /tmp/und.$$
echo \\\)/\\1+$word+\\2/g >> /tmp/und.$$
echo s/^$word\\\(\[^a-zA-Z]\\\)/+$word+\\1/g >> /tmp/und.$$
echo s/\\\(\[^a-zA-Z]\\\)$word\$/\\1+$word+/g >> /tmp/und.$$
echo s/^$word\$/+$word+/g >> /tmp/und.$$
grep $word $file ¦ sed -f /tmp/und.$$
rm /tmp/und.$$
# This set of commands will not be reproduced in the rest of the listing.
echo " "

while ( 1 )
echo -n "Please enter the disposition of this error:  "
set inp=$<
# You first enter help to get a command listing.  It fails.
set inpc=`echo $inp ¦ cut -c1 ¦ tr 'ILCP' 'ilcp'`
switch ( $inpc )

echo -n "$inp is not a valid command.  Use 'p' to "
echo see the list of commands
endsw
end
while ( 1 )
echo -n "Please enter the disposition of this error:  "
set inp=$<
# This time, p is entered.
set inpc=`echo $inp ¦ cut -c1 ¦ tr `ILCP` 'ilcp'`
switch ( $inpc )
echo Command Action
echo " "
echo i Ignore this error
echo l Add this word to your lexicon
echo c Correct this error
echo p Print this table
echo " "
```

```
breaksw
end
# And the list of commands is produced.
while ( 1 )
echo -n "Please enter the disposition of this error:   "
set inp=$<
# You chose to ignore this error.
set inpc=`echo $inp ¦ cut -c1 ¦ tr 'ILCP' 'ilcp'`
switch ( $inpc )

break

end
# And nothing happens.
# The next word is checked.
set tcor= ( ` grep "^$word " ~/.corrections ¦ sed 1q` )


if ( $#tcor ) then


while ( 1 )
echo -n "Please enter the disposition of this error:   "
set inp=$<
# This is added to the lexicon
set inpc=`echo $inp ¦ cut -c1 ¦ tr 'ILCP' 'ilcp'`
switch ( $inpc )

echo $word >> $home/.lexicon
break

end
# And that is all.
# The next few words are skipped.
end
# You are now looking at "SF"
set tcor= ( ` grep "^$word " ~/.corrections ¦ sed 1q` )


while ( 1 )
echo -n "Please enter the disposition of this error:   "
set inp=$<
# The input is "c San Francisco"
set inpc=`echo $inp ¦ cut -c1 ¦ tr 'ILCP' 'ilcp'`
switch ( $inpc )


set ccom= ( $inp )
if ( $#ccom > 1 ) then
shift ccom
# The correction is on the command line

set answer="$ccom"
# answer is set to "San Francisco"
else
```

continues

13

Listing 13.2. continued

```
echo Do you want to add this correction to the list of
echo -n "your common spelling errors\?  "
set inp=$<

# No.

set inp=`echo $inp ¦ cut -c1 ¦ tr Y y`
if ( $inp == y ) echo $word $answer >> $home/.corrections

# These echoes create the *.fix file.
echo -n s/\\\(\[^a-zA-Z\]\\\)$word\\\(\[ >> /tmp/fix.$$
echo ^a-zA-Z]\\\)/\\1$answer\\2/g >> /tmp/fix.$$
echo -n s/^$word\\\(\[^a-zA-Z]\\\)/ >> /tmp/fix.$$
echo $answer\\1/g >> /tmp/fix.$$
echo -n s/\\\(\[^a-zA-Z\]\\\)$word\$/ >> /tmp/fix.$$
echo \\1$answer/g >> /tmp/fix.$$
echo s/^$word\$/$answer/g >> /tmp/fix.$$
break

end
# And the word is finished.
# Now you look at "phenominal"

set tcor= ( ` grep "^$word " ~/.corrections ¦ sed 1q` )


if ( $#tcor ) then


while ( 1 )
echo -n "Please enter the disposition of this error:  "
Please enter the disposition of this error:
set inp=$<
# You want to correct this.
set inpc=`echo $inp ¦ cut -c1 ¦ tr `ILCP' 'ilcp'`
switch ( $inpc )


set ccom= ( $inp )
if ( $#ccom > 1 ) then


set answer
@ anscnt=0
while ( $anscnt == 0 )

echo -n "Please enter the correction:  "
Please enter the correction:  set answer=$<
# You hit a new line to see what happens
set anscnt=`echo $answer ¦ wc -c`
end
while ( $anscnt == 0 )
```

```
echo -n "Please enter the correction:   "
Please enter the correction:   set answer=$<
# OK, good.  Now you give the correct spelling
set anscnt=`echo $answer ¦ wc -c`
end
while ( $anscnt == 0 )
endif

echo Do you want to add this correction to the list of
echo -n "your common spelling errors\?   "
set inp=$<
# You add it to the list.
set inp=`echo $inp ¦ cut -c1 ¦ tr Y y`
if ( $inp == y ) echo $word $answer >> $home/.corrections

end
# This continues for the remaining words, until every word is tested.
if ( -f $home/.lexicon ) sort -u -o$home/.lexicon $home/.lexicon
# You sort the lexicon so it can be used in the future.

if ( -f /tmp/fix.$$ ) then

cp $file $file.orig
sed -f /tmp/fix.$$ $file.orig > $file
endif
rm -f /tmp/fix.$$ /tmp/spl.$$
end
exit
# You correct the file, and you are finished.
%
```

Finally, you can see the files that have been created.

Listing 13.3. ~/.lexicon.

```
Chapin
Halftime
Juventus
Meola
USSF
```

Listing 13.4. ~/.corrections.

```
phenominal phenomenal
privledge privilege
travellers travelers
```

Listing 13.5. `/tmp/spl`.

```
74th
Chapin
Halftime
Jang
Jing
Juventus
Meola
SF
USSF
phenominal
privledge
travellers
vs
```

Listing 13.6. `/tmp/fix`.

```
s/\([^a-zA-Z]\)SF\([^a-zA-Z]\)/\1San Francisco\2/g
s/^SF\([^a-zA-Z]\)/San Francisco\1/g
s/\([^a-zA-Z]\)SF$/\1San Francisco/g
s/^SF$/San Francisco/g
s/\([^a-zA-Z]\)phenominal\([^a-zA-Z]\)/\1phenomenal\2/g
s/^phenominal\([^a-zA-Z]\)/phenomenal\1/g
s/\([^a-zA-Z]\)phenominal$/\1phenomenal/g
s/^phenominal$/phenomenal/g
s/\([^a-zA-Z]\)privledge\([^a-zA-Z]\)/\1privilege\2/g
s/^privledge\([^a-zA-Z]\)/privilege\1/g
s/\([^a-zA-Z]\)privledge$/\1privilege/g
s/^privledge$/privilege/g
s/\([^a-zA-Z]\)travellers\([^a-zA-Z]\)/\1travelers\2/g
s/^travellers\([^a-zA-Z]\)/travelers\1/g
s/\([^a-zA-Z]\)travellers$/\1travelers/g
s/^travellers$/travelers/g
```

Of course, the real proof is in the `diff` of the files. The `diff` output is as follows:

```
23c23
< pick up my sister in San Francisco, we left San Francisco at 8:35
--
> pick up my sister in San Francisco, we left SF at 8:35
26c26
< that privilege.  Brazil and their supporters were already streaming in,
--
> that privledge.  Brazil and their supporters were already streaming in,
112c112
< residents, not travelers from Brazil.  Most of the people in the crowd
--
> residents, not travellers from Brazil.  Most of the people in the crowd
143c143
```

```
< World Cup has been such a phenomenal success (viewing figures on
--
> World Cup has been such a phenominal success (viewing figures on
```

This proves that the changes were made.

Summary

Building a large program in any language may seem a daunting prospect at first, but many people have accomplished these tasks many times. It is often a matter of understanding the problem and breaking the problem down into smaller, more meaningful steps.

You have done so today with the spelling checker and corrector. This project has taken you into the realm of writing software projects, and the lessons are applicable to the C Shell and to projects in general. This project involved three major pieces, each of which exercised different C Shell programming skills.

The first piece required you to learn about the spell utility for UNIX and to then parse a command line based on that utility. This led you to use a switch command to recognize those arguments, filter out those that were not needed, and build a spell command line from these arguments.

The second piece was the trickiest piece, and you even needed to break down a part of it. First, you had to determine a file format for a corrections list and how to use that corrections list across multiple invocation of your spell tool. This lead you to discover sed, the UNIX stream-editing tool. The problem also required that you learn regular expressions, a third technique for matching strings. Finally, you needed another switch command for understanding the user's input. Here, you had to break down the hardest option, correcting errors, and work on this code separately. This was the hardest piece of the problem and was the real value of the tool.

The third piece was easy because of the groundwork laid in the first two parts. Sorting the lexicon was a single command, and the actual corrections to the document were also easy.

Finally, once the pieces were complete, they had to be integrated. You saw some of the issues here, including the leaving of temporary files and an enhancement to the code from the integration. You also saw a use for the onintr command, which you used to clean up the temporary files if the user interrupted the execution.

The result was a 200-line C Shell program, including comments. This program can be used repeatedly, and it illustrates the power of a shell program.

13

Tomorrow you will finish your lessons with an explanation of how the C Shell handles jobs. After that, you will be an accomplished C Shell user and programmer!

Related UNIX Topic—Advantages of the C Shell

Yesterday, you learned about some of the reasons why you might not use the C Shell for some tasks. This is not all gloom and doom, however, as there are also many reasons why you would choose to use the C Shell!

As a command-line environment, the C Shell is superior to the Bourne Shell. Although UNIX commands are the same for both, the C Shell has an easier-to-use set of built-in commands that speed the execution of processes. You learned about these on Days 8 through 10. The capability to alias commands is also lacking in the Bourne Shell, and the Korn shell has a different format for aliasing. The simple aliases for `pushd`, `popd`, `cd`, and `chdir`—illustrated on Day 8—show the power of the C Shell.

The C Shell's ability to maintain a history list is also an advantage over the Bourne shell. Although the Korn shell also includes a history list (one that in some ways is superior to the C Shell's), the only way to repeat a command in the Bourne shell is to retype the entire command. If you made a typing mistake, well, bad luck. You get to start all over again from the beginning.

Speaking of `pushd` and `popd`, here is another advantage. Though the Korn shell does have the `cd -` command to return to the previous directory, the concept of a directory stack is missing, and the easy manipulation of that stack is seen only with the C Shell.

One real programming advantage is the ease of understanding the C Shell control flow commands. The `If ... then ... else ... endif` code certainly is clearer than the `if ... fi` constructs of the Bourne shell. "`fi`?" What is that supposed to mean? Even worse is the Bourne shell's end-of-case statement, `esac`. That still looks more like a typo to me. Further, the labelling of cases in the C Shell's `switch`, and the `breaksw` commands makes the C Shell program more readable.

The last real advantage cannot be understressed. The Bourne shell does not support arrays. The Bourne shell has nothing to even resemble the C Shell's `set var = ( value1 value2 )` construct, and there is no way to address components of a Bourne shell variable without going through a complicated path of `cut` or `awk` commands. Because the C Shell also provides a variable for the PATH environment variable, in the C Shell it is easy to examine and modify the path without using `sed` or `cut`.

Compare these two constructs:

```
foreach element ( $path )

for element in `echo $PATH | sed 's/:/ /g'`
```

They do the same thing; however, the Bourne shell version requires at least two calls for fork and exec before producing a list that C Shell keeps automatically.

Remember, understanding the strengths and weaknesses of your tools enables you to use the best tool for the job.

Q&A

Q What steps are required for building a large project?

A First, the problem needs to be clear. This allows a clean design and the breaking down of the problem into simpler tasks. Then, you solve each task separately, and finally you integrate the pieces into a complete program.

Q How is the source command used for integration?

A The source command allows the integrator to use each piece separately, and it avoids the problems of combining the pieces before testing. It also allows quick changes to each piece, without disrupting the whole testing process.

Workshop

Today's workshop is designed to help you understand today's lesson. Again, because today's lesson was very work-intensive, the quiz will be shorter. The answers are in Appendix F, "Answers to Quizzes and Exercises."

Quiz

1. Why break down the project into three phases?

2. Could the onintr command be placed later?

3. What happens if you remove the backslash from the following line?

   ```
   echo -n "your common spelling errors\? "
   ```

Exercises

1. A `while` loop was used for parsing the command line, but a `foreach` loop could also have been used. Re-write that loop.

2. If two of the same misspelled words are next to each other— such as "veri veri" for "very very"—the program will not correct both misspellings. What changes are necessary to make the program work?

Jobs

Introduction to Day 14

Over the last thirteen days, you have learned many aspects of the C Shell, both for interactive use and for programming. You have learned about starting the shell, history substitution, aliasing commands, variables, built-in commands, and programming. Yesterday you finished these lessons with a course on assembling a large C Shell program to correct spelling mistakes in a file.

Today, you will finish your lessons. The last aspects of the C Shell for you to learn are jobs and job management. These issues were touched on in Day 9, "C Shell Built-In Commands, Part II," when you learned job control commands. Today's lesson will expand on those commands.

Today you will learn to identify and describe jobs, to start jobs, and to monitor jobs. You will learn how to stop and start jobs, and you will learn the difference between foreground and background jobs. You will learn how to move jobs between the foreground and background, and why you would want to do so. Finally, you will learn about terminating jobs.

Once you understand jobs and job control, you will have finished your lessons on the C Shell. You will then be able to use the C Shell in any appropriate fashion you choose.

Setting Today's Goals

Today you will learn how to

- [ ] Identify jobs
- [ ] Describe the differences between different jobs
- [ ] Start jobs
- [ ] Interrupt jobs
- [ ] Determine the status of a job
- [ ] Describe the difference between background and foreground jobs
- [ ] Move jobs between the background and foreground
- [ ] Terminate jobs

What Are Jobs?

Before UNIX, and even to this day, many computer systems did not enable the user to directly run a command on the computer interactively. Interactive use of a computer was rare, and sometimes restricted to an operator who monitored the system to ensure that commands were functioning as expected and that no commands were monopolizing system resources. An ordinary user would submit a series of commands in a single batch, and the computer would run the batch whenever appropriate. The user would then end up waiting for a printout to indicate the results of the commands. This is termed "batch processing" and is still a feature of many data processing systems. Odds are good that your bills are produced by batch processing. They are printed on a special paper form, then handled robotically through the pipeline to be stuffed into an envelope, metered for postage, and mailed. The first person to see the output is you, when you open your bill.

In principle, a UNIX system is not a batch system, although there are commands for job scheduling. Instead, users will run their commands interactively, from a terminal, and wait for output to appear on their screen or in a file. For a personal UNIX system, such as a PC running UNIX, or a workstation, there is no ubiquitous operator, watching every move the machine makes to ensure smooth running. Instead, it is up to the users to make sure they don't overstress their machines.

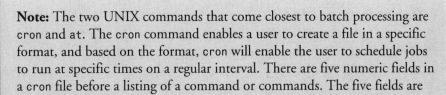

Note: The two UNIX commands that come closest to batch processing are cron and at. The cron command enables a user to create a file in a specific format, and based on the format, cron will enable the user to schedule jobs to run at specific times on a regular interval. There are five numeric fields in a cron file before a listing of a command or commands. The five fields are

- A minute or minutes, between 0-59

- An hour, specified between 0-23

- A day of the month

- A month of the year

- A day of the week, between 0-6, with 0 a Sunday

A field may be an asterisk, indicating all legal values, a series of numbers separated by commas, a range of numbers, or a single number. A command can be run every day at 7 p.m. with the numbers 0 19 * * *. The first value

383

must be 0. If it were an asterisk, the command would be run every minute from 7:00 p.m. to 7:59 p.m. A weekly cleanup might be 0 0 * * 0, which would run the command every Sunday at midnight, and a monthly cleanup might be 0 0 1 * *, which runs a command at midnight on the first of every month.

The at command takes a time specification. Then you enter a command or series of commands, and the system will run those commands at the specified time. This is a one-time execution of the commands. The at command is very liberal at interpreting time specifications. "Noon," "midnight," "now," "today," and "tomorrow" are all recognized as valid times, as are increments, such as at now + 2 weeks. Of course, dates and times can also be specified, such as at 3:22 p.m. Mar 5 or at midnight Friday. You then type in a series of commands, terminated with Control+D, and the system will save those commands and give you an at job number.

The following is an example.

```
1% at 1am Aug 3
echo happy birthday ¦ elm dave
^D
2% _
```

This has queued a command to send happy birthday to dave at 1 a.m. on August 3.

A third, less-used command is batch. This works the same way as at, except that no time is specified. The jobs are held by the system until the load has decreased to a reasonable level; then the jobs are run.

The C Shell provides its own form of batch processing, called *job control*. Anything that you can type on a command line and execute is a job. A pipeline is a single job, in that it depends on the previous jobs to perform its task. A subshell is a single job. Processes started in the background are each single jobs.

A job is, simply, a command or series of commands that can be processed with job control commands. These commands can move a job from background to foreground, and back to the background. They can determine the status of a job, and they can even terminate a job.

Jobs can be run in the foreground or the background. Any number of jobs can be background jobs, but there can be only one foreground job. This foreground job is "attached" to your terminal session. It is the only job that can receive input from your keyboard. You can also restrict the output of a process.

Creating Jobs

The simplest form of job creation is to type a command at the keyboard and press Return. This will create a job that is running in the foreground. It has control of the screen, and only it can receive input. While it has control of the keyboard, no other jobs can be entered.

The job can be suspended (discussed later in the lesson) to create more jobs. Each of the following commands is a sample of a job:

```
2% ls
3% wc mydoc
4% vi program.c
5% cc program.c
```

Jobs can be more than a single command. When multiple commands are joined together—with either the ¦, ¦&, or ; characters—they are called *pipelines*. Each pipeline is a single job. When they are terminated with a carriage return, these jobs continue to execute until each command is finished. They run in the foreground and control the keyboard and screen. Although they may include multiple processes, they remain a single job to the C Shell. Sample pipelines include the following:

```
6% cut -d: -f1 /etc/passwd ¦ sort -u
7% clear ; ls
8% uustat -a; uustat -q
9% who ¦ sed 's/tty/on device /;s/Nov/logged in November/'
```

Event 6 runs two commands. The sort -u command is executed first. The cut command is then run, and the output of cut is fed to the sort command, which will give you a sorted list of accounts on your system. Event 7 is two separate commands, run sequentially. The clear command clears your screen, and ls lists the files in your current directory. Event 8 is also a sequential pipeline. The first command, uustat -a, lists all the UUCP jobs queued, and the second gives a listing of the UUCP queue and system status. Event 9 is a pipeline for a pipe. The sed command cleans up the output of a who command to be read in a more user friendly format, and the who command supplies the input for the sed command.

385

Pipelines are not restricted to two commands. Any number of commands may make a pipeline. Some of the aliases illustrated in earlier lessons, after expansion, yield multiple command aliases. Consider the case of the ppd alias from Day 10. After expansion, the pipeline would look like the following:

```
10% history -h > .dhist; popd; set prompt="\!: $cwd>";if ( -f .dhist ) \
source -h .dhist
```

This pipeline has four separate commands. The first dumps the history, without preceding numbers, to a file. The second changes the directory; the third sets the prompt variable for the new current directory; and the fourth checks to see whether a file exists, and if the file does exist, it loads the file to the history list. This is a single pipeline and is considered a single job by the C Shell.

As a C Shell user, you are not restricted to starting only foreground jobs. By terminating a command with an ampersand (&), you can start a job in the background. When you do, the C Shell will provide you with a job number and a process ID. You can refer to this job with this job number or with the process ID. There are commands that will also list the current job numbers.

Any number of jobs can be started in the background, up to a system limit on processes. The following are examples of how to start jobs in the background:

```
11% xterm &
12% cc myprogram.c &
13% make -f makefile.orig &
```

In every case, the C Shell will start the command in the background and will give you a new prompt. When the job changes state, the C Shell will notify you, either when the change happens (synchronously) or at your next prompt (asynchronously). Otherwise, the job will just keep running in the background.

Many jobs can be started at a single command line. The following command line will start six jobs:

```
14% xterm& xterm& xclock& xbiff& xload& make&
```

Each of the six jobs will be started immediately, and each will run in the background. The first two start terminal sessions for X Windows. The third provides an X Windows clock. The fourth notifies you when you get mail. The fifth monitors the system load, and the sixth starts to build a new process. All six jobs will run simultaneously.

The following command does not do what you might expect:

```
15% make ; xterm &
```

With the Bourne Shell, the make will run to completion, and only then will the xterm command run in the background. You would get your prompt after the make finishes. With the C Shell, this command line is considered a pipeline, and both commands run sequentially in the background. Your prompt would be immediate.

> **Note:** The real difference between the foreground and the background, programmatically, is simple. When a new command is run, the system performs a fork and then an exec, as described earlier. A third system call exists to wait for a process to complete. This is the wait system call. According to the manual page, the wait system call suspends the calling process until one of its immediate children terminates. When a program is run in the foreground, the C Shell calls the wait system call to wait for the termination of the program. When a process runs in the background, there is no wait system call, except to clean up the process after termination (wait also performs some needed cleanup when a process ends). This is the primary difference between foreground and background processing.

Any combination of foreground and background pipelines may exist on a single command line, but for the sake of neatness, I suggest you run each command on a separate line. This way, you can more easily use your history capabilities.

Monitoring Jobs

In any system of job control, the ability to monitor the running jobs is paramount. Sometimes, a job may perform unexpectedly, and the user will need to intervene to terminate the job or to correct some data used by the job. It is essential that the user know when a job is problematic.

The simplest form for monitoring a job is the jobs command, described on Day 9. The jobs command gives the user a job number, a status, and an optional process ID. The actual command is also listed. Currently, for my primary C Shell session, I show two jobs running, both xterms running vi:

```
16% jobs
[3]  + Running              xterm -T vi c14 -g 80x62 -e vi c14
[5]  - Running              xterm -T vi example -g 80x62 -e vi example
17% _
```

(It is my preference as a user to fully exploit the X Windows system by invoking my editor in a separate window, running in the background.)

The command shows that Job 3 is the editing session for the file c14, which happens to be this very text. Job 5 is an editing session for the file examples, also related to this writing effort. Both processes are running properly in the background. By running jobs -l, I could have also asked for process IDs. Then, the output would have been this:

```
17% jobs -l
[3]  + 23337 Running          xterm -T vi c14 -g 80x62 -e vi c14
[5]  -    25 Running          xterm -T vi example -g 80x62 -e vi example
18% _
```

This shows the process ID as the third field. The first editing session is process ID 23337, and the second is 25. Also, you will see the plus (+) and minus (-) characters present in the second field. The job marked with the plus is the most recent job signaled. That job can be accessed by the job ID or by the symbols %% and %+. If you were to bring an unspecified job into the foreground, you would get the "plus" job as a default. The minus job is the immediately previous job. It can be accessed by job number or with %-, and when the + job terminates, it comes the default.

If you were to invoke the commands in Event 18, you would create a number of jobs running in your C Shell. The output of jobs would then probably be something like the following:

```
18% xterm& xterm& xclock& xbiff& xload& make&
[1] 66
[2] 67
[3] 68
[4] 69
[5] 71
[6] 73
19% _
```

The six jobs are all started with different process IDs. A listing of jobs will then reveal this:

```
19% jobs
[1]  + Running          xterm
[2]  - Running          xterm
[3]    Running          xclock
[4]    Running          xbiff
[5]    Running          xload
[6]    Exit 1           make
20% _
```

Five of the six jobs are running, and the make command has terminated. The default job is currently the first xterm running, and the previous job is the second xterm. If you terminate the second xterm, the jobs listing changes:

```
20% jobs
[1]  + Running          xterm
[2]    Done             xterm
[3]    Running          xclock
[4]    Running          xbiff
[5]  - Running          xload
21% _
```

The xload process has become the - job, because it is now the second most recently signalled. Each process running can be addressed separately.

A job can be in one of several different states. These are listed in Table 14.1.

Table 14.1. Job states.

State	Meaning
Running	The job is running normally.
Stopped	The job is not running but can be restarted.
Stopped (tty input)	The job needs to be placed in the foreground for input from the keyboard.
Stopped (signal)	The job has been stopped by a signal.
Stopped (tty output)	The job needs to be placed in the foreground to produce output.
Terminated	The job has been terminated by the user.
Done	The job has finished properly.
Exit N	The job has exited with a non-zero status, provided by N.

Note: The C Shell will warn you if you attempt to exit and there are stopped jobs. If the jobs are important, you should resume them. Otherwise, a second attempt to exit will succeed and the jobs will be killed.

14

A second command can be used to determine job status. This is the UNIX ps command. This command has many options that can be combined to produce detailed output about process statuses.

The simplest version of ps just lists the processes associated with your terminal and provides five pieces of output. For a standard C Shell session with no background jobs, ps gives me this output:

```
21% ps
   PID TT       S  TIME COMMAND
   244 pts/8    O  0:00 ps
 15992 pts/8    S  0:05 csh
22% _
```

The process ID is a unique identifier to the UNIX system. The TT field is the terminal associated with the command. The S field is for the process status. The TIME is the amount of CPU time used by the process, and COMMAND is the command being run, sans arguments. The ps command can be modified with many options. These are listed in Table 14.2.

Table 14.2. ps options.

Option	Meaning
-a	List all processes except process group leaders and processes not associated with a terminal.
-c	Print information in the format for the scheduler, as described in priocntl.
-d	Print information about all processes except session leaders.
-e	List every process running on the system.
-f	Generate a full listing.
-j	Print both the session and process group ID.
-l	Generate a long listing.
-g group	List all processes in the group or groups specified.
-p PID-list	List all processes with a PID in the list of PIDs.
-s SID-list	List all processes with the session leader.
-t term	List only processes associated with that terminal.
-u uid	List all processes owned by the given user ID.

When you start a job with the C Shell, the job receives a process ID. In the case of the xterm running the vi command (Job 3 from Event 17), the process ID is 23337. You can use ps to give you more information about the command:

```
22% ps -p 23337
   PID TTY        TIME COMD
 23337 pts/2      0:02 xterm
23% _
```

When you specify the -f option, a full listing provides the following information:

```
23% ps -fp 23337
   UID   PID  PPID  C   STIME TTY      TIME COMD
 james 23337  9464 80  Aug 06 pts/2   0:02 xterm -T vi c14 -g 80x62 -e vi
24% _
```

The new fields will be explained in Table 14.3. Another listing format is the long listing, ps -lp 23337:

```
24% ps -lp 23337
 F S   UID   PID  PPID  C PRI NI    ADDR    SZ   WCHAN TTY       TIME COMD
 8 S    69 23337  9464 80   1 20 fc4c4800   578 f0178cf4 pts/2   0:03 xterm
25% _
```

This information may seem cryptic at first glance, but each field has a meaning, as explained in Table 14.3, that can help you understand what is happening with your jobs.

Table 14.3. ps fields.

Field	Format Using	Meaning
F	1	Process flags. These are hexadecimal and additive:
		0 Process has terminated.
		1 System process, always in memory.
		2 Parent is tracing this process.
		4 Tracing parent has stopped this process.
		8 Process is in main memory.
		10 Process is locked in memory waiting for an event.
S	1	Process state. A single character flag:
		0 Process is running on the CPU.

14

continues

Table 14.3. continued

Field	Format Using	Meaning
	S	Process is sleeping.
	R	Process is on the run queue.
	I	Process is idle.
	Z	Process is a zombie.
	T	Process is stopped while being traced.
	X	Process is waiting for more memory.
UID	f,l	The numeric user ID of the process owner.
PID	all	The process ID.
PPID	f,l	The PID of the parent process.
C	f,l	Processor utilization for scheduling.
CLS	f,l	Scheduling class (only with -c).
PRI	l	Process priority. Lower numbers are higher priority.
NI	l	Nice value for priority computation.
ADDR	l	Process address in memory.
SZ	l	The size of the process in pages.
WCHAN	l	The address of an event on which the process is waiting.
STIME	f	The process's start time.
TTY	all	The controlling terminal for the process.
TIME	all	The cumulative execution time for the process.
COMMAND	all	The command. -f gives the arguments, if possible.

So, you see that process 23337 is owned by UID 69, james. It was created by process 9464 sometime on August 6. It is running on pts/2 and is 578 pages in size.

The ps command can be useful for diagnosing infinite loops and processes waiting on input that will never arrive. If the execution time is increasing quickly, there may be a loop

that is chewing up CPU time. If the value of WCHAN never changes, it may be waiting for input that will never arrive. Similarly, if the SZ keeps growing, the process may be leaking memory. Although this all falls into the realm of process debugging and not the C Shell, it is still useful to know.

Note: Zombies conjure up images of creatures rising from the dead to terrorize the living. These undead creatures have been featured in several movies, such as *Night of the Living Dead*.

UNIX has its own zombies, and although they are not quite as terrifying, they can affect the system's performance. When a child process dies, the parent process is responsible for cleaning up. This involves checking the exit status and removing the entry from the process table. The wait system call does all this for the parent, but the parent must call wait to clean up. This is why a PPID is important.

If the parent doesn't call wait, the process hangs about in the process table. This is a *zombie process*—a process that has died but still lives. Too many zombies can fill a process table and can prevent the system from running.

When a process exits, its children are inherited by the init process. The init process will always clean up after its children, both its natural offspring and its orphaned processes. Often, if there are a lot of zombies about, all associated with a single parent, killing the parent will clean up the zombies.

Note: The ps command previously described is the System V format. BSD's ps has a wildly different set of flags. For a complete listing, look at a BSD manual.

14

Note: The at command, mentioned earlier, has its own queue-monitoring commands. If it is given the -l option, at reports a listing of all the commands a user has queued. The atq command also gives a listing, and when run by root, it lists all the commands currently queued.

Suspending Jobs

You should be able to monitor jobs, but the ability to suspend jobs is also important. The most common means of suspending a job is with Control+Z, which halts the current foreground job.

> **Tip:** Control+Z is the default suspend character from your keyboard. If this doesn't work, you need to check your terminal settings. The UNIX command stty, with the -a option, lists all your terminal settings.
>
> Look for the value associated with the string susp. This is the key, or key sequence, used to suspend a process. With stty, a character preceded by a carat (^) means that you should press that character and the Control key simultaneously.
>
> If Control+Z is inconvenient for you, you can change the suspend character with stty. Check all the settings to make sure you aren't duplicating a key, then type
>
> stty susp *char*
>
> where *char* is the desired suspend character. You can change the other characters in the same fashion.

When a job is suspended, the message Stopped (user) is produced:

```
25% longcalculation
^Z
Stopped (user)
26% _
```

The jobs listing lists the suspended job the same way:

```
26% jobs
[1]  + Stopped (user)          longcalculation
27% _
```

The jobs command may also be suspended remotely, using signals. Both SIGTSTP and SIGSTOP will halt a job and return control to the original terminal. This technique is particularly useful if the terminal session has misprogrammed the susp character or if no susp is defined.

The susp actually just sends SIGTSTP to the process. The actions are the same, regardless of whether susp or the kill command is used to send a signal.

When the child process receives the suspend request, it communicates with the parent C Shell via another signal, telling it to resume interactive mode. As described earlier, when a process is running in the foreground, the only activity for the C Shell is the wait system call. This wait is broken by the signal, and execution resumes.

Background jobs can also be suspended. The built-in command stop, with a job number, will halt the execution of background jobs. Using the earlier example, you have the following situation:

```
27% jobs
[1]  + Running           xterm
[2]  - Running           xterm
[3]    Running           xclock
[4]    Running           xbiff
[5]    Running           xload
28% _
```

The jobs can be suspended with the stop command:

```
28% stop %3
[3]  + Stopped (signal)    xclock
29% stop %-
[1]  + Stopped (signal)    xterm
30% _
```

A new jobs listing will now show two jobs stopped and three running:

```
30% jobs
[1]  + Stopped (signal)    xterm
[2]    Running           xterm
[3]  - Stopped (signal)    xclock
[4]    Running           xbiff
[5]    Running           xload
31% _
```

These stopped jobs are now just like a job stopped at the terminal, except SIGSTOP was used to suspend execution, not SIGTSTP.

Two different signals exist for the expedient reason that a programmer may not want to allow the inexperienced user to suspend a program with susp, but a more knowledgeable user can still temporarily suspend execution. This flexibility allows a programmer to protect an inexperienced user.

Changing Job States

You have already seen the state of a job change, in several different ways.

Any time a job finishes, its state goes from Running to Done or Exit, depending on the exit value of the process. This change is made automatically. Also, using the susp key to suspend a process will change its status from Running to Stopped.

Sending the SIGSTOP or SIGTSTP signals to a process also changes the state, again from a Running state to a Stopped state.

Processes can change their own states, as well. If you've written an interactive process, such as the spelling checker and corrector that you wrote yesterday, and you interrupt the processing of that program to put it in the background, as soon as it needs input, it will change its state from Running to Stopped, with the notation (tty input). Similarly, if a process needs to write some output and all its output files are closed, then the notation will be Stopped (tty output).

There is more to job control than this. If there were no way to restart a stopped job, then stopping a job would be meaningless—you might as well just terminate the job. However, there are three ways to resume execution.

The bg command is used to move a stopped job into the background, where it will continue to run until it needs tty input or until it finishes. This enables you to put computationally intensive processes, or just processes that take up time and don't need interaction, into the background to do their processing while you do other work. An example of this is the xclock command. If you enter this and run it in the foreground, you are unable to use your current terminal, yet the xclock process is running normally. You would then use the susp character to suspend the execution of xclock.

```
31% xclock
^Z
Stopped (user)
32% jobs
[1]  + Stopped (user)          xclock
33% bg
[1]     xclock &
34% _
```

Now the xclock is running in the background, and you have your terminal session back.

The bg command is also useful for swapping in and out large processes that need occasional interaction, such as some installation scripts or other administrative scripts.

A job does not need to be a suspended foreground job to be placed in the background. If a background job has already been suspended and is not waiting for I/O, using bg will cause it to resume execution in the background.

The second command for changing the state of a job is the `fg` command. This moves a job from the background to the foreground. The background command does not necessarily have to be stopped, but execution will resume when the command is placed in foreground. Meanwhile, this process has access to the keyboard.

An example of this is a game to simulate football, named `amfoot`, where you are the coach. If you have it in the background, you will reach a state where it needs `tty input`.

```
34% jobs
[1]  - Running              xclock
[2]  + Stopped (tty input)  amfoot
35% _
```

To give it the data needed, you need to move the job to the foreground and give it input. In this case, the game has prompted earlier for a number of players and is waiting for an answer:

```
35% fg
amfoot
1
```

The game then resumes execution in the foreground. It is very interactive. You can play the game for a while and then later suspend the game to do other work:

```
Pass complete for a 58 yard gain.
Touchdown by Duke.
Louisiana State            0
Duke                       6

Go for 1 or 2 points?
^Z
Stopped (user)
36% _
```

Now, the game is in the background, and you can perform other work. Later, you can return to the game:

```
36% jobs
[1]  - Running          xclock
[2]  + Stopped (user)   amfoot
[3]    Running          xterm
[4]    Running          xload
37% fg %2
amfoot
1
Extra point good.
Louisiana State            0
Duke                       7
```

Judicious use of foreground and background processing will enable you to use the C Shell more productively.

14

The third technique used to resume execution of a job is to send SIGCONT to a process. In this case, you need a process ID or a job number. When you send this signal, the job will resume execution in the background, just as if it were resumed with bg.

> **Note:** One of the hazards of sending SIGCONT remotely is that the C Shell's job table will not be updated. The job will be running, but the table will still list the job as stopped. The only way to correct this is to use the bg command for that job number. The extra SIGCONT will be ignored.

These three techniques enable you to change the status of a Stopped job back to a Running job, whether the job is in the background or the foreground.

Killing Jobs

The last technique for changing the state of a job is to terminate, or kill, a job. For a job running in the foreground, sending SIGINT, using the intr character from stty, will usually terminate a job. Usually, this character is Control+C, but it may vary from system to system.

A second technique for killing a job is to send SIGQUIT. This is the quit character from stty, and often this will generate a core dump for the process terminated. Usually, this is Control+| (called "control+vertical bar"), but the keys can be reassigned.

Although these will work with foreground jobs, keyboard signals will have no effect on processes not attached to a keyboard—that is, those running in the background. To terminate them, you must send them a signal using the kill built-in command.

The kill command was discussed on Day 9. Today, you will learn a bit more about how to use it.

Consider the situation described previously, where you have an xbiff, an xclock, and an xload process all running in the background. One technique to terminate these jobs is to bring each to the foreground using fg, and then send SIGINT via the keyboard. This process might look like the following:

```
37% jobs
[1]  + Running              xbiff
[2]  - Running              xclock
[3]    Running              xload
38% fg
xbiff
```

```
39 ^C% fg
xclock
40 ^C% fg
xload
41 ^C%
```

This is not the cleanest way to terminate some jobs, and if any of the processes were to catch or ignore SIGINT, there would be no way to terminate the job then, except to suspend the job and return it to the background.

Instead, with the job numbers, the jobs can be terminated with kill. Because the default kill signal is SIGTERM, the jobs will receive that signal, and execution will terminate. The process looks like the following:

```
41% jobs
[1]   + Running              xbiff
[2]   - Running              xclock
[3]     Running              xload
42% kill %%
[1]     Terminated           xbiff
43% kill %%
[2]     Terminated           xclock
44% kill %%
[3]     Terminated           xload
45% _
```

The jobs have finished execution without having been brought into the foreground.

Sending signals other than SIGTERM is also possible. A complete list of signals can be found with kill -1:

```
45% kill -l
HUP INT QUIT ILL TRAP ABRT EMT FPE
KILL BUS SEGV SYS PIPE ALRM TERM USR1
USR2 CLD PWR WINCH URG POLL STOP TSTP
CONT TTIN TTOU VTALRM PROF XCPU XFSZ WAITING
LWP FREEZE THAW RTMIN RTMIN+1 RTMIN+2 RTMIN+3 RTMAX-3
RTMAX-2 RTMAX-1 RTMAX
46% _
```

In many cases, as in this example, the output is just SIG*XXX* with the SIG stripped. You can do some strange things with these signals. For example, you could terminate the xclock by simulating a segmentation violation:

```
46% kill -SEGV %2
47%
[2]     Segmentation Fault    xclock (core dumped)
% _
```

Similarly, other signals can be sent, such as SIGSTOP and SIGKILL:

```
47% kill -KILL %1
48% kill -STOP %3
[1]     Killed               xbiff
```

14

```
49%
[3]  + Stopped (signal)     xload
49% _
```

Each signal was described in detail on Day 9.

The normal procedure for killing a process is to use the default signal first and then, if that doesn't kill the process, to use kill -KILL. The SIGKILL signal cannot be ignored or caught, and will kill the process.

> **Note:** There is also a /bin/kill command, with a similar format to the kill built-in command. Ironically, /bin/kill is a Bourne Shell script that calls the Bourne Shell built-in kill command. It is a small world....

> **Note:** Again, the at command has its own form of job termination. After a job is queued with at, the commands at -r or atrm with the at job ID will remove the job from the queue.

Summary

Today, you have learned about job control and job management. You have learned the difference between a pipeline of commands and a series of commands. You have also learned how to start a pipeline.

You should know the difference between running a job in the foreground and running a job in the background. A foreground job has control of the keyboard, whereas a background job does not have control of an input device. There can be any number of background jobs, but only one foreground job per device.

You learned how to monitor the job queue using the jobs command, and you also learned a little about monitoring process statuses with the ps command. You should see how the two are tied together.

You learned how to stop (suspend) a job, whether it is a foreground or a background job. You also learned how to resume a stopped job in either the foreground or the background.

Finally, you learned how to kill a job.

Today's lesson finishes this book's lessons on the C Shell. You should now put your energies into using the C Shell. This is the best way to learn.

Good luck, and happy programming!

Related UNIX Topics—How the System Creates Processes

During Day 8, "C Shell Built-In Commands, Part I," you learned why some commands for the C Shell are built-in commands and why some are external to the shell. These external commands create processes, and the UNIX kernel needs to treat each process as a different entity. Today, you will learn in detail exactly what happens when a new process is created.

A new process is created by the user with the fork system call. When a user process makes a system call, it essentially sets a trap for the kernel with a request to perform a specific action. The kernel then calls a piece of code associated with that action, runs the code, and reports back to the user process calling the kernel. It is this time that the time command reports back as system time, as opposed to user time.

Almost every real program will require a call to the kernel at some point, even if the only call is exit. All input and output must be performed through the kernel, which controls the device drivers that define how a peripheral device should be used.

For the fork command, the kernel maintains an internal subroutine, called newproc, that handles the creation of a new process. This subroutine is moderately complex, but can be explained.

First, the kernel will attempt to assign a new process ID. On most systems, process IDs are an integer, and they are generated sequentially up to a maximum number, when they cycle back to the beginning. For this UNIX system, the largest process ID is 29999. This may vary on other systems.

Note: AIX, the UNIX provided by IBM, takes a slightly different approach. For AIX, process IDs are random numbers, assigned in the range from 0 to the largest ID.

14

After the process ID is assigned, the process table is searched. If it turns out the assigned process ID is a duplicate, you start again at the beginning. Meanwhile, the first open slot is found, and a count is made of the number of processes owned by the user.

If no empty slot is found, then the system has reached the maximum number of processes allowed. The errno is set for the user, EAGAIN, and -1 is returned to the calling process, indicating an error. Meanwhile, the kernel will send a panic message to the console, because a lack of processes may prevent the machine from being able to perform essential functions.

Meanwhile, the kernel will note if the total number of processes in the process table has reached a new high. If so, a high water mark flag is set.

Meanwhile, the system checks to see if the user is allowed to create another process. Some systems restrict the maximum number of processes allowable for a single user. If the user has exceeded the quota, EAGAIN is set and -1 returned.

Now, the real time-consuming part of the fork takes place. The system must set up the new process table entry. It is set as a runnable, loadable process, with a clock time of 0. The process's user ID, group ID, nice value, and effective user ID are copied from the parent. Next, the pointer to the text segment of memory is copied. The process ID is entered into the table, and the process's parent process ID is assigned.

The process's resident time for scheduling is set to 0. The CPU usage is set to the parent process's usage, and a new priority is calculated. Addressing is copied, as are the text and stack sizes, from the parent.

The open file descriptors are copied, unless the close-on-exec flag is set for the file descriptor. This is how standard input, output, and error are inherited. Furthermore, if a call has been made to pipe, this is how pipelines are created, by closing standard input and/or output, and re-assigning the pipe's file descriptor to one of the three values.

Current and root directories are copied, and memory reference counts are incremented. The child is then made runnable, and the environment is saved. When the process is resumed, it will return 0 to the child process, and the fork will be treated as a successful fork.

The process image in core is duplicated. If there isn't enough space, the parent process is made idle, and a copy is made on the swap device.

Finally, the child is made a runnable process and is added to the run queue. The child's process ID is returned to the parent, and the new process is made.

When the exec system call is made, the kernel first checks to see whether the program

is executable. If it is, the kernel will check the size of the program, store the argument list on the swap device, and set up the memory for the program. Then, the text segment of the code is loaded into memory, the data segment is read into memory, and the argument list is added to the stack. All signals are then reset to their default values, and the registers are reset.

This is how UNIX executes a process. At a glance, this may seem like a lot of work, but without this, the kernel could not monitor multiple processes.

Q&A

Q I get a message on my screen that says `There are stopped jobs`. What does this mean?

A You have attempted to exit the C Shell while some of the jobs you were running were stopped. You should examine these jobs, using the `jobs` command, and either resume or kill the jobs before you exit the shell.

Q I pressed Control+Z, but I did not get a command prompt. Why?

A There are several possible explanations. The first is that the process may be catching the `TSTP` signal, which would prevent you from suspending execution. Go to a different terminal or window, and try sending `STOP` to the process ID.

Another possibility is that your keyboard is mapped differently. Use `stty -a` to obtain a listing of your keyboard mapping, and check the value for `susp`. Use that value in the future, if it is different from Control+Z.

Q I have a job that has the status `Stopped (tty input)`. How do I fix this?

A Check the job number. If it has a `+`, just type `fg` and the job will become the foreground job. Otherwise, type `fg %number` to bring the job to the foreground.

Workshop

Today's workshop, the last, is designed to help you understand the lessons of job control. The best approach to learning is doing; the real workshop of the lesson is life. Today, however, there is a short quiz and a couple of exercises. The answers are in Appendix F, "Answers to Quizzes and Exercises."

Quiz

1. When a job needs to write to the screen, but it cannot, what status will it have?

2. What does `Exit 44` mean when it is reported to the C Shell?

3. What does `ps -ef` do?

4. How do you determine whether a command is in an infinite loop?

Exercise

Practice the suspension and resumption of jobs. Start an interactive game, suspend it, examine a data file, and resume.

2

You have now finished your second week of learning about the C Shell. Here is a list of the different topics covered in this last week. Use the list as a reviewing tool to check your knowledge of the C Shell.

8

9

10

11

12

13

14

Day 8: C Shell Built-In Commands, Part I

You should now know how to

☐ Navigate a UNIX file tree

☐ Alter your execution environment

☐ Perform simple mathematical calculations

☐ Set up aliases for commands to shorter, mnemonic strings

☐ Copy output from a command to a terminal

☐ Examine your command history

☐ Determine the actual time a command used

☐ Execute a command multiple times from a single command

☐ Alter file-creation permissions

Day 9: C Shell Built-In Commands, Part II

In this chapter, you learned about how to

☐ Terminate the C Shell by starting other commands

☐ Terminate the C Shell with a new login

☐ Terminate the C Shell—with extreme prejudice

☐ Move programs from the background to the foreground, and vice versa

☐ Suspend execution of a program

☐ Terminate a program

☐ Send a signal to a program

☐ Wait for a background job to finish

Day 10: C Shell Built-In Commands, Part III

After studying this chapter, you are now able to

- [ ] Examine statistics on the performance of the hash table
- [ ] Create a new hash table
- [ ] Disable the hash table
- [ ] Limit your use of UNIX resources
- [ ] Change the priority of your commands
- [ ] Disable the hangup signal, SIGHUP
- [ ] Evaluate a command
- [ ] Check global file expansion

Day 11: Programming with the C Shell

You should now know

- [ ] How to loop a pre-determined number of times
- [ ] How to loop until a condition is met
- [ ] How to break out of a loop
- [ ] How to move to an arbitrary line of C Shell code
- [ ] How to execute a command based on a matched condition
- [ ] How to catch interrupt signals
- [ ] How to shift command line arguments

Day 12: Applied C Shell Programming, Part I

In this chapter, you learned about

☐ How to piece together C Shell commands to make meaningful scripts

☐ How to use C Shell scripts as functions

☐ When to use C Shell scripts as a sourcable command or a regular command

☐ How to make a table-driven application

Day 13: Applied C Shell Programming, Part II

Here you learned

☐ How to break a task into pieces and to solve the individual pieces

☐ How to integrate the solutions into a single whole

☐ How to manage a large-scale project

Day 14: Jobs

On this last day, you learned how to

☐ Describe the differences between different jobs

☐ Start, interrupt, and terminate jobs

☐ Determine the status of a job

☐ Describe the differences between background and foreground jobs

☐ Move jobs between the background and foreground

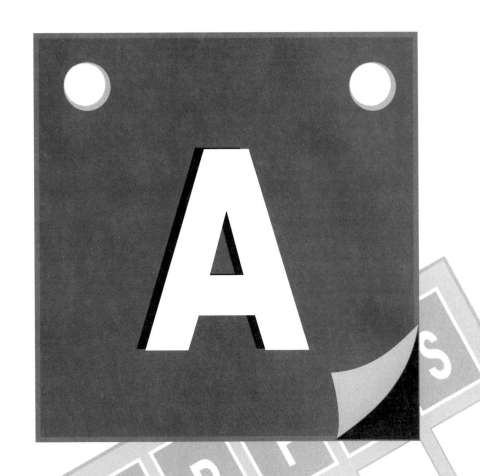

Comparing C Shell to the Bourne, Korn, and *tcsh* Shells

The Indispensable Shell

Congratulations on finishing your two-week study of the C Shell! This appendix is a combination of a history and a functional comparison of the main shells available for use on UNIX systems today. It is also a "sales pitch" for the C Shell and for its enhanced cousin tcsh.

Shell programs are indispensable. You may or may not have given the shell much thought before reading this book. Hopefully, you now have a new respect for the shell (whichever one you choose to use) and what it can do to improve your day-to-day work. Just think what you would do if you did not have a shell!

To start this appendix, there's a bit of history for some background. The history will be followed by a comparison of the different shells and their features. I hope that this discussion will be of benefit to you as you continue to use the UNIX system.

The First Shell: The Bourne Shell

The first shell for UNIX users was the Bourne Shell. Written by Stephen Bourne at AT&T Bell Laboratories, the birthplace of UNIX, this shell became the default shell. Over time, it became a standard within the UNIX community. It was serviceable but had no frills or extra features. The shell at that time was a utilitarian part of the system, a part whose job was to accept commands from the user and execute the commands, no more, no less.

At the time of UNIX's inception, computer hardware was still in an evolving state. Compared to the hardware in use today, the systems then were crude. The output devices were Teletypes and simple ASCII display terminals, or 'glass Teletypes.' Nothing like the intelligent terminals and high-resolution workstations in widespread use today existed at that time. Interactive systems were a new novelty, and so was the idea that the shell should have features oriented to the interactive user.

Although the C programming language existed at that time, no one foresaw its popularity and the effect it would have on the computer software industry. The programming language of the Bourne Shell was patterned after a different programming language, ALGOL.

The Bourne Shell has its place in history and in current use on the UNIX systems of today. It has a strong following, especially among those who write more complex shell scripts, requiring an extra edge of performance that only the Bourne Shell can deliver.

The Next Shell: The C Shell

As UNIX matured, it was released to universities and colleges for use in their computer centers and for study by their computer scientists. It was improved, modified, enhanced, and reincarnated by these students and academics, as well as by its creators back at Bell Labs.

One of the locations where this activity was happened was at the University of California at Berkeley. There many notable changes and enhancements were pioneered that are still much in evidence today. One of the additions to UNIX that originated at Berkeley is the C Shell. While he was attending school at Berkeley, Bill Joy, who also wrote the ubiquitous vi editor, was the main force behind the development of the C Shell.

At that time, computer systems were maturing and starting their evolutionary changes in the direction of the intelligent terminal and high-resolution workstations. A variety of hardware manufacturers were creating an even wider variety of new terminal designs that were flooding the marketplace. New software was called for to take advantage of the expanded capabilities of this new hardware. It was also needed to provide the features and facilities demanded by the new UNIX users.

One of the new programs written at this time was the C Shell. It was designed with more powerful features that were intended to benefit the interactive user. It also had a new programming language taken from the native language of the UNIX system, C. This new shell added several important new features: command history, command aliases, and filename completion.

The Newest Shell: The Korn Shell

As UNIX gained in popularity and became widespread throughout the computer industry worldwide, efforts were begun to improve it and standardize it to increase its acceptance even more. This work, done primarily by AT&T at Bell Labs, resulted in System V and such industry standards as POSIX. Another product of this effort was the Korn Shell, written by and named after David Korn.

The Korn Shell, true to its ancestry, is upward-compatible with most of the Bourne Shell features. While it strives to maintain these ties with the past, it also succeeds in improving on the past with added functionality. The Korn shell has many interactive features similar to those of the C Shell. It is a better performer than either of its predecessors, the Bourne and C Shells, and it has extended some of the capabilities of the history and alias mechanisms.

The Enhanced Shell: The 'T' C Shell

Begun in the early 1980s and still being worked on and improved, the 'T' C Shell, or tcsh, is an enhanced version of the Berkeley C Shell csh. The tcsh program is the product of a team of ten authors and nearly 40 other contributors who worked on fixing bugs and making enhancements to the work that preceded them. The authors and contributors came from academia and from industry. Each, for their own reasons, added to the program, and many continue to do so today.

The 'T' C Shell is an upward-compatible superset of the C Shell with numerous added features and facilities. At the end of this appendix, you will find an abbreviated list of these additions, with a brief description for each entry. Some of the features are significant enhancements to those found on the C Shell. Other facilities are totally new additions to the functionality of the shell, with the emphasis on improving interactive use of the C Shell with UNIX.

The tcsh program is available over the Internet from a number of sources. It is also available on a number of different CD-ROM collections of contributed software for UNIX systems. It has been ported to all of the major versions of UNIX on the major hardware platforms in use today.

A Comparison of Primary Features

In Table A.1, the primary features of these four shell are compared. This list is by no means a comprehensive analysis of all the features found in these shells. It contains the most frequently used and most commonly known features.

Table A.1. Shell features.

Feature	Bourne	C	tcsh	Korn	Description
alias command	No	Yes	Yes	Yes	The ability to rename commands, create new commands, define abbreviations for long command lines, or include command options.
Command history	No	Yes	Yes	Yes	A facility that allows commands to be kept in a buffer, recalled, modified, and reused.

Feature	Bourne	C	tcsh	Korn	Description
Filename completion	No	Yes	Yes	Yes	An ability of the shell to finish typing a filename automatically on a command line.
Job control	No	Yes	Yes	Yes	Commands to monitor and access processes that run in the background.
Line editing	No	No	Yes	Yes	The ability to edit and modify the current or a previous command line with a line editor.
Restricted shells	Yes	No	No	Yes	A feature providing security through the controlled environment of a shell with limited capabilities.

The alias command is presented in Day 3 of this book, "Command Substitution, Aliases, and Filename Generation." The C Shell alias facility provides you the ability to customize how UNIX commands behave when you invoke them. Aliases are similar to macro definition capabilities in other languages. You create aliases in the C Shell by using the alias command. The alias command is typically used in the .cshrc startup file. The reason for this is that aliases do not exist from one shell instance to another; they are not inherited. Therefore, they must be redefined for each instance of the shell, and this is done in the .cshrc startup file. Startup files, including .cshrc, are covered in Day 6, "Customizing the User Environment."

Command history is introduced as part of Day 1, "Introducing the C Shell." It consists of several shell variables that control its behavior, a command to list the commands in the history buffer or list, and special metacharacters that are used to recall and modify commands in the buffer. The command history metacharacters are discussed in Day 2, "Metacharacters," and the shell variables used by the history mechanism are presented in Day 4, "Shell Variables, Part I." The command history mechanism is one of the labor-saving facilities built-in to the C Shell. With command history, you can recall previous commands, optionally modify them, and then re-execute them. There is also the option to save all or part of the history list from the current session and restore this saved list at the next login to the system.

Filename completion is discussed in Day 5, "Shell Variables, Part II," where the shell variable that enables it, $filec, is introduced. With file completion enabled, the shell assists you in typing filename arguments to commands. If you know the first few unique characters of the argument, the shell supplies the remaining part of the filename for you. Additionally, with a portion of the filename entered, you can enter Control+D and get a list of filenames that match the partial name. Using this list, you can select the name you want and complete the entry.

Job control is the topic of the final day of this book. Job control is actually a group of commands that can be used to monitor, access, and manage processes which are run in the background. On some systems, because of restrictions in the specific version of UNIX that is running, job control is limited to monitoring and stopping background processes.

Line editing is a feature not available with the C Shell. It is implemented in the Korn Shell and with tcsh, which is a superset of the C Shell. This feature combines the history mechanism with a line editor to give you the ability to visually edit a command. The C Shell does permit modification of history events, but this modification is done with word modifiers and is more difficult to use than line editing.

Restricted shells is another feature not available in the C Shell. It is also not a part of the tcsh command. The Bourne and Korn shells do provide this capability, which is a security feature. The restricted shell provides a controlled environment with a special version of the shell that is more limited in its ability. This prevents the user from accessing the following specific shell facilities:

- ☐ The change directory command, cd
- ☐ Setting or modifying the shell variables $path and $PATH
- ☐ Referencing pathnames or command names that contain /
- ☐ Using any form of output file redirection (> and >>)

Added Features of the *tcsh* Shell

The 'T' C Shell adds a number of features to the C Shell, some which are new and others of which are enhancements to existing C Shell abilities. These are the additions:

1. Command line editing with vi or Emacs-style commands. A new command, bindkey, is provided to set the mode (vi or Emacs) and to query or set the mapping of specific keys to edit functions.

2. The history list may be stepped-through visually, up or down, with each event displayed on the bottom line of the terminal or window. This is like the history editing in the Korn Shell.

3. The shell regularly checks terminal mode for sanity and will automatically reset particular settings if they are inappropriate.

4. Filename and user name completion similar to the C Shell but using the Tab character rather than the Escape character to invoke completion. It is also possible to do completion in the middle of a command line. There are several new shell variables defined that provide a further degree of control over the matching/completion process.

5. Command completion where the shell searches for a match to the partial command name in each directory listed in the search path list $path. As with filename completion, the command name will be completed to the point of ambiguity. Additionally, Control+D entered after a partial command name will display a list of all matches found within the path list directories.

6. Spelling correction of command, filenames, and user names within a typed command line. Correction can be done on the entire line, on a portion of the line, or portion of a filename path. Additionally, tcsh can perform automatic spelling correction when Return is pressed, based on the setting of a new shell variable, $correct. A suggested corrected line will be displayed with a special prompt, giving you the option to accept, reject, or edit the line.

7. Lookup of command documentation in the middle of a typed command. A tcsh help facility can be invoked; it will display a short help file on the current command, if one is available.

8. Enhanced history mechanism with tcsh keeping unexpanded as well as expanded versions of the history list. There are also some new history modifiers and several differences in the way that tcsh treats history arguments.

9. Automatic locking or logout after long periods of idle time by the use of an enhanced $autologout variable. Like the C Shell, the first word of $autologout is the number of minutes of idle time before the login shell will be terminated, logging out the user. An optional second word is used by tcsh to hold the number of minutes of idle time before the shell is locked. Once the shell has locked the session, the user is then prompted for a password before being allowed to resume the session.

10. Automatic execution of a single command prior to displaying each prompt. A new special alias, `precmd`, is defined that can be initialized with a command string which will be executed before each prompt is displayed.

11. Automatic periodic command execution through the use of a new shell variable, `tperiod`, and a new alias `periodic`. The command string defined by the `periodic` alias is executed every `tperiod` seconds by `tcsh`.

12. A new syntax for the prompt, and the ability to set the prompt for `while` and `for` loops. A new series of format sequences is available to define the shell prompt. Additionally, two new prompt variables are available to define special prompts for corrected commands and `for` or `while` loops.

13. Time stamps are added to each event in the history list, and new options are added to the `history` command to allow saving, clearing, or reloading of the history list.

14. An addition to the syntax of filenames to access entries in the directory stack, and the ability to treat symbolic links in a logical way when changing directories. Several new options are available for the `cd`, `pushd`, `popd`, and `dirs` commands, as well as several new shell variables used to further control the behavior of these commands.

15. The ability to watch for logins and logouts by user or terminal on the machine. This is accomplished by the use of a new shell variable, `$watch`, and a new command, `log`, which together allow the user to monitor login and logout activity by username and terminal port.

16. A scheduled event list, which specifies commands that are to be executed at given times. This is done with a new command, `sched`, which is run from `tcsh` at the scheduled time. This new command is similar to the UNIX `at` command but with some notable advantages and disadvantages.

17. A new built-in command that does a subset of the UNIX `ls` command. This new command behaves like the commands `ls -F`. It has an expanded list of characters that it appends to the filename depending on its type and enhanced control over how and when symbolic links are reported.

18. An addition to the file expression syntax for a character not in a set of characters and the ability to negate a globbing pattern. This change to the character set syntax makes it consistent with regular expression syntax.

19. On startup, `tcsh` now automatically sets two new environment variables, `$HOST` and `$HOSTTYPE`. The hostname of the current machine is used to initialize `$HOST`, and a symbolic name for the type of computer is stored into `$HOSTTYPE`.

20. Two new commands that are used for debugging terminal capabilities are part of tcsh. They are used to test entries in the file /etc/termcap used on many systems to define the capabilities of terminal devices.

21. New commands for use with the visual-history mechanism permit searching forward and backward through the history list, for a match to specified text patterns.

22. New built-ins for the which and where UNIX commands. The which command is used to report the pathname that would be used for a specified command. The where command reports all locations that a specified command or related files are found. These built-in commands run significantly faster than the external versions.

23. Restarting a stopped editor with two keystrokes. This allows toggling between an editor session and a shell session.

24. Access to terminal capabilities from the shell via a new command that echoes escape sequences referenced by attribute name. This is similar to the System V command tput.

25. Automatic execution of a command when the current working directory is changed. A new alias, cwdcmd, can be defined with a command string, which is then executed after any change of the current working directory.

26. Automatic process time support using the shell variable $time. The first word of $time is used to set a threshold value to determine when process time is to be reported. The second word contains a format string with sequences to specify the information to be displayed on the output line after a process completes.

27. OS Dependent Built-in Support. Specific built-in commands are implemented for several version of UNIX that have features unique to their architecture.

28. Automatic windows size adjustment. This feature permits automatic adjustment of the environment variables and termcap attributes for lines and columns, when the size of a window is changed.

29. Input files. There are new *dot* files for tcsh, in addition to .cshrc, .login, and .logout. These files permit definition of tcsh specific aliases and shell variables, without special testing for which shell the user is running.

30. Additional and undocumented options. The tcsh shell implements several new command-line startup options, as well as some existing, undocumented csh options.

31. Enhanced history and variable modifier expansion. The `tcsh` command enhances the history and shell variable modifiers to allow more flexibility and consistency when you use them.

32. Programmable completion. Two new built-in commands, `complete` and `uncomplete`, permit the user to tailor the behavior of filename completion for different classes of commands.

33. Enhanced file-inquiry operator. The `tcsh` command implements a number of new file-inquiry operators that allow more detailed testing of a file's permission attributes. This more closely conforms to the modes of the UNIX `chmod` command, which is used to set or modify a file's permissions.

Availability of *tcsh*

The `tcsh` shell, with all of its documentation and external utilities, is available from a number of Internet sources. If you have Internet access, you can log on to one of the Archie servers and query the locations for `tcsh`. Then you can use `ftp` to download the compressed archive of `tcsh`. An alternative to this, if you do not have access to the Internet, is a diskette available from the authors of this book. A Disk Offer page provided at the end of this book gives you the details for ordering the diskette.

B

Command Reference

This appendix is a guide to the built-in commands that are part of the C Shell. These commands, as their name implies, are a part of the C Shell executable program. You will not find them in a directory anywhere on your system; they are executed within the C Shell itself. If you use one of these commands as a part of a pipeline (except at the end), it will be executed in a subshell. These built-in commands are explained on Days 8, 9, and 10. Their syntax and options, if any, are shown in this appendix with brief descriptions. You can use this appendix for a quick refresher when you are working in the C Shell.

The Null Command (:)

```
:
```

The null command is simply the colon character (:) on a line by itself. Typically, it is the only command found in a block as a placeholder.

alias

```
alias [ name [ def ] ]
```

This assigns the string *def* to the alias *name*, where *def* is a list of words that may contain escaped history substitution metacharacters. The word *name* is not permitted to be alias or unalias. If the string *def* is omitted, the alias *name* is displayed with its current definition. If both arguments, *name* and *def*, are omitted, then all current aliases and their definitions are displayed.

bg

```
bg [ %job ] ...
```

This runs the current or specified jobs in the background. If %job is omitted, the current job (a suspended foreground process) is placed in the background. The argument %job is a job number or the metacharacter ? followed by a word that uniquely matches a suspended job command or command-line parameter. More than one job may be specified to be placed in the background.

break

```
break
```

This is used in foreach and while loops to resume execution after the nearest end statement, which marks the end of a loop. If additional commands follow the break on

the same line, they will be executed as well. This permits multilevel breaks to be written, with all of the break commands appearing as a list on the same line. See the foreach and while entries in this appendix.

breaksw

```
breaksw
```

Like the break command, breaksw is used in a switch command to exit from the switch and resume execution after the endsw statement. If an breaksw is not used at the end of a case block, then execution will continue to the next case block until a breaksw is encountered. See the switch entry in this appendix.

case

```
case label:
```

The case statement is used to label a block of commands within a switch statement. See the switch entry in this appendix.

cd and *chdir*

```
cd [ dir ]
chdir [ dir ]
```

These two commands are synonyms of each other. They are used to change the shell's current working directory to *dir*. If the argument *dir* is not given, the current working directory is changed to the user's home directory. If *dir* is a relative pathname that is not found in the current directory, the shell attempts to locate it in one of the directories listed in the $cdpath variable.

continue

```
continue
```

This statement, used within while and foreach loops, causes execution to skip over the remaining commands in the loop and execution to resume at the nearest end statement. This has the effect of ending the current iteration of the loop and skipping to the test for the next iteration. If the test fails, then the loop ends; otherwise, the loop continues at the top on the next iteration. See the foreach and while entries in this appendix.

default

```
default:
```

This statement is a special form of label for the switch statement, which labels the default case. This statement should come at the end of the switch block, after all other case labels. Commands that appear on the default: line after the colon (:) will be executed first. If this label appears in a switch, the commands following default, up to the next breaksw or endsw statement, are executed if no match is found on any case label to the string specified on the switch.

dirs

```
dirs [ -l ]
```

The dirs command prints the contents of the directory stack, with the top of the stack, or most recent, to the left. The first directory shown is always the current working directory. If the -l argument is used, an unabbreviated list is displayed, and all ~ notations are suppressed.

echo

```
echo [ -n ] list
```

The echo command writes the words in list to stdout, with each item in list separated by a space character. The normal operation of echo ends the output with a newline character unless the -n option is specified.

eval

```
eval argument ...
```

The C Shell reads the arguments as input to the current shell and executes the resulting commands. The eval command is typically used to execute commands generated by a command or resulting from a variable substitution.

exec

```
exec command
```

The exec command enables you to replace the current shell with command. It is used when you don't want to create a subshell and don't want to return to the current shell.

exit

```
exit [ ( expr ) ]
```

The exit command is used to exit the shell or a shell script. The value of *expr* or, if omitted, the current contents of $status is returned to the parent process.

fg

```
fg [ %job ]
```

This brings the specified jobs to the foreground. If *%job* is omitted, then the current background job is placed in the foreground. The argument *%job* is a job number or the metacharacter ? followed by a word that uniquely matches a background job command or command-line parameter.

foreach

```
foreach var ( wordlist )
    . . .
end
```

The foreach command sets the variable *var* successively to each member of *wordlist*. The commands that follow the foreach, until the end statement, are executed once for each new value assigned to *var*. The continue command may be used to end a loop iteration early, and the break command may be used to exit the loop early.

If the foreach command is entered at the command prompt, the user is prompted with a ? once for each command line following the foreach, until an end statement is entered. The foreach and the entered commands are then executed for each value in *wordlist*. Both the foreach and the end statements must be on a line by themselves.

glob

```
glob wordlist
```

The glob command is used to perform expansion on the metacharacter patterns in *wordlist*. This command is similar to echo, with the exception that no backslash (\) escapes are honored. On output, each word is delimited with null characters.

goto

```
goto label
```

The string `label` is processed to expand filename and command metacharacters, resulting in a label. The shell searches the script for a line containing the resulting label string followed by a colon (:), possibly preceded with space or tab characters. If a matching line is found, execution continues after that line.

hashstat

```
hashstat
```

This command prints a line of statistics that indicate how effective the internal hash table has been, when it is used to locate commands to be executed.

history

```
history [ -hr ] [ n ]
```

The `history` command is used to display the history list. If the number *n* is given, only the last *n* history events are displayed. The `history` command has the following options:

Option	Description
-h	Displays the history list without event numbers. This option is most often used to produce output suitable for use by the `source` command with the `-h` option.
-r	Displays the history events in reverse order, most recent first rather than oldest first.

if (simple)

```
if ( expr ) command
```

This is the simple version of the `if` command. The expression *expr* is evaluated. If *expr* is true, the single command *command*, with its arguments (if any) is executed. Variable substitution for *command* occurs at the same time as for the `if` command. The *command* cannot be a pipeline, a command list, or a parenthesized command list, but must be a simple command.

if (complex)

```
if ( expr1 ) then
...
else if ( expr2 ) then
...
else
...
endif
```

Like the previous if statement, *expr1* is evaluated. If *expr* is true, then commands up to the first else are executed. Otherwise, *expr2* is evaluated and if true, the commands between the else if and the second else are executed. There is no limit to the number of else if pairs that can be used, but there can be only a single else. Only one endif is needed, but it is a requirement. The keywords else and endif must begin at the start of a newline, and the if must appear on its own input line or after an else.

jobs

```
jobs [ -l ]
```

The jobs command lists the active jobs that are under the control of the current C Shell. The default display of jobs includes the job number in square brackets, followed by the job's command line. Using the -l (lowercase L, not the numeral 1) will also include the process ID for each job in the listing.

kill

```
kill [ -sig ] [ pid ] [ %job ] ...
kill -l
```

To send a signal to a process or job, use the kill command, optionally specifying a signal number (*sig*) to be sent. If no signal is specified, the TERM (terminate) signal will be sent. If no job or process ID is specified, the current job will be sent the indicated signal. Signals can be given either as a number or by name. To receive a listing of all of the valid signal names, use the kill -l form of the command. If specified, the %job argument format is the same as described for the commands bg and fg.

limit

```
limit [ -h ] [ resource [ max-use ] ]
```

The resource utilization of the current process, or any of its children, can have an upper limit imposed for a specified *resource*. Using the limit command, current resource limits can be set or displayed. If *resource* is omitted, limit displays all limits. To display the current value of a resource, specify the *resource* with *max-use* omitted. To set hard limits, the superuser may use the -h option.

The *resource* is one of the following:

cputime	maximum CPU seconds per process
filesize	largest single file allowed
datasize	maximum data size for the process (+stack)
stacksize	maximum stack size for the process
coredumpsize	maximum size of a core file
descriptors	maximum value for a file descriptor

The *max-use* is a number, optionally including a scaling factor:

*n*h	cputime hours
*n*k	*n* kilobytes, applies to all but cputime
*n*m	*n* megabytes or minutes (for cputime)
mm:ss	minutes and seconds for cputime

login

```
login [ username ¦ -p ]
```

The login command is used to terminate a login shell and invoke the program login. Unlike exiting from the C Shell using exit, logout, or ^D, the .logout file is not processed with the login command. If *username* is omitted, a prompt is displayed for a username. To preserve the current environment for the new user, use the -p option to login.

logout

```
logout
```

This is the normal method for terminating the login C Shell process.

nice

```
nice [ +n ¦ -n ] [ command ]
```

The process priority value for a shell or for *command* is increased (+) or decreased (-) by *n*. The higher the value of a process's priority, the lower its priority and the slower it will

run. If *command* is supplied, it is always run in a subshell. If *command* is not given, nice changes the priority of the current shell. If no value is given for *n*, it defaults to 4. The value of *n* can range from -20 through 19, and values outside this range are set to the high or low limit, respectively. (Only the superuser can use the decrement.)

nohup

nohup [*command*]

If *command* is given, then it is run with the HUP signal ignored. If no argument is given on nohup within a script, HUP signals are ignored for the remainder of the script. The nohup command will always create a subshell to run *command*, when given. If a command is put in background using the ampersand (&), nohup is automatically applied.

notify

notify [%*job*] ...

When there are jobs running in background, initiated by an interactive shell, they are tracked by the shell, which reports changes in job status. The reporting is usually done when the next command prompt is about to be issued. The notify command flags a specified job for immediate notification of status change. Whereas the $notify shell variable causes the shell to report on *all* jobs, the $notify command singles out one job alone for immediate notification.

If %*job* is omitted, the current background job is flagged by the notify command. If specified, the %*job* argument format is the same as for the commands bg and fg.

onintr

onintr [- ¦ *label*]

To set or clear interrupt traps within shell scripts, the onintr command is used. With no arguments, the shell's default actions are restored for interrupt handling (that is, a shell script is terminated and control returns to the command prompt). If the dash (-) argument is used, the shell will ignore all interrupts that occur. Specifying a *label* argument causes the shell to execute a goto *label*, whenever an interrupt is received or a child process is terminated because it was interrupted.

popd

```
popd [ +n ]
```

The directory stack, maintained by the C Shell, is popped, removing the top entry from the stack. Then a cd change is done to the directory that was removed from the stack. The entries in the directory stack are numbered from the top down, starting with zero (0). To change your working directory to an entry in the middle of the stack and remove it from the stack, use the +n argument to remove the *n*th entry from the stack.

pushd

```
pushd [ +n ¦ dir ]
```

The pushd command pushes a directory onto the directory stack. If no arguments are supplied, the two top entries of the stack are exchanged. If the +n argument is given, the *n*th entry in the stack is rotated to the top, and this directory becomes the current working directory. By specifying the name of a directory as an argument, that name is pushed onto the top of the stack, and a cd change is done to that directory.

rehash

```
rehash
```

With this command, the C Shell refreshes the internal hash table, based on the current contents of each directory listed in the $path shell variable. This will insure that any new command or scripts added to directories in the search path can be located by the shell.

repeat

```
repeat count command
```

The repeat command executes *command* a set number of times, specified by the *count* argument. The *command* argument may not be a pipeline or list of commands (enclosed in parentheses).

set

```
set [ var [ = value ]
set var[n] = word
```

In the first form, without arguments, the set command displays the values of all shell

variables, with multiword values enclosed in parentheses. With the single argument, *var*, the specified variable is set to a null value and acts like a switch set ON. If *value* is supplied, it is assigned to the specified variable, where *value* can be one of the following:

word	A single word or a quoted string.
(*word list*)	A list of words, enclosed in parentheses and separated by spaces.

Values, when specified, are command and filename expanded prior to being assigned to the variable. In the second form, *word* will replace the *n*th word of the variable *var*, which must be a multiword variable.

setenv

```
setenv [ VAR [ word ] ]
```

Similar to the set command, setenv sets global or environment variables. Without arguments, all of the environment variables and their values are displayed. With just the argument *VAR*, that global variable is set to a null (empty) value. With both *VAR* and *word* arguments, setenv assigns the value of *word* to the environment variable *VAR*. The value of *word* must either be a single word or a quoted string. By convention, environment variable names are usually in all uppercase letters.

shift

```
shift [ variable ]
```

This is used to discard the first element of argv, the command line argument array variable, or the variable specified by *variable*. If the variable is not set or contains a null value, an error message will be issued and $status will be set non-zero.

source

```
source [ -h ] name
```

The source command, a C Shell built-in command, reads from the file *name*. The contents of *name* are assumed to be C Shell commands that are executed by the current shell. The source command can be nested, but if an error occurs while processing a sourced file, at any level, input from *all* files is terminated. With the -h option specified, commands read from file *name* are placed directly in the history list without being executed.

stop

```
stop [ %job ] ...
```

The current background job, or the background job specified by `%job`, is stopped. If specified, the `%job` argument format is the same as for the commands `bg` and `fg`.

suspend

```
suspend
```

This is used to stop the current shell, as though it were sent a stop signal with `^z`. Typically, this command is used to stop shells that were started using the `su` command. The suspended shell can be restarted using the `fg` command.

switch

```
switch (string)
case label:
...
breaksw
...
default:
...
breaksw
endsw
```

The value of `string`, after being command and filename expanded, is matched against each `label`, in turn, until a match is found. Case labels may contain filename metacharacters, `*`, `?`, and `[...]`, which if present, are variable expanded. If none of the label strings matches `string` and `default` is specified, execution begins after the `default:` statement. Each of the `case` and `default` statements must be at the beginning of the line, preceded only by whitespace. If `breaksw` is used, it causes execution to continue after the `endsw` statement. Without `breaksw` execution will continue through subsequent `case` and `default` statements until a `breaksw` or `endsw` statement is encountered.

time

```
time [ command ]
```

This is used to print a summary of the time used by the current C Shell, and its child processes, if no argument is specified. Otherwise, if `command` is given, it executes `command` and displays a summary of its time utilization.

umask

```
umask [ value ]
```

This displays the current value for the file creation mask if no argument is given. With the argument *value*, specified in octal, this sets the creation mask by XORing *value* with 666 for files and 777 for directories. The results of the XOR operation is the permissions to be assigned to new files and directories. A common value for *value* is 002, which grants complete access to the group and read (directory search) access to others. Another common value is 022, which grants read (directory search) access to group and others, without granting write permission.

unalias

```
unalias pattern
```

This removes all aliases that match (with filename substitution) *pattern*. If the *pattern* is *, all aliases will be removed.

unhash

```
unhash
```

This turns off the internal hash table used by the C Shell to locate executable files contained in the search path directories. This forces the shell to perform a search each time a command is executed, in lieu of doing a hash table lookup.

unlimit

```
unlimit [ -h ] [ resource ]
```

The reverse of the limit command, unlimit removes any limit set for *resource* if specified. If no argument is given, *all* resource limits are removed. To remove the corresponding hard limits, use the -h argument (restricted to use by the superuser).

unset

```
unset pattern
```

This removes all local shell variables that match (with filename substitution) *pattern*. All variables are removed if *pattern* is *.

unsetenv

```
unsetenv variable
```

This removes the global (environment) shell variable `variable`. Unlike unset, no pattern matching is performed.

wait

```
wait
```

This waits for all background jobs to finish (or be interrupted) before continuing (or prompting in an interactive shell).

while

```
while ( expr )
...
end
```

This repeats commands between the while and matching end statement, while `expr` is true (expression equals zero). The break and continue statements may be used to terminate or continue the loop early. Each of the statements, while and end, must be alone on their own lines. If used with an interactive shell, a question mark prompt will be displayed after the while for commands, until the end statement is entered; then the loop will be executed.

%

```
% [ job ] [ & ]
```

This brings the current or specified `job` to the foreground (without the & ending the line). With the &, `job` continues to run in background.

@

```
@ [ var [ = expr ]
@ var[n] = expr
```

In the first form, without arguments, the @ command displays the values of all shell variables, with multiword values enclosed in parentheses. If `expr` is supplied, its result is assigned to the specified variable. If the expression, `expr`, contains the metacharacters <, >, & or ¦, that portion of `expr` must be enclosed within parentheses. In the second form, `expr` replaces the *n*th word of the variable `var`, which must be a multiword variable.

C

Metacharacters

Metacharacters are explained in detail in Day 2, "Metacharacters." For ready reference, this appendix contains tables that summarize each group of metacharacters.

Syntactic Metacharacters

The syntactic metacharacters in Table C.1 are used as special punctuation characters between and around commands and also are used to combine multiple UNIX commands to make a single logical command. They provide a means to effect conditional execution of a command or commands, based on the outcome of a previous command.

Table C.1. Syntactic metacharacters.

Metacharacter	Description of Function
;	Separator between sequentially executed commands.
¦	Separator between commands that are part of a pipeline. In a pipeline, commands execute sequentially. The output of the command to the left of the separator becomes the input to the command on the right of the separator.
()	Used to isolate commands separated by semicolons (;) or pipelines (¦). The commands within the parentheses are treated as a unit and appear to be a single command. Enclosing pipelines in parentheses enables them to be included in other pipelines.
&	Background command indicator. It tells the shell to execute the commands as a background process.
¦¦	Separator between commands, where the command following the (¦¦) is executed only if the preceding command fails.
&&	Separator between commands, where the command following the (&&) is executed only if the preceding command succeeds.

Filename Metacharacters

Filename metacharacters, shown in Table C.2, are used on command lines to form match patterns for filename substitution and to identify or form abbreviations.

Table C.2. Filename metacharacters.

Metacharacter	Description of Function
?	Filename expansion character that matches any single character.
*	Filename expansion character that matches any sequence of zero or more characters.
[ ]	Filename expansion designating a character or range of characters that, as a class, are matched against a single character. A range is shown by the first and last characters in the range, separated by a dash (-).
{ }	Used for abbreviating sets of words that share common parts.
~	Used to abbreviate the path to a user's home directory.

Quotation Metacharacters

The quotation metacharacters in Table C.3 are used to selectively control when metacharacters from other groups are protected from expansion or interpretation by the C Shell. Judicious use of these characters allows construction of more sophisticated scripts.

Table C.3. Quotation metacharacters.

Metacharacter	Description of Function
\	Prevents the next character following it from being interpreted as a metacharacter by the shell.
"	Prevents the string of characters enclosed within a pair of double quote characters (") from being interpreted as metacharacters. Command and variable expansion are not affected by the double quotes.
'	Prevents the string of characters enclosed within a pair of single quote characters (') from being interpreted as commands or metacharacters.

Input/Output Metacharacters

Input/output metacharacters, shown in Table C.4, are used for file redirection and pipes. With these metacharacters, you can direct the output of a command to a file or pipe it through other UNIX commands. You can also cause a command to take its input from a disk file or pipe rather than from your keyboard. Additionally, with these metacharacters, you can merge stderr with stdout.

Table C.4. Input/Output metacharacters.

Metacharacter	Description of Function
<name	Redirected input to command is read from *name*.
>name	Output from command is redirected to *name*. If *name* exists it is overwritten, provided $noclobber is not set.
>&name	Output from stderr is combined with stdout and written to *name*.
>! name	Output from command is redirected to *name*. If *name* exists, it is overwritten. This form is used when one desires to override the effect of $noclobber when $noclobber is set.
>&! name	Output from stderr is combined with stdout and redirected to *name*. If *name* exists, it is overwritten. This form is used when one desires to override the effect of $noclobber when $noclobber is set.
>>name	Output from command is appended to the end of *name*. If $noclobber is set and *name* does not exist, an error message is issued.
>>&name	Appends output from stderr combined with stdout and appended to the end of *name*.
>>! name	The same as >>, used when $noclobber is set. When *name* does not exist, it is created without an error being issued.
>>&! name	Appends output from stderr combined with stdout and appended to the end of *name*. The same as >>&, used when $noclobber is set. When *name* does not exist, it is created without an error being issued.

Metacharacter	Description of Function
<<word	Input is read from stdin to the shell, up to the first input line that contains only *word*. No command, filename, or variable substitution is performed on *word*. Prior to any expansion or substitution being done on each input line, the text of the input line is examined for *word*.
¦	Creates a pipeline between two commands. The output of the command to the left of the pipe (¦) is connected to the input of the command to the right of the pipe.
¦&	Creates a pipeline between two commands, with the output from both stderr and stdout of the command to the left of the pipe (¦) combined and connected to the input of the command to the right of the pipe.

Expansion/Substitution Metacharacters

Expansion/substitution metacharacters act as special indicators to the C Shell. The shell uses these metacharacters, shown in Table C.5, to determine which words on a command line are shell variables or history events, with or without modifiers.

Table C.5. Expansion/Substitution metacharacters.

Metacharacter	Description
$	Variable substitution indicator. A word preceded by the $ is interpreted by the C Shell as a variable, and the contents of that variable are substituted for the string $*word*.
!	History substitution indicator. The exclamation character precedes all history event references.
?	History substitution modifier. The question mark, preceded by the ! and followed by a word, indicates that the most recent event which contains the word is to be substituted.
:	Precedes substitution modifiers.

Other Metacharacters

The metacharacters in Table C.6 do not fit into any of the previous groups. They are used to indicate the start of comments, to prefix command line options, and to prefix job name specifications.

Table C.6. Other metacharacters.

Metacharacter	Description
#	Indicates the start of C Shell comments.
-	Prefixes option flag arguments to commands.
%	Prefixes job name specifications.

D

C Shell Operators

C Shell Operators

C Shell operators are explained in Day 5, "Shell Variables, Part II." This appendix contains tables that summarize each group of operators for ready reference.

Table D.1. C Shell operators.

Parentheses

Operator	Description
(...)	Used for grouping expressions to force the order of evaluation. Because the parentheses are evaluated first, any expression they enclose will be evaluated before expressions that are not within parentheses.

Unary Operators

Operator	Description
~ expr	One's complement, complements *expr*.
! expr	Logical negation (NOT). Used to reverse the sense of the expression it prefixes (*expr*). Typically used with file-inquiry operators.

Arithmetic and Postfix Operators

Operator	Description
*	Multiplication
/	Division
%	Remainder
+	Addition
-	Subtraction
++	Postfix addition
- -	Postfix subtraction

Shift Operators

Operator	Description
expr << bits	Bitwise shift left. Shift *expr* left by *bits* number of bits.

`expr >> bits`	Bitwise shift right. Shift *expr* right by *bits* number of bits.
`expr1 < expr2`	Compare *expr1* to *expr2* and return TRUE if *expr1* is less than *expr2*.
`expr1 > expr2`	Compare *expr1* to *expr2* and return TRUE if *expr1* is greater than *expr2*.
`expr1 <= expr2`	Compare *expr1* to *expr2* and return TRUE if *expr1* is less than or equal to *expr2*.
`expr1 >= expr2`	Compare *expr1* to *expr2* and return TRUE if *expr1* is greater than or equal to *expr2*.

Boolean Operators

Operator	Description
`expr1 == expr2`	Compare *expr1* to *expr2* and return TRUE if they are equal.
`expr1 != expr2`	Compare *expr1* to *expr2* and return TRUE if they are not equal.

Pattern Match Operators

Operator	Description
`expr =~ pattern`	Filename-substitution pattern match. Test *expr* against *pattern* and return TRUE if *expr* is a match to the metacharacters in *pattern*.
`expr !~ pattern`	Filename-substitution pattern mismatch. Test *expr* against *pattern* and return TRUE if *expr* is not a match to the metacharacters in *pattern*.

Bitwise Operators

Operator	Description
`expr1 & expr2`	Bitwise AND of *expr1* with *expr2*.
`expr1 ^ expr2`	Bitwise XOR of *expr1* with *expr2*.
`expr1 ¦ expr2`	Bitwise inclusive OR of *expr1* with *expr2*.

continues

D

Table D.1. continued

Logical Operators

Operator	Description
&&	logical AND
¦ ¦	logical OR

Assignment Operators

Operator	Description
=	Assignment
+=	x += y is the same as x = x + y
-=	x -= y is the same as x = x - y
*=	x *= y is the same as x = x * y
/=	x /= y is the same as x = x / y
%=	x %= y is the same as x = x % y
^=	x ^= y is the same as x = x ^ y

File Inquiry Operators

Operator	Description
-r *filename*	If the user has read access to *filename*, return TRUE. Otherwise, return FALSE.
-w *filename*	If the user has write access to *filename*, return TRUE. Otherwise, return FALSE.
-x *filename*	If the user has execute access to *filename* (or search permission on a directory) return TRUE. Otherwise, return FALSE.
-o *filename*	Return TRUE if the user owns *filename*. Otherwise, return FALSE.
-d *filename*	Return TRUE if *filename* is a directory. Otherwise, return FALSE.

Operator	Description
-e *filename*	Return TRUE if *filename* exists. Otherwise, return FALSE.
-f *filename*	Return TRUE if *filename* is a plain file. Otherwise, return FALSE.
-z *filename*	If the length of *filename* is zero (empty), return TRUE (1). Otherwise, return FALSE.

Examples of *Dot* Files

In this appendix, you will find examples of the C Shell startup *dot* files. These files are explained in greater detail in Day 6, "Customizing the User Environment." Additional information on the contents of these files can also be found in the material on shell variables, metacharacters, aliases, and C Shell built-in commands.

An Example of a *.cshrc* Startup File

The following example shows a typical .cshrc startup file that you can use on your system. It defines aliases, initializes environment as well as local variables, and also does some setting of terminal characteristics:

```
#!/bin/csh
#
#  .cshrc: C Shell Startup File
#
#  This file is sourced everytime a CSH is started.
#
#-----------------------------------------------------------------

# Editor related Environment Variables (Additional settings in .exrc)
setenv EDITOR    vi
setenv VISUAL    vi

# Set  EXINIT environment variable to 'vi' options; or use .exrc file
setenv EXINIT    'set ts=8 sw=8 autoindent ignorecase wm=8 showmode'

# Miscellaneous Environment Variables
if ( -f /usr/local/bin/less ) then
    setenv PAGER '/usr/local/bin/less'    # set pager to less
    setenv LESS '-ceoMqs'                  # favorite options for 'less'
else
    setenv PAGER 'more'                    # set pager to more
    setenv MORE '-cds'                     # favorite options for 'more'
endif

# Set USER environment var; useful in many scripts for filenames etc.
setenv USER      `logname`

# Define search path for libraries used by linker/loader
setenv LD_LIBRARY_PATH    "/usr/lib/X11:/usr/lib"
setenv MANPATH "/usr/local/man:/usr/local/X11/man:/usr/man:$HOME/man"

#
# Set local variables for ALL shell invocations
#
set path = (/usr/bin/X11 $HOME/bin /usr/local/bin)
set path = ($path /bin /usr/ucb /usr/bin /usr/etc /etc /usr/5bin .)

#
# Set default directory search path
#
```

```
set cdpath = (. .. $HOME)

#
# Set file protection mask which control permissions for all new files.
# 022 mask results in -> owner:rwx  group:r-x  other:r-x
#
umask 022

if ($?USER == 0 || $?prompt == 0) exit  # Stop if NOT an interactive shell

#
# set local variables for interactive shell invocations
#
set filec
set ignoreeof
set noclobber
set notify
set autologout = 0
set mail = (30 /usr/spool/mail/$USER)
set history = 500
set savehist = 100
set time=100

set prompt="% "
if ( $SHELL == '/bin/tcsh' ) then
#    set prompt = "%d : `whoami`@%M\!%h % "     #tcsh
     set prompt = "%B%c4%b@%U%m%u%%%h%# "       #tcsh
     set correct = all
     set autocorrect
     set pushdtohome
     set pushdsilent
     set rmstar
     set dextract
     set listjobs
     #set printexitvalue
     alias cd pushd
     alias dirs "dirs -v"
     alias ls 'ls-F'
     alias lf 'ls-F'
else
    if ( `whoami` == "root" ) then
        set id='#'
    else
        set id='$'
    endif
    set prompt = "${id}\! `hostname`:`pwd`> " #csh
endif

#
# Define command aliases
#
alias    h      'history | tail -20'
alias    hp     'history | less'
alias    rt     'reset;tset -Q'      # restore sanity
alias    more   $PAGER
alias    mroe   $PAGER               # correct the spelling ;)
```

E

```
alias     m         $PAGER

alias     page      $PAGER
alias     pg        $PAGER                   # for sysV fans

alias     cd        'chdir \!*;set prompt = "${id}\! `hostname`:`pwd`> "'
alias     ..        'set dot=$cwd;cd ..'
alias     ,         'cd $dot '

#
# X11 Windows screen dump alias prints to Postscript printer w/grayscale
#
alias     sdump     'echo "place cursor on window to dump," \
                    " press LEFT button — output goes to lpt1 ..."; \
                    /usr/bin/X11/xwd ¦ /usr/bin/X11/xpr -device ps -gray 4 ¦ \
                    lpr -Plpt1 -h;lpq -Plpt1'

#
# Aliases for the ls command
# the following alias allows easy switching between ls versions
#
alias     ls        '/bin/ls -CF'    # set default options for all uses of ls
alias     la        'ls -a'
alias     lt        'ls -lt'
alias     ll        'ls -l'
alias     ll.       'ls -lisa .[a-z]*'
alias     lld       'ls -lisad \!*'
alias     lm        'ls -lisa'
alias     lx        'ls -x'

#
# chmod aliases
#
alias     +w        'chmod go+w'
alias     -w        'chmod go-w'
alias     +x        'chmod +x'

#
# pushd/popd aliases
#
alias     po        'popd; set prompt = "$cwd> "'
alias     pp        'pushd; set prompt = "$cwd> "'

#
# exit aliases
#
alias     lo        exit
alias     bye       exit
alias     quit      exit
alias     adios     exit

#
# find command aliases
#
alias     findbig   'find . -size +1000 -exec ls -l {} \;'
alias     findold   'find . -atime +125 -exec ls -l {} \;'
```

```
alias    findnew    'find . \( -ctime -1 -type f \) -exec ls -l {} \;'
alias    lsnew      'find . \( -ctime -\!* -type f \) -exec /bin/ls {} \;'
alias    finddirs   'find . -type d -exec ls -ld {} \;'
alias    findman    'find / -type d -name "man?" -exec ls -ld {} \;'
alias    findname   "find . -name '\!*' -print"


#
# find filename, file with word, file with expression
#
alias    findfile   'find . -name "\!*" -exec ls -ld {} \;'
alias    findword   'find . -type f -exec grep -wil -e "\!*" {} \;' #SunOS only
alias    findwords  'find . -type f -exec grep -wi \!:1 {} /dev/null \;'
#SunOS only
alias    findexp    'find . -type f -exec grep -il -e "\!*" {} \;'
alias    findexps   'find . -type f -exec grep -i \!:1 {} /dev/null \;'


#
# The following aliases print out the command history in 2 and 3 column
# format.  By Robert Kaminsky  11/19/90
#
alias    h2    '(history 30 | pr -2 -l15 -t | expand | cut -c1-79,80)'
alias    h3    '(history 45 | pr -3 -l15 -t | expand | cut -c1-79,80)'


#  The following aliases allow for editing commands given in the csh.
#    e n  -  visual edits command n (as numbered by history)
#    ee   -  visual edits last command
#  Note: Both use an invisible work file called ".e_cmd" in the home directory.
#  From Robert Kaminsky 11/19/90 modified by Bob Weissman
alias    e     '( history | sed -n -e "/^ *\!*[^0-9]/ s/......//p" ) \
                >&! ~/.e_cmd ; \vi -w2 ~/.e_cmd ; source -h ~/.e_cmd ; \
                source ~/.e_cmd'
alias    ee    '( history 2 | sed -n -e "1 s/......//p" ) \
                >&! ~/.e_cmd ; \vi -w2 ~/.e_cmd ; source -h ~/.e_cmd ; \
                source ~/.e_cmd'

/bin/stty -tabs erase ^H kill ^U intr ^C susp ^Z dsusp ^Y tostop ixon ixoff


#
# Set the default X Windows server name - set to the name of the host
# the user logged in from. If $DISPLAY is already  set, leave it alone.
#
if ( ! $?DISPLAY ) then
    setenv DISPLAY "${HOST}:0"
    tty -s
    if ( "$status" == "0" ) then
#add -R option to the who am i command on the next line for HP UNIX systems
        set disphost = `who am i | sed -s 's/.*(//' -e 's/).*$//'`
        if ( "$#disphost" == "1" ) then
            setenv DISPLAY $disphost\:0
        endif
        unset disphost
    endif
endif

# End of $HOME/.cshrc file
```

E

449

An Example of a *.login* Startup File

The following example shows a typical .login startup file that you can use on your system. It defines aliases, initializes environment as well as local variables, and also does some setting of terminal characteristics:

```
#! /bin/csh
#
#   .login: C Shell Startup File
#
# This script is used by the login C Shell **ONLY**
# It is 'sourced' in after the .cshrc file is read by the login shell
#


#
# Set terminal characteristics.
#
stty -tabs erase ^H kill ^U intr ^C susp ^Z dsusp ^Y tostop ixon ixoff


#
# Set terminal type.
# Note: This script uses 'favterm' which is the users favorite terminal
#       type. The assumed default if not given is 'vt100'.
#
if ( "$?favterm" == "0" ) set favterm = vt100

if ( "$?term" == "0" ) set term = $favterm
if ( "$term" == "" )   set term = $favterm
if ( "$term" == "unknown" )   set term = $favterm
set oldterm = $term
while ( "0" == "0" )   # infinite loop until user answers question from tset
    set noglob
    set term = ( `tset -Q -I -S ?$term` )
    unset noglob
    if ( "$term" != "" && "$term" != "unknown" ) break
    set term = $oldterm
end
unset oldterm
stty -tabs

if ( "$term[1]" == "xterm" || "$term[1]" == "xterms" \
   || "$term[1]" == "aixterm" || "$term[1]" == "hpterm" ) then # cover all bases
    if ( -f /usr/bin/X11/resize ) then
        set noglob
        eval `/usr/bin/X11/resize`    # do resize twice due to problem with
        eval `/usr/bin/X11/resize`    #  HP "broken pipe" brain-damage
#eval `/usr/openwin/bin/resize` #for SunOS only
        unset noglob
     else
        echo "*** Problem: no X11 'resize' for xterm - setting 24x80 ***"
        stty rows 24 columns 80
    endif
 else
    stty rows 24 columns 80          # default if not an X Windows client
```

```
endif

setenv TERM $term[1]
setenv TERMCAP $term[2]


#
# Display last login info.
#
if ( -f "$HOME/.lastlogin" ) then
   cat $HOME/.lastlogin
endif
tty -s
if ( "$status" == "0" ) then
   set loghost = `who am i -R ¦ sed -e 's/.*(//' -e 's/).*$//'`
   if ( "$#loghost" != "1" ) then
      set loghost = "display $DISPLAY"
   endif
   echo "Last Login: `date` on `hostname` from $loghost."\
                        >! $HOME/.lastlogin
   unset loghost
endif


#
# Other useful stuff
#
mesg y                        # allow messages from other users to display


#
# Optional user-selectable parameters and commands.
#
biff Y                        # report "You have mail" if true.
set mail = ( 60 /usr/mail/$USER )
cd
# End of $HOME/.login file
```

An Example of a *.logout* File

When the login C Shell terminates, it examines $HOME to see if a file exists with the name
.logout. If one is found, then the C Shell reads that file and executes the commands it
contains. These commands can be used to do any form of processing appropriate for the
end of a session:

```
#
# .logout file - run for every C Shell interactive logout.
#

clear                  # clear the screen
/usr/games/fortune     # end the day with a wise word
echo "."
date

exit
# End of $HOME/.logout file
```

F

Answers to Quizzes
and Exercises

Day 1, "Introducing the C Shell"

Quiz

1. To find out the values currently assigned to shell variables, the easiest and most effective way is to use the C Shell built-in command set. This command, used by itself with no arguments, displays all of the current shell variables, with their names and values. To display the value of a single variable, use the built-in command echo, followed by the variable name, for example:

```
% set
argv     ()
autologout     10
cwd     /usr/dave
history     15
home     /usr/dave
ignoreeof
noclobber
path     (/bin /usr/bin /usr/lib . /usr/dave/bin)
prompt     ! %
shell     /bin/csh
status     0
term     vt100
% echo $home
/usr/dave
%_
```

2. The C Shell's two modes, interactive and noninteractive, are distinguished mainly by whether you are entering commands at a shell prompt in the foreground, or running them in background. Foreground commands communicate with you at your terminal, soliciting input from the keyboard and displaying output to the display. Background commands, on the other hand, typically take input from and write output to disk files. In most cases, when a command running in background attempts to communicate with a terminal, the command is stopped and the user is notified.

3. a) To recall an event by number, use the history substitution metacharacter (!) followed by the event number. The following example recalls history event number 5:

```
% !5
```

To recall an event using a *relative* event number, follow the history substitution metacharacter with a minus sign (-) and the number of events back to recall. The following example recalls the command before the last one executed:

```
% !-2
```

b) The *command word* of an event is the first word of the command line. It can be matched for recall by following the history substitution metacharacter by the command word to be matched. The most recent event that begins with the command word will be recalled if one is found. This example shows how to recall the most recent command line that started with a grep command:

```
% !grep
```

c) Recalling a command by searching for a word within the line is similar to recalling by command word. The history substitution modifier metacharacter (?) is used after the history substitution metacharacter (!), and before the search word, to indicate that the word search includes words within the command line (whereas the bang ! followed by a search word without the ? indicates a match to only the first word). The next example shows how to recall the last command containing the word datafile:

```
% !?datafile
```

4. Table 1.1 shows event word designators. These designators can be used to recall arguments from a specified history event and include them within the current command line. To recall the first argument of the previous command, use the following:

```
% grep -v ^# !!:1
```

In this example, using the grep command, all lines that *do not* start with a pound sign (#) are found in the filename which is the first argument of the previous command. This is indicated by the characters !!:1 in the example. The !! indicates the previous command and the :1 modifies it to select the first argument.

5. As in the previous question, you would indicate the previous command with !! and modify it with the : modifier. In this case, because the last argument is desired, use the $ metacharacter rather than the argument number, and the last argument will be substituted.

455

Exercises

Your results will vary, depending on your experiments.

Day 2, "Metacharacters"

Quiz

1. The special syntactic metacharacter pair ¦¦ is used for conditionally executing one command if another fails. It causes the C Shell to test the return status of the first command and, if the status is non-zero, execute the second command.

   ```
   % grep daphne /etc/passwd ¦¦ echo "There is no user daphne."
   ```

   The `grep` command returns a non-zero status if no match is found. Here this status is tested and a message displayed to report the results. To reverse the test and execute the second command if the first *succeeds*, use the metacharacter pair && instead of ¦¦. If the preceding example is changed to use &&, then it might become this:

   ```
   % grep daphne /etc/passwd && echo "User daphne was found."
   ```

   Here the message is displayed only if a match is found, so the text of the message has been changed appropriately.

2. Specifying a search for a subset of letters, such as vowels only, requires the metacharacters [ ], which define a class of characters—in this case, the class of all vowels. To find all files in /bin that begin with a vowel, enter the following:

   ```
   % ls /bin/[aeiou]*
   ```

   The `[aeiou]` will eliminate all files beginning with consonants. The asterisk (*) that follows will match any and all (or none) characters after the first character, regardless of what they may be.

   To find the files starting with consonants, change the contents of the class to `[bcdfghjklmnpqrstvwxyz]` *or* `[^aeiou]`. Both of these classes do the same thing. The first explicitly states the characters *included* in the class. The second version specifies the characters *excluded* from the class by prefixing them with the ^ metacharacter, which reverses the definition of the characters within the brackets.

3. To get to a subdirectory of your home directory using a shortcut, simply prefix the directory name with ~/. To get to the `bin` subdirectory in your home directory, use ~/bin. The ~ expands to your home directory path, followed by the slash (/).

```
% cd ~/bin
```

The tilde metacharacter (~) can also be used to generate the home directory pathname of another user. If it is followed immediately by the username of that user, it will expand to that user's home directory pathname, rather than yours. To get to Maggie Smith's home directory, use the following:

```
% cd ~msmith
```

4. The difference between enclosing metacharacters in double quotes (") rather than single quotes (') is whether some of the metacharacters get expanded or not. If a double-quoted string contains shell variable references or command substitution, these metacharacters will be interpreted and expanded. All other metacharacters contained within double quotes will be protected from expansion. Enclosing a string containing metacharacters within single quotes inhibits any expansion or interpretation of those metacharacters by the shell.

```
% echo "My home directory is $home."
My home directory is /usr/dave.
% echo 'My home directory is $home.'
My home directory is $home.
%_
```

5. If the built-in shell variable `$noclobber` has been set, override it by prefixing the filename with the ! metacharacter. Therefore, to write `stdout` to a file `script.log` and override `$noclobber`, use >!script.log rather than >script.log. Likewise, if you are using the >& or >> forms of output redirection, they can also be modified with ! to override `$noclobber`.

6. The answer is similar to the answer for question 5. The metacharacter & is used to suffix the output redirection. This indicates to the C Shell that the output written to `stderr` is to be merged onto `stdout`. To modify standard output file redirection, > becomes >&. To append to a file and merge `stderr` and `stdout`, add the & after the append operator >> to make it >>&.

Remember that the & and ! metacharacters can also be combined to override `$noclobber` *and* merge `stderr` with `stdout`. See Table 2.4 for a complete list of input/output redirection metacharacters with a description of their function.

Exercises

Your results will vary.

Day 3, "Command Substitution, Aliases, and Filename Generation"

Quiz

1. Using the C Shell built-in command `alias` without arguments will display a listing of all current aliases. The listing only applies to the current shell and not to any other shell processed, even if it is owned by the same user. Aliases are local to a shell and are not passed on to subshells.

2. The semicolon metacharacter (;) is used simply as a delimiter, separating multiple commands on a single command line. It is most frequently used when two or more commands are enclosed within () to create a subshell. Two commands separated by the pipe metacharacter (¦) are connected such that the output of the first command becomes the input to the second command. Pipes are created, using *filters*, to accomplish more complex tasks by combining the functions of multiple UNIX commands.

   An example that combines the use of both of these metacharacters is this:

   ```
   % (cd ~jeffc/data ; tar cf -) ¦ (cd ~/data ; tar xvf -)
   ```

   This command uses the UNIX `tar` command to copy a group of files from one subtree to another, traversing the full extent of the first tree to find all the files. Unlike the UNIX `cp` command, this method maintains the file permissions and creation dates in their new location.

   Here two subshells are created and each is then joined by a pipeline. The first subshell changes directories (using `cd`) to `jeffc`'s `data` subdirectory and initiates a `tar` command to create an archive image to `stdout`, indicated by the `f -` arguments. The second subshell changes directories (using `cd`) to the current user's data directory and also starts a `tar` command. The second `tar` command will extract from `stdin` again indicated by the `f -` argument. It will also list each file as it is extracted. The output of the first `tar` becomes the input to the second `tar`. Each of the `tar` commands is prepositioned by the `cd` command that precedes it delimited with a ;.

3. When the C Shell processes a command line, the shell checks the first word for an exact match to a defined alias. Aliases are almost always defined with simple alias names. If you want to use a command's unaliased version, use its full pathname on the command line to avoid the match (that is, use /bin/ls rather than ls if you have an ls alias). The command with its full pathname will not match to a defined alias and thus you will get the original command to execute.

4. Enclosing an alias containing arguments in single quotes protects the substitution metacharacters from being interpreted immediately by the current shell. Instead, these metacharacters are stored as part of the alias and expanded when the alias is used. Using double quotes instead of single quotes allows the current shell to expand them immediately. The expanded results of the metacharacters are then stored instead, and the alias will not operate as intended. Instead, the alias will continually report the constant values that are now a part of its definition.

5. To substitute the last argument on a command line into an alias, you would use \!:$ as the event designator. The backslash (\) escapes the exclamation point (!) from the shell. The exclamation point indicates the current event, and the colon (:) precedes the event modifier $. The dollar sign event modifier is what selects the last argument of the current command line.

6. Alias definitions are temporary and exist only within the local shell that defined them. To make an alias definition permanent, add it to your .cshrc startup file. Because this file is read by every C Shell process when it starts, your alias will be defined for each shell instance.

7. Keep in mind that you cannot create an alias definition with the name alias. The shell specifically prohibits this and issues an error message. Second, an alias cannot reference itself more than once. Doing so is considered an alias loop and is illegal. An alias can reference other aliases, which will be handled appropriately when the alias is used.

8. The following metacharacter patterns will match the list of filenames that includes test, tent, talent, and tempest:

```
t[ae]*t
t{es,en,alen,empes}t
t{,al,emp}{es,en}t
```

Note that the last pattern would also match filenames talest and tempent, if they exist. The middle pattern is the most exact of the three, because it will match only these four filenames.

Exercises

Your results will vary.

Day 4, "Shell Variables, Part I"

Quiz

1. Use the UNIX command set without arguments. This will display a list of all local variables and their contents.

2. These two variables are related functionally, but different in how they are defined and displayed. The variable $path is a local shell variable, defined and displayed using the set command. The $PATH variable is a global or environment variable, which is defined and displayed using the setenv command. The C Shell will update the other of these two variables when either one of them is changed. The content of $path is accessible only to the current C Shell process, whereas the content of $PATH is passed on to any and all child processes created by the current shell.

3. Like the variables, $path and $PATH, in the previous question, $cwd and $PWD are related. One ($cwd) is a local variable, and the other ($PWD) is an environment variable. Each is defined with the set and setenv commands, respectively. When the contents of one variable is modified, the other is automatically updated to reflect the change. The C Shell built-in command cd updates $cwd as a part of its operation and thus affects $PWD as well.

4. The special shell variable $autologout is intended for just this purpose. If you set $autologout with the value 10 in your .cshrc startup file, when ten minutes of inactivity is reached, the shell will automatically kill your login shell process (even if not the current shell), causing you to be logged off the system.

5. Whenever the C Shell finds the tilde (~) metacharacter within a command line, the content of the variable $home is used to expand the tilde. Normally, $home is set by the login shell and is not modified. If the content of $home is changed, then later expansions of ~ will use the new value.

6. Any change to $path causes the C Shell to recompute its hash table. Because this table is used to locate commands and scripts that are not absolute paths, a change to $path could affect the operation of the shell. Resetting $path to NULL will make the shell unable to locate any commands or scripts. Otherwise,

changing the contents of $path, by appending to it or reordering its list, will affect only the order in which directories are searched.

7. The environment variable $USER is set to the user's account name by the login C Shell. Because environment variables are inherited by all child processes of the login shell, $USER is available to all C Shell processes for setting the $prompt variable. The following example shows one of many ways to include the username in a prompt definition:

```
set prompt = '$USER:$cwd % '
```

8. The three built-in variables that are used by the C Shell history mechanism are the following:

$histchars	Used to change the history substitution metacharacter to a character other than !.
$history	Used to define the number of history events kept by each instance of the shell.
$savehist	Used to define the number of history events that will be saved by the login shell when it terminates.

Exercises

Your results will vary.

Day 5, "Shell Variables, Part II"

Quiz

1. Within a shell script, a built-in C Shell switch variable can be tested for existence using the $?name form, which returns a value of 1 if the variable is set or 0 if the variable is not set. Using the C Shell set command with no arguments displays switch variables as simply their names if they are set. If a particular variable is not set, its name is not displayed by the set command.

2. When debugging a shell script, you often need to see the results from the shell-expanded metacharacter expressions. Using one of the switch variables $echo or $verbose will cause the shell to display each line before or after metacharacter expansion. These variables can also be enabled by using the shell options -v, -V, -x or -X on the first line of the shell script.

F

3. If you know in advance that you want to be informed as soon as a job has a status change, you can set the built-in shell variable $notify. Without $notify being set, the C Shell will wait until the current command has completed before displaying the completion or other job status message. By setting $notify, you let the shell know not to wait when a job's status changes. The C Shell will then display any messages immediately, regardless of what command you may currently be running.

4. When you have enabled C Shell file completion by setting the built-in shell variable $filec ON, the shell will beep when you press Escape if it cannot further complete the current filename. To disable this beeping for an ambiguous filename, you must also set another built-in shell variable, $nobeep, to ON as well. When $nobeep is ON, the shell will not beep during filename completion if the current filename cannot be completed.

5. To test a file to see whether it is writable, you would use the file inquiry operator -w. This operator will return the TRUE value, a numeric 1, if the file is writable by the current user. If the current user is not permitted to write to the specified file, the -w operator will return FALSE, which is numeric 0. To test a file with this operator in an if statement, you might do the following:

```
if ( -w /tmp/testdata ) then
    echo "The file /tmp/testdata is writable by $USER"
else
    echo "The file /tmp/testdata cannot be written by $USER"
endif
```

The if statement evaluates the results returned by the -w operator, testing /tmp/testdata to see whether it is writable by the current user. If -w returns TRUE, then the first echo command is performed, displaying the message that the file is writable. Otherwise, the second echo command is executed to tell you that the file is not writable. Because you know that the environment variable $USER contains the name of the current user, it can be included in the message to make it more personal and to display the account name of that user.

6. The C Shell, like the C programming language, allows the use of the postfix operators ++ and -- to do *autoincrementing* and *autodecrementing* of numeric shell variables. Using these operators would be the easiest way to add or subtract one from a variable in a script. To use these operators, you simply suffix the name of the variable with the operator on a @ command, as shown here:

```
@ addone++         # add 1 to the variable $addone
```

```
@ subone--            # subtract 1 from the variable $subone
@ results = counter++ # see the explanation below
```

In the third line of the example, the value contained in `$counter` is being incremented by the postfix operator `++`. As in the programming language C, the value contained in `$counter` is first assigned and then it is incremented. If, for example, the value initially in `$counter` is 5, that is the value that `$results` will contain. If you were to display the contents of `$counter`, you would see that it is now 6. Remember this important aspect of postfix operators when you use them in scripts as part of an assignment expression.

7. The special pattern-match operators, `=~` and `!~`, test a string against a metacharacter match pattern for a match or mismatch. The string can be a quoted literal or a shell variable that contains the string value. The string value is to the left of the operator, and the match pattern is to the right. The evaluated expression returns TRUE, the value 1, or FALSE, the value 0, depending on the operator and whether or not the string value matches the match pattern. In the following example, a shell variable `$dotfile` is tested against a match pattern. This test will check to see whether the filename contained in `$dotfile` is a UNIX *dot* file:

```
if ( $dotfile =~ '.??*' ) then
    echo "The file \"$dotfile\" is a \'dot\' file"
else
    echo "The filename \"$dotfile\" is not a \'dot\' file"
endif
```

Notice that the double quotes, surrounding `$dotfile` on the `echo` command lines, are escaped using backslashes. This keeps them from being taken for string delimiting metacharacters, and instead they become literal quotes included in the displayed message. The same applies to the single quotes used around the word `dot` in the messages. The metacharacter match pattern in the `if` will return FALSE for the special files *dot* (`.`) and *dot dot* (`..`) but not for any other file beginning with a dot and followed by two or more characters.

8. Say you want to test for a subdirectory called `data` in a user's home directory, and it if it does not exist, you want to create this directory. The following example will do just that using file inquiry operators:

```
# test $home/data for existence and also that it is a directory
# if this is not true then create it
if ( -e $home/data ) then        # $home/data exists
```

```
       if ( ! -d $home/data ) then  # but is isn't a directory
           rm -f $home/data         # so remove it and
           mkdir $home/data         # re-create it right
       else
           echo "$home/data already exists as a directory"
       endif
   else
       mkdir $home/data             # it doesn't exist so create it
   endif
```

Exercises

Your results will vary.

Day 6, "Customizing the User Environment"

Quiz

1. When a C Shell process starts executing, it looks in the home directory of the current user for dot files, .cshrc and .login, created by or for that user. These are the files that will be used to tailor or customize the environment for that C Shell process. If the particular shell process is a login shell, then it will read in the .login file, *after* it finishes reading and processing the contents of the .cshrc file, if one is found. Some versions of the C Shell will also look in the /etc system directory for a cshrc file (note the missing dot) before reading the user's .cshrc and .login files. The system administrator can use this file to setup a system-wide environment that will be the default for all users. The user's .cshrc and .login then supersede this setup, as desired.

2. The .cshrc file should contain the set commands for all local shell variables. This includes any of the C Shell built-in variables. Because these variables cannot pass on their values to child processes, they must be initialized by each shell process to take effect. The .cshrc file, because it is read by each C Shell process, is the ideal place to set these local variables.

   The only exception to this are the local variables, like $path, which have an environment variable partner that the shell updates to match the local variable.

These local variables can be set in .login, because the environment variable partner will pass the values onto later shell processes. These child shell processes then update the local variable from the environment variable partner.

3. The *kill* character, which tells the C Shell to erase the current command line, can be changed using the UNIX stty command. After this character—or any other terminal parameter set using stty—is established, it remains in effect until the user logs off the system. Because these terminal line-editing control characters only need to be set once, the stty command is usually placed in the .login startup file and executed by the login C Shell. To set the line erase or kill character to ^x, you would put the following command line in your .login startup file:

```
stty kill ^U
```

The ^U on this line is not entered as Control+U by holding down the Control key and typing U. Instead, it is entered as a carat character (^) followed by the letter U. The same is true for any other terminal parameter set to a control character using stty.

4. The C Shell prereads the directories in your search path and puts all the executable files in a hash table. This is done when the shell first begins execution, and normally the table is not updated unless requested by the user. If you add a shell script or executable program to one of these directories, it will not be found until the hash table is updated because the C Shell consults the table rather than the actual directories.

   There is a special built-in C Shell command, rehash, used for the specific purpose of requesting an update of the hash table. If a script or command is reported as not found, and if the ls command shows it to exist in a search path directory, you need to run rehash so that it will be added to the hash table:

```
% rehash
```

5. As a rule, you would want to set up your environment variables in your .login file. The exception to this is if you are regularly using the rlogin command to access other computers on a local network. Because the rlogin command starts the remote shell as a nonlogin shell, it will not read the .login file on the remote host. In this case, it is necessary to set up your environment variables within the .cshrc file so that they will be set for the shell started by rlogin.

6. The .login startup file is read only once by the login C Shell process. Because local variables are not passed on to child processes, if you set them in .login,

they would be established only for your login shell and not for its children. If you want only a specific variable to be set for the login shell, then the `.login` file is the appropriate place to do the setup. But the usual case is that you want these shell variable settings to be in effect for all shells that you start up, and the only way to accomplish that is to set them in `.cshrc`.

7. When a C Shell process starts, it always reads the contents of the `.cshrc` file in the current user's home directory. Then it checks to see if it is a login shell, and if so, reads the contents of `.login`. Since the `.login` file is read only once and always AFTER the `.cshrc` file, you should not put anything in your `.cshrc` file which depends on something which occurs in your `.login` file. For any shell process, either `.login` is not read at all or read after `.cshrc`, so the dependency will never be met at the time the `.cshrc` file is processed.

8. The `.login` startup file is only read by the login C Shell process, and only after the `.cshrc` file has been read. So, `.login` is not read by any shell process that is a child of the login shell.

Exercises

Your results will vary.

Day 7, "File Redirection, Pipes, and Filters"

Quiz

1. On any command line, output file redirection normally writes to the `stdout` file. By adding an ampersand metacharacter (&) suffix to the redirection characters, you then specify that you want `stderr` output to be merged with `stdout`. The following example illustrates this by first redirecting the output of `grep` to a file, with `stderr` going to the terminal. Then it is changed, adding the & to merge `stderr` output onto the same file with the output from `stdout`:

```
% grep -v ^# *.csh > nocomments        # matched line output only
cannot read /tmp/frank.csh
cannot read /tmp/mary.csh
cannot read /tmp/fido.csh
% grep -v ^# *.csh >& nocomments.err # matched lines & errors
```

2. To do a similar merging of stderr with stdout through a pipeline, you again add an ampersand (&). This time, it is added to the pipe metacharacter (¦), making it ¦&. The command that receives the output of the pipe gets the contents of stderr and stdout mixed or combined together. The exact order of the output from these two files is not predictable and is often intertwined.

3. A normal pipeline only connects the output from stdout of one command to stdin of the next. The output, if any, going to stderr from either of the two commands still goes to the terminal, unless it is explicitly merged with stdout.

4. The UNIX command tee is the filter you would need to save a copy of an output stream from the middle of a pipeline. The tee command takes the data read in from stdin and writes the data to stdout as well as to the filename specified as an argument on the command line. In the following example, the output from ls is saved to a file before being further processed by the pipeline:

```
% ls -l ¦ tee complete.ls ¦ grep 'data' >dataonly.ls
```

5. To look at the ten most recent files, you first need to order the output of the ls command by date and time. You can do this by using the -t option to the ls command. This will sort the output of the ls command by date and time, reporting the most recent files first, on through to the oldest files at the end of the list. You can then use the head command to output only the initial portion of the ls report. The head command takes an argument -#, where the # character is a number that specifies the number of lines to output from the start of the input stream. If no argument is given, head will default to 10 lines. Combining ls with head in a pipeline will give the desired results of displaying the ten most recent files.

```
% ls -lt ¦ head
-rw-r--r--   1 dave     users        4004 Feb 28 16:58 ar_data.02
-rw-r--r--   1 dave     users        4322 Feb 28 16:58 ar_data.03
-rw-r--r--   1 dave     users        4170 Feb 28 16:58 ar_data.04
-rw-r--r--   1 dave     users        4256 Feb 28 16:58 ar_data.05
-rw-r--r--   1 dave     users        2532 Jan 31 17:05 gl_data.03
-rw-r--r--   1 dave     users        2380 Jan 31 17:05 gl_data.04
-rw-r--r--   1 dave     users        2466 Jan 31 17:05 gl_data.05
-rw-r--r--   1 dave     users        6530 Jan 31 17:05 in_data.01
-rw-r--r--   1 dave     users        6314 Jan 31 17:05 in_data.02
-rw-r--r--   1 dave     users        6642 Jan 31 17:05 in_data.03
```

Exercises

Your results will vary.

Day 8, "C Shell Built-In Commands, Part I"

Quiz

1. `pushd +2`. This will rotate down two directories, to the third entry on the directory stack.

2. `popd +2`.

3. `unset *element`. But be careful. If any other variables end in `element`, they, too, will be deleted.

4. `alias` *command*. If there is no output, the command is not aliased.

5. It denies access to the world for any file created, and it denies other members of your group the privilege to write to the file.

Exercises

You will need to create aliases for the `cd`, `chdir`, `pushd`, and `popd` commands. To make it easier to understand, a fifth alias will set the prompt:

```
alias pathprompt set prompt=\"\\\!: \$cwd\>\"
alias cd cd \!\*\;pathprompt
alias chdir chdir \!\*\;pathprompt
alias pushd pushd \!\*\;pathprompt
alias popd popd \!\*\;pathprompt
```

The first alias, `pathprompt`, sets the prompt to the current path. Then, the four commands that change directory are aliased to also execute `pathprompt` after performing their normal functions. The backslashes are necessary to prevent the C Shell from interpreting the arguments when the aliases are created.

Day 9, "C Shell Built-In Commands, Part II"

Quiz

1. Use `exit 3`.

2. The `.logout` script is a set of C Shell commands that are executed when a terminal session is finished. It is run from `exit` and `logout`.

3. The `jobs` command will provide a list of jobs and their status.

4. When a program is stopped for input, use `fg %job` to move the program to the foreground for input.

5. `kill %job` or `kill -KILL %job` will terminate the background job.

6. The `suspend` command will put the current C Shell in the background, if it isn't the login shell.

Exercises

Your results will vary.

Day 10, "C Shell Built-In Commands, Part III"

Quiz

1. The `unhash` command removes the hash table from the C Shell. No longer will the hash data be available for path improvement.

2. By examining the hit rate, the command history, and the path variable, you can re-order the directories in the path to optimize the hit rate. The most frequently used directories should be first.

3. The `datasize` resource restricts the amount of memory available for malloced memory in a process.

4. When you set `coredumpsize` to 0, no core files will be generated. Use `limit coredumpsize 0`.

5. The `-h` option on `source` enables you to read a file and add the commands to the history list.

Exercise

The alias for `cd` is `dhist\;chdir \!\*\;pathprompt\;lhist`. You need the following for the other commands:

```
alias chdir dhist\;cd \!\*\;pathprompt\;lhist
```

The `pushd` and `popd` commands cannot be aliased with this scheme, because using the same name will create an alias loop. Instead, you will need to create two new aliases:

```
alias ppd dhist\;popd \!\*\;pathprompt\;lhist
alias psd dhist\;pushd \!\*\;pathprompt\;lhist
```

If there were ten basic commands, let's assume they are in a file in your home directory, `.Hist`. You'd need to change the `lhist` alias like so:

```
alias lhist if \( -f .dhist \) source -h .dhist\;source -h ~/.Hist
```

Day 11, "Programming with the C Shell"

Quiz

1. A label for a `switch` command must be located between the `switch` and the `endsw` and is preceded by the word `case`.

2. The `shift` will eliminate the first element of a variable and move all the other elements one place to the left.

3. `SIGTERM` and `SIGKILL` cannot be caught in a C Shell. For `SIGHUP`, use the `nohup` command, and for `SIGINT` use `onintr`.

4. Use this command (assume the file in question is named `file`):

```
if ( -d $file ) then
    if ( -r $file ) then
        commands
    endif
endif
```

Alternatively, you could use `test` and check the return value:

```
test \( -d $file -a -r $file \)
if ($status == 0 ) then
    commands
endif
```

5. `break;break;continue`

All must be on the same line.

Exercises

1.

```
switch ( $j )
case blue:
    echo Now it is green
    breaksw
case cat:
    echo Now it is mouse
    breaksw
case hot:
    echo Now it is cold
    breaksw
default:
    echo No match
    breaksw
endsw
```

2.

```
@ i = $number % 2
if ( $i == 1 ) then
    echo $number is odd
else
    echo $number is even
endif
```

Day 12, "Applied C Shell Programming, Part I"

Quiz

1. The -f option is for a fast start; the user's .cshrc file is not loaded into the shell. This appears in C Shell scripts because often you may not know the changes a user has made. This prevents any user aliases or variables from preventing your script from running.

2. a and d are `foreach` loops. b and c are `while` loops.

Exercises

1. You need to unset the temporary variables. You should also check to see whether the variables already exist; if so, you need to save the values. A temporary file works well for this. To make this truly useful, you should trap SIGINT. The script would then be the following:

```
onintr breakout
if ($?newpath) then
    echo set newpath = \( $newpath \) >> /tmp/reload$$
endif
if ($?element) then
    echo set element = \( $element \) >> /tmp/reload$$
endif
if ($?needed) then
    echo set needed = \( $needed \) >> /tmp/reload$$
endif
if ($?newelement) then
    echo set newelement = \( $newelement \) >> /tmp/reload$$
endif
set newpath
foreach element ( $path )
    if ( -d $element ) then
        set needed
        foreach newelement ( $newpath )
            if ( $element == $newelement ) then
                unset needed
                break
            endif
        end
        if ( $?needed ) set newpath = ( $newpath $element )
    endif
end
set path = ( $newpath )
breakout:
unset newpath newelement needed element
if ( -f /tmp/reload$$ ) source /tmp/reload$$
```

2. Instead of running a `foreach` loop, you'd need to parse the addresses into an egrep pattern:

```
set pat = ( `cat ~/.bounce` )
set pat2 = $pat[1]
shift pat
foreach elem ( $pat )
    set pat2 = "$pat2¦$elem"
end
set returns=`/usr/ucb/mail -H ¦ egrep $pat2 ¦ cut -c1-5`
set count=`/usr/ucb/mail -H ¦ egrep $pat2 ¦ wc -l`
if ( $count > 0 ) then
    /usr/ucb/mail << EOF
    d $returns
EOF
endif
```

3. Catch the flag early, and set a variable. Check it later, before running the xsetroot commands:

```
if ($#argv==2 ) then
    if ($argv[1] == "-r" ) then
        set REVERSE
        shift
    endif
endif
if ( $#argv < 1 ) then
    echo an argument is expected.
endif
cd /usr/share/roots
set args = ( `grep "${1}:" index` )
if ( $?REVERSE ) then
    xsetroot -bitmap $1 -fg $args[3] -bg $args[2]
    xsetroot -cursor ${1}_cur ${1}_mask -fg $args[5] -bg $args[4]
else
    xsetroot -bitmap $1 -fg $args[2] -bg $args[3]
    xsetroot -cursor ${1}_cur ${1}_mask -fg $args[4] -bg $args[5]
endif
```

Day 13, "Applied C Shell Programming, Part II"

Quiz

1. Using smaller pieces makes the task of coding easier.

2. Yes. Because the only reason to catch the interrupt is to clean up the temporary files, the `onintr` could have been placed before the first temporary file is created, before the `spell` command.

3. Just remove the backslash:

```
echo -n "your common spelling errors?   "
```

Exercises

1.

```
foreach arg ( $argv )          # Look at each argument
    set optc=`echo $arg | cut -c1`
                  # Since arguments start with either '-'
                  # or '+', we chop the argument to check
                  # this character
        switch (optc)
        case +:
            procarg $arg         # '+' is always added.
            breaksw
        case -:
            set opt2c=`echo $arg | cut -c1-2`
            switch (opt2c)       # '-' takes a second letter
                        # to indicate the option.
            case -b:
            case -l:
                    # Both -b and -l take the same processing
                procarg $arg
                breaksw
            case -v:
            case -x:
                    # Both -v and -x are ignored.
                echo -n $arg is supported by spell,
                echo but not supported by $argv[0]
                shift
                breaksw
            case -d:
            case -s:
                    # Both -d and -s need a second argument,
                    # and take the same processing.
                addarg $arg
                addarg $argv[2]
                set skipthis
                shift
                breaksw
            default:
                echo $arg is not supported.
                shift
            endsw
            breaksw
        default:
         if (! $?skipthis) set files = ( $files $arg )
         if ( $?skipthis ) unset skipthis
            shift
                    # Default on the outerloop is a file
                    # to be checked.
        endsw
    end
```

The $argv variable is expanded before the loop is entered, so the shifts have no effect. The skipthis variable needs to be set to prevent the arguments to the -d and -s options from also being added to the files list.

2. This solution is simple. The bug happens because sed will not match overlapping regular expressions. In this case, the space between the two words is a part of both regular expressions. The solution is to run the sed command twice: first to create a temporary file, and the second time on the temporary file. This will catch both occurrences.

Note that you'll need to add the temporary file to the cleanup label, in case somebody hits interrupt. The changes are these:

```
        sed -f /tmp/fix.$$ $file.orig > /tmp/$file.$$
        sed -f /tmp/fix.$$ /tmp/$file.$$$file.orig > $file
    endif
    rm -f /tmp/fix.$$ /tmp/spl.$$
end
exit
cleanup:
rm -f /tmp/*.$$
exit
```

Day 14, "Jobs"

Quiz

1. The status will be Stopped (tty output).

2. The job exited with the value 44. This is probably an error condition and should be checked.

3. This will give a full listing of every command running on the system.

4. Watch the CPU time from the ps command. If the CPU time value is increasing quickly, and nothing else seems to be happening, the command may be in an infinite loop. One way to confirm this is to send the SIGQUIT signal and generate a core dump to examine the values with a debugger.

Exercises

Your results will vary. Happy programming!

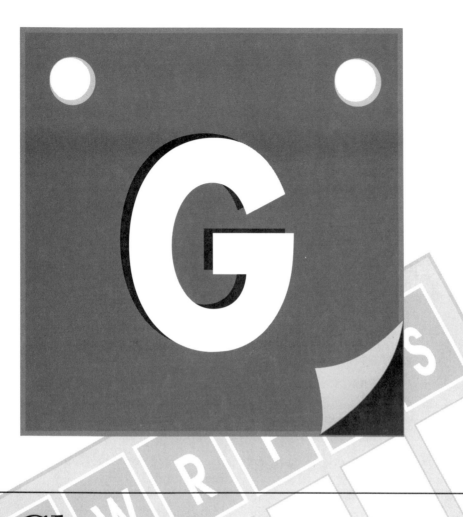

Glossary

$ignoreeof   A built-in variable that changes the effect of the character which indicates an end of file (EOF). The default for this character is ^D, but it can be changed using the stty command. Normally, when the C Shell receives an EOF character on stdin, it terminates. If it is the login shell and EOF is entered, the shell exits and you are logged off the system. Setting $ignoreeof forces you to use either exit or logout to leave a shell process. This is a Boolean variable and is either set or unset—it does not take a value.

$noclobber   A built-in variable that prevents accidental overwriting of a file when you redirect output. When you use append redirection with this variable set, the target file must exist or the operation will not proceed. To override the effect of this variable, you must add an exclamation point character (!) after the redirection metacharacters. This is a Boolean variable and is either set or unset—it does not take a value.

absolute path   A filename that begins with a slash (/) which equates to the root directory. A filename specified in this way locates a file without reference to the current working directory. See also **relative path**.

ambiguous filename   A filename that contains metacharacters or is described by metacharacters. It does not refer specifically to any one file, but rather to a potential group of files that match the metacharacter pattern. The shell expands the metacharacters to a list of filenames that match the pattern.

Bourne Shell   The original shell program distributed with the UNIX operating system. It is named after its author, Stephen Bourne. Like the C Shell, it has a programming language for writing scripts. It does not have the history mechanism, alias mechanism, or job control features that the C Shell has.

command history   A facility where previously executed commands are kept in a list. These commands can be recalled, modified, and executed from the history list. The number of entries in the list is controlled by a number stored in the shell variable $history. Another shell variable, $savehist, controls how many history commands are saved at the end of the shell session. Saved history is recalled automatically at the start of the next shell session.

command prompt   The string of characters displayed by the shell, in interactive mode, to indicate that it is ready to accept another command line. The contents and format of the command prompt can be customized by the user by using the built-in shell variable $prompt.

command substitution   An operation in which the results of a command enclosed in backticks (`) are substituted for the entire expression, including the backticks. Using this method, you can use one command to prepare arguments or parameters for another command.

current working directory The directory, represented by the special filename *dot* (.), where simple filenames are read from or written to. Relative pathnames start from this directory. The contents of the built-in shell variable $cwd always contain the current pathname of this directory, and the UNIX command pwd always displays this pathname as well.

dot file Any filename that begins with a period (.) is considered one of these files. They are also referred to as *silent files* or *hidden files* on some versions of UNIX. Dot files are found most frequently in a user's home directory, and typically they contain configuration or other pertinent information for a UNIX command. For example, .cshrc is a dot file used to set up a specific environment for the C Shell when it starts execution. These files are not displayed as part of the output of the ls command, unless the special option -a is used or a specific metacharacter pattern is used to match one or more of these files.

environment variable A shell variable that is created and initialized with the setenv command. These variables are also known as global variables. The contents of an environment variable are accessible to the current shell and any child processes that it creates. Environment variables are one of the ways that one process can communicate information to another. These variables are removed or deleted by use of the unsetenv command.

event number A unique number associated with each command, known as a history event, kept in the C Shell history list. The event number can be used to recall a specific command from history by prefixing it with an exclamation point at a command prompt.

exec() The UNIX function call that locates a command file or script and replaces the current process image with that command. It is used by the shell and any other command to initiate a new command as a child process. The exec() function does not close any files open at the point that it is called. The command that is initiated inherits these files opened and positioned, as they were for the calling program.

expansion/substitution metacharacters A group of special characters that act as special indicators to the C Shell. They include $, ! and :, which are used to indicate the start of shell variables, history events, and substitution modifiers on a command line. The shell acts accordingly to expand the items prefixed with $ or !, and it modifies accordingly those suffixed with :.

file redirection The process of reading input for a command from a disk file rather than from stdin, or writing the output of a command to a disk file rather than to stdout. It also includes appending output to a disk file. Although file output redirection normally writes stdout to a file, it can also merge the output from stderr to the same destination as that of stdout. There is also an option to override the protection offered by setting the shell variable $noclobber.

filename completion   A shell mechanism, optionally enabled by the existence of the shell variable $filec. It completes the current filename on a command line, when the user presses the Escape key, up to the point where the name is ambiguous. Typing Control+D at any time in a search displays a list of filenames that match the pattern entered, up to the current point.

filename metacharacters   The special characters used on a command line to form filename match patterns. They are also used to identify or form abbreviations.

filter   A command that takes input from stdin and writes output to stdout as its default operation. Filters are usually not interactive and do not issue prompts for input. Instead, they read stdin continuously until they reach EOF.

foreground command   A command that is run from the command prompt and stays attached to the terminal until it completes processing. You must wait for the foreground command to finish before you receive a shell prompt and can enter another command.

fork()   The UNIX function call that creates a new child process that is an exact duplicate of the process which called fork(). Any program, including the C Shell, that initiates new commands or creates subprocesses uses this function. The new child process will then usually call the exec() function to actually start the command in its place in memory.

globbing   The expansion process in which filename metacharacters are replaced by a list of matching filenames. When globbing is inhibited with the noglob command, filename metacharacters on a command line are passed to the command literally, rather than being replaced with a list of matching filenames.

here document   A type of input redirection indicated by the << metacharacters. A here document, used in a shell script, takes its input from the script file lines that immediately follow the command line. Following the << characters on the command line is a word used to indicate the end of the here document.

history event   The commands in the C Shell history list are history events. Each event has a number associated with it, which starts at 1 when the session begins and is increased with each new command line entered.

home directory   The directory which is a user's initial working directory after logging onto the system. It is the directory referenced by the shorthand metacharacter tilde (~). When the cd command is entered without an argument, it changes to the user's home directory by default.

input/output metacharacters   The special metacharacters that preface a filename to be used for file redirection. These metacharacters permit a command to take its input

from a file rather than from stdin or write output to a file rather than to stdout. They can also be used to indicate a merging of output to stderr with output going to stdout.

job control   The ability to manipulate processes that are either attached to a terminal and running in foreground, or detached and running in background. Job control permits the suspension of processes and also the changing of process states to any of three states— foreground, background, or suspended. The status of all jobs can also be reported.

Korn Shell   The latest shell program distributed with many versions of the UNIX operating system. It is named after its author, David Korn. This shell is 95 percent compatible with the Bourne Shell. It also has many features similar to those of the C Shell, such as command history and editing, aliases, and job control.

local variable   A shell variable that is created and initialized with the set command. These variables, unlike environment variables, are only accessible by the shell process that created them. They cannot be passed on to a child process. Local variables can be Boolean or can contain strings or numbers on which simple arithmetic operations can be performed.

login shell   The initial shell process that is created after a user logs in to the system. When running the C Shell, the login shell reads the .login startup file after reading .cshrc. Other C Shell processes started as children of this shell only read the .cshrc file. When this shell terminates, the user is logged out of the system.

metacharacter   Any of the special characters which, in different contexts, have special meaning or significance to the C Shell. These characters are interpreted by the shell when the command line is read and processed, prior to being executed. See also **syntactic metacharacters**, **filename metacharacters**, **quotation metacharacters**, **input/output metacharacters**, and **expansion/substitution metacharacters**.

multiword variable   A local variable that has multiple elements, one for each word or quoted string in its assigned value. Multiword variables are similar to array variables in many programming languages. Individual words of the variable can be addressed directly by the use of subscripts enclosed in square brackets.

pager   One of several UNIX commands used to process long input and break it up into screen pages. These commands cause a pause at the bottom of the screen after each page is displayed and wait for user input before proceeding. They have different capabilities as far as searching for text, moving forward or backward through the text, and controlling how the screen pages are displayed. The three most common paging commands are more, pg, and less.

pathname   An optional string of directory names, separated by slashes and followed by a filename, which locates where the filename resides. A pathname is absolute if it starts with the root directory (/), or relative if it starts with a directory name, or the special directories *dot* (.) or *dot dot* (..).

pattern matching   The process of interpreting metacharacter patterns, and replacing them with lists of filenames or with strings that match the patterns. Pattern matching is used on command lines to generate filename arguments and in text-processing commands to match strings of text.

pipeline   A connection of two or more commands, where the standard output of one command is joined to the standard input of the next in the pipeline. The vertical bar character (¦) is used to indicate the creation of a pipeline to the shell.

process   An instance of a command running in its own environment in memory. Each process on the system is unique and is assigned an ID number, known as a PID. A process provides an environment, which is a copy of its parent's environment, for the command that it is running.

process ID   The unique number, known as a PID, by which a specific process can be referenced. The PID can be used to kill a process or otherwise change its run state. Commands such as ps report PIDs for each running process on the system.

quotation metacharacters   The special characters used to create strings for arguments to commands or for assignment to variables. These metacharacters can control when other metacharacters, contained within the strings, are expanded or protected from expansion by the shell. They can also singly protect specific metacharacters from being interpreted by the shell.

relative path   A filename that is qualified relative to the current working directory. A relative path begins with a directory name or one of the special directory files *dot* (.) or *dot dot* (..), which denote the current directory or its parent, respectively. See also **absolute path**.

search path   A list of directories that is used to search for a command file. The order of the directories in this list controls the order in which the search is performed. If a command with the same name exists in two directories, both of which are in the search path, the command will be located and run from the first of the two paths. The C Shell creates a hash table containing all of the executable files in each of the search path directories except for *dot* (.), which is searched directly when required.

shell script   A text file containing a shell program comprised of command lines and shell control structures. Shell scripts can be used as direct input to a shell process or can be made executable and run by name.

shell variable   A name and its associated value, which can be a character string, a number, or a Boolean on/off setting. Variables can be defined by the user or can be part of the set of built-in shell variables used to affect the environment in which the shell operates.

stderr   The file available to a program for error, diagnostic, or informational messages. The default destination for the output to this file is the terminal, display device, or window associated with the program.

stdin   The file from which a program can read input. The default source for this file is the keyboard, unless file redirection is used to cause input to be received from an alternate location.

stdout   A file available to a program for writing regular output to. By default, this file is directed at the terminal, display device, or window associated with the program. By use of file redirection, this output can be written to a different destination. This output is what is normally passed through a pipeline when the pipe (¦) metacharacter is used to connect two commands.

subshell   When a shell explicitly starts another copy of itself, or when a shell calls the `fork()` system function, the resulting child process that is created is known as a subshell. In the case where `fork()` is called, this subshell usually also calls the `exec()` function to start a specified command.

syntactic metacharacters   The special characters used as punctuation characters between and around commands. They are also used to combine multiple UNIX commands to make a single logical command. Syntactic metacharacters provide a means to effect conditional execution of a command or commands, based on the outcome of a previous command.

wild-card characters   Filename metacharacters are often referred to as wild-card characters.

Index

files

SAMS
Learning
Center

SAMS
PUBLISHING

Disk Offer

Many of the scripts in *Teach Yourself the UNIX C Shell in 14 Days* are available on disk from the authors. Fill out this form and enclose a check for only $10.00 to receive a disk. Please make the check payable to David Ennis. Sorry, no credit card orders. Mail this form to

David Ennis
2829 N. Glenoaks, Suite 106, Box 193
Burbank, CA 91504

Name _____

Company (for company name) _____

Street _____

City _____

State/Province _____

ZIP or Postal Code _____

Country (outside the USA) _____

Disk format (check one):

5.25-inch _____   3.5-inch _____

Add to Your Sams Library Today with the Best Books for Programming, Operating Systems, and New Technologies

The easiest way to order is to pick up the phone and call

1-800-428-5331

between 9:00 a.m. and 5:00 p.m. EST.
For faster service please have your credit card available.

ISBN	Quantity	Description of Item	Unit Cost	Total Cost
0-672-30551-8		Exploring the UNIX System, 4th Edition	$29.99	
0-672-30402-3		UNIX Unleashed	$49.99	
0-672-30460-0		Absolute Beginner's Guide to UNIX	$19.99	
0-672-48448-X		UNIX Shell Programming, Revised Edition	$29.95	
0-672-30464-3		Teach Yourself UNIX in a Week	$28.00	
0-672-30457-0		Learning UNIX, Second Edition (Book/Disk)	$39.95	
0-672-22715-0		UNIX Applications Programming: Mastering the Shell	$29.95	
0-672-30583-6		Teach Yourself UNIX Shell Programming in 14 Days	$29.99	
0-672-30448-1		Teach Yourself C in 21 Days, Bestseller Edition	$24.95	
0-672-30471-6		Teach Yourself Advanced C in 21 Days (Book/Disk)	$34.95	
❏ 3 ½" Disk		Shipping and Handling: See information below.		
❏ 5 ¼" Disk		TOTAL		

Shipping and Handling: $4.00 for the first book, and $1.75 for each additional book. Floppy disk: add $1.75 for shipping and handling. If you need to have it NOW, we can ship product to you in 24 hours for an additional charge of approximately $18.00, and you will receive your item overnight or in two days. Overseas shipping and handling adds $2.00 per book and $8.00 for up to three disks. Prices subject to change. Call for availability and pricing information on latest editions.

201 W. 103rd Street, Indianapolis, Indiana 46290

1-800-428-5331 — Orders   1-800-835-3202 — FAX   1-800-858-7674 — Customer Service

GO AHEAD. PLUG YOURSELF INTO
MACMILLAN COMPUTER PUBLISHING.

Introducing the Macmillan Computer Publishing Forum on CompuServe®

Yes, it's true. Now, you can have CompuServe access to the same professional, friendly folks who have made computers easier for years. On the Macmillan Computer Publishing Forum, you'll find additional information on the topics covered by every Macmillan Computer Publishing imprint—including Que, Sams Publishing, New Riders Publishing, Alpha Books, Brady Books, Hayden Books, and Adobe Press. In addition, you'll be able to receive technical support and disk updates for the software produced by Que Software and Paramount Interactive, a division of the Paramount Technology Group. It's a great way to supplement the best information in the business.

WHAT CAN YOU DO ON THE MACMILLAN COMPUTER PUBLISHING FORUM?

Play an important role in the publishing process—and make our books better while you make your work easier:

- Leave messages and ask questions about Macmillan Computer Publishing books and software—you're guaranteed a response within 24 hours
- Download helpful tips and software to help you get the most out of your computer
- Contact authors of your favorite Macmillan Computer Publishing books through electronic mail
- Present your own book ideas
- Keep up to date on all the latest books available from each of Macmillan Computer Publishing's exciting imprints

JOIN NOW AND GET A FREE COMPUSERVE STARTER KIT!

To receive your free CompuServe Introductory Membership, call toll-free, **1-800-848-8199** and ask for representative **#597**. The Starter Kit Includes:

- Personal ID number and password
- $15 credit on the system
- Subscription to CompuServe Magazine

HERE'S HOW TO PLUG INTO MACMILLAN COMPUTER PUBLISHING:

Once on the CompuServe System, type any of these phrases to access the Macmillan Computer Publishing Forum:

GO MACMILLAN   **GO BRADY**
GO QUEBOOKS   **GO HAYDEN**
GO SAMS   **GO QUESOFT**
GO NEWRIDERS   **GO ALPHA**

Once you're on the CompuServe Information Service, be sure to take advantage of all of CompuServe's resources. CompuServe is home to more than 1,700 products and services—plus it has over 1.5 million members worldwide. You'll find valuable online reference materials, travel and investor services, electronic mail, weather updates, leisure-time games and hassle-free shopping (no jam-packed parking lots or crowded stores).

Seek out the hundreds of other forums that populate CompuServe. Covering diverse topics such as pet care, rock music, cooking, and political issues, you're sure to find others with the same concerns as you—and expand your knowledge at the same time.